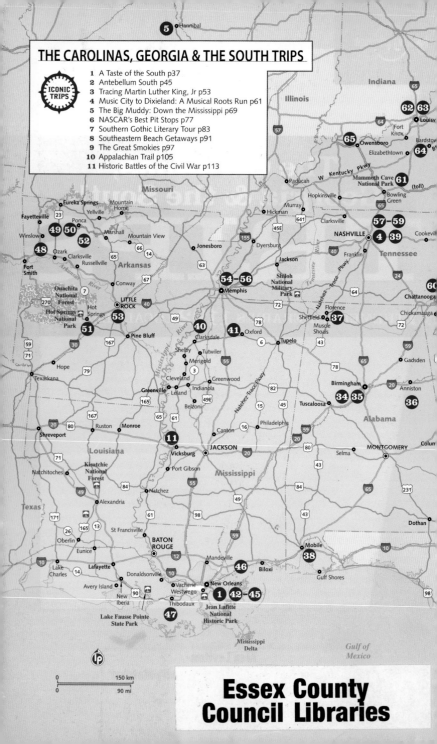

THE CAROLINAS, GEORGIA & THE SOUTH TRIPS

ICONIC TRIPS

Essex County Council Libraries

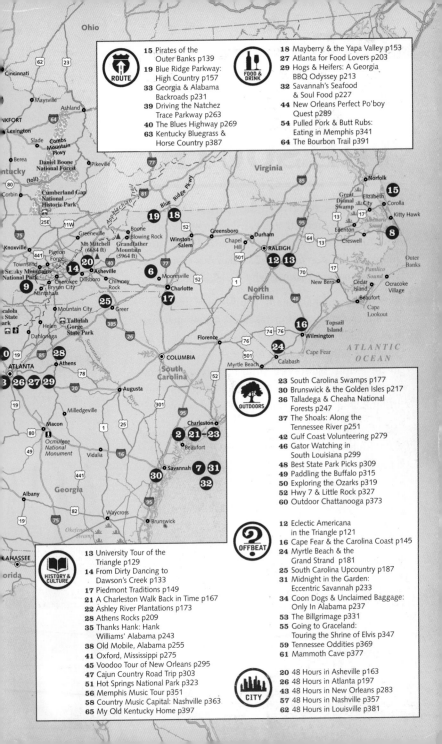

THE CAROLINAS, GEORGIA & THE SOUTH

Whether you have lived in the heart of Dixie your entire life, have recently relocated or are just visiting, you might think you know the South. Forget, for a moment, the stereotypes and infamous history, as we want to show you just why we love the South.

You're not imagining it; people here really are friendlier, and tradition takes on a new meaning below the Mason Dixon line. History permeates the South like one of Scarlett O'Hara's lingering sighs in an empty ballroom. Almost every American-born music style originated here, from bluegrass to funk, and rock and roll to soul.

And yes, so did slavery. And the Civil War. And the Civil Rights movement. And the work of Dr Martin Luther King, Jr. We'll show you all of it as we weave through 65 trips in nine states.

It's the natural beauty – the off-the-beaten-track treks – that provides some of the best road trip destinations. Rock out to zydeco after a day canoeing past swamp gators. Sip ice tea on a breezy veranda in Kentucky's Bluegrass Country. Kayak along Georgia's relatively undiscovered Golden Isles. There's an experience here for every mood.

And if you're not yet convinced a Southern road trip is for you, we have one word for you: barbecue.

 THE GREAT SMOKIES p97
Mountain Farm Museum, Great Smoky Mountains National Park, Tennessee

"It's the natural beauty – the off-the-beaten-track treks – that provides some of the best road trip destinations."

SWEET TEA

If you order "tea" from just about any Southern restaurant, expect a cold, tall glass of sweetened iced tea. A sugar solution is added during brewing, so if you'd like tea without sugar, you'll have to specifically request unsweetened iced tea.

Iconic Trips

ICONIC TRIPS

Although we love many things about the South, we especially love its iconic influence – from **antebellum architecture** (p45) to diverse **music** (p61). Take a page from our Iconic Trips and learn to fluff biscuits at a New Orleans **cooking school** (p37) or sleep at the hike-in Hike Inn on the **Appalachian Trail** (p105). You can also follow in the footsteps of **Martin Luther King, Jr** (p53), **Mark Twain** (p69), **William Faulkner** (p83) and **Dale Earnhardt** (p77), or explore battlefields with a die-hard, Zen-minded **Civil War reenactor** (p113).

THE VINE THAT ATE THE SOUTH

Perhaps the best way to decipher whether or not you're in the South is if you spot kudzu, the Japanese flowering vine that now covers the Southeast. Growing as much as 60ft during steamy summers, kudzu is known to cover everything in its path – including trees, stop signs and old barns.

![ROUTE] Routes

From the 1930s CCC (Civilian Conservation Corps) building of the Blue Ridge Parkway to the 1960s film *Easy Rider*, a road trip through the American South has become an iconic milestone for all ages. Hop from antebellum mansion to emerald mound along the elegant **Natchez Trace Parkway** (p263) or feast on pecan pie and peach cobbler on Georgia's **back roads** (p231). Along the **Blue Ridge Parkway** (p157), stop at a different traditional music venue each night or follow the history of the delta blues in **Mississippi** (p269). Down the **Outer Banks** (p139), cruise your convertible past lighthouses, and hang gliders launched from huge sand dunes. Whether your rig is an RV or a chopper, the road is your (fried) oyster.

BEST SHORT DRIVE: ASHLEY RIVER ROAD PLANTATIONS

Starting with the 17th-century Charles Towne Landing State Historic Site and passing through three antebellum plantation mansions, the Ashley River is a tour of the American South in miniature.

"Whether your rig is an RV or a chopper, the road is your (fried) oyster."

61

The CROSSROADS

Food & Drink

From duck **po'boys** (p289) to **butt rubs** (p341), and **candied yams** (p227) to **fried pig ears** (p203), Southern cuisine is nothing if not eclectic. Food is central to entertainment and it's not uncommon to see a fish fry for a church fundraiser or a pig pickin' at a black-tie wedding. While New Orleans is most famous for its po'boys, gumbo, jambalaya, *muffalettas* and beignets, culinary hotspots like Atlanta, the Triangle (Raleigh–Durham), Charleston and Savannah attract foodies like Elvis to a peanut butter and banana sandwich. Guilty pleasures are a culinary mainstay 'round these parts, but nowadays you'll also find Lowcountry **cooking classes** (p227), **wine-tasting tours** (p153) in central North Carolina and an expert-led **barbecue trip** (p203) through Georgia.

"Culinary hotspots attract foodies like Elvis to a peanut butter and banana

BARBECUE

No one quite knows where the word originated, but barbecue (the noun, not the verb) has been a Southern tradition for coming on 200 years and continues to be cooked over wood (hickory or mesquite is best) or charcoal at many restaurants.

"Try canoeing languidly alongside gators and tupelos through a moss-covered swamp in Louisiana."

OLYMPIC RAFTING

Take a day trip to the US National Whitewater Center outside Charlotte, NC, where layfolk can raft down Olympic-grade rapids (and ride back to the top on a ski lift contraption).

Outdoors

Some of the oldest mountains in the world are in the South. You can almost feel the age of the Appalachian or Blue Ridge Mountains as they roll peacefully across the horizon, content to let those young guns out in Colorado or California host heli-skiing or base jumping. Adrenaline junkies can get their fix rafting past 525ft granite rock faces on the **Buffalo River** (p315) in Arkansas or spelunking the Raccoon Mountain Caverns outside **Chattanooga** (p373) in Tennessee. If you'd like to slow down the pace, try canoeing languidly alongside gators and tupelos through a moss-covered swamp in **Louisiana** (p299) or lending a hand on the hurricane-ravaged **Gulf Coast** (p279).

PADDLING THE BUFFALO p315
Canoeing the Buffalo River, Arkansas

GATOR WATCHING IN SOUTH LOUISIANA p299
Inhabitant of the bayous and backwaters, Louisiana

CHATTANOOGA OUTDOORS p373
Ruby Falls underground waterfall at Lookout Mountain, Chattanooga

APPALACHIAN TRAIL p105
Picturesque Carvers Gap on the Appalachian Trail, Tennessee

History & Culture

The history of the South is inextricably linked to some of the United States' most shameful moments. Within this infamy is a storied and fascinating past dating back to not too long after the *Mayflower*'s arrival. In Charleston, sleep at an inn where George Washington once stopped for breakfast, or walk through the **island fort** (p167) where the Civil War began. Peruse a French fort in **Mobile** (p255), Alabama or head to the heart of **Bluegrass Country** (p397). The newer cultural offering of the South is as diverse as it gets: follow North Carolina's **film industry** (p133), perform **voodoo spiritual rituals** (p295) in New Orleans or soak with the ghost of Al Capone in **Hot Springs** (p323), Arkansas.

VOODOO TOUR OF NEW ORLEANS p295
Altar at a voodoo temple, New Orleans

A CHARLESTON WALK BACK IN TIME p167
The elegant John Rutledge House Inn, Charleston

MY OLD KENTUCKY HOME p397
Craftsman at Louisville Slugger Museum, Louisville

OLD MOBILE, ALABAMA p255
Musketeer firing a 1700s rifle at Fort Condé, Mobile

"In Charleston, sleep at an inn where George Washington once stopped for breakfast."

FAULKNER SLEPT HERE

Spend a few days creatively inspired by the historic town square, antebellum mansions and Southern nouvelle cuisine of Oxford, Mississippi, where legions of fans channel William Faulkner's literary genius in his impeccably preserved former home.

Offbeat

From Graceland's tiki-styled **Jungle Room** (p347) to the world's longest **yard sale** (p369) and **corn-on-the-cob lollipops** (p187), the South does quirky like no place else in the world. Jog to Bill Clinton's favorite chili-covered tamale restaurant on a **Billgrimage** (p331), or just try to avert your eyes from the glitter- and ostrich-fest that is **Dolly Parton's Dixie Stampede** (p181) in Myrtle Beach, South Carolina. But put together a boll weevil monument, a coon dog cemetery and the world's **largest chair** (p237) for the quirkiest of our offbeat offerings. We'll also take you through the metaphorical garden of good and evil in **Savannah** (p223), from hula hoop clinics to chainsaw wood creatures in the **Triangle** (p121), and to where poisonous snakes and killer plants top off a day at the beach in **North Carolina** (p145).

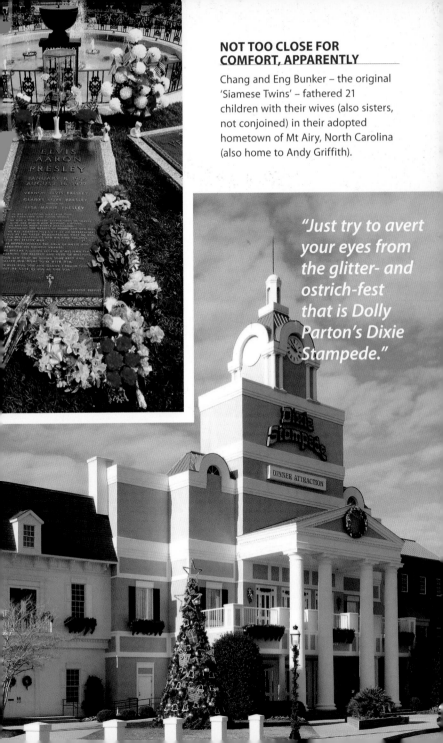

NOT TOO CLOSE FOR COMFORT, APPARENTLY

Chang and Eng Bunker – the original 'Siamese Twins' – fathered 21 children with their wives (also sisters, not conjoined) in their adopted hometown of Mt Airy, North Carolina (also home to Andy Griffith).

"Just try to avert your eyes from the glitter- and ostrich-fest that is Dolly Parton's Dixie Stampede."

Cities

Cosmopolitan **Atlanta** (p197) is the South's largest city, and its world-class restaurants and museums don't disappoint. Mythic **New Orleans** (p283) needs little introduction, but we offer four trips to show you all its different facets. But it is perhaps the midsize Southern city that best encapsulates the New South. Towns like hippified **Asheville** (p163), true-blue **Louisville** (p381) and irascible **Nashville** (p357) show why so many folks are flocking here.

BEST TRIPS

THE BEST TRIPS

COUNTRY MUSIC CAPITAL: NASHVILLE p363
Musical monuments on Broadway, Nashville

SAVANNAH'S SEAFOOD & SOUL FOOD p227
Serving up Lowcountry boil, Georgia

Contents

GEORGIA & ALABAMA TRIPS 195

MISSISSIPPI, LOUISIANA & ARKANSAS TRIPS 261

TENNESSEE & KENTUCKY TRIPS   339

BEHIND THE SCENES   405

INDEX   409

GREENDEX   422

Trips by Theme

 ROUTES

 FOOD & DRINK

 HISTORY & CULTURE

 OUTDOORS

Trips by Season

SUMMER

AUTUMN

Expert-Recommended Trips

The Authors

ALEX LEVITON
After getting a master's degree in journalism from UC Berkeley in 2002, Alex bought a tobacco warehouse loft in downtown Durham and has split her time between North Carolina and San Francisco ever since. She loves both places, but has a special fondness in her heart for the porches, fireflies and pace of life in North Carolina.

EMILY MATCHAR
Emily was raised in the Tar Heel State and can still sometimes be found around Chapel Hill. She coauthored Lonely Planet's *USA* guide, and writes on food and travel for magazines and newspapers. Her favorite trip was Pulled Pork & Butt Rubs: Eating in Memphis. She can be seen here at Sun Studio in Memphis, where Elvis, Johnny Cash and Roy Orbison were discovered.

KEVIN RAUB

Kevin grew up in Atlanta and attended the University of Georgia in Athens. He has previously worked on Lonely Planet guides to Mexico, Brazil and Chile. For this book, Kevin drove through Georgia and Alabama, stopping off here for a picture at Little St Simons Island, the jewel of the Golden Isles.

ADAM SKOLNICK

Adam covers travel, culture and health for Lonely Planet and several magazines. His Mississippi, Louisiana and Arkansas odyssey was one extended overdose of live music, lush landscapes and insanely good regional food. He has authored and coauthored six Lonely Planet guidebooks. Read more of his work at www .adamskolnick.com.

LONELY PLANET AUTHORS

Why is our travel information the best in the world? It's simple: our authors are independent, dedicated travelers. They don't research using just the internet or phone, and they don't take freebies, so you can rely on their advice being well researched and impartial. They travel widely, to all the popular spots and off the beaten track. They personally visit thousands of hotels, restaurants, cafés, bars, galleries, palaces, museums and more — and they take pride in getting all the details right, and telling it how it is. Think you can do it? Find out how at lonelyplanet.com.

CONTRIBUTING EXPERTS

John T Edge is the author of a number of books, including a four-book series on iconic American eats. He most recently released a revised edition of *Southern Belly: The Ultimate Food Lover's Companion to the South*. John contributes to the Hogs & Heifers: A Georgia BBQ Odyssey trip.

Philip Grymes is the director of Outdoor Chattanooga, a city agency dedicated to promoting the outdoor lifestyle. He is a Wilderness First Responder and an avid hiker, kayaker and rock climber. Philip shares some of his favorite spots in the Outdoor Chattanooga trip.

Dixie Hibbs is the former mayor of Bardstown, Kentucky, the "Bourbon Capital of the World." She has written several books on local history and culture, including *Bardstown: Hospitality, History and Bourbon*. She shares her insider knowledge in The Bourbon Trail trip.

Robert Lee Hodge has been engaging in Civil War reenactments for three decades as a self-proclaimed "hardcore" reenactor, and was the subject of Tony Horwitz's *Confederates in the Attic*. Robert lends his expertise to the Historic Battles of the Civil War trip.

Jordan Johnson, JD, spokesman for the Clinton Foundation and director of public policy at Cranford Johnson Robinson Woods, was born and raised in Arkansas. He spends his downtime with his family hiking, paddling and fly-fishing. Jordan contributed to The Billgrimage trip.

Victoria Logue first hiked the Appalachian Trail in 1988 and has since written several books on

hiking the trail. Victoria assisted on the Appalachian Trail trip.

Mike Mills is a world-class paddler and the longest tenured outfitter on the Buffalo. In the 1980s he served as Arkansas' Minister of Tourism under then Governor Clinton. In the off-season you'll find him flying his Cessna or hot-air balloon. Mike contributed to the Paddling the Buffalo trip.

Connie Nelson is the coauthor of *The Film Junkie's Guide to North Carolina*. She lives in Wilmington, North Carolina. Connie offers an insider's insight in the From Dirty Dancing to Dawson's Creek trip.

Scott Peacock, chef and Southern food expert, is the executive chef at Watershed in Atlanta. In 2007 he won a James Beard Award, and is coauthor of *The Gift of Southern Cooking: Recipes and Revelations from Two Southern Chefs*, with the late Edna Lewis. Scott shares his foodie insights in the Atlanta for Food Lovers trip.

Simona Rabinovitch writes about pop culture, travel and entertainment for Canada's national newspaper the *Globe and Mail* and international magazines including *Zink*, *Nylon* and *SPIN.com*. Simona's interview with Terrance Simien appears in the Cajun Country Road Trip.

Jack Thomson runs a Civil War walking tour of Charleston and has published a photography book entitled *Charleston at War*. To take one of his tours, go to www.civilwarwalk.com. We joined Jack for a walk in A Charleston Walk Back in Time.

THE CAROLINAS, GEORGIA & THE SOUTH ICONIC TRIPS

ICONIC
TRIPS

While each region of each state in the South has a distinct character (and often, a unique cuisine, and landscape, and accent), some things are just plain ol' Southern – antebellum mansions, kudzu and the ability to deep-fry just about anything (fish, chicken, sweet potatoes, unripe green tomatoes, an entire turkey, Twinkies...).

In these 11 Iconic trips, we'll weave you through all nine states, from the top of the Great Smokies in Tennessee to an island inhabited by wild ponies in North Carolina, and from William Faulkner's Oxford to Dale Earnhardt, Jr's Talladega. Honor the memory of Dr Martin Luther King, Jr by retracing his footsteps and contemplate the brutality of the Civil War with a reenactor-turned-preservationist.

And, of course, eat. Beignets, po' boys and fried alligator in New Orleans and Lowcountry, black-eyed peas, okra and shrimp in Charleston, and barbecue, well, just about everywhere. To work off all that soul and Southern food, take a stroll on the Appalachian Trail, or shake your tail feathers to practically any style of American music – most of it was invented here.

PLAYLIST ♫ Many of our Iconic Trips bring you to the root of the Southern experience, so we're bringing you back to where it all began musically, as well. While you're driving the open road, here is a selection of songs to keep you going.

- "Cross Road Blues," Robert Johnson
- "Boom Boom," John Lee Hooker
- "Jambalaya (On the Bayou)," Hank Williams
- "Coal Miner's Daughter," Loretta Lynn
- "Heartbreak Hotel," Elvis Presley
- "The Man in Black," Johnny Cash
- "The Thrill is Gone," BB King
- "Crazy," Patsy Cline
- "When the Saints Go Marching In," Louis Armstrong
- "9 to 5," Dolly Parton

BEST ICONIC TRIPS

THE CAROLINAS, GEORGIA & THE SOUTH ICONIC TRIPS

A Taste of the South

WHY GO For Southerners, food means family, friends and a good time, whether eating gumbo in Louisiana or ribs in Tennessee. For a hefty sampling of regional cuisines, trip it from New Orleans to Memphis to Charleston, stopping for plenty of boiled peanuts and MoonPies along the way.

TIME
1 week

DISTANCE
1170 miles

BEST TIME TO GO
Year-round

START
New Orleans, LA

END
Charleston, SC

ALSO GOOD FOR

"Southern food" is a vast category. While some elements remain constant – you can have fluffy biscuits and grits for breakfast almost anywhere in the South – others are micro-regional. Just try finding Frogmore Stew outside of South Carolina's Lowcountry or locating barbecued spaghetti anywhere but Memphis.

Start your food trip by filling your belly by the bayou in ❶ New Orleans. Many books have been written about the Cajun and Creole cuisine of Southern Louisiana; you could happily spend weeks searching the alleys of the Big Easy and the back roads of swampy Cajun Country for the best andouille sausage and po'boys (po'boys, New Orleans' indigenous fast food, are sublime French-bread sandwiches packed with anything from fried shrimp to duck meat). But even a day or two in the area is time enough for a sampling of this region's marvelous cooking. If you're wondering what the difference between Cajun and Creole food is, the jury is still out. While it's agreed that Cajun food is somewhat more rustic, Creole food somewhat more refined, the subtleties are still a matter of raging debate.

Breakfast on beignets (delectable powdered sugar-coated donuts) at 24-hour ❷ Café Du Monde in the iconic French Quarter. Sit under the striped awning and watch the street vendors and crowds of tourists as you sip your café au lait. Bright yellow tins of its chicory-laced coffee make cool gifts – buy them in the gift shop across the street.

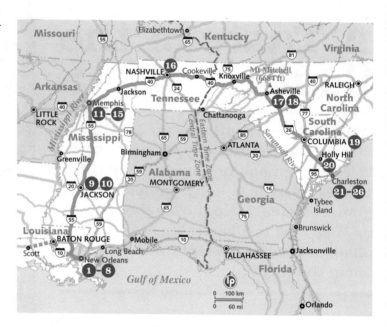

For lunch, don't miss nearby ❸ **Johnny's Po-Boy** on St Louis St. This bustling family-run joint has been around since 1950, serving up roast beef po'boys and ham po'boys, and fantastic hot sausage. Sit down at one of the checkered tablecloth–covered tables and watch the fry cooks work at warp speed. Alternatively, you could head over to Decatur St for a *muffaletta* at ❹ **Central Grocery**. This beloved ham, salami and olive-salad sandwich on round Italian bread was invented here by a Sicilian immigrant in 1906.

Spend happy hour with a lager and a heap of fresh-shucked oysters at noisy ❺ **Felix's Oyster Bar**, also in the French Quarter. Tourists and locals have been piling in for nearly six decades to suck down raw, grilled and fried crustaceans. Try boiled crawfish, a seasonal Cajun specialty. Crawfish, aka crayfish (or crawdads or mudbugs), are freshwater crustaceans that look like the love child of a shrimp and a lobster. They star in crawfish étouffée, a classic Cajun dish of seafood in a spicy reddish sauce served over rice.

"Spend happy hour with a lager and a heap of fresh-shucked oysters."

For upscale neo-Cajun dining, you can't beat ❻ **Cochon**. Classics like catfish courtbouillon, and red beans and rice are terrific, but don't shy away from offbeat dishes such as fried alligator with aioli or the grilled beet and pickled pork-tongue salad. James Beard award-winning chef Donald Link draws trendy crowds to this contemporary renovated warehouse; make reservations.

Want to get interactive with your food? Head over to the **7** **New Orleans School of Cooking**, where spirited, wisecracking chefs like former pro-football player Kevin Belton will teach you how to make Big Easy classics such as shrimp remoulade, jambalaya and pecan pie. The price includes an open bar with wine and local Abita beer – careful with that butcher knife!

Spend the night at the **8** **Melrose Mansion**, a restored Victorian home of wide verandas and graceful white columns. In the evening, guests nibble hors d'oeuvres and sip cocktails in the parlor; in the morning they dine on fresh pastries and quiche in the sunny dining room. Rooms have high ceilings and elegant antiques.

Head out of New Orleans and cut north through Mississippi. In Jackson, stop at **9** **Walker's Drive-In**, a 1940s diner serving sophisticated takes on down-home cooking. Try the Redfish Anna or the Mississippi tamales with sweet corn sauce. Mississippi tamales? Yep. Known here as

> **DETOUR** A sausage made of pork, rice and spices, boudin (pronounced "BOO-dan"), is one of the most memorable Cajun foodstuffs. Innumerable gas stations and small-town butchers throughout swampy Cajun Country claim to have the "best". We recommend the **Best Stop**, a family-run meat shop in the town of **Scott**, about 2½ hours west of New Orleans. Also try its spicy andouille sausage and the tasso ham.

"red hot tamales" or "Delta tamales," they were introduced by Mexican laborers around the turn of the century and are a popular street snack in the Delta region. Just up the block from Walker's is the magical **10** **Fondren Beverage Emporium**, specializing in rare sodas and bizarre candies. Fancy a celery soda and a bacon-flavored mint?

Roll into **11** **Memphis**, on the banks of the muddy Mississippi. This gritty, brightly colored patchwork of a city is known for two things – blues and barbecue. Both are high art forms, requiring complete dedication to the discipline and years of toil, whether that means singing your heart out to drunks in a dingy bar or tending the hog cooker at 4am on an obscure city side-street. Barbecue is usually one of two things here: slow-cooked pulled-pork shoulder or glossy mahogany ribs. Ribs can be either "wet" with barbecue sauce or "dry" with a powdered spice rub. Try them both.

On the south side of town, **12** **Jim Neely's Interstate Bar-B-Que** serves the quintessential Memphis pulled-pork sandwich, with tangy tomato-based sauce and a dollop of coleslaw on a soft white bun. Get a side of barbecue spaghetti, an eccentric only-in-Memphis creation. It's just chopped noodles with barbecue sauce and lumps of pulled pork. Weird, ugly, but oddly satisfying.

13 **Cozy Corner**, in a wood-paneled bungalow with peeling vinyl booths, is famous for its barbecued Cornish game hen. True connoisseurs know how to strip every bit of meat from the tiny wings and legs, leaving nothing but a miniature carcass and a pile of napkins. The ribs, thick bologna sandwiches and barbecue turkey are also big sellers.

TABASCO SAUCE

Across the South and beyond, Tabasco sauce livens everything from collard greens to scrambled eggs. Banker Edmund McIlhenny invented it just after the Civil War to add kick to the boring Reconstruction-era diet, planting Tabasco peppers in the loamy soil of his Avery Island, Louisiana home. Peppers are still grown and bottled on the island today, and the super-secret recipe remains in the McIlhenny family. You can tour the **Tabasco factory** (www.tabasco.com) for $1.

Don't let hoards of tourists scare you away from ⑭ **Charlie Vergos' Rendezvous.** The cavernous subterranean restaurant is noisy and crowded for a good reason. Propping your elbows on the red-and-white checked tablecloth to devour a rack of succulent dry-rub ribs has been a Memphis dining experience since 1948.

Nearby Beale St is all about blues, beer and tourists; head over to South Main for quirky, more sophisticated nightlife options. Crash downtown at the Renaissance Revival–style ⑮ **Peabody Hotel,** Memphis' grandest digs. A troop of pampered ducks waddles around the lobby during daylight hours, taking dips in the marble fountain while guests sip cocktails beneath the chandeliers.

The four-hour drive from Memphis to Nashville should work up your appetite. That's a good thing, because you'd be remiss to so much as set foot in central Tennessee without stopping at ⑯ **Prince's Hot Chicken.** A fluorescently lit storefront in a decaying north Nashville strip mall, Prince's has a few white tables and no decor to speak of. Order your chicken (leg quarters are best) at the hole in the kitchen wall, choosing from mild, medium, hot or extra-hot. Try the medium. We don't know anyone who has eaten an entire extra-hot quarter and lived. All the chicken is pan-fried in a cast iron skillet; if the restaurant's crowded it can take up to an hour. Your chicken comes crackling hot and dripping with juices, slapped atop two slices of white bread with a pickle. Your lips go numb, your eyes water. You want more.

ASK A LOCAL
"Learn how to trim meat, to skin the membrane off the ribs. They'll look a whole lot better. Use good charcoal and good wood – we use apple wood and cherry wood. Get yourself a good dry rub and a good sauce. Play around with it until you find your own flavor. Cooking time is about 20 hours for a whole hog. You can cook it faster but it won't be nearly as good."

John Wheeler, barbecue pitmaster, Southhaven, Mississippi

While passing through Tennessee, remember to stop for a MoonPie and an RC Cola. MoonPies – chocolate-covered marshmallow and cookie sandwiches – have been baked in Chattanooga for nearly 100 years and are a gas station staple across the South. Georgia-based RC Cola came onto the scene in the 1930s, and the two treats have been inseparable ever since.

Cross the Great Smokies and spend the night in Asheville, North Carolina. A favorite of jazz-age luminaries such as F Scott Fitzgerald, this stylish mountain town is notable for its art deco architecture and arty, liberal-minded residents. Spend the night at the **17** **Grove Park Inn**, an Arts and Crafts–style colossus of red tile and gray stone clinging to the side of a mountain like a fairy-tale castle. Inside are 510 rooms, numerous shops and restaurants and a grotto-like basement spa complete with fake waterfall.

In the morning, call in to the self-consciously rustic **18** **Mast General Store** to load up on old-fashioned candy like horehound drops and Squirrel Nut Zippers. Pick up a jar of sourwood honey – a pale, slightly spicy honey gathered from bees that feed on the sourwood trees of the southern Appalachians. You may see highway-side vendors in these parts hawking "authentic sourwood".

BOILED PEANUTS

If you spot a hand-lettered sign on a house or gas station window advertising the sale of "BPs" while you're driving, you know you're in boiled peanut territory. These Carolinas roadside delicacies are immature or "green" peanuts boiled in their shells, then scooped right out of the salty brine and into a big Styrofoam cup. They're much softer than roasted peanuts, with a mildly nutty flavor.

They're not always telling the truth. Grab a cold Cheerwine for the road – the syrupy burgundy-colored soda is made in Salisbury, NC.

If you're passing through South Carolina's sleepy state capital of Columbia around lunchtime, stop in for a pimento cheeseburger at the **19** **Rockaway Athletic Club**. Pimento cheese consists of grated cheddar, mayo and chopped sweet peppers. Spread on white bread, it's a staple of Southern school cafeteria lunches. The Rockaway, a rather ordinary sports bar and grill, creates an aura of secretiveness by forgoing a sign and having its main entrance in a parking lot facing away from the street. But the thick, drippy pimento cheeseburgers are worth the search.

A short detour off Hwy 26 takes you into the town of Holly Hill, where the **20** **Holly Hill Country Restaurant** serves up retro country cooking in a cafeteria setting. Stop off for an enormous plate of fried chicken, okra and mac 'n' cheese or whatever else is on the daily menu.

Gardenia-scented **21** **Charleston** is heaven for food and architecture lovers. Downtown is neatly contained on a small peninsula; most of the action is found below Calhoun St. Stroll the cobblestone back streets admiring the multicolored antebellum mansions before digging into the port city's refined seafood delicacies.

Right in the middle of the historic downtown action, casual **22** **Hyman's Seafood** is always slammed with tourists, local families and College of Charleston students. Expect a wait. The sherried she-crab soup, a Charleston classic, is worth it. Or go for one of the irrationally huge made-for-two (or five!) mixed seafood platters.

The **23** **Charleston Cooks!** kitchen store (owned by the same people who run S.N.O.B.) offers "Taste of the Lowcountry" cooking classes. Guests sit back and sip wine as instructors prepare dishes like stuffed squash, red rice and blackened pork tenderloin.

Just across Charleston Harbor is the resort community of Mount Pleasant. Some of the area's best seafood can be found around Shem Creek, where fishermen bring in their catch in the evenings. On an unpaved road overlooking the water, **24** **The Wreck of the Richard and Charlene** exemplifies the truism that in the South, some of the best eats are usually found in the dingiest places – gas stations, fishermen's shacks and cinderblock bunkers with hog cookers smoking out back. In an old bait warehouse, The Wreck serves sloppy piles of fried shrimp and red rice at plastic tables. There's no sign outside; just look for the cars.

LOWCOUNTRY CUISINE

South Carolina's central and southern coastline, known as the Lowcountry, has its own unique culture and cuisine. Here, the West African roots of the Gullah people shine through, with heavy use of okra, sweet potatoes and rice. Parties here often feature a Lowcountry boil (also known as Frogmore Stew) – shrimp, crab legs, sausage and corn cooked in a big pot then served on a newspaper-covered table. Another typical dish, Hoppin' John, is made from rice, black eyed peas and onions.

Sleep in the French Quarter at **25** **Vendue Inn**, a boutique hotel on a historic lane by the water. While some Charleston inns can have a bit of a formal, twin-set-'n'-pearls vibe, the Vendue is all about trendy exposed brick and quirky antiques. Rooms have deep soaking tubs and gas fireplaces; the two-story rooftop bar has live music and the best views of the skyline at sunset.

Before you leave town, swing by **26** **S.N.O.B.** (it stands for Slightly North of Broad) for self-described "maverick Southern cooking" in a trendy, exposed brick dining room. Think pan-fried Carolina quail, house-smoked salmon, and luxe banana cream pie. Try their funky take on shrimp and grits, a classic Charleston fisherman's breakfast. S.N.O.B.'s version, featuring homemade sausage, will keep you full for the journey home.

Emily Matcher

TRIP INFORMATION

GETTING THERE

From Houston, take I-10 east for about 350 miles and follow the signs for New Orleans.

DO

Charleston Cooks!

Watch a Lowcountry cooking demo at this downtown cooking store. ☎ 843-722-1212; www.mavericksouthernkitchens.com; 194 E Bay St, Charleston, SC; class $25

Fondren Beverage Emporium

Taste dozens of kinds of root beer and other rare and forgotten sodas at this one-of-a-kind soft drink and candy shop. ☎ 601-321-0806; 3030 N State St, Jackson, MS; ⏱ 10am-6pm Tue-Sat; ♿

Mast General Store

This old-time general store sells "penny" candy from barrels and mountain foodstuffs like honey and blackberry preserves. ☎ 828-232-1883; www.mastgeneralstore.com; 15 Biltmore Ave, Asheville, NC; ⏱ 10am-6pm Mon-Fri, later on weekends; ♿

New Orleans School of Cooking

Sip a cold beer as you watch personable chef-instructors cook up classics like gumbo and pralines. ☎ 504-525-2665; www.new orleansschoolofcooking.com; 524 St Louis St, New Orleans, LA; class $27

EAT

Café Du Monde

The floors are coated with powdered sugar from the famous beignets at this 24-hour French Quarter café. ☎ 504-525-4544; www .cafedumonde.com; 800 Decatur St, New Orleans, LA; beignets $1.75; ⏱ 24hr

Central Grocery

The original *muffalettas* are big enough for four people at this small Italian deli. ☎ 504-523-1620; 923 Decatur St, New Orleans, LA; mains $7-13; ⏱ 9am-5pm Tue-Sat; ♿

Charlie Vergos' Rendezvous

Rib-hungry diners pack this subterranean institution. ☎ 901-523-2746; www.hogsfly .com; in the alley off Second St btw Union & Monroe, Memphis, TN; mains $7-18;

⏱ 4:30pm-10:30pm Tue-Thu, 11am-11pm Fri & Sat

Cochon

This James Beard award-winner does amazing upscale Cajun. ☎ 504-588-2123; www .cochonrestaurant.com; 930 Tchoupitoulas St, New Orleans, LA; mains $7-22; ⏱ 11am-10pm Mon-Fri, 5:30pm-10pm Sat

Cozy Corner

Barbecued Cornish game hen is an offbeat delicacy at this family-run bungalow. ☎ 901-527-9158; 745 N Pkwy, Memphis, TN; mains $5-16; ⏱ 10:30am-5pm Tue-Sat, later in summer

Felix's Oyster Bar

Crowds pack in for the fresh market oysters prepared every which way. ☎ 504-522-4440; www.felixs.com; 739 Iberville St, New Orleans, LA; mains $12-20; ⏱ 10am-10pm Mon-Thu, to midnight Fri & Sat, to 9pm Sun

Holly Hill Country Restaurant

Pile your plate high with rib sticking soul food like collards and fried chicken at this cafeteria-style buffet. ☎ 803-496-1211; 8637 Old State Rd, Holly Hill, SC; mains from $5; ⏱ 7am-8pm Mon-Wed & Sat, to 9pm Fri, to 4pm Sun

Hyman's Seafood

Join the crowds waiting outside this casual favorite for she-crab soup and crispy flounder. ☎ 843-723-6000; www.hymanseafood .com; 215 Meeting St, Charleston, SC; mains $8-24; ⏱ 11am-11pm daily; ♿

Jim Neely's Interstate Bar-B-Que

Order a pulled-pork sandwich with a side of barbecue spaghetti and allow yourself to swoon with pleasure. ☎ 901-775-1045; www.interstatebarbecue.com; 2265 S Third St, Memphis, TN; mains $5-9; ⏱ 11am-11pm Mon-Thu, to midnight Fri & Sat; ♿

Johnny's Po-Boy

This family-run sandwich joint has been going strong since the 1950s. ☎ 504-524-8129; www.johnnyspoboy.com; 511 St Louis St, New Orleans, LA; mains $6-10; ⏱ 9am-3pm Mon-Fri, 8am-4pm Sat & Sun; ♿

Prince's Hot Chicken

Cayenne-laced fried chicken is worth the long wait in a dingy strip mall. ☎ 615-226-9442;

123 Ewing Dr, Nashville, TN; mains $4-8;
ⓦ noon-10pm Tue-Thu, to 4am Fri & Sat

Rockaway Athletic Club

Sink your teeth into a sloppy pimento cheeseburger at this hidden sports bar. ☎ 803-
256-1075; 2719 Rosewood Dr, Columbia, SC;
mains $9-12; ⓦ 11am-11pm

S.N.O.B.

Think upscale Southern food with an attitude –
grilled barbecue tuna, sour-cream apple pie –
cooked up in a contemporary open kitchen.
☎ 843-723-3424; www.slightlynorthof
broad.net; 192 E Bay St, Charleston, SC;
mains $18-34; ⓦ 11:30am-3pm Mon-Fri &
5:30pm-10pm daily

Walker's Drive-In

Try the upscale version of the famous Delta
tamale at this critically acclaimed neo-
Southern restaurant. ☎ 601-982-2633;
www.walkersdrivein.com; 3016 N State St,
Jackson, MS; mains $24-32; ⓦ 11am-2pm
Mon-Fri & 5:30-9:30pm Tue-Sat

Wreck of the Richard and Charlene

Chow on fried shrimp with a side of boiled
peanuts in this creekside former bait warehouse. ☎ 843-884-0052; www.wreckrc.com;
106 Haddrell St, Mount Pleasant, SC; mains
$12-20; ⓦ 5:30pm-8:15pm Tue-Thu, to
9:15pm Fri & Sat

SLEEP

Grove Park Inn

This massive 1913 stone lodge sits high
above Asheville in the Blue Ridge mountains;
don't miss the underground spa. ☎ 828-252-
2711; www.groveparkinn.com; 290 Macon
Ave, Asheville, NC; r from $155

Melrose Mansion

This graceful Victorian mansion has rooms
furnished with antiques, and wide verandas.
☎ 504-944-2255; www.melrosemansion
.com; 937 Esplanade Ave, New Orleans, LA;
r $225-450

Peabody Hotel

Watch the ducks swim in the marble lobby
fountain at this well-appointed downtown
hotel. ☎ 901-529-4000; www.peabody
memphis.com; 149 Union Ave, Memphis, TN;
r from $240

Vendue Inn

This hip boutique hotel, resembling a tiny
Parisian row house, has an always-packed
rooftop bar. ☎ 843-577-7970; www.vendue
inn.com; 19 Vendue Range, Charleston, SC;
r $179-399

USEFUL WEBSITES

www.gumbopages.com
www.southernfoodways.com

LINK YOUR TRIP

www.lonelyplanet.com/trip-planner

TRIP
44 New Orleans Perfect Po'Boy Quest p289
54 Pulled Pork & Butt Rubs: Eating in Memphis p341

Antebellum South

WHY GO The Civil War decimated the South, but several elegant plantation homes built in the 30 years leading up to the war avoided the Union's fiery wrath. Referred to as antebellum, they not only represent some of the most astounding architecture on American soil, but also offer a glimpse into a bygone era.

TIME
8 days

DISTANCE
1100 miles

BEST TIME TO GO
Mar – Jun

START
Charleston, SC

END
Vacherie, LA

ALSO GOOD FOR

HISTORY &
CULTURE

Many people's idea of antebellum architecture, whether they realize it or not, is Tara Plantation, the fictional abode of Scarlett O'Hara in Margaret Mitchell's 1946 novel, *Gone with the Wind* – but you can only visit that one in your own fantasyland. In the book, Tara is spared the fiery wrath of the Union's matchbook warfare, surviving untorched while its neighbors are burnt to the ground. That's pretty much how it went, and why antebellum architecture is so vehemently preserved today: there just isn't very much of it left.

Antebellum refers to a time and place in history – the 30 years leading up to the Civil War, from 1831 to 1861 – not an architectural style as some people think. Most antebellum homes are actually one of three styles: Greek Revival, Classical Revival Tidewater or Federal style. They are boxy, grand mansions with central entrances in the front and back, impressive columns and sizable covered porches made for lazily watching the days go by while sipping on homemade lemonade or backyard hooch (as the case may be). These are typical architectural features introduced by Anglo Americans who settled in the area after the Louisiana Purchase in 1803. Today, antebellum homes conjure up romanticized images of Southern opulence, owned by folks with so much money, they'd gladly give you some (just ask nicely, hon); but in reality, folks with this much money usually "owned" slaves, so most of these antebellum homes aren't without their dark side.

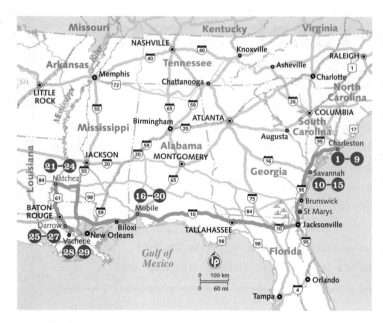

Bookending this trip are two evocative river roads – Ashley in Charleston, South Carolina and the Great Mississippi in Vacherie, Louisiana – that together represent the most picturesque destinations to take in the refined elegance of antebellum architecture in a concentrated area. But there is no shortage of impressive stops along the way – small patches of the Deep South, like the fictional Tara, were left untouched, while others suffered damage but not irreparably so, leaving behind one of America's most endearing architectural legacies.

1 Charleston, South Carolina offers its visitors an unparalleled continuum of classical American architecture, ranging from early colonial through Federal, antebellum and Victorian styles, unmatched anywhere else in the United States. Despite being the cradle of the Civil War and its succession movement, a surprising amount of buildings here eluded destruction or irreversible damage. The **2 Aiken-Rhett House** is the only surviving urban plantation. Built in 1818, it was described in a 19th-century newspaper ad as: "Twelve upright rooms, four on each floor, all well finished, the material of the piazzas and fences all of cypress and cedar; underneath the house are large cellars and storerooms." Confederate President Jefferson Davis slept here on a visit to Charleston in 1863.

Everywhere you turn in Charleston, an historic inn or hotel beckons. Try the **3 Mills House Hotel**, which is slightly hipper than most. Owned by Holiday

Inn, it's anything but a typical highway-exit haunt. An ornate $17 million restoration has returned it to the glory of its original opening date (1853). The staircases and chandeliers are original. Inside a 19th-century shipping warehouse a few blocks west, you'll find **4** **S.N.O.B.** which stands for Slightly North of Broad, but order the Carolina quail breast over cheese grits and your graduation to food snob will be complete.

A few miles west of town is the impossibly scenic **5** **Ashley River Rd**, a picturesque glimpse into once-thriving South Carolina Lowcountry wealth. The oldest *preserved* plantation in the US is the pre-revolutionary **6** **Drayton Hall**, built in 1738 and unique here for its Georgian-Palladian architecture. If it all goes down while you're in the area, this is a good place to seek shelter; it has survived the American Revolution, the Civil War, the earthquake of 1886, and Hurricane Hugo. A few clicks northwest is the **7** **Magnolia Plantation** (1676), known for its exquisite formal gardens – said to be the origin of azaleas in the US – and 19th-century slave cabin.

Your bed for the night is at the **8** **Inn at Middleton Place** on the sprawling **9** **Middleton Place Plantation**, another 4 miles or so down Ashley River Rd. The main house (c 1730) is home to the oldest landscaped gardens in the US. Several generations of influential Middletons stomped these gorgeous grounds, including the president of the first Continental Congress (Henry), a signer of the Declaration of Independence (Arthur) and a governor of South Carolina (Henry). The inn is cozy, and noted for its wide plantation shutters, hardwood floors and braided rugs. The whole property has also been designated a National Wildlife Federation (NWF) Backyard Wildlife Habitat site and offers memorable kayaking and birding. Allow a few hours to visit the plantations on Ashley River Rd.

Leave Ashley River Rd on Hwy 61, which takes you to Hwy 17 Alt (south bound) and I-95 (south bound) on to **10** **Savannah**, Georgia's Belle of the Ball. For a good comparison of middle-class versus high falutin' antebellum life, two good examples spell it out for you here. The **11** **Davenport House Museum**, a 200-year-old mansion built in Federal style is credited with spawning Savannah's historical preservation movement when it avoided demolition in 1955. Built by Isaiah Davenport in the 1820s, the simply appointed home boasts an impressive entrance hall

ASK A LOCAL

"Beloved in Southern history, the **Olde Pink House** is my favorite of Savannah's antebellum structures. Today, as a fine-dining restaurant, the graceful dining rooms are dressed in white tablecloths and candles, while the grandeur and pioneering adventures of the 18th century seem to hover gracefully. My vivid imagination has often taken me on a time travel to the Planters Tavern, at basement level, to watch and listen as Liberty Boys plotted and put in motion Georgia's role in the united colonies' fight for independence from England."
Sandy Traub, Savannah

with two iconic columns, a spiral staircase and Palladian window. There is, however, questionable – though period-perfect – wallpaper.

A block away, but worlds away in social status, one of the wealthiest men in America, cotton merchant Richard Richardson, built the ⓰ **Owens-Thomas House** between 1816 and 1819. This ornate English Regency mansion features rare *Haint* Blue ceiling paint, made from crushed indigo, buttermilk and wine, in the slave quarters. *Haint* means "haunt" in the Gullah language (still spoken by some Lowcountry African Americans), and the paint was used to ward off spirits. The home also boasts a gorgeous upstairs bridge connecting two sides of the house, impressive curved doors in the dining room and a beautiful Russian harp belonging to Isabella Habersham. The home is part of Savannah's ⓭ **Telfair Museum of Art**, the oldest museum in the Southeast.

MO-BEEL'S HISTORIC HOMES

Residents of Alabama's oldest city throw open the doors to their most preciously preserved historic homes for two days every March for the **Mobile Historic Homes Tour** (*Mo-beel*, not a bunch of trailers!). Mobile's diverse architectural styles are all represented on the tours: Creole cottages, Greek Revival mansions, Victorian and neoclassic residences, among others. It's a one-shot chance to get inside some of the country's most antique abodes.

Savannah is an ideal spot for a sleepover. Dine on the signature crispy scored flounder at ⓮ **Olde Pink House**, a 1771 National Landmark that turned from white to Jamaican pink after the original bricks "bled" through the plastered walls. The ⓯ **Kehoe House**, a romantic Renaissance Revival B&B built in 1892 and said to be haunted, is where you'll find your historic bed. Twins are said to have died in a chimney here, so they are boarded up. The skittish should steer clear of rooms 201 and 203!

Continue on I-95 (south bound) to Jacksonville, FL, where you'll pick up I-10 (west bound) across the entity of the Florida Panhandle all the way to ⓰ **Mobile, AL**. It's risky to stop first and drop your bags at the ⓱ **Kate Shepard House**, historic Mobile's must-sleep. Innkeeper Wendy James is as gracious a host as humanly possible. The meticulous restoration of this gorgeous 1897 Queen Anne–style home by Wendy and her husband deserves the museum treatment itself. You won't want to leave. But it's the pecan praline French toast that ensures this wonderful find won't soon be forgotten. Ask about the long lost Civil War papers found in the attic. This surely must be where the phrase "Southern hospitality" was first uttered. The house is across the street from Katharine Philips, who played a role in the Ken Burns documentary, *The War*.

Located in one of Mobile's eight National Register Historic Districts, the main T-shaped Greek Revival mansion at the ⓲ **Oakleigh Historic Complex** dates back to 1833. Its distinct cantilevered front staircase and grand double parlors offer a peek in to the Gulf Coast's high society lifestyle, while the Cook's House (1850), originally built for slaves, and Cox-Deasy Cottage (1850), built by a brick mason for his wife and 11 kids, show how the working and servant classes lived. Spend your evening in the classic ⓲ **Pillars** restaurant; they do wonderful things with blackened cow.

Before hopping on I-10 (west bound) towards Natchez, stop off at the ⓴ **Bragg-Mitchell Mansion** (1855), one of the most splendid Greek Revival mansions on the Gulf Coast. It closes without notice for special events though, so call ahead. From there, it's a 4½ hour drive to southwest Mississippi, where ㉑ **Natchez, Mississippi**, the oldest civilized settlement on the Mississippi River (beating out New Orleans by two years), stands perched on a bluff. Settled by the French in 1716, it remains a living antebellum museum (when it's not getting pounded by hurricanes) and boasts more antebellum homes than any other US city. If you can get here during spring and fall pilgrimage, many private residences are open to the public – but there is plenty to do and see here year-round.

㉒ **Longwood Plantation**, a six-story, 30,000 sq ft, Greek Revival monster is considered the grandest octagonal house in America (rumor has it a sassy hexagonal number from Tallahassee is looking to unseat Longwood for most striking geometric dwelling). When the Civil War broke out during construction, the workers hightailed it out of here (damn straight), leaving the home unfinished. It's still unfinished (not cool, yet fascinating). You can sleep in Natchez most well-known antebellum attraction, the Federal-style ㉓ **Monmouth Plantation** (1818). Union soldiers almost took this one out, due to the succession cries of its original owner, Mexican War hero General John A Quitman. He died before war broke out, but if it weren't for his two daughters pleading with Union soldiers on their way to declaring allegiance to the United States, Monmouth would have been a smoldering mess in no time. Toast to the daughters' quick-thinking resilience over mint juleps at the ㉔ **Carriage House** on the grounds of Stanton Hall (1857). It's famous for fried chicken and tiny buttered biscuits.

> **ASK A LOCAL**
>
> "The historic homes are certainly the main attraction, but we also have a vineyard and winery, Old South Winery, and a great exhibit of photographs of life in Natchez from the mid-1800s to about 1920 at the Stratton Chapel. We have seasonal pilgrimages in the spring and fall, when more of the homes are open to the public for tour than usual, and that's when we enjoy more visitors because the seasons are milder."
>
> *Charles Burns, Natchez*

A little over two hours' travel south along the Mississippi River's scenic ㉕ **Great River Rd** lands you in Darrow, Louisiana, worth a stop for the ㉖ **Houmas House Plantation** and its excellent restaurant, ㉗ **Latil's Landing**. The former is a grand mansion so unmistakably *Cribs*-worthy, it sold for

$1 million in *1857*, and is notable as one of the few antebellum homes that remain an active residence (no, Snoop Dogg doesn't live here). The restaurant is set inside the 230-year-old French House on the same grounds, complete with original beamed ceilings, cypress mantels, wood-burning fireplaces and original wood floors. It's the foodie highlight of the trip.

Continue east along Great River Rd to the Louisiana's two most adored plantations. **28 Laura Plantation**, built in 1805, stands out for its whimsical exterior (canary yellow with a bright-red roof, pine-green shutters, and mauve and grey trim) and its fascinating tour – far and away the most interesting along the road for its deep-rooted Creole past, its slave quarters and the slaves' affiliation with the West African folktale of Br'er Rabbit (the American version of which was said to have originated here among slaves). The backbone of the tour is based on 5000 pages of documents related to the plantation found archived in Paris, plus the memoirs of Laura Locoul Gore, for whom the house is named. These written accounts from generations of the Creoles who lived here (the women who ran the plantation and the slaves who lived here) will inspire laughter one minute, tears the next, but it's never boring.

"A grand mansion so unmistakably Cribs-worthy, it sold for $1 million in 1857."

The easiest plantation on the eyes is **29 Oak Alley Plantation**, with its 28 perfectly symmetrical live oak trees naturally framing the 28-column entrance corridor to this majestic Greek Revival beauty from 1837. Arrive early or stay late for that postcard-perfect shot without a bunch of gawking tourists mucking up your photos. Like elsewhere on Great River Rd, countless movies have been filmed here, most notably *Primary Colors* and *Interview with the Vampire*. It runs a B&B, so you can sleep here, too, dreaming of a simpler time, wondering if the South were to rise again, what would become of its most treasured possessions?

Kevin Raub

TRIP INFORMATION

GETTING THERE
From Atlanta, take I-20 (east bound) to I-26 (east bound) into Charleston.

DO

Aiken-Rhett House
Charleston's most intact antebellum mansion. Many pieces are still sitting in the same rooms for which they were purchased. ☎ 843-723-1159; www.historic charleston.org; 48 Elizabeth St, Charleston, SC; adult/child $10/5; 🕙 10am-5pm Mon-Sat, 2-5pm Sun; 🎫

Bragg-Mitchell Mansion
This Greek-Italianate mansion (1855) is the grandest of the surviving Gulf Coast antebellum homes. It does close sporadically though. ☎ 251-471-6364; www.bragg mitchellmansion.com; 1906 Springhill Ave, Mobile, AL; adult/child $5/3; 🕙 10am-4pm Tue-Fri; 🎫

Davenport House Museum
This 200-year-old Federal-style mansion kicked off Savannah's preservation movement. ☎ 912-236-8097; www.davenport housemuseum.org; 324 E State St, Savannah, GA; adult/child $8/5; 🕙 10am-4pm Mon-Sat, 1-4pm Sun; 🎫

Drayton Hall
The oldest surviving Georgian Palladian structure in the US and the only originally intact plantation along the Ashley River. ☎ 843-769-2600; www.draytonhall.org; 3380 Ashley River Rd, Charleston, SC; adult/child $14/8; 🕙 8:30am-5pm Mar-Oct, to 4pm Nov-Feb; 🎫

Houmas House Plantation
Exquisite 1828 Greek Revival mansion originally owned by Houmas Indians. There's a fantastic restaurant here too. ☎ 225-473-9380; www.houmashouse.com; 40136 Hwy 942, Darrow, LA; adult/child $20/10; 🕙 9am-5pm Mon & Tue, to 7pm Wed-Sun; 🎫

Laura Plantation
This 1805 Creole plantation runs exceptional tours of the colorful manor house, formal French gardens and historic outbuild-ings. ☎ 225-265-7690; www.laura plantation.com; 2247 Hwy 18, Vacherie, LA; adult/child $15/5; 🕙 10am-4pm; 🎫

Longwood Plantation
The Civil War interrupted the construction of Longwood (1861), the grandest octagonal house in the US. ☎ 601-442-5193; www.natchezpilgrimage.com; 140 Lower Woodville Rd, Natchez, MS; adult/child $10/8; 🕙 9am-4pm; 🎫

Magnolia Plantation
Exquisite gardens (some parts as old as 325 years) and main home dating back to 1676. ☎ 843-571-1266; www.magnolia plantation.com; 3550 Ashley River Rd, Charleston, SC; adult/child incl house tour $22/17; 🕙 8am-5:30pm; 🎫

Middleton Place Plantation
Sprawling 18th-century Lowcountry plantation and America's oldest landscaped gardens. ☎ 843-556-6020; www.middleton place.org; 4300 Ashley River Rd, Charleston, SC; adult/child $25/5; 🕙 9am-5pm; 🎫

Oakleigh Historic Complex
A three-home museum highlighted by the main Greek Revival house (1833) and its 1840 rosewood piano with mother-of-pearl keys. ☎ 251-432-6161; www.historicmobile .org; 300 Oakleigh Pl, Mobile, AL; adult/child $10/5; 🕙 10am-4pm; 🎫

Owens-Thomas House
Ornate English Regency mansion that's part of Savannah's Telfair Museum of Art. ☎ 912-233-9743; www.telfair.org; 124 Abercorn St, Savannah, GA; adult/child $10/4; 🕙 noon-5pm Mon, 10am-5pm Tue-Sat, 1-5pm Sun

Telfair Museum of Art
Three unique buildings make up the Telfair, which isn't antebellum, but dates back to 1886. ☎ 912-233-1177; www.telfair.org; 121 Barnard St, Savannah, GA; adult/child $10/5; 🕙 10am-5pm Mon, Wed, Fri & Sat, to 8pm Thu, noon-5pm Sun

EAT

Carriage House
Southern fried chicken, tiny buttered biscuits and mint juleps top the fare at this restaurant on the grounds of 1857 Greek Revival Stanton

Hall. ☎ 601-445-5153; 401 High St, Natchez, GA; mains $10-15; ⏱ 11am-2pm Thu-Mon

Latil's Landing
Inside the 1770 French House on the grounds of Houmas House, chef Jeremy Langlois' discriminating cuisine will leave you feeling like a sugar baron. ☎ 225-473-9380; 40136 Hwy 942, Darrow, LA; mains $25-35; ⏱ 6-10pm Wed-Sat, 2-9pm Sun

Olde Pink House
This 1771 pink mansion on Reynolds Square epitomizes antebellum romance. The nouveau Southern cuisine ain't bad, either. ☎ 912-232-4286; 23 Abercorn St, Savannah, GA; mains $17-29; ⏱ 5pm-10:30pm Sun & Mon,11am-10:30pm Tue-Thu, 11am-11pm Fri & Sat

Pillars
Historic 1904 mansion-turned-restaurant, serving up excellent steaks (the Queen filet, blackened – trust us) and seafood, served in a space boasting picturesque original checkerboard-tile floors. ☎ 251-471-3411; 1757 Government St, Mobile, AL; mains $29-49; ⏱ 11am-3pm Mon-Fri & 5pm-10pm Mon-Sat

S.N.O.B.
An eclectic menu, and decor carved from a 19th-century shipping warehouse. ☎ 843-723-3424; 192 E Bay St, Charleston, SC; mains $10-34; ⏱ 11:30am-3pm & 5:30pm-10pm Mon-Thu, 11:30am-3pm & 5:30-11pm Fri, 5:30-10pm Sat & Sun

SLEEP

Kate Shepard House
This 1897 Queen Anne–style B&B isn't antebellum, but don't fret. The only thing more gorgeous than the home is the pecan praline French toast. ☎ 251-479-7048; www.kateshepardhouse.com; 1552 Monterrey Pl, Mobile, AL; r $155

Kehoe House
An intimate, 13-room Renaissance Revival B&B on beautiful Columbia Square. ☎ 912-232-1020; www.kehoehouse.com; 123 Habersham St, Savannah, GA; r $200-400

Inn at Middleton Place
Inviting cypress paneling, warm hardwood floors and wood-burning stoves are a highlight of this romantic inn at Middleton Place. ☎ 802-496-2276; www.theinnatmiddletonplace.com; 4300 Ashley River Rd, Charleston, SC; r $189-235

Mills House Hotel
Originally opened just before the Civil War, this hotel features an opulent marble lobby and gilded elevators. ☎ 843-577-2400; www.millshouse.com; 115 Meeting St, Charleston, SC; r $209-379

Monmouth Plantation
A night at this regal Federal-style 1818 mansion and eight outbuildings is like sleeping *on* history. Good restaurant, too. ☎ 601-442-5852; www.monmouthplantation.com; 36 Melrose Ave, Natchez, MS; r from $195

Oak Alley Plantation
Slip into slumber in century-old plantation cottages on the grounds of Oak Alley Plantation (1841) and its famously photographed 28 classic columns. ☎ 225-265-2151; www.oakalleyplantation.com; 3645 Hwy 18, Vacherie, LA; r from $130

USEFUL WEBSITES
www.charlestoncvb.com
www.visitnatchez.com

LINK YOUR TRIP
www.lonelyplanet.com/trip-planner

Tracing Martin Luther King, Jr

WHY GO When a shot rang out in the Memphis sky on April 4, 1968, a true American hero was silenced. But the words and life of Rev. Martin Luther King, Jr will forever remain in the public consciousness as the soundtrack to civil rights. This eye-opening journey traces his revolutionary footsteps.

TIME
3 – 4 days

DISTANCE
600 miles

BEST TIME TO GO
Mar – May

START
Atlanta, GA

END
Memphis, TN

ALSO GOOD FOR

There once was a time in the frighteningly none too distant past when humankind was not equal. Men and women could not drink from the same water fountains, share the same seats on public transport, or eat in the same restaurants. The deciding factor was skin color, and the color black was on the losing end. It's a preposterous American story by today's standards, an embarrassing wound that is still healing. More scary still is the thought that were it not for one man, born in Atlanta in 1929, who knows how much longer this story called segregation would have continued.

Though he was far from acting alone, the Rev. Martin Luther King will forever remain the most prominent face of the struggle for civil rights for African Americans. King – preacher, motivational speaker, activist and promoter of non-violent social change – rose to prominence shortly after the Supreme Court unanimously ruled in 1954 in *Brown vs Board of Education of Topeka, Kans,* that segregation in public schools was unconstitutional. Though the ruling paved the way for large-scale desegregation, resistance was widespread and violent. A few months later, when Rosa Parks defied a Southern custom by refusing to give up her seat at the front of the colored section of a public bus to a white man, the year-long Montgomery Bus Boycott was launched, led by MLK, Jr.

This act of defiance set forth in motion the Civil Rights movement, one of the darkest periods in American history. For the next 14 years,

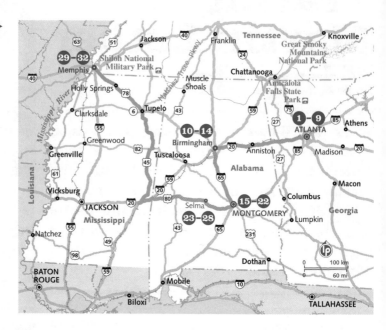

MLK, Jr would be the movement's poster boy, its catalyst and its leader, a man who dedicated his life to the greater good. He paid the ultimate price, as did many others before and after him, when he was shot dead in Tennessee in 1968. Though his voice was silenced, his legacy remains, a story that begins and ends in ① **Atlanta**, where he was born, raised and is now buried.

"Today you are not only listening to history, you are walking with history."

"Today you are not only listening to history, you are walking with history." No, that wasn't a famous phrase uttered by MLK, Jr but rather a close friend of his named Reverend Graham Williams, who remains the only living employee at the ② **Martin Luther King, Jr National Historic Site** who actually knew MLK, Jr. Do yourself a favor and get on a tour of the ③ **King Birth Home** with Williams, who marched with MLK and was otherwise in the thick of nearly everything you will read about on the Civil Rights movement. He does tours four days a week (days vary).

Reservations for the tour must be made at the ④ **Martin Luther King, Jr National Historic Site Visitor's Center**, home to a small interpretive museum chronicling MLK, Jr, who lays entombed in a watery grave at the nearby ⑤ **King Center**. The center also has a fascinating exhibit of MLK, Jr's personal items. One block away is the ⑥ **Ebenezer Baptist Church**, where

MLK, Jr was baptized and later preached. The church is the heart and soul of the **7** **Sweet Auburn** neighborhood, where MLK, Jr grew up.

If you get hungry while touring the area, **8** **Thelma's Kitchen** does righteous soul food in the former space of one of MLK, Jr's favorite haunts, the Auburn Ave Rib Shack. In downtown Atlanta, the **9** **Hyatt Regency** was the first area hotel to welcome African Americans – the King Center and the Southern Christian Leadership Conference (SCLC) still do events here today.

But as any good Alabamian will tell you, MLK, Jr might have been born in Atlanta, but it was in Alabama that he became famous. It's time to head west. From Atlanta, hop on I-20 (west bound) and make your way to **10** **Birmingham**, home to the **11** **Birmingham Civil Rights Institute**. This museum in the round does a wonderful – although scary – job of recreating the segregated world of Birmingham under Jim Crow laws, a series of mandates that ensured No Shirt, No Shoes, No Service included No Blacks. The museum chronicles the plight of Birmingham's civil rights struggle from the city to all the major hot points. There's also a rotating art gallery that often features African American artists. Across the street is the **12** **Sixteenth St Baptist Church**, bombed by the Ku Klux Klan (KKK) in 1963 after a ruling to desegregate Birmingham's schools. Four young schoolchildren were killed. It was here that same year that MLK, Jr was

REVEREND BERNICE KING

"The civil rights historic site that has the most inspirational resonance for me is **Ebenezer Baptist Church's Heritage Sanctuary**, where my father, uncle, grandfather and great grand-father all preached. There were civil rights meetings being held in Ebenezer even before my father was born. It is also the church I grew up in and where I developed a strong spiritual foundation. As a child, I always looked forward to getting dressed up and going to church on Sunday. Although on Sunday, June 30, 1974 my grandmother was assassinated while play-ing the Lord's Prayer on the church organ by a deranged young man. So many of the other memories are joyful – weddings, baptisms, great singing and often laughter, as well as the inspirational sermons. I'm sure those pre-cious memories contributed to me becoming a preacher. It was in Ebenezer's Heritage Sanctu-ary where I first preached and was ordained into the gospel ministry. I have also preached on special occasions, like the 25th Commemorative Holiday Service honoring my father. It's holy ground to me, and many others."

arrested and jailed for protesting anti-segregation laws. From his cell, he penned his famous *Letter from Birmingham Jail*, arguing that human beings have a moral duty to disobey unjust laws.

"We know through painful experience that freedom is never voluntarily given by the oppressor; it must be demanded by the oppressed," he wrote. "Frankly, I have never yet engaged in a direct action movement that was 'well timed,' according to the timetable of those who have not suffered unduly from the disease of segregation. For years now I have heard the word 'wait!' It rings in the ear of every Negro with a piercing familiarity. This 'wait' has almost always meant 'never.' We must come to see with the distinguished jurist of yesterday that 'justice too long delayed is justice denied.'"

While in town, be sure you grab a meal at ⑬ Café Dupont where wonderful upscale contemporary Southern cuisine emerges from the kitchen. The next stop is Montgomery, but if you want to sleep here (trust us, you do), try the ⑭ Tutwiler Hotel, one of the city's two historic choices. There is nothing anywhere near as appealing in Montgomery.

I-65 (south bound) out of Birmingham is a straight shot to ⑮ Montgomery, the armpit of America otherwise, but ground zero for the Civil Rights movement. It was here that the movement found its footing in 1955, when a member of the National Association for the Advancement of Colored People (NAACP) named Rosa Parks boarded a public bus and decided today wasn't going to be the day she moved seats because of the color of her skin. When she refused to obey bus driver James Blake's order that she give up her seat to make room for a white passenger, all hell broke loose. Though Parks wasn't the first to engage in this sort of civil disobedience, her actions and subsequent arrest sparked the Montgomery Bus Boycott, (conceived by MLK, Jr) turning her into an icon of non-violent social change and paving the way for the entire Civil Rights movement.

It wasn't until the city of Montgomery was hit in the pocketbook that change commenced (the year-long bus boycott by African Americans resulted in a massive revenue hole for the city's public transit system as African Americans were its bread and butter). In 1956, the Supreme Court upheld a lower court's ruling that Alabama's racial segregation laws on public buses had run their course. A month later, the boycott ended, and the Civil Rights movement scored its first major victory. The bus ride itself is recreated at the ⑯ Rosa Parks Museum, located in the former spot of the Empire Theater, in front of which Parks took her defiant stand. You can also take a photo next to a sculpture of Parks seated on the bus.

Nearby, the ⑰ Civil Rights Memorial Center, with its circular memorial designed by Maya Lin, is a haunting eye-opener for anyone who only learned about the struggle for civil rights in eighth grade American History class. It focuses on 40 martyrs of the movement, all murdered for countless reasons; many of the murders have never been solved. MLK, Jr was the most famous, but there were many 'faceless' deaths along the way, white and black alike, that here provides the most somber moments while tracing the footsteps of MLK, Jr. You can walk over to ⑱ Dexter Ave King Memorial Baptist Church, where MLK, Jr preached his first sermon at the age of 24. The ⑲ Dexter Parsonage Museum, his home for six years during his tenure at the church, is less than 1 mile away on Jackson St. You're not too far from **20** Isaiah's restaurant inside Montgomery's first African American–owned B&B, the **21** **Butterfly Inn**. This is the spot to enjoy some fine lemon-pepper catfish while rapping with the friendly and welcoming owners. Or you could hit **22** **Martin's**, for the best fried chicken in Montgomery, located 1.5 miles southeast on Carter Hill Rd.

Out of Montgomery, take Hwy 80 (west bound) towards **23** **Selma** – you are now traveling the path of one of the Civil Rights movement's darkest hours, the **24** **Selma-to-Montgomery National Historic Trail**. As you near Selma, stop at the **25** **Lowndes County Interpretive Center**, which commemorates the 1965 Voting Rights March, and "Bloody Sunday" – the day Alabama State troopers greeted over 500 non-violent marchers on the **26** **Edmund Pettus Bridge** in Selma and attacked them with billy clubs and tear gas. The whole thing was captured on video, marking one of the first time Americans outside the South had witnessed firsthand the horrifying images of the struggle. Shock and outrage ensued, and support for the movement grew. You can see it all here in a 25-minute documentary.

For supreme views of the bridge and river, book a room in the historic **27** **St James Hotel** in Selma itself, where balconies stare right into the heart of this infamously bloodied battlefield. It's not far from where the small **28** **National Voting Rights Museum** is located, ironically enough in a building formerly occupied by the White Citizen's Council, a now-defunct white supremacy group. The most shocking thing here is a cattle prod belonging to a defiantly racist local sheriff named Jim Clark, used routinely on African Americans.

GONE BUT NOT FORGOTTEN

Martin Luther King, Jr is the most famous casualty of the Civil Rights movement in the US, but he was hardly a unique case. The following also lost their lives:

- Lamar Smith: Shot dead on a courthouse lawn in Brookhaven, Mississippi.

- Viola Gregg Liuzzo: White housewife murdered in Selma for offering rides back to Montgomery to marchers from the Edmund Pettus Bridge.

- Emmet Louis Till: 14-year-old murdered in Money, Mississippi, for flirting with a white girl.

Head west out of Selma on Hwy 80 to Hwy 45 (north bound) through Tupelo, Mississippi to catch Hwy 78 (west bound) to **29** **Memphis** and check into the **30** **Inn at Hunt Phelan** – you've come a long way and deserve a little pampering, antebellum-style in this 1828 mansion on 5 acres, 1 mile northeast from civil rights central. It was here that MLK, Jr's crusade was abruptly halted in April 1968, when he visited in support of the black sanitation workers. The visit was tense, as violence had erupted on MLK, Jr's previous visit to town for the same reason, and MLK, Jr's entourage noticed he was more nervous than usual. On April 3, MLK, Jr delivered the following lines in a speech at the Mason Temple: "Well, I don't know what will happen now. We've got some difficult days ahead. But it really doesn't matter with me now, because I've been to the mountaintop."

The next day, while standing on the balcony outside room 306 at the Lorraine Motel on the south end of downtown Memphis, a shot rang out that took off half of MLK, Jr's neck and jaw. He collapsed, one foot hanging off the railing, and died. Two months later, James Earl Ray was captured at London's Heathrow Airport (on the same day that Senator Robert Kennedy, who was also assassinated, was laid to rest) and later convicted of MLK, Jr's murder. Ray's participation in the assassination, however, is debated and doubted to this day, especially by the King family. Ray died in prison in 1998. Both the Lorraine Motel and the boarding house from where the shot was allegedly fired are now part of the **31** **National Civil Rights Museum**. Memphis' oldest café, **32** **Arcade Restaurant**, is a block away on S Main St. Munch here – as Elvis Presley once did – on hearty breakfast plates and lunch treats like fried peanut butter and banana sandwiches. Eating here is like stepping back in time to 1919, when it first opened. Not much has changed since, except, of course, that African Americans and whites are now both welcomed with open arms. We have MLK, Jr to thank for that.
Kevin Raub

TRIP INFORMATION

DO

Birmingham Civil Rights Institute
Interactive museum showcasing the struggle for voting rights and desegregation. It does a fascinating job of recreating a segregated world. ☎ 866-328-9696; www.bcri.org; 520 Sixteenth St, Birmingham; adult/child $10/4; ⊙ 10am-5pm Tue-Sat, 1-5pm Sun; ♿

Civil Rights Memorial Center
A haunting memorial focused on some 40 'faceless' individuals who were murdered in the civil rights struggle. ☎ 334-956-8200; www.civilrightsmemorialcenter.org; 400 Washington Ave, Montgomery; adult/child $2/free; ⊙ 9am-4:30pm Mon-Fri, 10am-4pm Sat; ♿

Dexter Ave King Memorial Baptist Church
The only church where MLK, Jr was a full-time preacher. ☎ 334-263-3970; www.dexterkingmemorial.org; 454 Dexter Ave, Montgomery; adult/child $5/3; ⊙ tours 10am, 11am, 1pm, 2pm, 3pm Tue-Fri; 10am, 11am, noon, 1pm Sat; ♿

Dexter Parsonage Museum
King's home from 1954 to 1960 still houses some of his family's furniture. ☎ 334-261-3270; 309 S Jackson St, Montgomery; adult/child $5/3; ⊙ tours 10am, 11am, 1pm, 2pm, 3pm Tue-Fri; 10am,11am, noon, 1pm Sat; ♿

Ebenezer Baptist Church
The church where MLK, Jr was baptized, and was later co-pastor. It's closed until 2010 for renovations. ☎ 404-331-5190; www.nps.gov/malu; 407-413 Auburn Ave, Atlanta; ⊙ 9am-6pm

King Birth Home
Go on a tour of MLK, Jr's 1895 birth home, guided by Rev. Graham Williams, who marched with MLK, Jr. Reservations essential; book at Martin Luther King, Jr National Historic Site Visitor's Center. ☎ 404-331-5190; www.nps.gov/malu; 501 Auburn Ave, Atlanta; admission free; ⊙ 9am-6pm

King Center
Don't miss the small exhibition here of MLK, Jr's personal items, including his key from the Lorraine Motel, where he was assassinated. ☎ 404-526-8900; www.thekingcenter.org; 449 Auburn Ave, Atlanta; admission free; ⊙ 9am-6pm

Lowndes County Interpretive Center
Showcases the 1965 historic Selma to Montgomery march for voter rights, a day known as "Bloody Sunday." ☎ 334-877-1984; www.nps.gov/semo; 7002 Hwy 80 W, Hayneville, AL; admission free; ⊙ 9am-4:30pm; ♿

Martin Luther King, Jr National Historic Site Visitor's Center
A small interpretive museum and the spot to make reservations to tour the King birth home. ☎ 404-331-5190; www.nps.gov/malu; 450 Auburn Ave, Atlanta; admission free; ⊙ 9am-6pm

National Civil Rights Museum
The site of MLK, Jr's assassination is now a startling museum covering the entirety of the Civil Rights movement. ☎ 901-521-9699; www.civilrightsmuseum.org; 450 Mulberry St, Memphis; adult/child $12/9; ⊙ 9am-5pm Mon & Wed-Sat, 1-5pm Sun

National Voting Rights Museum
An ex-Selma sheriff's cattle prod is the haunting highlight at this museum as seen through Selma's eyes. ☎ 334-418-0800; 1012 Water Ave, Selma, AL; adult/child $6/4; ⊙ 9am-5pm Mon-Fri, 10am-3pm Sat; ♿

Rosa Parks Museum
A recreation of Parks' infamous bus ride highlights this museum dedicated to her and the Montgomery Bus Boycott. ☎ 334-241-8615; 252 Montgomery St, Montgomery; adult/child $5.50/3.50 ⊙ 9am-5pm Mon-Fri, 9am-3pm Sat; ♿

Sixteenth St Baptist Church
The site of a 1963 KKK bombing that killed four young school children. ☎ 205-251-9402; www.bcri.org; 1530 Sixth Ave N, Birmingham; tour donation $2; ⊙ 10am-4pm Tue-Fri, to 1pm Sat

EAT & DRINK
Arcade Restaurant
A classic soda fountain serving up some of Memphis' finest home cooking, including a wealth of breakfast choices, sandwiches

and pizza. ☎ 901-526-5757; 540 S Main St, Memphis; mains $4-7; ⊗ 7am-3pm daily, dinner Fri; ⑤

Café Dupont
Upscale contemporary Southern. If the buttermilk fried chicken in lemon basil sauce is available, that's the way to go. ☎ 205-322-1282; 113 20th St N, Birmingham; mains $25-28; ⊗ 11am-2pm Tue-Fri, 5pm-10pm Tue-Sat

Isaiah's
It's all about the fried lemon-peppered catfish and peach cobbler at this super-friendly soul food spot. ☎ 334-265-9000; 135 Mildred St, Montgomery; mains from $8.50; ⊗ 11am-2pm Tue-Fri

Martin's
Fried poultry you'd kill your grandmother for, served up Americana-style in a Winn-Dixie parking lot. ☎ 334-265-1767; 1796 Carter Hill Rd, Montgomery; mains $8-13; ⊗ 11am-3pm & 4-7:45pm Mon-Fri, 10:45am-1:45pm Sun; ⑤

Thelma's Kitchen
This no-frills soul-food stop occupies the former space of MLK favorite, Auburn Ave Rib Shack. The food hasn't changed much, though. ☎ 404-688-5855; 302 Auburn Ave; mains $8-9; ⊗ 8am-6pm Sun-Fri, to 8pm Sat

SLEEP

Butterfly Inn
Montgomery's first African American–owned B&B is a real charmer, but Isaiah's restaurant on site is the real coup. ☎ 334-230-9708; www.butterflyinn.net; 135 Mildred St, Montgomery; r $89-119

Inn at Hunt Phelan
Sitting on five downtown Memphis acres, this historic 1828 antebellum mansion is a welcome urban retreat. ☎ 901-525-8225; www.huntphelan.com; 533 Beale St, Memphis; r $185-295

Hyatt Regency Atlanta
We don't normally recommend chains, but this Hyatt was the first in Atlanta to welcome African Americans. ☎ 404-577-1234; www.atlantaregency.hyatt.com; 265 Peachtree St, Atlanta; r $195-255

St James Hotel
This landmark hotel – Selma's only surviving hotel in the historic district – offers rooms with spectacular balconies overlooking the river and Edmund Pettus Bridge. ☎ 334-872-3234; www.stjameshotelselma.com; 1200 Water Ave, Selma, AL; r $105-205; ⑤

Tutwiler Hotel
In 2007 Hampton Inn purchased this historic hotel (originally opened in 1914) and spruced it up – it's Birmingham's best. ☎ 205-322-2100; www.thetutwilerhotel.com; 2021 Park Pl, Birmingham; r $199; ⑤

USEFUL WEBSITES
www.thekingcenter.org
www.nps.gov/malu

LINK YOUR TRIP   www.lonelyplanet.com/trip-planner

Music City to Dixieland: A Musical Roots Run

WHY GO Waylon Jennings once said, "I've always felt that blues, rock and roll, and country are just about a beat apart." And a few miles. Get your motor runnin' on this musical tour of the South, where country, rock and roll, blues and jazz were all born within 500 miles of each other.

There isn't a spot on planet earth that has seen a soundtrack as influential as the American South. Go on – just try and name a region, anywhere in the world, that can sing a sweeter song than this: blues, rock and roll, country and jazz were all born here; gospel, bluegrass, soul, funk and R&B all grew up here; alternative and indie rock came here for college; and hip-hop settled here after graduation. Ethnically, politically and economically diverse, the sounds of the Southland cut through lines of race, color and creed and, in fact, owe a mound of debt to the composition of the South as a racially mixed land of milk and honey. How sweet it is.

Fire up a good road-trip mix tape and make your way to Music City, **1 Nashville**, home to country music and the most musicians per capita than any other city in the US (two for every 1000 residents, and those are just the serious ones). Drop your bags at **2 Loews Vanderbilt Hotel**, a chain hotel anywhere else, a spot steeped in local music memorabilia here. Toss some funds in the jukebox and get your dancing shoes on.

Nashville's honky tonk history begins at the **3 Country Music Hall of Fame & Museum**, a straight shot east on West End Ave from the hotel. This 40,000-sq-ft facility will teach you everything you need to know about the origins of country music, from its humble beginnings in rural Tennessee to where we're at today: if you don't live in Nashville and are trying to make it in country music, well, you're gonna find a lot of tears in your beers.

TIME
8 days

DISTANCE
660 miles

BEST TIME TO GO
Mar – May

START
Nashville, TN

END
New Orleans, LA

ALSO GOOD FOR

HISTORY & CULTURE

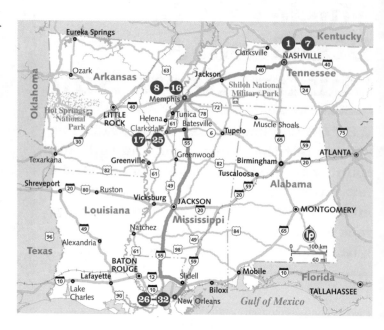

Just down the road is the historic ❹ **Ryman Auditorium**, originally built as a church in 1892, though preaching nothing but the country music gospel these days. The Grand Ole Opry, the longest running radio show in the world, lived here from 1943 to 1974, but the venue fell into neglect when the Opry jumped ship to Music Valley. In 1994, a renovated and revitalized Ryman opened its doors and has never looked back. You can take a self-guided tour or, better yet, check out who's playing and catch a show. It's gonna be a long night, so you might want to fill up on a "Cheeseburger in Paradise" at ❺ **Rotier's**, rumored to be the burger Jimmy Buffet was singing about, served here on French bread.

Nashville is home to countless live music venues, but two stand out. Garth Brooks and Kathy Mattea were discovered at the ❻ **Bluebird Café**, where aspiring songwriters, talent scouts, tourists and wannabe Tim McGraws all converge among tightly spaced tables and a whole lot of hootin' and hollerin'. The musicians here perform right in your face. Early performances by aspiring musicians are often free and there is some real talent. The other spot to drown your sorrows in some tell-it-like-it-is sonic therapy is ❼ **Tootsie's Orchid Lounge**, where Willie Nelson, Waylon Jennings and Kris Kristofferson found their careers nurtured by legendary owner Tootsie Bess, a den mother of country music who died in 1978. Hank Williams, Patsy Cline and Waylon Jennings have all been famously drunk here. Aspiring talents show up at 10am in hopes of discovery (and you thought Los Angeles was bad).

It's located on the stretch of Broadway known as the Honky Tonk Highway for its plethora of bars and live-music venues.

Trade in your Stetsons for Stratocasters and leave country in the dust on I-40 (west bound) to **8 Memphis**, the birthplace of rock and roll. When Elvis Presley walked into Memphis Recording Services, part of the now legendary **9 Sun Studio**, in 1954, he was little more than a truck driver for an electric company. When he walked out that July, with a $4 10-inch acetate carrying the songs, "I Love You Because," "Blue Moon of Kentucky," and "That's all Right," in hand, he was days from becoming the world's first true rock and roll star, and is still its biggest.

They say timing is everything and nobody knows that better than Elvis. Though rock and roll had begun to take shape in the beginning of the decade, it lacked sex appeal and soul. Bill Haley & His Comets are most often credited with charting the first rock and roll song ("Rock Around the Clock") in 1955, but it wasn't exactly rough around the edges, nor sexy. It was right around that time that record producer Sam Phillips uttered the very un-PC, and now infamous, quote: "If I could only find a white boy who could sing like a Negro." In walked Elvis. There's so much history in that one simple room at Sun Studio, it has been known to bring grown men to tears, including this author. There's a free shuttle between here and **10 Graceland** that runs every hour.

Don't be shocked at the green shag carpet that lines the walls and ceiling in the Jungle Room; the 350 yards of multicolored fabric that covers nearly everything in the Pool Room; and the mirrored ceiling in the TV room – Graceland is star-studded grandiosity, and it's obvious *Queer Eye for the Straight Guy* hasn't been anywhere near it. Elvis Presley's 1939 Colonial Revival–style mansion and 14-acre estate is a pilgrimage even a gay interior designer could love. You'll want to spring for the Platinum Package tour, which also includes Elvis' automobile museum and his two airplanes.

 **DETOUR** When the Grand Ole Opry departed from its former home in Ryman Auditorium, it moved to the 4400-seat **Grand Ole Opry House** (www.opry .com) east of Nashville in Music Valley. This squarish modern building hosts the Opry Friday and Saturday from March to November. Guided backstage tours are offered daily by reservation. Out this way, you'll want to hang your hat at the 2881-room **Gaylord Opryland Hotel** (www.gay lordhotels.com), a tourist attraction in itself.

From Nashville, exit 215 on I-40 to Briley Pkwy and follow the signs – it's just over 11 miles (about 20 minutes).

If Graceland doesn't suck the charmed life out of you, begin your evening with burgers at former brothel **11 Earnestine & Hazel's**, once a hangout of Stax recording folk like Otis Redding and Booker T & the MGs' Steve Cropper. Yes, Elvis ate here too. From here it's a quick trolley ride along Main St to

12 **Beale St.** Back in the 1860s, African American traveling musicians would perform here; in the early-20th century it was a debauched thoroughfare of gambling, drinking, prostitution, murder and voodoo; today, it is home to the blues (and lots of drunks). These days it is perhaps a little too Bourbony, but there are still plenty of good live-music venues to get your groove on along this historical stretch of 30 nightclubs. The most authentic of the lot is classic juke joint **13** **Mr Handy's Blues Hall**, which is attached to the Rum Boogie Café.

Stumble like a rock star back to **14** **Madison Hotel**, a whimsical boutique hotel with soulful tunes pumped right into the lobby inside a renovated 100-year-old bank building. If you're on an Elvis pilgrimage, you're sleeping out by Graceland at **15** **Heartbreak Hotel**, where B&W photos of the King don the walls, and four themed suites evoke the true spirit of Presley's gaudiness.

Stop at the **16** **Memphis Rock 'n' Soul Museum**, done up by the excellent Smithsonian Institute, before skipping town. This seven-gallery museum covers rock and roll, and soul, from rural roots to modern-day hit makers. It's here at this corner of Beale and 3rd that your adventure continues: head south from here and you are on the legendary Blues Highway, otherwise known as **17** **Hwy 61**. It's a 70-mile drive from here to **18** **The Crossroads**, the intersection of Hwy 61 and Hwy 49 just north of **19** **Clarksdale, Mississippi**. This is where legend says Delta blues henchman Robert Johnson sold his soul to the devil at midnight in exchange for mastery of the guitar. Johnson went on to become one of America's first guitar heroes and one of the most influential blues musicians of all time, but the devil don't play that: he cashed in on his side of the deal when Johnson was just 27-years-old. Three blue guitars mark the spot.

The awesomely named **20** **Shack Up Inn** is the place to stay (B&B here meaning Bed & Beer as opposed to Bed & Breakfast) as much for its renovated shotgun shacks as for proclamations like, "The Ritz we aint!" and "If you like 5-star shit, go somewhere else." It's 3 miles from the Crossroads on the old Hopson Plantation. A few miles north in downtown Clarksdale, everything old is becoming new again, all in the name of paying homage to the blues. **21** **Delta Blues Museum**, in the old train depot, hosts an impressive collection of blues memorabilia.

But Clarksdale's blues heritage is hardly a thing of the past – stop in at the
22 **Cat Head Delta Blues & Folk Art, Inc** for kitschy blues memorabilia and
CDs, but also to pick owner Roger Stolle's brain about what music to take in
during your visit. He owns a blues record label and is also
the booking agent for actor Morgan Freeman's blues club,
23 **Ground Zero**, a must-stop but not nearly as authentic
as **24** **Red's**, a nitty-gritty, smoked-out juke joint rubbed
with the kind of musical spices that makes the blues the
sonic equivalent of a 60-day dry aged porterhouse. Speaking of which, **25** **Abe's** does the kind of gut-sticking bar-

> *"Clarksdale's blues heritage is hardly a thing of the past."*

becue that will have you singing the blues on the toilet, but you won't much
care at this stage, they are teeth-pickin' good. Save some room, though;
26 **New Orleans** may be the birthplace of jazz, but it's not a bad spot to chew
the bone, either.

From Clarksdale, take Hwy 6 (east bound) to Batesville and catch I-55 (south
bound) to I-10 (east bound) straight into the heart of the **27** **French Quarter**.
You are now in jazz country, where jazz has been wizzled and spit out
here dating back to the days when African and Caribbean slaves pounded
out their rhythmic postcards home on Sunday in Congo Square (now
28 **Armstrong Square**, named after jazz great Louis Armstrong). Once European instruments and ragtime piano ditties in brothels were stirred into the
pot, jazz was born like an improvised stew. Shockingly, New Orleans does
not have a jazz museum, so you must resort to listening to music – not a bad
deal at all, actually.

3 DOORS DOWN'S MISSISSIPPI – BRAD ARNOLD

"As a musician, there are not many places you can be more proud to be from than Mississippi. It all started right here on a little rural road in the middle of nowhere Mississippi.
I can't put my finger on what it is in that area that breeds the music that comes from
there, but it's something special. It cannot be replicated. People in Mississippi are very set
in their ways, and believe what they believe. I've always believed myself if you're going
to sing something, you better believe it and live it yourself. Those old blues guys down
there, they live those blues.

I was in a bar down in Pascagoula not too long ago and there were a few guys onstage
playing covers. An old African-American man came in the door, 75- or 80-years-old – he'd
been hitting the bottle – and asked the band, 'Do y'all mind if I play a song or two?' The
guys reluctantly agreed. This old man never got through a full song, and the band went up
there a few times to stop him, but I said, 'Don't you dare take the guitar away from that guy.
That man stumbled in here off the street, asked nicely to borrow your guitar, and played
something sincere. You ain't taking that guitar away from him until he puts it down. You're
looking at the blues.'"

Brad Arnold, vocalist, 3 Doors Down

The genre has since branched off on numerous notes since inception, but traditional New Orleans–style jazz is preserved vehemently at **㉙ Preservation Hall** on St Peter St, a muggy, dirty, Prohibition-inspired hothouse with no air conditioning and no beverages (although you are welcome to BYO *water*). Of course, as the name implies, all of this preserves the throwback feel – you think folks were comfortable back then? Um, no. They got their comfort from food.

For the quintessential Nola meal with a soundtrack to boot, head to the jazz brunch at **㉚ Commander's Palace** and save room for the bread-pudding soufflé. The rest of the week, tuneful meals are served at post-Katrina newcomer **㉛ Club 300 Jazz Bistro**, which offers jazz seven nights a week – bottom line, it ain't difficult to find yourself a little boogie-woogie wallop in which to shake your bones. With your ears still ringing, lay yourself to sleep at **㉜ The Columns**, a lovely and quieter spot in the Garden District (though there's live music there nightly, too).

Elvis once said, "I don't know anything about music. In my line you don't have to." Now you know a little more than he did.
Kevin Raub

TRIP INFORMATION

DO

Cat Head Delta Blues & Folk Art, Inc
This kitschy, blues-themed shop is full of regional folk art and, more importantly, knowledge. ☎ 662-624-5992; www.cathead.biz; 252 Delta Ave, Clarksdale, MS; 🕑 10am-5pm Mon-Sat; ♿

Country Music Hall of Fame & Museum
A $37 million slap on country music's ass. Historic Studio B tours also leave from here. ☎ 615-416-2001; www.countrymusichalloffame.com; 222 Fifth Ave S, Nashville; adult/child $20/10; 🕑 9am-5pm; ♿

Delta Blues Museum
The top blues museum in the region, housed inside the old train depot in Clarksdale. ☎ 662-627-6820; www.deltabluesmuseum.org; 1 Blues Alley, Clarksdale, MS; adult/child $7/5; 🕑 9am-5pm Mon-Sat; ♿

Graceland
The King's home is the king of all decorating nightmares, but you gotta see it. ☎ 802-578-9093; www.elvis.com; 3765 Elvis Presley Blvd, Memphis; platinum package tour adult/child $33/15; 🕑 9am-5pm daily summer, 10am-4pm Wed-Mon winter; ♿

Memphis Rock 'n' Soul Museum
Immerse yourself in the origins of rock and roll and soul music at this excellent museum from the Smithsonian folks. ☎ 901-205-2533; www.memphisrocknsoul.org; 191 Beale St, Memphis; adult/child $10/7; 🕑 10am-7pm; ♿

Ryman Auditorium
Tour this venue of biblical importance to country music (the Grand Ole Opry stayed here for 31 years) or catch a show if you can. ☎ 615-889-3060; www.ryman.com; 116 Fifth Ave N, Nashville; adult/child $12.50/6.25; 🕑 9am-4pm

Sun Studio
If music were Christianity, this would be the birthplace of Jesus himself. It was here that Elvis changed the world. No children under four. ☎ 901-521-0664; www.sunstudio.com; 706 Union Ave, Memphis; adult/child $10/free; 🕑 10am-6pm

EAT

Abe's
Bone-sticking good barbecue is the calling at this road-food classic immortalized everywhere from blues tunes to Mississippi Delta novels. ☎ 662-624-9947; 616 State St, Clarksdale, MS; mains $3-12; 🕑 10am-9pm Mon-Thu, to 10pm Fri & Sat, 11am-2pm Sun; ♿

Commander's Palace
A Nola classic with a weekend jazz brunch and the best bread-pudding soufflé in town. ☎ 504-581-2534; 1403 Washington Ave, New Orleans; mains $27-38; 🕑 11:30am-2pm & 6:30-10pm Mon-Fri, 11:30am-1pm Sat, 10:30am-1:30pm Sun

Club 300 Jazz Bistro
French Quarter newcomer serving fine Creole cuisine over live jazz performances, beginning at 6:30pm (Sat & Sun) and 7:30pm (Sun-Thu). ☎ 504-899-8221; 300 Decatur St, New Orleans; mains $15-43; cover $5; 🕑 meals 5pm

Earnestine & Hazel's
Former brothel-turned-juke joint serving up memorable "Soul Burgers." Otis Redding, James Brown and Elvis Presley would concur were they alive. ☎ 901-523-9754; 531 S Main St, Memphis; mains $4-7; 🕑 7am-3pm daily, dinner Fri; ♿

Rotier's
The cheeseburger served here, served on French bread, is rumored to be the one Jimmy Buffet was talking about in his famous song. Its near the Vanderbilt campus. ☎ 615-327-9892; 2413 Elliston Pl, Nashville; mains $4-14; 🕑 10:30am-10pm Mon-Sat

DRINK

Bluebird Café
This divey institution is the place to get discovered in Nashville (just ask Garth Brooks). ☎ 615-383-1461; 4104 Hillsboro Rd, Nashville; cover free-$15; 🕑 5:30pm-1am Mon-Sat, 6pm-midnight Sun

Ground Zero
Actor and owner Morgan Freeman's take on an old-school juke joint inside a former cotton warehouse. ☎ 662-621-9009;

www.groundzerobluesclub.com; 0 Blues Alley, Clarksdale, MS; ☺ 11am-2pm Mon & Tue, to 11pm Wed & Thu, to 1am Fri & Sat

Mr Handy's Blues Hall

A classic juke joint, stale from the scent of 100 years of cigarettes and hard times. ☎ 901-528-0150; 182 Beale St, Memphis; cover weekends $5; ☺ 6pm-12:30am

Preservation Hall

The Preservation Hall Jazz Band holds court in this sonic museum of traditional Dixieland jazz. ☎ 504-522-2841; 726 St Peter St, New Orleans; cover $10; ☺ 8-11pm Thu-Sun

Red's

Rusted grills pepper the outside; spicy, stick-to-your-gut barbecue beckons inside. ☎ 662-627-3166; 395 Sunflower Ave, Clarksdale, MS; cover $5; ☺ 9pm-late Fri & Sat

Tootsie's Orchid Lounge

There's enough purple here to make Prince sick, but the talent and history make it a must-stop. Live music starts at 10am. ☎ 615-726-0463; 422 Broadway, Nashville; no cover; ☺ 9:30am-2:30am

SLEEP

Heartbreak Hotel

Elvis-themed hotel steeped in '50s kitsch and chic, just steps from Graceland. ☎ 901-332-1000; www.heartbreakhotel.net; 3677 Elvis Presley Blvd, Memphis; r from $125

Loews Vanderbilt Hotel

Its lobby jukebox is stocked with tunes from past VIP guests and its walls are lined with impressive music memorabilia. ☎ 615-320-1700; www.loewshotels.com; 2100 W End Ave, Nashville; r from $125

Madison Hotel

This music-themed boutique hotel is where rock stars stay in Memphis. You think you're a rock star, right? ☎ 901-333-1200; www.madisonhotelmemphis.com; 79 Madison Ave, Memphis; r from $280

Shack Up Inn

Shotgun sharecropper shacks run by a straight-talking owner, and cozy retro rooms inside an authentic cotton gin on Hopson Plantation. You need to be over 25 to sign for a room. ☎ 662-624-8329; www.shackupinn.com; 1 Commissary Circle, off Hwy 49, Clarksdale, MS; r from $75

The Columns

A lovely 1883 Victorian choice on St Charles Ave in the Garden District with live music nightly, and jazz on Friday and Sunday. ☎ 504-899-9308; www.thecolumns.com; 3811 St Charles Ave, New Orleans; r $160-230

USEFUL WEBSITES

www.clarksdaletourism.com
www.neworleanscvb.com

LINK YOUR TRIP

www.lonelyplanet.com/trip-planner

The Big Muddy: Down the Mississippi

WHY GO She gave us Budweiser, Huck Finn and the blues. Meriwether Lewis kissed her goodbye. The Civil War streaked her with blood. Plantation owners loaded her with commerce. Slaves used her to escape. So make like Mark Twain and follow America's most important river from Missouri to the Gulf of Mexico.

TIME
4 – 6 days

DISTANCE
777 miles

BEST TIME TO GO
Apr – Jun

START
Hannibal, MO

END
New Orleans, LA

ALSO GOOD FOR

HISTORY & CULTURE

The Mississippi River bubbles up in Minnesota, where it's still fairly wild and narrow enough to swim across. But as it winds 2430 miles south toward New Orleans, it widens and becomes increasingly industrialized. In the Deep South, it is a commercial artery that continues to ferry fuel, goods and people to the Midwest and back again, just as it has for hundreds of years.

Your journey begins in Hannibal, Missouri where the great Mark Twain (1835–1910), aka Samuel Langhorne Clemens, grew up on the riverside. Missouri was a slave state back then, and Hannibal's characters, scenery and politics would later inspire the fictional town of St Petersburg, home of the joyously conniving Tom Sawyer and his best friend, the mischievous hero, Huckleberry Finn. You'll enjoy all the scenes of Tom's greatest adventures – including the fence he did not paint and the cave where he and Becky Thatcher got lost. The ❶ **Mark Twain Boyhood Home & Museum** is a complex of seven buildings, including two homes Twain lived in and the home of Laura Hawkins, the true-life inspiration for Thatcher. July 4 weekend brings National Tom Sawyer Day, which features frog jumping and face-painting contests, among other events.

In his 20s, Twain was a commercial steamboat pilot on the Big Muddy, and he got to know all the bends and eddies, towns and outlaws, islands and sandbars that made Huck's grand escape with

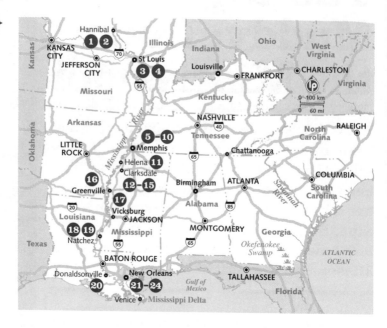

Jim, the runaway slave, so true to life. In fact, when it was published in 1880, *The Adventures of Huckleberry Finn* was considered the first Great American Novel. But you don't have to pilot a driftwood raft to honor that legacy; you can float the Mississippi on a dinner cruise aboard the ❷ **Mark Twain Riverboat**.

Follow the river, and Hwy 61, for 100 miles further south and you'll reach the ❸ **Gateway Arch** in St Louis. You've probably seen it on TV, but in person it is mind-bending. Its sheer size (630ft tall) and gentle arc against the (hopefully) blue sky may inspire you to laze on the grass and stare a while as sunlight flashes off the steel. In the arch's basement you'll find the Museum of Westward Expansion, chronicling Lewis & Clark's expedition into the American West. Lewis famously left St Louis on horseback and connected with Clark further north in Illinois on May 14, 1804 before they rafted wild rivers and paved the way for countless western pioneers.

> *"When it was published, 'The Adventures of Huckleberry Finn' was considered the first Great American Novel."*

Make sure you don't leave St Louis until you've grabbed a Bud at ❹ **Anheuser-Busch Brewery**. The tour through this cereal-smelling, Victorian-era multiplex is damned interesting. You'll see the Clydesdales, and learn that at one time the brewery used Mississippi River water to make beer, and stored barrels in man-made caves dug into the cool riverbanks. Afterward you'll be rewarded with two frosty ones.

From St Louis follow I-55S to Memphis, one of the river's most soulful cities. Here you'll find Graceland, Sun Studio, Stax Records and Beale Street. There's blues and barbecue almost everywhere you turn. The Smithsonian's ❺ **Memphis Rock 'n' Soul Museum** examines the social and cultural history that produced the blues in the Mississippi Delta. That sound eventually morphed into rock and roll when Elvis sang "Hound Dog," an old blues tune, in Sun Studio.

But long before Elvis-mania, this section of the river was used to shepherd slaves to freedom. Learn the details at the ❻ **Slave Haven Underground Railroad Museum**. It's set in a modest clapboard house laced with tunnels fed by trapdoors.

The ❼ **Mississippi River Museum** is the place to learn more about the cultural and natural history of the Big Muddy. Check out the scaled model of the lower Mississippi and the interactive 1-acre pool that doubles as the Gulf of Mexico. The museum is part of ❽ **Mud Island River Park**, and is linked to Memphis by a monorail. There are kayaks, canoes and bikes for rent, and it's a decent place to while away a couple of hours if the sun is shining. Mud Island made international news when Jeff Buckley drowned here in 1997.

Spend the night at the handsome ❾ **Peabody Hotel**, where a flock of ducks is marched from the penthouse to the marble lobby fountain every morning. And when your stomach growls seek spicy, saucy salvation at ❿ **Cozy Corner**, on a rather bleak stretch of North Parkway. Don't let the chipped wood paneling and shredded vinyl booths scare you off. This family-run spot is famous for its barbecue Cornish hen. You tear the bird apart with your hands and suck every bit of brick-red sauce off its wings. It also serves a mean rack of ribs.

Pick up the Blues Highway (Hwy 61) in Memphis and drive through the Mississippi Delta, where the blues were born. Robert Johnson, the original blues star, was born in Tunica, Mississippi, but this small riverside town has morphed into a maze of casinos, which aren't worth your time. Roll on to Helena, Arkansas, a depressed mill town, and home to the late Sonny Boy Williamson, a regular on King Biscuit Time, the first blues radio show. BB King listened religiously as a child, and considers Sonny Boy a major influence. The show, which begins weekdays at 12:15pm, is still running (on KFFA 1360AM, and via King Biscuit Time podcast) and has been hosted by Sunshine Sonny Payne for 57 years. It broadcasts out of the ⓫ **Delta Cultural Center**, which is also a terrific blues museum. You can listen to the show live, and may even get on the air.

Clarksdale is the hub of Delta blues country. This is where you'll find the Crossroads, at the intersection of Hwy 61 and Hwy 49, where Robert Johnson made his famous deal with the devil and became America's first guitar hero. And it's here where live music and blues history are most accessible. Stay at the ⓬ **Shack Up Inn**, an old plantation where a cotton gin and sharecroppers cabins have been converted into guestrooms stuffed with kitsch antiques. The owners are warm and fun, and are tuned in to the local live-music scene.

The ⓭ **Delta Blues Museum**, in downtown Clarksdale, has the best collection of blues memorabilia in the Delta, including Muddy Waters' reconstructed Mississippi cabin. It will soon move, along with his instruments, records and costumes, in to the Muddy Wing. Creative, multimedia exhibits also honor BB King, John Lee Hooker, Big Mama Thornton and WC Handy, whose original 1912 compositions popularized the 12-bar blues. Swing back to the Crossroads for dinner. That smoky sweetness in the air is coming from ⓮ **Abe's**, a local barbecue joint that's been in business since 1924. The ribs melt off the bone, and its barbecue beef, pork and ham sandwiches are popular too. Apparently when Robert Johnson was mingling with Satan, old Abe was getting a barbecue sauce recipe from Jesus. At least that's what the menu reports.

OIL SPILL

On July 24, 2008 a cargo barge collided with an oil tanker on the Mississippi in New Orleans, causing a 500,000-gallon oil slick. In minutes, 100 miles of the river was closed to boat traffic, costing the Port of New Orleans up to $250,000 per day. Downriver, waterfowl were covered in the sludge, and there were concerns about contamination of urban tap water supplies and the estuaries along the Gulf Coast. Clean up was swift, but the spill served as a reminder that this great river is not indestructible.

There's live music in Clarksdale at least four nights a week. Morgan Freeman's Ground Zero lures the tour buses and has the most professional venue and sound system, but if you land here on a weekend head to ⓯ **Red's**, a ragged downtown juke joint run with in-your-face charm by its namesake. Red has hosted legends like Robert "Wolfman" Belfour for years. Sometimes he has homemade corn liquor behind the bar. Ask nicely.

Hwy 61 parallels the Mississippi all the way to the Louisiana border, but even though it's nearby, you won't actually see it unless you detour on Hwy 82 to Greenville, another Mississippi casino enclave. ⓰ **Doe's Eat Place** is a legendary steakhouse that poses as a neighborhood dive. The tamales and porterhouse steaks are sensational here, and after you eat you can (and you should) walk it off along the river.

Further south off Hwy 61, the ⓱ **Vicksburg National Military Park** honors one of the turning points of the Civil War. In June, 1863 the Union launched a major siege and eventually took the Confederacy's Vicksburg fortress located on high ground above the river. Robert E Lee surrendered on July 4, and gave the North undisputed control of the Mississippi. You can drive along the

16-mile Battlefield Drive, which winds past 1330 monuments and markers – including statues, battle trenches, a restored Union gunboat and a national cemetery. It makes for a fascinating afternoon. It's also a fabulous bike ride if you're traveling with bicycles.

Historic antebellum mansions will greet you in Natchez, Mississippi. In the 1840s, there were more millionaires per capita here than anywhere in the world. When Union soldiers marched through with orders to torch the place during the Civil War, there weren't any men in town. They were all off fighting. Legend has it that the women greeted the soldiers at their doors and said something like, "Now boys, leave your guns outside and come sit a spell. You must be exhausted." Yes, Southern hospitality saved the city. And the mansions are still open to visitors during the twice annual pilgrimage seasons held in the spring and fall.

Care to taste mansion life? Dine at 18 **The Castle**, a restaurant set at the Dunleith, a gorgeous mansion ringed with Corinthian columns. The night scene, when the house is illuminated, is unforgettable, and it's widely considered the best kitchen in town. But Natchez gets down and dirty too. When Mark Twain passed through during his riverboat captain days, he crashed in a room above the local saloon. 19 **Under the Hill Saloon** remains the best bar in town, with terrific (and free) live music on weekends. The name works, because the saloon is built into a hillside and overlooks the wide, languid Mississippi. And you can still crash upstairs at what is now called the Mark Twain Guesthouse. Reserve your bed at the bar.

Cross the Louisiana state line and the 61 bleeds into the I-110S, which merges with I-10 in Baton Rouge. Take Hwy 44S to Hwy 70W to Hwy 18 toward Donaldsonville, just off Louisiana's River Rd (actually a series of highways that skirt both sides of the Mississippi all the way to the Gulf of Mexico). There are some antebellum mansions in the area, although most were torched by Union troops. If you've already seen the mansions in Natchez, step into the 20 **River Road African American Museum** and learn about the region's seldom told African American history. You'll learn the truth about slave ships, the vicious toils of slavery, slave revolts, the Underground Railroad, reconstruction and Jim Crow from displays crafted from antiques, artifacts, photographs and video interviews. When slaves escaped the Donaldsonville plantations, they ran or floated south

THE PHATWATER CHALLENGE

If you're into aquatic self-propulsion (ie you dig kayaking) then you'll enjoy the **Phatwater Challenge** (www.kayakmississippi.com), a marathon kayak race (the future Olympic sport you've never heard of) that runs 45 miles downriver from the Port of Grand Gulf to Natchez, MS. For one day, barge traffic is halted as paddlers own the Mississippi. Join the party, stopping for breaks on beaches and sand bars; you may even see a gator. The race wraps with a bluegrass jam at the **Under the Hill Saloon**.

to New Orleans (where they could blend in with free blacks), rather than hike north, where they would have to cross Mississippi, Tennessee and Missouri to find freedom.

From Donaldsonville, make your way to Hwy 90W toward New Orleans. At Lake Pontchartrain you'll cross a 24-mile long causeway, the largest bridge in the world. When you get into the city limits you'll traverse the gorgeous Cresecent City Connection, a four-lane cantilever bridge that crosses the Mississippi and leads into downtown.

DETOUR The River Rd continues on Hwy 23 along the west bank, where it ends 70 miles south of New Orleans, amid the stilted vacation homes, oil infrastructure and sport-fishing marina of **Venice**, Louisiana. This is the mouth of the Mississippi and you'll see the river spread into rivulets that flood a vast estuary known as the **Delta National Wildlife Refuge**, which is protected by the Fish & Wildlife Service. There are redfish and speckled trout in the wetlands, and tarpon, snapper and grouper in the Gulf. Charter a boat for a day, and you can cast off a defunct offshore oil platform. Tens of thousands of migrating water fowl and shorebirds descend here, including osprey, three kinds of hawks, avocets, killdeer and dowitchers.

Don't miss the French Market. New Orleanians have been trading goods for over 200 years from this spot on the Mississippi riverbanks. In addition to the famous **㉑ Café Du Monde**, where you can snack on fried and sugared beignets, there's a flea market, gift stalls and a produce market. If you haven't yet floated down the river, board the **㉒ Steamboat Natchez** at Canal St. It offers historic dinner and day cruises that are great for families. If you don't mind brown-bagging lunch, head to **㉓ Crabby Jacks** and order a smoked duck po'boy and a salad to go, then take it to one of dozens of riverside benches and picnic. You can access the river from Decatur in the French Quarter or from Canal St in the CBD. And when it's time for shuteye, float to the upper reaches of the **㉔ W New Orleans** in the CBD, where swank rooms and suites have exquisite views of the city, and that sweet, brown, sinuous river that has formed, flooded, and nourished the continental United States for centuries.

Adam Skolnick

TRIP INFORMATION

GETTING THERE
From Hannibal take Hwy 61S to Hwy 55S through St Louis to Memphis. Continue on Hwy 61S through Mississippi to the 110S in Louisiana which merges with I-10E toward New Orleans.

DO

Anheuser-Busch Brewery
Tour the largest brewery on earth. ☎ 314-577-2626; www.budweisertours.com; 12th & Lynch St, St Louis; admission free; ⏱ 9am-4pm Mon-Sat, 11:30am-4pm Sun Mar-May, Sep & Oct; 9am-5pm Mon-Sat, 11:30am-5pm Sun Jun & Jul; 10am-4pm Mon-Sat, 11:30am-4pm Sun Nov-Feb; ♿

Delta Blues Museum
Peruse memorabilia, video installations and coming soon…the Muddy Wing. ☎ 662-627-6820; www.deltabluesmuseum.org; 1 Blues Alley, Clarksdale; adult/child $7/5; ⏱ 9am-5pm Mon-Sat; ♿

Delta Cultural Center
Helena's glorious musical past is distilled into this fine museum. ☎ 870-338-4350; www.deltaculturalcenter.com; 141 Cherry St, Helena, AR; admission free; ⏱ 9am-5pm Tue-Sat; ♿

Gateway Arch
Stare at the elegant arch from below, then ride the tram to the top. ☎ 877-982-1410; www.gatewayarch.com; the Gateway Arch Riverfront, St Louis; tram adult/child $10/7; ⏱ 8am-10pm Jun-Aug, 9am-6pm Sep-May; ♿

Mark Twain Boyhood Home & Museum
Fans of the eminently quotable author/traveler will enjoy this blast from Twain's past. ☎ 573-221-9010; www.marktwain museum.org; 415 N Main St, Hannibal; adult/child $8/4; ⏱ 8am-6pm, call for abbreviated winter schedule; ♿

Mark Twain Riverboat
Twain piloted a river boat just like this. ☎ 573-221-3222; www.marktwainriver boat.com; Center St, Hannibal; 1hr sightseeing cruise adult/child $13/10, 2hr dinner cruise $35/20; ⏱ Apr-Nov, schedule varies; ♿

Memphis Rock 'n' Soul Museum
Get primed on the Mississippi Delta blues. ☎ 901-205-2533; www.memphisrocknsoul .org; Lt George W Lee Ave & 3rd St, Memphis; adult/child $10/7; ⏱ 10am-7pm; ♿

Mississippi River Museum
Enjoy a natural history lesson on Mud Island. ☎ 901-576-7241; www.mudisland .com; Center St, Hannibal; adult/child $8/5; ⏱ 10am-5pm Apr & May, Sep & Oct; to 6pm Jun-Aug, closed Mon; ♿

Mud Island River Park
Paddle, cycle or stroll, then take a monorail back to Beale St. ☎ 901-576-7241; www .mudisland.com; 125 N Front St, Memphis; ⏱ 10am-5pm Apr & May, Sep & Oct, to 6pm Jun-Aug, closed Mon; ♿

River Road African American Museum
Details the harsh reality, heroes and triumphs of Louisiana's African-American history. ☎ 225-474-5553; www.africanamerican museum.org; 406 Charles St, Donaldsonville; admission $4; ⏱ 10am-5pm Wed-Sat, 1-5pm Sun; ♿

Slave Haven Underground Railroad Museum
An old safe-house for escaped slaves depicts this dangerous, 19th-century humanitarian effort. ☎ 901-527-3427; 826 N 2nd St, Memphis; adult/child $6/4; ⏱ 10am-1pm Mon-Sat; ♿

Steamboat Natchez
Float the Mississippi on a steamboat, but skip the buffet. ☎ 504-586-8777; www .steamboatnatchez.com; Toulouse St, New Orleans; adult/child $19.50/10; ⏱ lunch & dinner; ♿

Vicksburg National Military Park
Stroll, pedal or drive through arguably the most strategically important Civil War battlefield. ☎ 601-636-0583; www.nps .gov/vick; 3300 Clay St, Vicksburg, MS; per car $8; ⏱ 8am-5pm; ♿

ICONIC TRIPS

EAT & DRINK

Abe's
Don't miss the slow-burning tamales and melt-off-the-bone ribs. ☎ 662-624-9947; 616 State St, Clarksdale; mains $3-12; 🕙 10am-9pm Mon-Thu, to 10pm Fri & Sat, 11am-2pm Sun; ♿

Café Du Monde
Famous purveyors of greasy, sugary beignets. ☎ 504-525-4544; 800 Decatur St, New Orleans; 🕙 24hr; ♿

Cozy Corner
A spectacularly delicious dive. ☎ 901-527-9158; www.cozycornerbbq.com; 745 N Parkway, Memphis; mains $5-16; 🕙 10:30am-5pm Tue-Sat, open later in summer; ♿

Crabby Jacks
New Orleans' best po'boys are served here. ☎ 504-833-2722; 428 Jefferson Hwy, New Orleans; mains $6-12; 🕙 10am-5pm Mon-Fri, 11am-4pm Sat; ♿

Doe's Eat Place
The chili tamales are wonderful, and so are the steaks. ☎ 662-334-3315; www.doeseatplace.com; 502 Nelson St, Greenville, MS; mains $15-30; 🕙 5pm-9pm Mon-Sat

Red's
The ramshackle environs may intimidate, but you're welcome here. ☎ 662-627-3166; 395 Sunflower Ave, Clarksdale; cover $5; 🕙 9pm-late Fri & Sat

The Castle
Upscale continental cuisine is served on the grounds of the sensationally illuminated

Dunleith Plantation. ☎ 601-446-8500; www.dunleith.com; 84 Homochitto St, Natchez; mains $18-34; 🕙 7:30-10am, 11am-2pm, 6pm-9pm Mon-Thu, to 10pm Fri & Sat

Under the Hill Saloon
A tremendously fun and historic bar that was once a favorite haunt of Samuel Clemens, riverboat pilot. ☎ 601-446-8023; www.underthehillsaloon.com; 25 Silver St, Natchez; 🕙 9am-late

SLEEP

Peabody Hotel
It's been considered Memphis' glamour girl since she opened in the 1930s, and they have had a morning duck procession through the lobby since day one. ☎ 901-529-4000; www.peabodymemphis.com; 149 Union Ave, Memphis; r from $245

Shack Up Inn
Grab one of the old sharecropper shacks. It has kitchens for self-catering. ☎ 662-624-8329; www.shackupinn.com; off Hwy 49, Clarksdale; r from $75; ♿

W New Orleans
This fashionable, bustling hotel attracts a young, hip crowd, with a dash of business traveler. ☎ 504-525-9444; www.whotels.com; 333 Poydras St, New Orleans; d from $210

USEFUL WEBSITES
www.greatriverroad.com
www.experiencemississippiriver.com

LINK YOUR TRIP
www.lonelyplanet.com/trip-planner
TRIPS

NASCAR's Best Pit Stops

WHY GO Witnessing the breathtaking raw power of a Ford Fusion pushing 200mph can convert staunch NASCAR naysayers into genuflecting devotees. Bristol, Daytona, Lowe's and Talladega have become synonymous with full-throttle, pedal-to-the-metal adrenaline overload – this is NASCAR holy ground.

Admit it: you've been fascinated with stock car racing since Kenny Rogers' 1982 film, *Six Pack*. Or maybe it was more recently, when you rooted on Ricky Bobby to whup Borat's ass in *Talladega Nights*. Or maybe you just think Tom Cruise looked cute in his fire suit in *Days of Thunder*. Point being, unless you already spend your Saturday afternoons glued to the NASCAR Sprint Cup Series, you probably owe the full sum of your NASCAR knowledge to Hollywood. Well, it ain't like that. NASCAR (National Association for Stock Car Auto Racing) is a well-oiled machine that employs mechanics with engineering degrees from MIT, boasts 75 million fans, counts $3 billion in licensing revenue, and is the second most popular sport on American TV. Start your engines: it's time to see what all the fuss is about.

The Charlotte area is the undisputed capital of NASCAR, where the majority of teams, owners, governing bodies and fans are based. ❶ **Memory Lane Motorsports & Historic Automotive Museum** in nearby Mooresville, north of Charlotte, is a good spot to brush up on a little car history – it features one of the largest private collections of retired NASCAR vehicles. Pay homage to NASCAR's most revered driver, the late Dale Earnhardt, at ❷ **Dale Earnhardt, Inc.,** about 9-miles southeast. Earnhardt was killed when he slammed into the wall at the Daytona 500 in 2001. This is the corporate headquarters of all things Earnhardt, but the showroom, museum and store are open to the public.

TIME
8 days

DISTANCE
1120 miles

BEST TIME TO GO
Feb – Nov

START
Mooresville, NC

END
Daytona Beach, FL

ALSO GOOD FOR

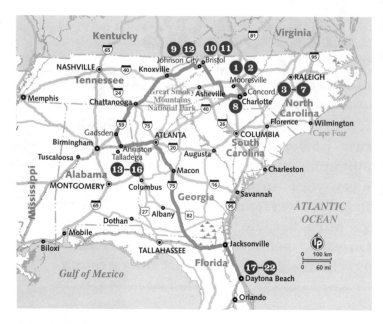

Head back to I-85 (south bound) to exit 49 for Speedway Blvd to Concord, and stop in for some hot wings at ❸ **Quaker Steak & Lube**. It claims to be America's number-one motorsports-themed family restaurant (but competition is surely clamoring to dethrone them soon). At any rate, it's full of race fans and 21 different hot wing sauces ranging from Ranch to Atomic. There are also plenty of beers and margaritas flowing, so we're questioning that family claim.

"You can book a ride-along experience on race weekends that could soon have you riding shotgun..."

From Quaker, it's 2 miles to ❹ **Lowe's Motor Speedway**. Catching a race here is like watching the *Joga Bonito* in Brazil. Getting out on the track yourself is like jumping in the goal for penalty kicks against Ronaldinho, so ditch your car keys and get suited up for the ❺ **Richard Petty Driving Experience**. You can book a ride-along experience on race weekends that could soon have you riding shotgun in a two-seat stock car pushing speeds upwards of 150mph. If you've got the cash, you can get behind the wheel and roar off into the sunset yourself (the sunset to the left). Another interesting stop near the track is the ❻ **Sam Bass Gallery**, home to the gallery of NASCAR's first sanctioned artist. Tired of driving? Good thing the ❼ **Embassy Suites** is here, a 10-minute walk from the track. Location, location, location. Don't leave the area without stopping into Dale Earnhardt, Jr's sleek bar and live-music venue ❽ **Whiskey River**, in Uptown Charlotte.

From Charlotte, head on 150 miles north on I-77 and east on Hwy 421 to Johnson City, TN and drop your bags at the ❾ **Carnegie**, the nicest hotel in town and nearest to the ❿ **Bristol Motor Speedway**, your next pit stop. The track is located 20 miles north in Bristol, where the curvy hills of Eastern Tennessee will do little to prepare you for the drama elicited from this driver-favorite track and the steepest banking in NASCAR. A night race here is said to be a once-in-a-lifetime experience. You can tour the track here, which includes a lap around the "world's fastest half mile," a visit to Pit Road, and a tour of the Dragway.

Sustenance in these parts means barbecue. Four miles south of the track is ⓫ **Ridgewood Barbecue** in Bluff City, a Tennessee institution and road-food classic. It's all about the pork – fresh ham to be specific – smoked over hickory wood in a little smokehouse that backs up against the wooded hillside out back. Race-centric nightlife means ⓬ **Bailey's**, where on any given race weekend, you'll find loads of sauced motor-sport fans slobbering all over their favorite NASCAR driver's number.

DETOUR If your need for speed is still not satiated, head two-hours southwest to Sevierville, TN and the **NASCAR SpeedPark** (www.nascarspeedpark .com). Adults and kids alike can test their racing skills on the eight tracks of adrenaline-pumping pavement. For $32, you can race until you singe your eyebrows off.

From Bristol, take Hwy 394 (south bound) to I-81 (south bound) to I-40 (west bound) to Hwy 66 (south bound) and follow the signs to the park.

Wipe your mouth off and head deeper south still on I-40 (west bound) to I-59 (south bound) to Talladega, AL, home to the ⓭ **Talladega Superspeedway**. The largest, fastest track in NASCAR is a monster: staring into its massive, wind-blown grandstands has been known to send shivers down the spine of even the most casual car enthusiast. It says one thing: speed. But not so fast, you need a bed nearby and the pickin's are scarce in these parts. ⓮ **Race Lodging**, actually based in Bristol, can place you in a private home on race weekends in both Bristol and, more importantly, Talladega.

Back at the track, you can spend a considerable chuck of time wandering the various halls of the ⓯ **International Motorsports Hall of Fame**, full of retired NASCAR vehicles, including a load of heaped wrecks that are terrifying (yet fascinating) to feast your eyes on – kind of like a five-car pileup. The car Ricky Bobby drove in *Talladega Nights* is here, as is an impressive 1919 Ford Racer. But where is the one Kenny Rogers drove in *Six Pack*? Where is Brewster Baker's badassmobile? Huh?

A few miles from the track is the ⓰ **Montana Saloon**, serving fat burgers under the even fatter stuffed water buffalo's head. The long bar here is classic saloon territory, but with friendlier faces and better food. Fully refueled, it's time to head to Florida, where the mecca of NASCAR awaits.

Charlotte may be the home of NASCAR, but the Daytona 500 is its birth-place, its most coveted Victory Lane and home to its biggest party. Each February, the season-opening race draws the largest crowd in motor sports: ⑰ **Daytona International Speedway** seats 168,000, but there are at least 50,000 more folks hyped on Heineken and dripping sweat in and around the track. Though the annual Georgia-Florida football game hordes the phrase, this is actually the "World's Largest Outdoor Cocktail Party". Not only that, but Daytona Beach is better equipped for tourism than anywhere else on the NASCAR circuit, with a wealth of attractions and sandy beaches all around. But this ain't no story about Disney World!

The ⑱ **Daytona 500 Experience** is sort of like the world's largest NASCAR theme park. If you want to tour the track at Daytona, you can do it here (via a 30-minute tram tour). It's located just outside Turn 4. Otherwise, race fans play along ⑲ **Atlantic Ave**, the requisite beach-paralleled main drag that all beach towns must have. ⑳ **Racing's North Turn**, a beach bar-and-grill, sits on the very spot that NASCAR began, on these hard-packed sands that were once home to world-record setting land speed automobile races. Doesn't sound too inviting for sunbathing, does it? You can dine inside a booth carved from a stock car at ㉑ **Cruisin' Café**, part museum, part restaurant and full of memorabilia and retired stock cars.

Atlantic Ave is literally lined with lodgings, all of which cater to race fans one way or another in February. For a touch of extra class, head to the ㉒ **Shores**, a boutique property with a nice spa and sophisticated color palette if you're suffering from beach-décor overkill. You deserve it. After all, you're the new face of NASCAR.
Kevin Raub

TRIP INFORMATION

GETTING THERE

From Charlotte, take I-77 (north bound) to Hwy 150 toward Lincolnton/Mooresville.

DO

Bristol Motor Speedway

Bristol tours include a lap around the track — you can even get out and walk on its famous 36-degree banking. ☎ 423-989-6933; www.bristolmotorspeedway.com; 151 Speedway Blvd, Bristol, TN; adult/child $5/3; ⊙ 9am-4pm Mon-Sat, noon-4pm Sun; ⑤

Dale Earnhardt, Inc

This museum, showroom and retail store pays tribute to NASCAR legend Dale Earnhardt, who died in 2001. ☎ 877-334-9663; www.daleearnhardtinc.com; 1675 Dale Earnhardt Hwy, Mooresville, NC; admission free; ⊙ 9am-5pm Mon-Fri, 10am-4pm Sat; ⑤

Daytona International Speedway

Every February, the largest audience in motorsports descends upon Daytona for the season-opening Daytona 500. Some come just to drink. ☎ 800-748-7467; www.daytonainternationalspeedway.com; 1801 W International Speedway Blvd, Daytona Beach, FL; ⑤

Daytona 500 Experience

Interactive, multi-million dollar NASCAR entertainment facility featuring IMAX, motion simulators and a tram track tour. ☎ 386-681-6800 www.daytona500experience.com; 1801 W. International Speedway Blvd, Daytona Beach, FL; adult/child $24/19; ⊙ 9am-7pm; ⑤

International Motorsports Hall of Fame

Honors not only drivers but also car designers, crew chiefs and sponsors. Highlights include numerous racing vehicles, including Ricky Bobby's from *Talladega Nights*. ☎ 256-362-5002; www.motorsportshalloffame.com; 3198 Speedway Blvd, Talladega, AL; adult/child $10/5; ⊙ 9am-4pm; ⑤

Lowe's Motor Speedway

Tours of this 165,000-seat speedway in the NASCAR Holy Land run hourly during non-race weeks. ☎ 704-455-3200; www.lowesmotorspeedway.com; 5555 Concord Pkwy, Concord, NC; tours $5; ⊙ 9:30am-3:30pm Mon-Sat, 1:30pm-3:30pm Sun; ⑤

Memory Lane Motorsports & Historic Automotive Museum

Private collection of retired NASCAR and vintage rides, including those by Dale Earnhardt and Bill Elliott. ☎ 704-662-3673; www.memorylaneautomuseum.com; 769 River Hwy, Mooresville, NC; adult/child $10/6; ⊙ 10am-5pm Mon-Sat, 9am-5pm race week

Richard Petty Driving Experience

Reservations are required in advance to get behind the wheel at this ultimate speed-freak fantasy. Available at numerous tracks including Lowe's and Daytona. ☎ 800-237-3889; www.richardpetty.com; Lowe's Motor Speedway, Concord, NC; ⑤

Sam Bass Gallery

3500 sq ft of NASCAR-themed artwork, limited edition framed prints and fine-art posters from the sport's first sanctioned artist. ☎ 704-455-6915; www.sambass.com; 6105 Performance Dr, Concord, NC; ⊙ 10am-5pm Tue-Fri; ⑤

Talladega Superspeedway

You can tour NASCAR's largest, fastest track in a combo tour with the International Motorsports Hall of Fame. ☎ 877-462-3342; www.talladegasuperspeedway.com; 3366 Speedway Blvd, Talladega, AL; adult/child $5/4; ⊙ 9am-4pm; ⑤

EAT & DRINK

Bailey's

A great race weekend hangout, with pool tables, a huge flat-screen TV and loads of loaded race fans. ☎ 423-929-1370; 2102 N Roan St, Johnson City, TN; mains $8-18; ⊙ 11am-1:30pm & 5pm-10pm Mon-Thu, 11am-10pm Fri-Sun

Cruisin' Café

Dine in a stock car, on specialty burgers inspired from various NASCAR tracks around the country at this race-fan favorite. ☎ 386-253-5522; 2 S Atlantic Ave, Daytona Beach, FL; mains $7-18; ⊙ 11am-late; ⑤

Montana Saloon

Just off I-20 near Talladega Superspeedway, this charismatic saloon serves manly American food and gets crazy on race days. ☎ 205-763-1225; 75023 Hwy 17, Lincoln, AL; mains $8-18; ◔ 11am-1:30pm & 5pm-10pm Mon-Thu, 11am-10pm Fri-Sun

Quaker Steak & Lube

Motor sport–themed hotspot for outrageously hot chicken wings and all the alcohol you'll need to drown the burn. ☎ 704-979-5823; 7731 Gateway Ln NW, Concord, NC; mains $8-19; ◔ 11am-1am Sun-Thu, to 2am Fri-Sat; ⓐ

Racing's North Turn

Rowdy Ponce Inlet bar-and-grill on the very spot that NASCAR began. The oceanfront deck swells in February. ☎ 386-322-3258; 4511 S Atlantic Ave, Ponce Inlet, FL; mains $7-21; ◔ 11am-11pm

Ridgewood Barbecue

A Tennessee barbecue institution, featuring slow-smoked pork over hickory from a small smokehouse north of the restaurant. ☎ 423-538-7543; 900 Elizabethtown Hwy, Bluff City, TN; mains $3-17; ◔ 11am-7:30pm Mon-Thu, to 2:30pm & 4:30-8:30pm Fri & Sat; ⓐ

Whiskey River

Dale Earnhardt, Jr–owned bar/club in uptown Charlotte, catering to plenty of beautiful folk and one monstrous mechanical bull. ☎ 704-749-1097; 210 E Trade St, Charlotte; cover $5-7; ◔ 9pm-2am Tue & Wed, 5pm-2am Thu & Fri, 7pm-2am Sat, noon-midnight Sun

SLEEP

Carnegie

This upscale choice, 20 minutes from Bristol, can sell out two years in advance for race weekends. ☎ 423-979-6400; www.carnegie hotel.com; 1216 W. State of Franklin Rd, Johnson City, TN; r from $124

Embassy Suites

Walking distance from Lowe's Motor Speedway, this new resort hotel is the best option for race fans in Concord. ☎ 704-455-8200; 5400 John Q Hammons Drive NW, Concord, NC; r $119-169; ⓐ

Race Lodging

This Bristol-based service can hook you up with accommodations in private homes near tracks in Bristol and Talladega, sometimes within walking distance. ☎ 423-764-5454; www.racelodging.com; 637 Rose St, Bristol, TN; r from $125-250

Shores

A classier option on Daytona Beach's endless drag, with a full-service spa and Italian marble bathrooms. It's probably where Kenny Rogers would sleep. ☎ 386-767-7350; www.shoresresort.com; 2637 S Atlantic Ave, Daytona Beach, FL; r $139-339

USEFUL WEBSITES

www.nascar.com
www.rowdy.com

LINK YOUR TRIP

www.lonelyplanet.com/trip-planner

Southern Gothic Literary Tour

WHY GO Legendary Southern authors William Faulkner, Tennessee Williams and Harper Lee are among those who channeled regional drama (think obscene riches, crippling poverty, brutal racial oppression), garnished with the South's signature sweltering nights and powerful storms, into its own literary genre.

TIME
7 days

DISTANCE
1274 miles

BEST TIME TO GO
Mar – Jun

START
Savannah, GA

END
New Orleans, LA

ALSO GOOD FOR

No wonder then that the South has produced some of America's most glorious writers, novels and characters. William Faulkner, Tennessee Williams, Carson McCullers and Flannery O'Connor have roots in Southern soil, as do the unforgettable Vampire Lestat, the brave Atticus Fitch, and wily Huckleberry Finn and his friend Jim. The Great American novel was invented here, and the Southern Gothic genre flourished here. There have been countless bestsellers, Pulitzers and one Nobel Prize.

Of course, commercial and critical success did not necessarily bring inner peace to all the authors. But we won't get into the details behind the drunken loneliness, suicides, bankruptcies, or one author's curious leap from erotic, Gothic horror to an embrace of evangelical Christianity. Yes, these things happened, but our tour is a celebration of the people, places and histories that nurtured our heroes – both real and fiction – in their prime of life. We are here for inspiration, people, not judgment. So bring along a six-pack of Southern literature and drive to that place where truth and fiction collide.

Our journey begins at *Midnight in the Garden of Good and Evil*, also known as Savannah, Georgia. This opulent, historic town is nestled on the Savannah River, 18 miles from the Atlantic. Lowcountry swamps and massive oaks heavy with Spanish moss surround its countless antebellum mansions and colonial relics. It's a beautiful place, and you're here because of one of the more recent books on our list. *Midnight* was

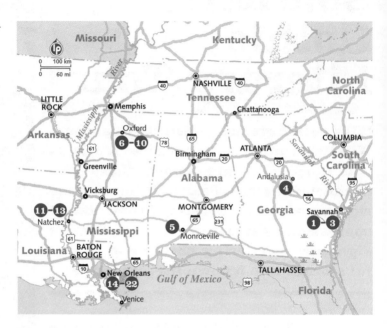

written by John Berendt in 1994, and though it's classified as non-fiction, it reads like a novel. Written in the Southern Gothic tone, this distinctively 1980s tale revolves around the murder of a local hustler, Danny Hansford, by respected art dealer, Jim Williams – an event that triggered four murder trials. We won't ruin it for you but, yes, the hustler and the dealer were lovers. Berendt doesn't shy away from painting an eccentric picture of Savannah society and you'll love the Lady Chablis, a local drag queen. The book eventually became a major Hollywood film starring John Cusack and Kevin Spacey. While in town stop by the ❶ **Mercer-Williams House Museum**, where Williams lived, and may have killed Hansford. Williams died in 1990 and the house opened for tours in 2004. The garden of good and evil refers to Savannah's Bonaventure Cemetery. If you visit, look for the Bird Girl statue, which graced the book's front cover, and sparked a lawsuit when the film's producers had a reproduction made for the shoot. Stay the night in one of the 16 rooms or four villas available at ❷ **Bed & Breakfast Inn**, just down the road from the Mercer-Williams House, and dine at ❸ **Walls Bar-B-Que**, a divine little hut on E York Lane. The deviled crab and smoked pork nourish body and soul; or maybe just soul.

From Savannah, Carson McCullers fans may want to take I-16 to Hwy 25 to I-20 to Columbia, Georgia. McCullers, Tennessee Williams' favorite protégé, was born here and her home served as inspiration for the mill town depicted in her first and greatest novel, *The Heart is a Lonely Hunter*. It's a beautifully sad, yet ultimately hopeful, tome centered on an enlightened deaf mute and his various friends and confidantes (including an adolescent girl, an African-American doctor, a business owner and a hard-drinking communist) during the Great Depression. Or you can bypass Columbia, and stay on I-16 to Hwy 441 which will take you toward Flannery O'Connor's home, **④ Andalusia**. O'Connor was raised on this farm property when her family moved from Savannah. After attending the Writers Workshop at the University of Iowa, she returned here to write. Her acclaimed short story collection, *A Good Man is Hard to Find,* was published in 1955. Like her father, she died of lupus. She was just 39. Before she passed she published two novels and two short story collections. She won the National Book Award for her compilation, *The Complete Stories,* published posthumously.

SOUTHERN GOTHIC EXPOSED

Gothic literature was born in England, when writers took on the moral blindness of the medieval era through supernatural tales. Southern writers, for the most part, muted the supernatural in their work. Instead they plumbed the characters and communities damaged by a regional history of Christian supremacy, frosted with an "everything-is-just-fine-as-it-is" veneer. Writers knew that such social tension led to years of brutality, as well as economic and moral bankruptcy, because they lived it. Which makes their stories more dramatic and poignant.

From here you'll head west into Alabama on Hwy 80 and I-85. At Montgomery, head south on I-65 to Hwy 84 and Monroeville, a small Alabama town that gave us both Truman Capote, the progenitor of the non-fiction novel, and his childhood friend, Harper Lee of *To Kill a Mockingbird* fame. *To Kill a Mockingbird,* written in the Southern Gothic style, takes aim at the institutional racism of the South. It was a runaway hit, and earned Lee the 1961 Pulitzer Prize. It takes place in the fictional town of Maycomb, a mirror image of Monroeville. The plot revolves around the trial of a young black man who is wrongfully accused of raping a white woman during the Great Depression. It's narrated by six-year-old Scout Finch, whose dad, Atticus, risks his and his family's safety to defend his railroaded client. If you've never read it, this book is an absolute must! Each May, curtains rise on a production of *To Kill A Mockingbird* at the **⑤ Old Courthouse Museum**, which also has permanent exhibits on both Lee and her pal, Capote.

When the curtain drops, find Hwy 45 north and take the long drive to Hwy 6 and Oxford, Mississippi. Nobel Prize winner William Faulkner may be long dead, but he still owns this town. It's home to the lovely University of Mississippi, and has a certain literary panache to it. **⑥ Rowan Oak**, Faulkner's fine, 33-acre estate, nurtured many novels, but required him to slum in Hollywood as a studio-owned screenwriter in order to pay it off. Check out the Coen brothers' *Barton Fink* to glimpse a less than sympathetic picture of Faulkner's Hollywood days. Ninety-percent of Rowan Oak's original furnishings are in tact – you'll see Faulkner's prized typewriter, rusted golf clubs, an outline for a never-written fable written on the walls, and a half bottle of Jack left on the mantle above the kitchen fireplace. His 1950 Nobel Prize is on permanent display at the **7 Center for Southern Culture** on the Ole Miss campus. Faulkner never actually thought much of the award and didn't even wish to accept it in person, but his daughter forced him to make the trip. The Center has a copy of Faulkner's acceptance speech, which became an instant classic.

> *"Even with its sense of tradition and history, Oxford isn't all about the past."*

Even with its undeniable sense of tradition and history, Oxford isn't all about the past. **8 Square Books** is one of the last, and very best, indie bookstores in America. It's set on the Square, the heart of downtown Oxford. Visiting authors read from their newly published works, and autographed copies of hot novels abound. If you're hell-bent on Billy, there's a Faulkner section upstairs, next to the café.

And Oxford is still prowling with literary lions. Larry Brown and Tom Franklin can be found swilling adult liquids from time to time at the **9 City Grocery**, a restaurant and bar on the south end of the Square. The Creole-spiced lamb meatloaf and the Southern classic, shrimp and grits, are both exceptional. The bar, with a balcony overlooking the outdoor action, is upstairs. You can stay in one of the cheap motor inn chains off the highway, or spend and enjoy **10 Puddin' Place**, a cozy B&B set in a turn-of-the-century home filled with antiques, and within walking distance of the Square.

After enjoying Oxford (and you will), detour through Tupelo, the birthplace of King Presley, and hop on the glorious Natchez Trace Parkway. Folks have been traveling through this oak-and-swamp-studded countryside since before Europeans landed in America. But things don't get literary until you land in Natchez proper, where the woods part to reveal historic antebellum mansions. But Natchez isn't all old-world glamour. It has dirt under its fingernails too.

THE FRENCH QUARTER LIT TOUR

Hungry for more dirt on the French Quarter literary set of years gone by? Join one of Professor Ken Holditch's **New Orleans Literary Tours.** The two-hour walking tour is led by one of the professor's knowledgeable guides, and makes for a great way to take in the sights and sounds of what Tennessee Williams called Little Bohemia. Call Professor Holditch at 504-949-9805.

The Big Muddy meanders through town, and back when Mark Twain was steamboat pilot Samuel Clemens, he visited countless times. He drank at the **11 Under the Hill Saloon** (still a local hot spot with live music on weekends), and he crashed upstairs at what is now the **12 Mark Twain Guesthouse**. The three rooms vary in size and aren't fancy, but they're inexpensive and comfortable. It offers up free laundry facilities, and rooms on the riverside have a balcony overlooking the mighty Mississippi River.

Mark Twain is synonymous with this great river. His years as a riverboat pilot remained with him for the rest of his life, and helped him bring Huck's adventures with Jim to life in *The Adventures of Huckleberry Finn*, widely considered the first Great American Novel. While in Natchez, dine with a river view at ⓭ **Magnolia Grill**, a casual spot for tasty salads and grilled fish, shrimp and steaks. It's down the block from Under the Hill Saloon.

Eventually, all southern roads pass through New Orleans, and the literary one is certainly no exception. From Natchez drive south on 61 until it merges with I-110E in Baton Rouge and then I-10E towards New Orleans.

ADAPTATION

The book is always better, but that doesn't mean we don't love movies. Here are three Southern Gothic dramas that made the leap with style:

- *A Streetcar Named Desire* (1951) Brando's Stanley Kowalski loves STELLA! Four Oscars, Marlon becomes a star.

- *To Kill a Mockingbird* (1962) Best actor, Gregory Peck, is Atticus Finch.

- *Interview With a Vampire* (1994) An unintentional comedy. Tom Cruise and Brad Pitt vamp around New Orleans in wigs and makeup.

This is the town of Tennessee Williams, Anne Rice and Ignatius J Reilly. Some of the first women-only literary salons were held in New Orleans. Faulkner, Twain, and William Burroughs – an original Beat who Jack Kerouac's fictional self visited in Louisiana in *On The Road* – settled here for a spell.

Perhaps no writer is better associated with New Orleans than Tennessee Williams, a playwright who gave us the Pulitzer Prize–winning *A Streetcar Named Desire*, and *Cat on a Hot Tin Roof*. He also won a Tony award for best play with *The Rose Tattoo*. When he moved to New Orleans in 1939 he was dead broke. But President Roosevelt's Works Progress Administration was in the business of funding struggling writers through the Writers and Arts Program, and Williams won a grant. During those days he would write from 5am to 11am and then hit ⓮ **Lafitte's Blacksmith Shop** to drink with his fellow artists while a pianist played whatever sheet music Williams brought him that day. This candle-lit, hole-in-the-wall is purported to have been smuggler Jean Laffite's workshop and French Quarter hideout. Today the piano music is gone, but it remains a grungy oasis of the authentic on cheese ball Bourbon St.

Williams' fortunes took a significant turn skyward when he penned *Streetcar* at ⓯ **632½ St Peter**, a town-home with a wide veranda in the French Quarter – or as Williams called it, Little Bohemia. Soon Tennessee was flush with cash, and he would often enjoy a late brandy at ⓰ **Napoleon House**, an attractive bar set in a courtyard building erected in 1797. It also has a terrific menu if you're hungry. On hot days sit in the courtyard and order a scoop of shrimp *remoulade* served in a half avocado. When Williams craved a bit of luxury, he checked into the **17 Maison de Ville**. Ask for Room 9 – that was Williams' suite.

William Faulkner also got his start in the Crescent City. Fellow author Sherwood Anderson hosted literary salons at his 1920s residence, **18 540 St Peter**, where Faulkner first earned critical praise. Gertrude Stein, Carl Sandburg and John Dos Passos were also launched by Anderson's salons. Anderson's was not the first, or the only, exclusive literature salon in the Quarter. The turn-of-the-century **19 Writers Club**, led by authors Grace King and Kate Chopin, was for women only. But it was Anderson who buoyed young William with confidence, and convinced him to hole up on Pirate's Alley and write his first novel, *Soldiers' Pay,* in 1926. Today, the canary-yellow building where Faulkner wrote the novel has been converted into a dusty new-and-used bookseller, **20 Faulkner House Books**. Poke around for first editions!

Modern literature has been nourished by New Orleans as well, or have you forgotten the Vampire Lestat? He, and all of his nefarious French Quarter adventures were created at the rambling and leafy **21 Anne Rice House** in the Garden District. And don't leave until you've paid homage to that overweight, counter–cultural, hot-dog selling, rabble-rousing elitist, **22 Ignatius J Reilly**, at his statue on Canal St. Ignatius is immortalized in the brilliant *Confederacy of Dunce,* written by local author John Kennedy Toole (he actually wrote the book in Lafayette) and published after Toole's suicide. It hasn't yet made it to the screen despite decades of interest from a parade of comics including John Belushi and Will Ferrell. Perhaps it's just as well. Ignatius would have likely found the whole red carpet thing way beneath him.

Adam Skolnick

TRIP INFORMATION

GETTING THERE
Fly into Savannah and move northwest through Alabama and Mississippi before turning south to New Orleans.

DO
540 St Peter
A literary landmark you'll enjoy curbside, this is the site of Sherwood Anderson's legendary salons. **540 St Peter St, New Orleans;** 🚹

632½ St Peter
An early–French Quarter home of Tennessee Williams. Observe it from the street. **632½ St Peter St, New Orleans;** 🚹

Andalusia
Visit the house and farm where Flannery O'Connor was raised and wrote her masterworks. ☎ **800-653-1804; www.andalusiafarm .org; Greene St, Milledgeville; admission by donation;** 🕑 **tours by appointment only;** 🚹

Anne Rice House
This gorgeous Garden District mansion is where the horror-novelist-turned-erotica-temptress-turned-Christian penned the Vampire Chronicles. **1239 First St, New Orleans;** 🚹

Center for Southern Culture
Faulkner's Nobel Prize is on permanent display on the top floor of the JD Williams library. There's a brilliant blues archive here, as well. ☎ **662-915-5855; 1 Library Loop, Oxford; admission free;** 🕑 **8am-9pm Mon-Thu, to 4pm Fri, to 5pm Sat, 1pm-5pm Sun;** 🚹

Faulkner House Books
New and used books are on sale in what used to be Faulkner's New Orleans abode. ☎ **504-524-2940; www.faulknerhousebooks.net; 624 Pirate's Alley, New Orleans;** 🕑 **10am-5:30pm, closed Mardi Gras;** 🚹

Ignatius J Reilly
This Canal St statue honors New Orleans' funniest protagonist. **Canal St btw Bourbon & Delphine, New Orleans;** 🚹

Mercer-Williams House Museum
Upstairs is off-limits, but the downstairs is an interior decorator's fantasy. Williams' sister gives lunchtime tours. ☎ **912-236-6352;** **www.mercerhouse.com; 429 Bull St, Savannah; adult/child $12.50/8;** 🕑 **10:30am-3:40pm Mon-Sat; 12:30pm-4pm Sun**

Old Courthouse Museum
In May, 30,000 people descend on tiny Monroeville for annual productions of *To Kill a Mocking Bird*. There are also Truman Capote and Harper Lee exhibits here. ☎ **251-575-7433; www.tokillamockingbird.com; 31 N Alabama Ave, Monroeville; admission free;** 🕑 **8am-4pm Mon-Fri, 10am-2pm Sat;** 🚹

Rowan Oak
This is the graceful 1840s home of William Faulkner, who authored many brilliant and slightly off-center novels about Mississippi and the South. He lived here from 1930 until he died in 1962. Tours are self-guided. ☎ **662-234-3284; off Taylor Rd, Oxford; admission adult $5, child & student free;** 🕑 **10am-4pm Tue-Sat, 1pm-4pm Sun;** 🚹

Square Books
The prolific Faulkner section is mind-boggling, but they have current titles and frequent readings from living, breathing authors, as well. ☎ **662-236-2262; www.squarebooks.com; 111 Courthouse Square, Oxford;** 🕑 **9am-9pm Mon-Thu, to 10pm Fri & Sat;** 🚹

Writers Club
Grace King and Kate Chopin held a women's lit salon in this lovely Jackson Square town home. **620 St Peter St, New Orleans;** 🚹

EAT & DRINK
City Grocery
Eclectic Southern cuisine is served at this place on the south side of the Square. Writers congregate at the stylish, funky upstairs bar. ☎ **662-232-8080; www.citygroceryonline .com; 152 Courthouse Square, Oxford; mains $10-25;** 🕑 **10am-2pm & 6pm-10pm Mon-Sat**

Lafitte's Blacksmith Shop
Bourbon St's most historic and soulful watering hole. ☎ **504-523-0066; 941 Bourbon St, New Orleans;** 🕑 **noon-late**

Magnolia Grill
Fresh continental fare served with fabulous Mississippi River views. ☎ **601-446-7670; www.magnoliagrill.com; 49 Silver St, Natchez; mains $13-29;** 🕑 **11am-9pm Sun-Thu, to 10pm Fri & Sat;** 🚹

Napoleon House

Wonderfully timeworn and just off Jackson Square. Most come for drinks, but the food is tasty. ☎ 504-524-9752; **500 Chartres St, New Orleans; mains $9-15; ⊙ 11am-5pm Mon, to midnight Tue-Thu, to 1am Fri & Sat, to 7pm Sun**

Under the Hill Saloon

A tremendously fun and historic bar that was once a favorite haunt of Samuel Clemens, riverboat pilot. ☎ 601-446-8023; www .underthehillsaloon.com; **25 Silver St, Natchez;** ⊙ **9am-late**

Walls Bar-B-Que

Tasty Southern-grill fare is yours at this Savannah institution. ☎ 912-232-9754; **515 E York Lane, Savannah; mains from $7;** ⊙ **11am-9pm Thu-Sat;** &

SLEEP

Bed & Breakfast Inn

Whenever a B&B serves blueberry pancakes for breakfast, that's a good thing. It's just down the street from Mercer-Williams House.

☎ 912-238-0518; www.savannah bnb.com; **117 W Gordon St, Savannah; r from $150;** &

Maison de Ville

Tennessee Williams preferred these luxe environs when he was flush. The antique furnishings and summer bargains are nice. ☎ 800-634-1600; www.maisondeville.com; **727 Rue Toulouse, New Orleans; r $100-700**

Mark Twain Guesthouse

Riverboat captain Clemens used to drink till late at the saloon and pass out in one of three upstairs bedrooms. Room 1 has the best view. ☎ 601-446-8023; www.under thehillsaloon.com; **25 Silver St, Natchez; r from $85**

Puddin' Place

A historical B&B within walking distance of the Square. Reserve ahead! ☎ 662-234-1250; **1008 University Ave, Oxford; r from $140;** &

USEFUL WEBSITES

www.beelerslife.wordpress.com

LINK YOUR TRIP

www.lonelyplanet.com/trip-planner

Southeastern Beach Getaways

WHY GO From playing pinball on neon-lit boardwalks to crabbing with raw-chicken bait on isolated barrier islands, experience the A to Z of the Southeast coast in just over 600 stunning, sandy miles. Hope you like fried shrimp!

Start on North Carolina's northern coast, where the windswept Outer Banks have always been a little apart from the mainland, both geographically and culturally. These shifting ribbons of sand trace the coastline for about 100 miles. While the northern towns are inundated with vacationers in high season, other parts of the Outer Banks remain nearly silent but for the waves and the occasional crackle of summer thunder. If you're driving from the mainland on Hwy 64, you'll cross onto ❶ Roanoke Island, site of the first English colony in the New World. The settlers (about 100 of them) disappeared without a trace in the late 1580s; their fate is still one of America's greatest mysteries.

Head across the causeway onto ❷ Bodie Island (pronounced "body"), where the contiguous villages of Kitty Hawk, Kill Devil Hills and Nags Head have laid-back beachy vibes. There is no shortage of 25-cent oyster bars and pirate-themed motels in these parts, no sir. Wilbur and Orville Wright made Kitty Hawk famous in 1903 when they launched the world's first airplane flight here (it lasted 12 seconds). You too can soar over the Sahara-like dunes of ❸ Jockey's Ridge State Park, a popular spot for hang-gliders. Take a lesson with ❹ Kitty Hawk Kites or, if you prefer to keep your feet on the ground, just fly a kite. Afterwards, dine on seared tuna at the ❺ Black Pelican, housed in an old lifesaving station decorated with funky knickknacks. Its bar is a local favorite in the early evening.

Follow Hwy 12 (also known as Virginia Dare Trail or "the coast road") south, crossing the bridge onto largely undeveloped ❻ Hatteras Island. Here, the ❼ Pea Island National Wildlife Refuge is a birder's

TIME
1 week

DISTANCE
630 miles

BEST TIME TO GO
May – Sep

START
Roanoke Island, NC

END
Cumberland Island, GA

ALSO GOOD FOR

OUTDOORS

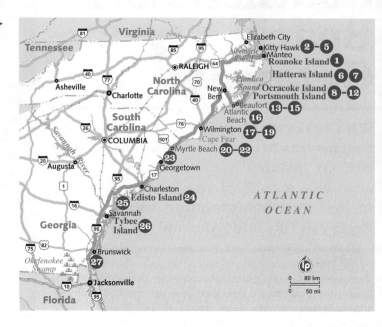

paradise – wander miles of nature trails with your binoculars in search of endangered Peregrine falcons. A 13-mile stretch of isolated beach is perfect for peaceful strolls and shell-gathering.

"Rooms have the feel of an eccentric great auntie's house, with old dolls and portraits."

Take the free car ferry to **8** **Ocracoke Island** and spend the day watching the wild horses run, or putt-putt around Ocracoke Village's narrow streets on a rented scooter – try **9** **Wheelie Fun Scooter Rentals** in the marina. Ocracoke's native population of fishermen and craftspeople were so historically isolated that some still speak with the brogues of their British ancestors, a dialect known as "Hoi Toider" for the way they pronounce "high tide." Buy one of the island's famous hammocks at **10** **Ocracoke Island Hammock Company** then check out the 1823 Ocracoke Lighthouse, North Carolina's oldest. For dinner, have a fried-oyster sandwich at **11** **Howard's Pub**, where visitors and salty locals alike drink beer on tap and listen to live music on the porch. At the end of the day, lay down your head in the you-know-it-*must*-be-haunted **12** **Island Inn**, built in 1901 entirely from shipwrecked wood. Rooms have the feel of an eccentric great auntie's house, with old dolls and oil portraits.

Cross back onto the mainland on the Cedar Island ferry and head south, where the Outer Banks give way to an area known as the Crystal Coast (or, as locals call it, "Down East"). Photogenic **13** **Beaufort** is one of the oldest towns in the state, with a truly Gothic history of piracy, rum-running and Civil War spying. Blackbeard himself lived here, in the so-called Hammock House off Front St. This treacherous stretch of coast was once known as "the Graveyard of the Atlantic," and numerous shipwrecks lie just off the shore.

14 **Discovery Diving** specializes in tours of spooky submerged wrecks. For a real treat, catch a private ferry from the boardwalk to **15** **Shackleford Banks**, inhabited only by wild ponies. You can camp on this giant sandbar overnight, or just spend a few hours wading and gathering seashells in solitude.

While Beaufort itself doesn't have a swimming beach, the smell of coconut sun block hangs heavily in the air in nearby **16** **Atlantic**, where the wide stretch of sand is always crowded with families, fishermen and surfers. Continue on to the Wilmington area, where several nearby beaches are popular surf and vacation spots. **17** **Wrightsville Beach**, closest to Wilmington, has a lively, youthful vibe with surf shops, souvenir stands and fried-fish restaurants. Nothing says summer more than lunch on the pier at the **18** **Oceanic Restaurant**, where you can chow on fish and chips above the waves. Afterwards, learn to surf in the warm Gulf Stream waters with a lesson from **19** **Wrightsville Beach Supply Company**. A private instructor will lead you into the fairly gentle waves, ideal for first-timers.

> **DETOUR** In the late 1700s, **Portsmouth Island** was the largest settlement on the Outer Banks. By 1971, the last two remaining islanders moved to the mainland, leaving Portsmouth a ghost town. From Ocracoke, hire a private ferry to the island (20 minutes), where you can camp overnight on the beach and wander around the deserted houses, post office, school and church. Bring all your own provisions, including *plenty* of bug spray.

Cross into South Carolina on Hwy 17 and you're now in the 60-mile stretch of beaches and resorts known as the Grand Strand. Here you'll find the thumping club music and neon lights of **20** **Myrtle Beach**, the Cancun of South Carolina. By day, lay on the golden sand on the crowded public beach, or shop at **21** **Broadway at the Beach**, an outlet mall the size of a small city. By night, slurp Jell-O shots with Harley riders and college Spring Breakers. There's not much in the way of nature here, but that's OK when you've got 50 mini-golf courses and the 87,000-sq-ft **22** **Ripley's Aquarium**. Walk through the glass tunnel in the shark-filled Dangerous Reef and stop to pet Cownose rays in the touch

BEACHES OF THE GULF COAST

While much of the Gulf Coast of Alabama, Mississippi and Louisiana consists of swampy marshland, there are a few nice beaches if you're dying for a dip.

- Alabama: The adjacent towns of **Gulf Shores** and **Orange Beach** feature high-rise condos overlooking sugar-white beaches.

- Mississippi: **West Ship Island's** green waters are the state's loveliest; accessible by ferry from Gulfport for day trips only.

- Louisiana: Swim in the warm Gulf waters off **Grand Isle State Park**, then camp on the beach.

tank. Have dinner in nearby Murrells Inlet, a longtime fishing community now home to a strip of good family-run seafood restaurants. **㉓ Lee's Inlet Kitchen** has been serving up shrimp cocktails and golden hush puppies in a large, noisy cottage since 1948. Expect crowds.

Further south, the Sea Islands range from isolated marshlands to tidy resort communities. This area, known as Lowcountry, is home to the African-American Gullah (sometimes known as Geechee) people, who retain strong cultural and linguistic connections to their African roots. **㉔ Edisto Island** is proud of its lack of traffic lights. Stop here for a morning of swimming and an afternoon of bike riding amid the palmettos, then tuck into a platter of shrimp at one of the half-dozen seafood restaurants. Across the St Helena Sound, **㉕ Hunting Island State Park** is South Carolina's most popular state park. Rent a cabin and hike the nature trails through the dense maritime forest. In the summer, if you're lucky, you might catch a nesting loggerhead turtle on the beach.

PLAYLIST 🎵

"Beach music," a mix of big band, doo-wop and rock 'n' roll sounds, was developed in the Carolinas in the 1950s. Dance the shag to these genre classics.

- "39-21-46," the Showmen
- "Carolina Girls," General Johnson & the Chairmen of the Board
- "Double Shot (of My Baby's Love)," the Swingin' Medallions
- "Girl Watcher," the O'Kaysions
- "I Love Beach Music," the Embers
- "Myrtle Beach Days," the Fantastic Shakers
- "Summertime's Callin' Me," the Catalinas
- "What Kind of Fool Do You Think I Am?," Bill Deal & the Rhondels

Down in Georgia, **㉖ Tybee Island** is popular with families for its wide, peaceful beaches and handful of moderately priced hotels and restaurants, just a stone's throw from downtown Savannah. It's also a great place for crabbing – try your luck on the rock jetty off the far north end of the island. About 1½ hours down the coast is the **㉗ Cumberland Island National Seashore**, with untouched beaches and 50 miles of hiking trails through deep, spooky maritime forest and marshes overhung with Spanish moss. Camp out and watch the stars above the swaying palmettos, or stay in the nearby village of St Mary's. Beware of gators.
Emily Matchar

TRIP INFORMATION

GETTING THERE
From Raleigh, head east on Hwy 64, or fly into Virginia's Norfolk International Airport and go south on Hwy 168.

DO

Broadway at the Beach
This city-sized outdoor mall has over 100 stores, plus dozens of bars and restaurants, an IMAX, mini-golf and a fake lake. ☎ 483-444-3200; www.broadwayatthebeach .com; 1325 Celebrity Cir, Myrtle Beach, SC; ⏰ 10am-11pm summer

Discovery Diving
Dive spooky shipwrecks in the "Graveyard of the Atlantic" with this Beaufort-based scuba shop. ☎ 252-728-2265; www.discovery diving.com; 414 Orange St, Beaufort, NC; half-/1-day dive $65/105

Jockey's Ridge State Park
Walking these dunes feels more like being in the Sahara than North Carolina. Watching the kite-fliers is an activity in itself. ☎ 252-441-7132; Milepost 12, Nags Head, NC; admission free; ⏰ 8am-9pm summer; ♿

Kitty Hawk Kites
This outfitter has locations all over the Banks, and offers hang-gliding lessons in Jockey's Ridge State Park. ☎ 252-449-2210; www .kittyhawk.com; 3933 Croatan Hwy, Nags Head, NC; beginners lesson $89

Ocracoke Island Hammock Company
The island is rightfully famous for its hammock makers; this shop's wares are woven on-premises from thick, white cotton. ☎ 252-928-4387; 201 British Cemetery Rd, Ocracoke, NC; ⏰ 10am-7pm Mon-Fri, varies on weekends

Pea Island National Wildlife Refuge
Unwind on miles of pristine beaches and hiking trails, or train your binoculars on the 365 species of birds. ☎ 252-473-1668; www.fws .gov/peaisland; Hatteras Island, NC; admission free; ⏰ daylight hrs

Ripley's Aquarium
This 87,000-sq-ft aquarium, in the Broadway at the Beach complex, features a great white shark display and a huge touch tank full of skates and rays. ☎ 800-734-8888; www.ripleysaquarium.com; 1110 Celebrity Cir, Myrtle Beach, SC; adult/child $19/10; ⏰ 9am-9pm; ♿

Shackleford Banks
From the Beaufort boardwalk, catch a water taxi to the uninhabited Shackleford Banks sandbar for an afternoon of watching wild horses. ☎ 252-728-7555; www.islandferry adventures.com; Beaufort boardwalk, Beaufort, NC; round-trip $15

Wheelie Fun Scooter Rentals
The best way to tour Ocracoke Village's quaint side streets is by scooter. ☎ 252-928-6661; Anchorage Marina, Ocracoke, NC; rental per hr $30

Wrightsville Beach Supply Company
This surf outfitter offers both private and group lessons in the fairly gentle waters of Wrightsville Beach. ☎ 910-256-8821; www .wbsupplyco.com; 1 N Lumina Ave Wrightsville Beach, NC; 2hr lesson $60

EAT

Black Pelican
Fish entrees and wood-fired pizza rule at this cozy, converted lifesaving station. ☎ 252-261-3171; www.blackpelican.com; Milepost 4, Kitty Hawk, NC; mains $11-22; ⏰ 11:30am-9:30pm

Howard's Pub
This rambling wooden building decorated with license plates is popular for oyster sandwiches, ribs, beer and live music. ☎ 252-928-4441; www.howardspub.com; Hwy 12, Ocracoke Village, NC; mains $7-24; ⏰ 11am-10pm Mon-Fri, to midnight Sat & Sun; ♿

Lee's Inlet Kitchen
Lee's has been serving deviled crab and hush puppies to crowds on Murrells Inlet's restaurant row since 1948. ☎ 843-651-2881; www.leesinletkitchen.com; 4460 Business Hwy 17, Murrells Inlet, SC; mains $18-33; ⏰ from 4:30pm high season; ♿

Oceanic Restaurant
Munch calamari and Oysters Rockefeller at sunset on the pier of this well-loved seafood restaurant overlooking the Atlantic. ☎ 910-256-5551; www.oceanicrestaurant.com;

703 S Lumina Ave, Wrightsville Beach, NC;
mains $7-26; 11:30am-10pm Mon-Sat

SLEEP

Cumberland Island National Seashore

Take the ferry over to this island park, which offers both backcountry and beach camping. ☎ 912-882-4336 ext. 254; www.nps .gov/cuis; Cumberland Island, GA; ferry $17, entry fee $4, campsite $4; (♿)

Hunting Island State Park

Rent a fully equipped cabin, complete with microwave, TV and central air, amid the palmettos in this popular seaside wilderness area. ☎ 843-838-2011; www.southcarolina parks.com; 2555 Sea Island Pkwy, Hunting Island, SC; cabins $89-172; (♿)

Island Inn

Sleep amid mismatched decor in a spooky turn-of-the-century building built from ship-wrecked wood. ☎ 252-928-4351; www .ocracokeislandinn.com; 25 Lighthouse Rd, Ocracoke, NC; r $99-169

USEFUL WEBSITES

www.discoversouthcarolina.com
www.nccoast.com

LINK YOUR TRIP

www.lonelyplanet.com/trip-planner

The Great Smokies

WHY GO The Cherokee Indians fell in love with these ancient, mist-shrouded mountains, which they named Shaconage (Place of the Blue Smoke). Lose yourself in their lush valleys and mossy, shaded trails. But lest you overdose on trees, there's plenty of man-made fun (hello, Dollywood!) on either side of the park.

The Great Smoky Mountains, a subrange of the Appalachians, straddle the North Carolina–Tennessee border. On a map, the southwestern corner of North Carolina looks like a lump of taffy being flattened by the rollers of Tennessee and Georgia. This "tail" – geographically part of the Tennessee Valley – is crisscrossed with thundering mountain rivers, and dotted with lakes and hidden waterfalls.

The terrain, unsurprisingly, is fantastic for whitewater rafting, kayaking and tubing. The ❶ **Nantahala Outdoor Center** (NOC) launches trips on the class II and III rapids of the Nantahala River from their main outpost west of Bryson City. Ride a group raft or a two-person ducky through the wide, brown river gorge, spinning through a dizzying whirlpool and splish-splashing over the Nantahala Falls. The NOC also offers whitewater trips for all ages and skill levels on a half-dozen other rivers in the Appalachians. Experienced paddlers can brave the 9-mile trip down the roiling class IV-V Cheoah, launching from nearby Robbinsville. After a long day on the river, put your sore muscles to bed at the NOC's ❷ **Nantahala Inn**, a rustic, pine-paneled motor lodge tucked into the trees.

Trips on the historic ❸ **Great Smoky Mountains Railroad** depart from Bryson City and plow through the dramatic Nantahala Gorge and across the Fontana Trestle. The former Murphy Branch Line, built in the late 1800s, brought unheard of luxuries like books, factory-spun cloth and oil lamps to these mountains, making rural Appalachian life a little

TIME
5 days

DISTANCE
180 miles

BEST TIME TO GO
Apr – Jun, Sep & Oct

START
near Bryson City, NC

END
Knoxville, TN

ALSO GOOD FOR

OUTDOORS

BEST TRIP

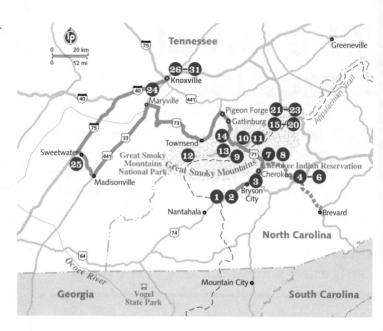

less tough. Themed trips on the red-and-yellow trains include a beer tasting, a Thomas the Tank Engine–themed ride for kids, and a mystery dinner theater.

Half an hour to the northeast is the town of ④ **Cherokee**, the major North Carolina gateway to the Great Smoky Mountains National Park. The Cherokee people have lived in this area since the last Ice Age, though many of them died on the Trail of Tears. The descendents of the people who escaped or returned are known as the Eastern Band of the Cherokee, about 12,000 of whom live on the Qualla Boundary reservation near town. Contemporary Cherokee can feel a bit sad, with "chiefs" hawking plastic headdresses on Tsali Blvd and elderly locals playing the one-armed bandits in the dim, smoky depths of Harrah's Cherokee Casino.

But several sights transcend the kitsch and stereotypes, and actually teach a thing or two about Cherokee culture and history. The cool, earth-colored halls of the ⑤ **Museum of the Cherokee Indian** have displays filled with artifacts such as pots, deerskins, woven skirts, eerie life-sized dioramas and a new animated exhibit on Cherokee myths.

In the summer, catch ⑥ **Unto These Hills**, an outdoor play dramatizing the Trail of Tears. Performed at the Mountainside Theater since 1950, it's the second longest–running outdoor drama in America (the oldest is *The Lost Colony*, in the North Carolina coastal town of Manteo).

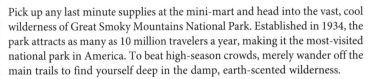

Pick up any last minute supplies at the mini-mart and head into the vast, cool wilderness of Great Smoky Mountains National Park. Established in 1934, the park attracts as many as 10 million travelers a year, making it the most-visited national park in America. To beat high-season crowds, merely wander off the main trails to find yourself deep in the damp, earth-scented wilderness.

Newfoundland Gap Rd/Hwy 441 is the only thoroughfare crossing the entire 521,000-acre park. And what a drive it is, traversing 33 miles of deep oak and pine forest, and wildflower meadows. Stop first at the **7** **Oconaluftee Visitor Center**, with interactive exhibits on the park's history and ecosys-tems. Pick up a map and stroll the Oconaluftee River Trail, which leaves from the center and follows the river for 1.5 miles to the boundary of the Cherokee reservation. Don't forget to pick up a free backcountry camping permit if you plan to go off-trail.

Also near the park entrance is the **8** **Mountain Farm Museum** and **Mingus Mill**. The museum, located next to the visitor center, is a 19th-century farmstead assembled from buildings from various locations around the park. The worn, wooden struc-tures, including a barn, a blacksmith shop and a smokehouse, give you a peek into the hardscrabble existence of early Appalachian settlers. A half-mile north, the 1886 Mingus Mill still grinds corn and wheat.

THE TRAIL OF TEARS

In the late 1830s, President Andrew Jackson ordered more than 16,000 Native Americans removed from their southeastern homelands and resettled in what's now Oklahoma. Thou-sands died of disease, exposure and exhaustion on the forced march west, now known as the "Trail of Tears." In Gatlinburg, see a **monument to Tsali**, the Cherokee hero who, according to legend, was executed for his part in an anti-relocation rebellion.

Further down the road, 6643ft **9** **Clingmans Dome** is the third-highest mountain east of the Mississippi. You can drive almost all the way to the top via Clingmans Dome Rd, then walk the rest of the way to the Jetsons-like concrete observation tower. From here you can see over the spruce- and pine-covered mountaintops for miles around.

Climbing 6593ft **10** **Mt LeConte** is probably the park's most popular chal-lenge, sure to give some serious hamstring burn. The Alum Cave Trail, one of five routes to the peak, starts out from the Alum Cave parking area on the main road. Follow a creek, pass under a stone arch and wind your way steadily upward past thickets of rhododendron, myrtle and mountain laurel. **11** **LeConte Lodge**, a collection of rough-hewn log cabins near the summit, is the park's only non-camping accommodation. There's no electricity, no real showers and all the food – beef and gravy for dinner, grits and ham for break-fast – is packed in by llamas three times a week. But you'll be amply rewarded by glowing purple sunsets from the eastern-facing cliffs at Myrtle Point.

Continuing on Newfound Gap Rd, turn left on Little River Rd, which becomes Laurel Creek Rd, running right into the 11-mile loop around ⑫ **Cades Cove**. This secluded (except for the glut of cars in summer) valley contains the remnants of a 19th-century settlement. Park your car to see the old churches and farmhouses up close, and to hike trails through postcard-perfect meadows filled with deer, wild turkeys and the occasional bear. Cyclists take note – cars are banned from the loop road until 10am every Wednesday and Saturday from May through September.

DETOUR In the Pisgah National Forest, one hour southeast of Cherokee, you'll find **Sliding Rock**, a 60ft-long natural waterslide. In summertime visitors wait their turn to swoosh down the slick rock face into the 7ft-deep pool below. The ride can be painful on the tailbone and the water is freezing, but you'll line up to do it again anyway. Nearby **Brevard** is a cute mountain town of B&Bs and candy shops.

Doubling back to Little River Rd, you'll find the ⑬ **Elkmont Campground**. The 220 wooded sites can fill up quickly in high season. Back at the juncture of Little River and Newfound Gap Rds is the ⑭ **Sugarlands Visitor Center**, park headquarters. There's a bookstore, exhibits on plant and animal life, and seasonal ranger-led talks and tours.

Driving out of the park on the Tennessee side is a bit disconcerting. All at once you pop out of the tranquil green tunnel of trees and into a blinking, shrieking welter of cars, motels and mini-golf courses, all blaring Christmas music and smelling of fried dough. Welcome to ⑮ **Gatlinburg**. It's Heidi meets Hillbilly in this vaguely Bavarian-themed tourist wonderland, catering to Smokies visitors since the 1930s. Turn off your cynical side and let the kitsch work its magic. Most of the tourist attractions are within the compact, hilly little downtown.

Pancakes are to Gatlinburg what pizza is to New York. Though there's a different pancake house on every corner proclaiming itself the best in town, ⑯ **Pancake Pantry** is the granddaddy of them all. Chow down on 24 varieties of pancake, cheese-swollen omelets or whipped cream–smothered waffles in a building that looks like an overgrown Smurf house.

The Ripley's franchise operates seven shock-and-awe-style attractions in town. The gargantuan ⑰ **Ripley's Aquarium of the Smokies** features sea turtles, piranhas and stingrays far, far from their homes. A 340ft-long moving sidewalk shunts you through the clear tunnel on the floor of the Shark Lagoon, where you can watch long, sinister shapes glide by overhead. Though the original ⑱ **Ripley's Believe it or Not!** burned down in 1992, taking with it nearly all the exhibits, the popular odditorium rose from the ashes twice as large. Join the crowds to gawk at the shrunken heads, the 6583½ft-long gum-wrapper chain and the 1840s vampire killing kit.

The **19** **Gatlinburg Sky Lift**, a repurposed ski resort chair lift, whisks you high over the Smokies. You'll fill up your camera's entire memory card with panoramic snapshots. At night, take your pick of a plethora of Appalachian-themed motels and lodges. **20** **Buckhorn Inn** is a tasteful bed and breakfast with views of Mt LeConte, and a flagstone terrace with rocking chairs.

A few miles north of Gatlinburg is the dismal stretch of chain motels, ye olde kountry shoppes and discount cigarette warehouses known as **21** **Pigeon Forge**. This town exists for one reason only: the worship of that big-haired, big-busted angel of East Tennessee, Dolly Parton. Dolly was born in a one-room shack in the nearby hamlet of Locust Ridge, started performing on Knoxville radio at the age of 11 and moved to Nashville at 18 with all her worldly belongings in a cardboard suitcase. She's made millions singing about her Smoky Mountain roots and continues to be a huge presence in her hometown, donating money to local causes and riding a glittery float in the annual Dolly Parade.

WATERFALLS OF THE SMOKIES

The Smokies are full of waterfalls, from icy trickles to roaring cascades. Here are a few of the best:

- Grotto Falls: you can walk behind these 25ft-high falls, off Trillium Gap Trail
- Laurel Falls: this popular 80ft fall is located down an easy 2.6-mile paved trail
- Mingo Falls: at 120ft, this is one of the highest waterfalls in the Appalachians
- Rainbow Falls: on sunny days, the mist here produces a rainbow

The **22** **Dollywood** theme park is an enormous, gushy love letter to mountain culture. Minivans full of families pour in each morning to ride the hee-haw themed thrill rides like the Mystery Mine Coaster and the Tennessee Tornado; see demonstrations of traditional Appalachian crafts such as wagon-making; and browse a plethora of shops hawking Christian-themed T-shirts and pink taffy. You can also tour the bald eagle sanctuary, attend Sunday services at the country chapel or worship at the altar of Dolly in the Chasing Rainbows life-story museum. The adjacent **23** **Dollywood's Splash Country** takes the same themes and adds water. Ride the Mountain Scream waterslides and the "whitewater rafting adventure" of Big Bear Plunge.

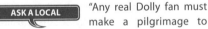

"Any real Dolly fan must make a pilgrimage to **Dollywood**. But there are also several less well-known stops in the area. Many fans visit the **Sevier County Courthouse** in Sevierville and get their picture made at the statue of her on the courthouse lawn. In Pigeon Forge you'll pass the **Little House of Prayer**, where her 'holy roller' Pentecostal grandfather preached, and **Caton's Chapel School**, one of the schoolhouses Dolly attended as a child."

Duane Gordon, webmaster, www.dollymania.net

Head out of town via Hwy 321. This rural highway gives you an idea of what a Tennessee road trip was like before I-40 sliced its way through the state.

Watch as the tree-covered peaks of the Smokies mellow into grassy green hills dotted with farmstands and flea markets; stop for an ice-cream cone as you pass through the time-warp town of **24** **Maryville**, where it still looks like 1955.

About two hours southwest of Pigeon Forge is the town of Sweetwater, home to America's largest underground lake. **25** **The Lost Sea** is a genuine country roadside attraction, where families and elderly couples with guidebooks queue up for hour-long tours. Before the modern tourist-era, the caves were used as a dance hall, as a venue for cockfighting and as a hiding place for moonshine stills. Descend into Craighead Caverns via a long metal tunnel and ride a glass-bottom boat across the eerie greenish lake, illuminated from below by underwater lights. If you're lucky you'll spot a silvery cave trout gliding through the murky depths.

"Ride a glass-bottom boat across the eerie greenish lake, illuminated from below by underwater lights."

Double back northeast for 45 minutes to hit **26** **Knoxville**. This funky little gem of a city is one of those places where, despite the lack of specific tourist attractions, you come away feeling like you might want to live there one day. Driving in, note the giant gold orb towering over the city skyline. That's the **27** **Sunsphere**, a relic of the 1982 World's Fair. You can walk up to the observation deck for free. Downtown Knoxville is full of splendid 19th-century warehouses and storefronts turned lofts and boutiques. Pedestrian-only **28** **Market Square** is the center of the action, with outdoor cafés and a public green that hosts summertime concerts and plays.

Grab a table in the crowded, art-filled dining room of the **29** **Tomato Head**, where tattooed hipsters will serve you a gorgonzola and free-range chicken calzone. Right around the corner, the **30** **Hotel St Oliver** is like something out of a Tennessee Williams play. The 28 rooms have the eccentric elegance of a slightly dotty Southern belle, with Victorian wingback armchairs and thick Persian carpets. Sit for a spell in the dim downstairs library with its crumbling leather tomes and gilt-framed oil paintings. Wind down with a night of music at the impeccably restored **31** **Bijou Theatre**. Built in 1909, the Bijou has hosted luminaries of the bygone era like Dizzy Gillespie and Groucho Marx. These days, Knoxville's old guard comes for the ballet, while the whippersnappers from the University of Tennessee bobble their heads to indie rock performers such as Bright Eyes.

Emily Matchar

TRIP INFORMATION

GETTING THERE
From Charlotte, NC, take I-85 South to I-26 West to I-40 W. Turn onto the Great Smoky Mountains Expressway and continue for 40 miles toward Bryson City.

DO

Bijou Theatre
Downtown Knoxville's opulent 19th-century theater hosts big-name rock acts, ballet and theater. ☎ 865-656-4444; www.knoxbijou .com; 803 S Gay St, Knoxville, TN; ☾ show times vary

Dollywood
Revel in the Appalachian-themed kitsch at this family-friendly amusement park, owned by East Tennessee's own darlin' Dolly. ☎ 865-428-9488; www.dollywood .com; 1020 Dollywood Ln, Pigeon Forge, TN; adult/child $50/39; ☾ hours vary by season, closed Jan-Mar; ♿

Dollywood's Splash Country
Cool off in the Mountain Waves pool at Dolly's 25-acre water park. ☎ 865-428-9488; www.dollywoodssplashcountry.com; 146 Middle Creek Rd, Pigeon Forge, TN; adult/ child $42/37; ☾ 10am-7pm high season, closed Oct-Apr; ♿

Gatlinburg Sky Lift
Ride this chairlift high into the mountains for incomparable views. ☎ 865-436-4307; www.gatlinburgskylift.com; Parkway light 7, Gatlinburg, TN; adult/child $12/9; ☾ 9am-10pm, to 5pm winter

Great Smoky Mountains Railroad
Choose from a variety of scenic train tours, including dinner and wine trips and kid-friendly rides. ☎ 800-872-4681; www.gsmr .com; 226 Everett St, Bryson City, NC; adult/ child from $34/19; ♿

Mountain Farm Museum and Mingus Mill
Be transported to the 19th century at this replica farm (next to Oconaluftee Visitor Center) and working grist mill (a half-mile up the road). ☎ 423-436-1200; www.nps .gov/grsm; ☾ 9am-5pm Mar-Dec

Museum of the Cherokee Indian
Artifact-filled exhibits trace the long, proud and often sad history of Native Americans in these mountains. ☎ 828-497-3481; www .cherokeemuseum.org; 589 Tsali Blvd, Chero-kee, NC; adult/child $9/6; ☾ 9am-5pm

Nantahala Outdoor Center
This trusted river outfitter has whitewater trips for all levels, with several outposts throughout the Appalachians. ☎ 828-488-2176; www .noc.com; 13077 Hwy 19/74, near Bryson City NC; guided rafting trips from $38; ♿

Oconaluftee Visitor Center
Pick up maps and camping permits at North Carolina's gateway to the Smokies. ☎ 423-436-1200; www.nps.gov/grsm; Hwy 441, near Cherokee, NC; ☾ 8am-4:30pm, until later spring & summer

Ripley's Aquarium of the Smokies
Take a walk through the shark tunnel and play with stingrays at this massive fish tank. ☎ 865-430-8808; www.ripleysaquarium ofthesmokies.com; Parkway light 5, Gatlin-burg, TN; adult/child $22/12; ☾ 9am-9pm Sun-Thu, to 11pm Fri & Sat; ♿

Ripley's Believe It or Not!
The shrunken heads are a major crowd pleaser at this house of oddities. ☎ 865-436-5096; www.ripleys.com; Parkway light 7, Gatlinburg, TN; adult/child $15/9; ☾ 9am-midnight; ♿

Sugarlands Visitor Center
Tennessee's main park entrance has a book-store and ranger tours in summer. ☎ 865-436-1291; www.nps.gov/grsm; Hwy 441, TN; ☾ 8am-4:30pm, until later spring & summer

The Lost Sea
Descend into Craighead Caverns and sail across a 4.5-acre underground lake. ☎ 423-337-6616; www.thelostsea.com; 140 Lost Sea Rd, Sweetwater, TN; adult/child $16/7.50; ☾ 9am-5pm, until later spring & summer; ♿

Unto These Hills
This summertime outdoor play dramatizing Cherokee history has been performed at the Mountainside Theater since 1950. ☎ 866-554-4557; www.cherokee-nc.com; Drama Rd, Cherokee; adult/child $18/8; ☾ 8:30pm Mon-Sat Jun-Aug

EAT

Pancake Pantry
Dig into an extra-tall stack at this beloved all-day breakfast joint. ☎ 865-436-4724; 628 Parkway, Gatlinburg, TN; mains $4-9, ☯ 7am-4pm; ♿

Tomato Head
Fill your belly with pizza and tofu burritos at this quirky locals spot. ☎ 865-637-4067; 12 Market Sq, Knoxville, TN; mains $5-9; ☯ 11am-9:30pm Tue-Thu, to 3pm Mon, to 10:30pm Fri & Sat, to 9pm Sun

SLEEP

Buckhorn Inn
Curl up by the fire and gaze out at the misty mountains from the parlor of this gracious bed and breakfast. ☎ 865-436-4668; www.buckhorninn.com; 2140 Tudor Mountain Rd, Gatlinburg, TN; r from $115

Elkmont Campground
The park's largest campground has 220 sites on the banks of the Little River. ☎ 865-436-1271; nps.gov/grsm; Little River Rd, TN; campsites from $17; ☯ Mar-Dec; ♿

Hotel St Oliver
Sleep amid quirky Southern antiques in this eccentric old downtown hotel, with a grand piano in the tiny lobby. ☎ 865-521-0050; www.hotelstolivertn.com; 407 Union Ave, Knoxville, TN; r from $75

LeConte Lodge
Hike up to these rustic cabins at the summit of Mt LeConte and enjoy a group meal and a stunning sunrise. ☎ 865-429-5704; www.leconte-lodge.com; cabins per person from $64

Nantahala Inn
Rafters crash at this simple wooden lodge amid the pines after a day on the river. ☎ 828-488-2176; www.noc.com; Hwy 19, 12 miles west of Bryson City, NC; r from $59

USEFUL WEBSITES
www.gatlinburg.com
www.nps.gov/grsm

LINK YOUR TRIP   www.lonelyplanet.com/trip-planner

TRIP
10 Appalachian Trail opposite
19 Blue Ridge Parkway: High Country p157

Appalachian Trail

WHY GO Three Southern states – Georgia, Tennessee and North Carolina – each claim a section of the 2175-mile Maine-to-Georgia trail. Victoria Logue, inveterate hiker and author of a half-dozen books including "The Best of the Appalachian Trail: Day Hikes" and "Overnight Hikes," gives readers a taste of the epic journey.

TIME
5 – 7 days

DISTANCE
618 miles

BEST TIME TO GO
Apr – Oct

START
Dawsonville, GA

END
Braemar, TN

ALSO GOOD FOR

There is no better way to get a feel for the grandeur of the Appalachian Trail than at its Georgian gateway, ❶ **Amicalola Falls State Park**. Amicalola, a Cherokee Indian word meaning "tumbling waters," is an appropriate name for these 729ft falls – the tallest cascading waterfall east of the Mississippi River. The park offers more than 12 miles of hiking trails, including the 8.5 mile approach trail to Springer Mountain.

The park's beautiful ❷ **Amicalola Falls Lodge** is popular with guests who prefer hotel-type comforts. Campsites and cottages are also available, and the casual ❸ **Maple Restaurant** is open year-round. But for a truly unique Appalachian Trail experience, strap on a backpack and hoof it up to the ❹ **Len Foote Hike Inn**. Its hike-in Approach Trail is a two- to four-hour hike through 5 miles of easy to moderate terrain, and culminates in a zone free of all modern trappings – TV, cars, cell phones. Dine family style with new friends or relax with a book in an Adirondack chair in front of the celestial calendar. Check in to the Hike Inn at the ❺ **Amicalola Falls State Park Visitors Center**, which also offers exhibits and a gift shop.

The Appalachian Trail officially starts at ❻ **Springer Mountain**. On the top of the mountain, you'll find the start of the trail, marked with a plaque: "A footpath for those who seek fellowship with the wilderness."

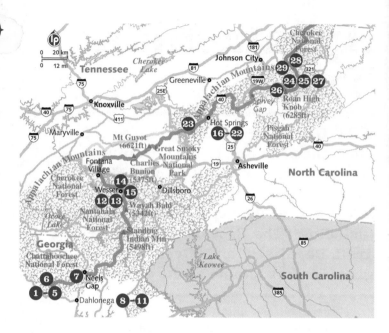

Most thru-hikers (or "2000 milers," as those who walk the Appalachian Trail in a single journey are known) usually start at the Georgia terminus (about two hours north of Atlanta) in the late spring and finish five to seven months later on Mt Katahdin in Maine, 2175 miles to the north. About 400 to 600 registered hikers complete the journey each year, about a quarter of those who set out. Altogether, only a little over 10,000 brave and hearty trekkers have ever completed the journey. A few of those thru-hike the entire route in one go, but many hike the trail in sections – a few months or weeks at a time.

If you're not ready for quite this level of commitment but still want to seek a bit of fellowship with nature, Victoria Logue – who thru-hiked the Appalachian Trail in 1988 and has returned many times since, and has written several books on hiking the Appalachian Trail – suggests several jumping-off points in the Trail's Southern region of Georgia, North Carolina and Tennessee.

Originally the idea of one man, Benton MacKaye, as an antidote to the busy, urban lifestyle of the East Coast in the 1920s, the Appalachian Trail (known as the AT) was completed in 1937. Until 1969, only 61 hikers reportedly thru-hiked the trail, but the endeavor took off after it was declared a National Scenic Trail. The entire route is marked by a series of 2in x 6in white blazes, and is for foot traffic only.

Thirty miles north of Springer Mountain by foot is your first stop in civilization, Mountain Crossings at ❼ **Mountain Crossings at Walasi-Yi** (if you're on wheels, it's 65 miles by car – take Service Road 42, make a right on Hwy 60 and a left on Hwy 19). The one and only man-made covered spot on the trail, the AT literally runs directly through the store, which has served as a resource center to AT hikers since it was completed by the New Deal's Civilian Conservation Corps in 1937. There are hostel beds for those who'd like to do the first part of the trail and then hike (or hitch-hike) back to Springer Mountain.

Thirty miles down Hwy 52 you'll hit the town of ❽ **Dahlonega, Georgia**. In the 1820s, the Dahlonega area was the site of the country's first gold rush. The gold that plates the dome of Georgia's state capitol in Atlanta is from Dahlonega. Today, the story of the gold rush is told inside the oldest courthouse in Georgia, built in 1836, and home of the ❾ **Dahlonega Courthouse Gold Museum**.

Bunk down for the night in Dahlonega at ❿ **Smith House Inn**, an 1895 home too close to downtown for the first owner's liking. When Captain Hall was excavating the land to build, he found a rich vein of gold ore. However, city fathers felt a mine one block from the public square was a bad idea, so the house still stands on that vein of Dahlonega gold. Its ⓫ **Smith House Restaurant** serves up boarding-style meals of fried chicken, baked ham, fresh vegetables and corn muffins.

Go a little wild at your next stop, the ⓬ **Nantahala Outdoor Center** (NOC), where the Appalachian Trail and Nantahala River meet. Nestled in a steep gorge, the Nantahala River lends truth to the meaning of its name – Land of the Noonday Sun. The river offers 8 miles of practice on easy class

ASK A LOCAL

"The Appalachian Trail is maintained by volunteers: more than 6000 people work to protect it each year. The **Appalachian Trail Conservancy's Trail Crews** are a way to give back, as volunteers come to base camp ready for adventure and the ATC provides the food, tools, safety equipment and leadership necessary for crews to get the job done. Want to meet some great folks, live on the AT for a week and paint a blaze? Join the Konnarock, Rocky Top or Mid-Atlantic crews and bust some trail! Check it out at www .appalachiantrail.org/crews."

Andrew Downs, Appalachian Trail Conservancy

II rapids before splashing through the exciting class III whitewater of Nantahala Falls. It's one of America's most popular whitewater runs, and rafters, kayakers and canoeists are often seen plying its waters.

The NOC's ⓭ **Nantahala Adventure Resort**, started in 1972, is situated at the intersection of the Nantahala River, the Appalachian Trail and the Great Smoky Mountains Railroad. The resort offers on-site lodging options and a variety of outdoor activities. Changing rooms, hot showers, full-service restaurants, a pub and a fully stocked Outfitter's Store are also available for your camping, clothing, souvenir and sundry needs. The Appalachian Trail literally passes through the resort. From the resort, it's a 4 mile (strenuous!) hike to **14 Jump Up**, a rocky outcrop boasting outstanding views, or a 6.5 mile hike to the top of **15 Wesser Bald** (4627ft) and the former fire tower, now an observation deck, offering panoramic views of the Great Smoky Mountains, Fontana Lake and the Nantahalas. Hiking north, it is a longer, more strenuous hike (8.1 miles) to the summit of Cheoah Bald (5062ft), which offers one of the most splendid panoramas of the Southern Appalachians. There are AT sleeping shelters all along the trails for overnight hikers.

ASK A LOCAL   The friendliness of mountain folk is nothing to be trifled with. Here's a conversation overheard one early afternoon at the Smoky Mountain Diner in Hot Springs, NC:
Customer to waitress: "Mornin' Sue!"
Waitress to customer: "Mornin' Tom."
"You still servin' breakfast?"
"You want breakfast?"
"Yup."
"Then we're still servin' breakfast."

Snake through Hwy 74 to I-23/Hwy 209 toward **16 Hot Springs, North Carolina**, situated near the French Broad River. Hot Springs is known for just that: hot springs. The postage stamp–sized town offers a range of fabulous lodging, including the historic **17 Mountain Magnolia Inn**, built in 1868, and featured in *This Old House*, HGTV and *Southern Living* magazine. The upscale inn offers visitors a chance to experience the health-giving properties of the springs, while its restaurant **18 Martha's** completes the experience with organic fare. Combine camping with a spa trip at the **19 Hot Springs Resort**. Campsites and simple cabins (with or without air conditioning and full bathrooms) are just a few hundred yards away from the **20 Hot Springs Spa & Mineral Baths**, which has French Broad–fronted hot tubs fed by natural hot springs, plus massage rooms and a pre- or post-massage fire pit for relaxing. If you want a more adventurous foray into the waters, sign up with **21 Huck Finn Rafting**, which runs whitewater rafting and canoeing trips down the French Broad. Hike two city blocks of the Appalachian Trail here, as it runs right through town on Bridge St. For a filling plate of breakfast potatoes or sandwiches, stop in at the **22 Smoky Mountain Diner**.

"Hike two city blocks of the Appalachian Trail, as it runs right through town on Bridge St."

To get to **23 Max Patch Mountain**, take NC 209 south for about 7 miles from Hot Springs, turning west on NC 1175 for 5.3 miles. Turn onto Max Patch Rd (NC 1182). The parking area at the foot of the bald is 3 miles down Max Patch Rd. While there is pleasant hiking both north and south, a short drive will take you to Max Patch and a 1.6 mile roundtrip hike to the Appalachian Trail's southernmost bald mountain. From atop the grassy summit of Max Patch, there are panoramic views of the Blacks, Balds, Balsams and Great Smoky Mountains. On a clear day, you can even see the highest point in the Eastern United States – Mount Mitchell (6684ft).

Hop over the border to Tennessee, then continue another 50 miles on Hwy 352 and I-26 to exit 32 to reach **24** **Roan Mountain State Park**, which encompasses 2006 acres of southern Appalachian forest at the base of 6285ft Roan Mountain. Recreational opportunities abound and the **25** **Roan Mountain State Park Lodge** offers 30 cabins with a chance to relax – each cabin has a front porch with rocking chairs, outfitted kitchen, full bath with tub and shower, wood-burning stove and heat. Campsites are also available in the park.

On the top of Roan Mountain, straddling the Tennessee/North Carolina border (literally; it even ran through the dining hall) are the ruins of the old **26** **Cloudland Hotel** site. The 300-room hotel was built in 1885 by Civil War General John T Wilder. Legend has it that North Carolinian sheriffs would hang out in the saloon, waiting for alcohol-imbibers from the Tennessee side to stray across the line, as North Carolina was a dry state back then.

Just 8 miles past Roan Mountain State Park on Hwy 143 you'll reach **27** **Carvers Gap**, where a set of log steps leads to a section of the Appalachian Trail which crosses a 10-mile series of grassy balds. Considered to be the Trail's most beautiful section, it includes a virtually treeless area whose origin still mystifies scientists. Theories for their evolution include everything from extensive grazing to creation by aliens. The balds offer unobstructed views of the Blue Ridge Mountains in Tennessee and North Carolina. To the south, the AT climbs to the high point of the Roan Mountain ridge, the 6285ft Roan High Knob.

ASK A LOCAL

"Thru-hikers invent trail names to shed their 'real world' identity and represent the transformative power of a thru-hike. It's common to hike with someone named Greyhound or Bloody Stumps for months and never know their real name. My friends named me Mr Magoo before the hike because of my dumb luck, and a thru-hiker named my hiking partner Lisa 'Cartwheel' because he thought her light pack would allow her to do cartwheels up the mountain."
Francis Tapon, Appalachian Trail thru-hiker & author of "Hike Your Own Hike: 7 Lessons from Backpacking Across America."

The Appalachian Trail can also be accessed at **28** **Shook Branch Recreation Area** where the AT crosses I-321. With picnic tables, restroom, water and a sandy beach on the lake, Shook Branch is a pleasant location to hang out and relax before or after a hike. A fairly strenuous hike from the recreation area is to **29** **Laurel Fork Gorge & Falls**. The vertical walls of the gorge rise 100ft on either side of the AT, the only trail through the gorge. But the gorge and the 40ft falls can also be shorter hikes – 5 miles roundtrip or 2.6 miles roundtrip.

To hike the former, access the blue-blazed Hampton Blueline Trail where I-321 crosses Laurel Fork in Hampton, TN (there's a parking lot for hikers here). The shorter hike can be reached by taking Hwy 67 in Tennessee from Hampton to Braemar, and USFS 50 (Dennis Cove Rd) in Braemar 3 miles to the parking area on the left. Both hikes use the Appalachian Trail.

Alex Leviton & Victoria Logue

TRIP INFORMATION

GETTING THERE

The Appalachian Trail runs 2175 miles, from Maine to Georgia. The trail can be accessed in many locations in Georgia, Tennessee and North Carolina for day or overnight hikes.

DO

Amicalola Falls State Park & Visitors Center

The series of waterfalls in this gateway to the Appalachian Trail are especially beautiful in the fall. ☎ 706-265-4703; www.ga stateparks.org/info/amicalola; 418 Amicalola Falls State Park Rd, Dawsonville, GA; 🕑 7am-10pm

Dahlonega Courthouse Gold Museum

In Georgia's oldest courthouse is an homage to the first American gold discovery, back in the 1840s. ☎ 706-864-2257; www .dahlonega.org; Public Square, Dahlonega, GA; adult/child $4/2.50; 🕑 9am-5pm Mon-Sat, 10am-5pm Sun

Hot Springs Spa & Mineral Baths

Hikers, campers and those just looking to relax can soak in hot spring-fed tubs along the French Broad, or book a massage service. ☎ 828-622-7676; www.nchotsprings.com; 315 Bridge St, Hot Springs, NC; mineral hot tubs $12-40, massage $40-100; 🕑 noon-10pm Mon-Thu, 10am-midnight Fri-Sun

Huck Finn Rafting

Canoe down the river or join a group tour for adventurous whitewater rafting or inner-tubing trips. ☎ 877-520-4658; www .huckfinnrafting.com; 158 Bridge St, Hot Springs, NC; trips adult/child from $35/25; 🕑 8.30am-6pm

Mountain Crossings at Walasi-Yi

All your thru- or day-hiking needs in one spot, including mail drops, food and back-packing gear, plus simple overnight accommodations. ☎ 888-MT-XINGS; www.moun taincrossings.com; 9710 Gainesville Hwy, Blairsville, GA; 🕑 9am-5pm Mon-Thu, to 6pm Fri-Sun; hostel per person per night $15

Nantahala Outdoor Center

Whitewater rafting, paddling school and fly-fishing, as well as a full-service outdoor shop. ☎ 828-488-2176; www.noc.com; 13077 Hwy 19/74, near Bryson City, NC; guided rafting trips from $38

Roan Mountain State Park

One of the most beautiful spots near the Appalachian Trail, with the stunning Catawba Rhododendron Garden and comfortable lodge accommodations. ☎ 800-250-8620; www.state.tn.us/environment/parks/roan mtn/; 1015 Hwy-143, Roan Mountain, TN; 🕑 8am-4:30pm

EAT

Maple Restaurant

Family-style buffet at the Amicalola Falls Lodge with an enormous Sunday brunch. ☎ 706-265-1521; 418 Amicalola Falls State Park Rd, Dawsonville, GA; buffet $5-13; 🕑 7am-10:30am & 11:30am-3pm daily; 5pm-9pm Sun-Thu, 5pm-10pm Fri & Sat

Martha's

It doesn't get any more organic, free-range or locally grown than the restaurant at Mountain Magnolia Inn. ☎ 828-622-3543; www .mountainmagnoliainn.com; 204 Lawson St, Hot Springs, NC; mains $11-29; 🕑 5-9:30pm

Smith House Restaurant

Communal tables host diners piling their plates hike-worthy high with Southern favorites. ☎ 706-867-7000; www.smith house.com; 84 S. Chestatee Rd, Dahlonega, GA; all-you-can-eat adult $15-18, child $8-10, 🕑 11am-3pm & 4pm-7:30pm Tue-Fri, 11am-8pm Sat, 11am-7:30pm Sun

Smoky Mountain Diner

Located directly on the Appalachian Trail running through town, with plates of eggs bigger than your whole head. ☎ 828-622-7571; 70 Lance Ave, Hot Springs, NC; mains $3-10; 🕑 7am-10pm Mon-Sat, to 5pm Sun

SLEEP

Amicalola Falls Lodge

The lodge is a full-service hotel with beautiful views from every room, while the rustic cottages sleep 4 to 10. ☎ 706-265-8888;

www.amicalolafalls.com; 418 Amicalola Falls State Park Rd, Dawsonville, GA; campsites $25, r $75-200, cottages $80-160

Hot Springs Resort

Varying degrees of creature comforts inhabit a range of cabins, campsites and recreational vehicle (RV) sites, all with fire rings and picnic tables nearby. ☎ 828-622-7676; www.nchotsprings.com; 315 Bridge St, Hot Springs, NC; campsites $20-40, RV sites $35-40, cabins $50-65

Len Foote Hike Inn

You will be far, far from the rat race at this hike-in-only lodge; 5 miles from the nearest road; you'll need to carry in everything, haul out your own trash and reserve in advance. It serves three meals a day. ☎ 800-581-8032; www.hike-inn.com; 240 Amicalola Falls State Park Rd, Dawsonville, GA; r $97-140; ☺ year-round

Mountain Magnolia Inn

Step out on your balcony and breathe in the smell of the magnolias before diving into a Southern home-cooked breakfast. ☎ 828-622-3543; www.mountainmagnoliainn.com; 204 Lawson St, Hot Springs, NC; r $95-270

Nantahala Adventure Resort

From simple campsites or bunk houses popular with AT hikers to fully stocked cabins and inn rooms. ☎ 828-488-2176; www.noc.com; Hwy 19, 12 miles west of Bryson City, NC; r & cabins $60-380; campsites & bunk lodging $7.50-16

Roan Mountain State Park Lodge

RV sites, campsites and cabins amid one of the trail's most beautiful locations. ☎ 800-250-8620; www.state.tn.us/environment/parks/RoanMtn/; 1015 Hwy 143, Roan Mountain, TN; ☺ year-round, tent camping Apr-Nov

Smith House Inn

In the heart of the Chestatee Village shopping area, with guest rooms in the inn or cottage and a 2-bedroom villa for longer stays. ☎ 706-867-7000; www.smithhouse.com; 84 S Chestatee Rd, Dahlonega, GA; r/2-bedroom villa $140-300

USEFUL WEBSITES

www.appalachiantrail.org
www.nps.gov/appa

LINK YOUR TRIP

www.lonelyplanet.com/trip-planner

TRIP

Historic Battles of the Civil War

WHY GO The Civil War shaped the South and the rest of the United States in ways unmatched by any other period in American history. Civil War expert and Zen-minded self-proclaimed "hard core" reenactor Robert Lee Hodge leads us on a visit through some of the most influential Civil War sites in the South.

TIME
5 – 7 days

DISTANCE
741 miles

BEST TIME TO GO
Apr – Jun

START
Vicksburg, MS

END
Atlanta, GA

ALSO GOOD FOR

HISTORY & CULTURE

"I've been wearing the funny clothes and shooting guns for 27 years," says Robert Lee Hodge, about his lifelong fascination with the Civil War. "My brother named me after Robert E Lee. My favorite book growing up was *The Golden Book of the Civil War*. I'd say my prayers with my mom and she'd ask, 'What battle do you want me to read from tonight?'"

For Hodge, visiting battlefields and Civil War sites is not about celebrating war but about creating a connection with the land and with the past. "For me," says Hodge, "it's kind of a low-key spiritual thing. It's respectful and almost Zen-like. I go to these places now and they're places of peace. There's this weird juxtaposition between war and death and the brutality that people can do to each other and the land, and then you have birds chirping and quiet fields and the sun shining. People who go to battlefields can relate to this."

Although it's not one of Hodge's favorite battlefields, ① Vicksburg National Military Park is first on the list of anyone who studied the Civil War in eighth-grade history class. The Vicksburg campaign came in the middle of the war, and was a turning point of sorts, especially for the beleaguered Union troops. For over six months, starting in December of 1862, Grant and his army staged 11 battles with the Confederate army, many of them naval battles along the Mississippi River. After Grant's final decisive victory on July 4, 1863, the Mississippi

BEST TRIP

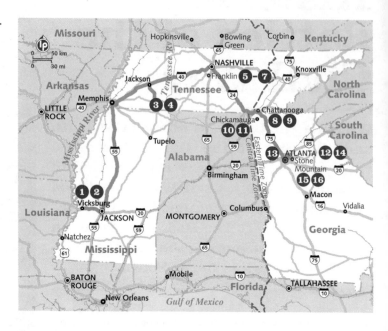

River was once again controlled by the Union forces, beginning a sea change in the direction of the war. Once you enter the battlefield grounds, you can drive along a 16 mile road that takes you past marked sites including trenches, a restored Union gunboat and a cemetery.

"The battlegrounds are some of the best preserved in the United States."

Stay the night at the historic ❷ **Cedar Grove Mansion Inn & Restaurant**. Feel like a Southern belle when you sip wine and nibble cheese in the parlor's afternoon reception or as you tuck yourself in under a romantic canopied bed. (Hint: history fans will want to stay in Rhett's Penthouse Suite, where you can still see a patched up hole from where a Union cannonball crashed through the wall during the Civil War.) The restaurant serves dinner only, but what a dinner it is. Taste 200 years of Southern culinary history with updated dishes like crab martini, pan-seared catfish on a bed of okra, and peppered risotto or quail with crawfish corn-bread dressing.

One of Hodge's favorite spots is ❸ **Shiloh National Military Park** in Hardin County, Tennessee. In one of the first of the ensuing mega-battles of the Civil War, over 109,000 Union and Confederate troops met near the Pittsburg Landing on the Tennessee River on April 6, 1862, resulting in a casualty rate of about 25%. The battlegrounds are some of the best preserved in the United States, partly because the area was designated a national landmark back in 1894. "Shiloh was one of the first preserved national military parks," says Hodge. "It's probably about 85% pristine. All these people of pedigree – senators, politicians – felt a strong desire to memorialize and interpret these places." After picking up a map at the visitors center, take a tour of the cemetery (eternal home to 4000 soldiers who died at the battle), Indian Mound and the site of the Methodist church that gave the battle its name.

"If you go to Shiloh," Hodge says, "you've got to go to Hagy's. They serve old-school Dr Pepper in bottles and have these pictures on the wall of old-time farmers plowing with mules, plus they serve all-you-can-eat catfish." Officially known as the **4** **Catfish Hotel**, the original 1825 shack on the park grounds burned down in 1975, but the third generation of the Hagy family rebuilt the institution. It is one of the oldest continually operating restaurants in the country. After eating a plate full of breaded frogs legs, fried oysters and hush puppies, or smoked baby back ribs, relax in a catfish-shaped Adirondack chair overlooking the Tennessee River.

ASK A LOCAL

"We can't change history, nor should we be ashamed of it, but we should learn from it and not repeat its errors. My reenactor friends yearn to know American history as told by all of its participants. The African-American perspective is still unique, but there are some of us in 'the hobby,' as reenactors call it. It's a joy to be with like-minded people who are just as passionate about history as I am."

Daniel J Johnson, aka Thomas Morris Chester, the only African-American war correspondent hired by a major daily newspaper during the war

Take Hwy 22 north for about 40 miles until you hit I-40, which will take you toward Nashville. Detour south to **5** **Franklin**, where the Battle of Franklin was fought and where, these days, a new battle for preservation is being waged. The historic downtown has many preserved buildings, but suburban sprawl has put the site of the Battle of Franklin on the Civil War Preservation Trust's most endangered sites list for several years in a row. First, head to the **6** **Carter House**, which holds the dubious record of sustaining more bullets (over 1000) than just about any other building during the Civil War. The Carter family went to sleep on November 29, 1864, only to be woken in the middle of the night by a brigadier army general, who turned the house into a Union command center for the battle that was to occur. What was to become known as the "five bloodiest hours in the Civil War" killed or wounded over 8500 mostly Confederate soldiers on and around the Carter farm. While 23 Carter family members and neighbors hid in the basement, Union and Confederate troops clashed, sometimes hand to hand, on their front porch. One of the arriving Confederate soldiers was Tod Carter, who was thrilled to see his home for the first time in three years. However, he later died inside after being mortally wounded (some say he never left and his ghost, along with dozens of others, still lingers).

The next stop in Franklin is **7** **Carnton Plantation**. On the New York *Times* best-seller list for months, *The Widow of the South* was based on the

life of Carrie McGavock, the mistress of the plantation during the Civil War. After the Battle of Franklin, the plantation – like many other large houses near battlefields – became an impromptu army hospital. McGavock cared for hundreds of wounded and dying men from both sides of the war, and in 1866, enlarged her own family's cemetery to bury 1500 troops. Tours now showcase the family's portraits and furnishings, much unchanged since the war. "On the floor, you can see imprints of bloody shoes from the Civil War," says Hodge. "They had tests done to make sure it wasn't oil from the 1950s, but no, it was blood."

On the anniversary of the battle, Franklin hosts thousands of die-hard Civil War reenactors, who spend days dressed in woolen shell jackets, camping out in A-frame canvas tents and eating Civil War rations from tin mess plates.

ASK A LOCAL

"You've got to hit a battlefield early in the morning. Sunrise to 8am is best. It's beautiful with the fog in the morning, or at twilight with the fading light. I'm a filmmaker, so I'll take my tripod and camera out and I'll film the historic vistas I'm enamored with. That's when the spiritual vibe gets me more."
Robert Lee Hodge

Hodge had never much thought about the environment before he began spending time in historic locations that were being swallowed up by suburban sprawl, or ignored out of budget constraints or apathy. But then he found reenacting and, "the Confederate flag made me an environmentalist," he says. "It's about being at Franklin, Tennessee, on November 30, and preferably on a Wednesday, because the battle was on a Wednesday. It's about knowing that you're stepping on the same ground at the same time where people you've read about stepped." Years ago, a Pizza Hut was built over soldiers' graves, but preservation groups have raised $2.5 million and reclaimed the area as a public green space, open to visitors.

If you'd like to bed down for the night somewhere a tad more comfortable, head into ❽ **Chattanooga** and the ❾ **Mayor's Mansion Inn**, a stately 1889 home with as many modern comforts as antique touches. Set your alarm to rise before dawn to head down Hwy 1/US-27 to the expansive ❿ **Chickamauga and Chattanooga National Military Park**. Chattanooga was a major railroad thoroughfare at the start of the Civil War, so whichever side claimed her would be able to boast a clear transportation advantage. The park was the first battlefield made into a national military park, back in 1890. From September 18 to 20, 1863, over 60,000 Union troops and 43,000 Confederate troops fought at Chickamauga. At the end of the battle, there were 34,000 soldiers wounded, killed or taken prisoner. The Union troops had retired to Chattanooga, where they gathered supplies. One month later, under the direction of General Ulysses S Grant, Union and Confederate forces once again fought, this time resulting in a clear Union victory, paving the way for

Union General William Tecumseh Sherman to start his eastward march to the sea from Chattanooga the following spring. Be sure to stop in at **11** **Lookout Mountain**, the site of much fighting. "I haven't been able to find it yet," says Hodge, "but there's an interpretive marker [somewhere on the mountain] where my ancestors fought with the Fourth Alabama Calvary."

Head toward **12** **Atlanta**, to the **13** **Kennesaw Mountain National Battlefield Park**, located just before the city beltline. It's surrounded by suburbs, but is easily accessible. Considered one of the events with the most needless waste of troops, the series of battles led by General Sherman saw 3000 Union and 1000 Confederate soldiers die without any ground gained. In the city, Hodge recommends the **14** **Atlanta History Center**. For him, museums are about the "stuff" that make the history books and battlefields real, and the history center is filled with enough "stuff" to bring a tangible connection to the history of the war. "There are all sorts of relics from the army – guns, uniforms, IDs from everyone who did heroic deeds to unknown soldiers. It gives you an idea of: what did the guns look like? What were the blankets like? What were their letters like?"

Don't miss sleeping in the **15** **Village Inn B&B**, one of only a handful of inns in the Southeast with a direct connection to the Civil War. It's 15 minutes east of downtown Atlanta. The only reason it wasn't burned down during Sherman's march was because it served as a Confederate hospital (there are a few reputed ghosts left over from days past). The inn was built in the 1840s and is as romantic as it gets – in-room spa tubs and fireplaces, homemade cookies waiting for you each afternoon and a veranda overlooking nearby **16** **Stone Mountain**. If you enjoy the breakfast so much you want to be able to make the raspberry-stuffed French toast or flaky biscuits at home, you're in good; the B&B publishes its own recipe book so you can take some of the South home with you.

Alex Leviton

A WAR BY ANY OTHER NAME

In the South, one conflict comes by many names.

- The Civil War: what the federals called it, simply a term for fighting within a country.

- War Between the States: used primarily by those in Confederate states, as states broke away and began fighting for independence.

- War of Northern Aggression: the South had the right to secede and the North attacked.

- War for Southern Independence: ditto.

- The Recent Unpleasantness: first used by Charlie Weaver on the Jack Paar's *Tonight Show* in the 1960s, when the events of the 1800s weren't a too distant memory.

- The War: across the South and in Charleston, everyone will know what you mean.

Jack Thomson, Civil War historian

TRIP INFORMATION

DO

Atlanta History Center
See hundreds of artifacts from the Civil War, including uniforms, ID tags and letters home. ☎ 404-814-4000; www.atlantahistorycenter .com; 130 West Paces Ferry Rd, Atlanta, GA; adult/child$15/10; ⏱ 10am-5:30pm Mon-Sat, noon-5:30pm Sun

Carnton Plantation
A mansion that became a makeshift Confederate hospital during the Battle of Franklin. ☎ 615-794-0903; www.carnton.org; 1345 Carnton Ln, Carnton, TN; adult/child $12/5; ⏱ 9am-5pm Mon-Sat, 1-5pm Sun

Carter House
Over 1000 bullet holes riddled this mansion, next to where the Battle of Franklin raged. ☎ 615-791-1861; www.carter-house.org; 1140 Columbia Ave, Franklin, TN; adult/child $8/4; ⏱ 9am-5pm Mon-Sat, 1-5pm Sun, shorter winter hours

Chickamauga & Chattanooga National Military Park
Site of the second deadliest battle in Civil War history. ☎ 423-752-5213; www.nps .gov/chch; 3370 S. Lafayette Rd, Fort Oglethorpe, GA; admission free; ⏱ 8:30am-6pm Apr-Sep, to 5pm Oct-Mar

Kennesaw Mountain National Battlefield Park
A full-scale battlefield with a scenic mountain and hiking trails. ☎ 770-427-4686; www .nps.gov/kemo; 905 Kennesaw Mountain Dr, Kennesaw, GA; admission free; ⏱ 8:30am-5pm Mon-Fri, to 6pm Sat & Sun

Shiloh National Military Park
Next to the Corinth Civil War Interpretive Center, with a driving tour of a historic battlefield. ☎ 703-689-5696; www.nps.gov /shil; 1055 Pittsburg Landing Rd, Shiloh, TN; admission free; ⏱ 8am-5pm Apr-Sep, to 6pm Oct-Mar

Vicksburg National Military Park
A 16-mile driving tour of the USS Cairo museum, Civil War ironclad gunboat display and national cemetery. ☎ 601-636-0583; www.nps.gov/vick; 3201 Clay St, Vicksburg, MS; vehicle $8; ⏱ 8am-5pm

EAT

Catfish Hotel
A catfish 'palace' right on the Tennessee River, serving dishes and tradition for almost 200 years. ☎ 731-689-3327; www.catfish hotel.com; 1005 Pittsburg Landing, Shiloh National Military Park, TN; mains $9-12; ⏱ 11am-9pm Sun-Thu, to 10pm Fri & Sat

Cedar Grove Mansion Inn & Restaurant
Decorated with furnishings brought back from an 1842 European honeymoon. The elegant mansion was once used as a Union hospital. ☎ 601-633-1000; www.cedar groveinn.com; 2200 Oak St, Vicksburg, MS; mains $18-32, r $100-215; ⏱ 5-10pm dinner

SLEEP

Mayor's Mansion Inn
The antebellum mansion is a registered historic landmark, as well as a gracious inn and four-star restaurant. ☎ 901-525-8225; www.huntphelan.com; 533 Beale St, Memphis, TN; r $180-265

Village Inn B&B
It doesn't get any more authentic than having a patched hole in your room from a Civil War cannon blast. ☎ 770-469-3459; www .villageinnbb.com; 992 Ridge Ave, Stone Mountain, GA; r $140-180

USEFUL WEBSITES
www.civilwar.org
www.civilwartraveler.com

LINK YOUR TRIP

www.lonelyplanet.com/trip-planner

NORTH CAROLINA & SOUTH CAROLINA TRIPS

Separated in 1729, North and South Carolina have been splitting apart culturally ever since, although beautiful rolling foothills and languid beach towns cover both states.

North Carolina has gently melded biotech, banking and university industries with down-home values, resulting in a state both cosmopolitan and homespun. In the mountains of Asheville, the grits are infused with basil and goat cheese, and the Saturday bluegrass jams at the Downtown Cinema Theater in Mount Airy (Andy Griffith's Mayberry) haven't changed much for 50 years, except now you can go wine tasting afterwards.

South Carolinians are ever so grateful to have stuck with a more genteel pace of life. You might be forgiven for wanting to stroll romantic Charleston with a parasol, and the blackwater swamps and inland foothills offer a geographic trip back in time.

PLAYLIST 🎵 The Carolinas don't have the famed musical roots as most of their Southern state neighbors, but South Carolina's beach music and "shagging" (platonically, of course), and North Carolina's traditional old-time and bluegrass music will send you back to a more simple time, while thoroughly modern folk and country-punk jazz things up a bit.

- "Carolina On My Mind," James Taylor
- "My Baby's Got the Strangest Ways," Southern Culture on the Skids
- "Broken," Tift Merritt
- "Shady Grove," Doc Watson
- "Oh My Sweet Carolina," Ryan Adams
- "Under the Boardwalk," The Drifters
- "Only Want to Be With You," Hootie & the Blowfish
- "What It Was, Was Football," Andy Griffith (spoken word comedy)

NORTH CAROLINA & SOUTH CAROLINA BEST TRIPS

NORTH CAROLINA & SOUTH CAROLINA TRIPS

Eclectic Americana in the Triangle

WHY GO The Triangle – Raleigh, Durham and Chapel Hill – may be one of the most livable places in the country. The rare blend of Southern hospitality, university culture, rural charm and big-city life, however, also makes it a spectacular place to visit...if you know where to look.

Downtown **1 Raleigh** is filled with all the usual capital city offerings – excellent museums, professional sports venues, historic homes, impressive governmental buildings and so on – but we trust our readers can find these on their own. Instead, we start our tour with a good, swift kick in the pants, descend into Hell, and then rise up to hog heaven. But first, spend a day absorbing culture at the **2 North Carolina Museum of Art**. Bring your picnic blanket on summer evenings, as outdoor concerts (from jazz to world music), films and events grace every weekend from May to September. Next head west on Hwy 70 to **3 Angus Barn**, a storied local steakhouse with several agents of death beckoning. Guns and taxidermied heads line the wall heading up to the Wild Turkey cigar lounge (cigars are for sale in the gift shop's walk-in humidor), while butter-smooth marbled steaks adorn most diners' plates. The legendary wine list is thicker than the Oxford American dictionary (unabridged). If you've ever uttered "I could just kick myself" drop by the parking lot's 1937 kicking machine for a self-booting.

The liveliest area at night in Raleigh is **4 Glenwood South**, a formerly gritty warehouse district turned bustling cultural mecca of restaurants, pubs, dance clubs, art galleries, shops, wine bars and coffeehouses where you're encouraged to stay out way past your bedtime. The neighborhood is bordered by Peace St to the north and Hillsborough St to the south, running along Glenwood Ave for half a mile of more than 100 businesses. Pull into **5 518 West**, an Italian restaurant

TIME
5 days

DISTANCE
128 miles

BEST TIME TO GO
Year-round

START
Raleigh, NC

END
Siler City, NC

ALSO GOOD FOR

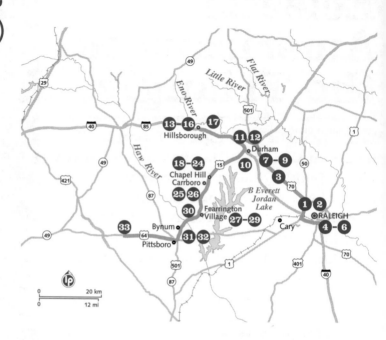

housed in a former train depot, now in the heart of the fine dining scene. Venetian plaster walls and a boldly offbeat wine list bring a taste of the good life to the gentrified neighborhood. Cap off your late-night adventure with the most local of treats, the North Carolina–born and bred hot glazed doughnut from **6** **Krispy Kreme**, whose 1950s sign glows on the edge of the historic Oakwood district of jaw-dropping Victorian beauties.

Start your second day in **7** **Durham**, whose past is inextricably tied to the tobacco that made the Duke family one of wealthiest in North Carolina history. Up until the 1990s, town residents say the smell of the sweet tobacco curing in downtown's brick warehouses would fill the streets. Just after the Civil War, Washington Duke planted several acres of the local Bright Leaf tobacco on his farm north of town. Millions of lung cancer diagnoses later, the **8** **American Tobacco Historic District** is now an entertainment complex, exhibition space and outdoor concert venue with five restaurants (all, ironically, smoke-free). Next door is the most famous minor league ballpark in the country, the **9** **Durham Bulls Athletic Park**, where, in between innings, mascot Wool E Bull shoots T-shirts from his miniature race car or referees wrestling matches between fans in inflatable sumo costumes.

Today science, medicine and art have replaced tobacco and farming as Durham's most prolific exports, and the Triangle has one of the most educated populations in the US, nowhere more apparent than in downtown Durham.

The city went through an ill-found "urban renewal" effort in the 1960s and '70s, but preservationists (including one woman who chained herself to the about-to-be-destroyed downtown theater, ensuring its survival to this day) eventually won out. These days, the "Durham Love Yourself" movement devotees (look for the T-shirts and bumper stickers everywhere) have an almost militant love for the city's revitalization of art galleries and restaurants. Join grad students, filmmakers and yoga teachers at the morning epicenter of the good fight, the ⑩ **Guglhupf Bakery and Patisserie**, a favorite for its European pastries and bread, outdoor patio, free wi-fi and inexpensive meals. If you want to go more upscale in the evening, the internationally recognized ⑪ **Magnolia Grill**, just north of Duke University's student hangout zone, ⑫ **Ninth Street**, has been wowing critics for the past decade with its Southern take on California-style cuisine.

FARMERS MARKETS

The Triangle's weather and agricultural roots make for spectacular farmers markets, some with traditional bluegrass or old-time entertainment, including:

- Durham: Saturday 8am to noon and Wednesday 3:30pm to 6:30pm in Central Park at 501 Foster St.

- Carrboro: Saturday 7am to noon and Wednesday 3:30pm to 6:30pm at 301 W Main St.

- Raleigh: Monday to Saturday 6am to 5pm and Sunday 8am to 6pm at 1201 Agriculture St.

From Durham, take Hwy 85 northwest to the historic town of ⑬ **Hillsborough**, whose heyday was around the Revolutionary War. The entire downtown is on the National Registry for Historic Places with more than 100 buildings from the 18th and 19th centuries. It's no wonder that dozens of writers have made it their home, including novelist Lee Smith and the late Doug Marlette, creator of the "Kudzu" comic strip. If you're here on the last Friday of the month from April to September, downtown turns into an art walk, with open studios, wine and cheese receptions and live music. If you're looking for lodging that's historical and charming, Hillsborough has several, including the ⑭ **Webb House B&B**, a 200-year-old Colonial home in downtown with claw-foot tubs, four-post beds and filling breakfasts. Start the next day at ⑮ **Ayr Mount**. The stately brick Federal-style home still has some of the original family furnishings from almost 200 years ago. The serene ⑯ **Poet's Walk** past the woodsy Eno River really shows off the beauty of the area. The ⑰ **Historic Occoneechee Speedway Trail**, off exit 165 from I-85, is, surprisingly, exactly as it sounds. It's not often you get to call a hiking trail "eclectic," but this one leads to the Occoneechee Speedway, used in NASCAR's inaugural 1949 season. The overgrown track and surrounding area, blanketed with pines and weepy thickets, has been turned into a 44-acre nature preserve, accessible to day hikers. The original oval track dates back to the early 1900s, when it was used to train horses, and backs up against the Eno River, the unexpected final resting place of many an out-of-control stock car.

From Hillsborough, head back to the I-40 and take exit 265 for Hwy 86 to dine and drink in collegiate ⓲ **Chapel Hill**. The University Tour of the Triangle trip will introduce you to university life, but the noncollege crowd will appreciate one of *Gourmet* magazine's top 50 restaurants in the country,

LIVING IN A TOBACCO WAREHOUSE

"In 2003, I bought a loft condo in the first to-bacco warehouse converted after Durham's cigarette industry died out in the 1980s. Next to the elevators, signs read: "Ironically, the hall-ways and common areas in this former tobacco warehouse are smoke-free." My neighbors and I still hear stories from teary-eyed visitors about how they loved the smell of cured Bright Leaf tobacco when visiting their dads or granddads at work here in the 1940s."

Alex Leviton, guidebook author, San Francisco, CA/ Durham, NC

⓳ **Lantern**. The chef and owner heads up a local Slow Food convivium and many of her ingredients are grown within a 50-mile radius. The sake- and tea-cured salmon bento box appetizer is like an edible toy set where adults are encouraged to play with their food. Stick with child-friendly food with dessert at ⓴ **Locopops**, a few doors down historic Franklin St. With flavors like Nilla wafer, mojito, plum black pepper and cherry hibiscus, you'll understand why obsessed locals are fiercely loyal to their gourmet Mexican popsicle parlor.

After dessert, go to Hell. No, really, go to ㉑ **Hell**. Hidden down a fittingly dank stairway, the seedy but chic late-night bar thumps with activity every night, especially on Monday when the John Waters-esque Mary K Mart hosts the Triangle's favorite pastime, Drag Bingo. Sleep off your hangover at ㉒ **Siena Hotel**, an upscale Tuscan-inspired hotel where the restaurant, ㉓ **Il Palio**, marries all that is holy about Italian cuisine with a few Southern touches – fried green tomatoes on *mozzarella di bufala* or fennel-crusted tuna with watermelon. Start the next morning fresh at ㉔ **A Southern Season**, a football field–sized gourmet food store that sells everything, and we mean everything, from Le Creuset cookware and imported prosciutto to artisanal North Carolina organic cheeses and 500 different types of candy bars on its "Wall of Chocolate." Book the restaurant or legendary cooking classes in advance, and bring your credit card; the wine department is easily the top in the state.

"Go to Hell, especially on Monday."

Bordering Chapel Hill is the quirky town of ㉕ **Carrboro**, whose most famous resident dances to his own beat…literally. The center of town is the Triangle's version of the village green, the lawn at ㉖ **Weaver Street Market**, which now has an "Open Space Policy" to make sure dancing alone (and, um, shirtless, with no music) isn't a crime. During the day, wi-fi users and fans of the organic salad bar and hot bar congregate at picnic tables to nosh, read Umberto Eco novels or discuss the nearby biodiesel fuel pumping station. Events run throughout the week, including Sunday morning jazz concerts,

Thursday evening After Hours concerts, and Friday night wine tastings. Hula-hoop clinics pick up during the summer.

Head west on Hwy 15/501 toward Pittsboro until a grain silo and colorful whirligigs welcome you to ㉗ **Fearrington Village**, home to the famed belted cows (the bovine version of the Oreo cookie). These black and white three-stripe cows, and goats, have been at this farm's location for generations. The tiny village deserves an afternoon wander through shops that sell books, garden supplies and gifts, but the night belongs to the famed ㉘ **Fearrington House Restaurant** – there's not an award it hasn't won. With dishes like duck breast and foie gras in a cherry cinnamon sauce or pork belly and lobster with shellfish cappuccino, it's no wonder. Get in touch with your inner Southern belle next door at ㉙ **Fearrington Inn**, where the exercise in sumptuous hospitality includes canopied beds, English high-tea finger sandwiches each afternoon and in-room massages. For lunch in the village, dine at the Old Granary Restaurant, where lighter fare like salad with cornmeal-fried oysters or sea scallops on cauliflower risotto have an equally gourmet feel. If you feel a sudden urge to retire here, you're not alone; Fearrington caters to well-heeled and active older folks (the housing wing of the village advertises in the back of *New Yorker* magazine).

If Fearrington is exquisite sophistication overlaid on farm fields, ㉚ **Allen & Son Barbecue** is as plain and genuine as North Carolina red clay. Here, before sunrise, owner Keith Allen loads hand-chopped hickory logs into a BBQ pit, lays out a pig and cooks his homemade sauce from scratch to maintain one of the last bastions of genuine pit cooking. Believe your waitress – who might or might not have a beehive hairdo and call you "Hon" – when she tells you to order the peanut butter pie.

> **ASK A LOCAL**
>
> "I like to go where the wild things are: like **Bynum**, a Chatham County mill village, home of stilt-walking puppeteers (www.paperhand.org) and famous artist, Clyde Jones. Amongs a frenzy of new construction in the Triangle, this oasis protrudes like an extra five pounds on a supermodel. Get to the Bynum General Store music series by 6:30pm to grab a seat, and you'll get to see the fireflies spring to life. Plus, it offers jam sessions and art shows on Saturdays."
>
> *Molly Matlock, director, Chatham County Arts Council, Bynum, NC*

Keep going down the road towards ㉛ **Bynum**, a tiny former mill village where intellectuals and artsy types dwell alongside longtime residents all in humble front-porch cottages. Lazed up against the Haw River, Bynum is perhaps best known for artist Clyde Jones and his colorful, chain saw–cut wooden critters. There's no museum or store, as Jones refuses to sell his creations for money (though he's given one away to Mikhail Baryshnikov), but it just takes a quick stroll through town to see dozens gracing front yards. On Friday nights in summer, mosey on down to the ㉜ **Bynum General Store** whose "Front Porch Music Series" draws an astoundingly wide variety of artists, including folk/country goddess Tift Merritt, who got her start hereabouts. The store provides the plastic chairs and hot dog vendor, you provide the toe tappin'.

SUNDAY SUPPER

On the third Sunday of each month, the **Sunday Dinner at the Celebrity Dairy** kicks off at 1:30pm with an all-afternoon Slow Food feast. Local farms contribute sustainably raised meats and fresh produce to create four mouthwatering courses, shared with 35 new friends over BYO wine in between tours of the dairy facilities, lazing on the tire swing and, in February's kidding season, cuddling baby goats in the barn.

The tour ends at the ❸ Inn at Celebrity Dairy, the culmination of all that is good and right about the Triangle's eclectic side. If you liked the goat cheese at Lantern, Weaver Street Market, Fearrington House Restaurant, the Carrboro farmers market or Magnolia Grill, you can thank Celebrity Dairy, a working organic goat dairy farm. Each spring and fall, the dairy welcomes all to its Open Barn weekends, a feast of goat cheese, farm lessons and baby goat cuddles. The inn's seven rooms are antiqued but comfortable – there's a bay window seat in the 3rd-floor attic room (shared bath), and an 1887 log cabin cottage with a private front porch. In the winter, curl up with Wordsworth in front of the fireplace; in summer, take Kerouac out to the front porch, shared with the farm kittens and chickens.

Alex Leviton

TRIP INFORMATION

DO

A Southern Season
Sixty thousand square feet of the world's best culinary finds, with a popular cooking school and restaurant. ☎ 800-253-3663; www.southernseason.com; 201 E Estes Dr, Chapel Hill; 🕑 10am-9pm Mon-Sat, 11am-6pm Sun; ♿

American Tobacco Historic District
Five restaurants, including sushi, pub food and pizza; Friday evening summer concerts; temporary art exhibits and history, next door to the Athletic Park. ☎ 919-433-1566; www.americantobaccohistoricdistrict.com; 318 Blackwell St, Durham; ♿

Ayr Mount and Poet's Walk
A homage to Revolutionary era homes and gardens. ☎ 919-732-6886; www.classicalamerican.org; 376 St Mary's Rd, Hillsborough; admission $10; 🕑 tours 11am Wed-Sat & 2pm Thu-Sun

Bynum General Store
Old-time summer front porch music series. bynumfrontporch.googlepages.com; 950 Bynum Rd, Bynum; suggested donation $3-7; 🕑 7pm Fri; ♿

Durham Bulls Athletic Park
In 2008, Kevin Costner returned to this iconic stadium to jam with his band. ☎ 919-956-BULL; www.durhambulls.com; 409 Blackwell St, Durham; baseball tickets $6-16; ♿

Historic Occoneechee Speedway Trail
A historic NASCAR speedway that's now a 3-mile walking trail reclaimed by nature (and Preservation North Carolina). www.presnc.org; Elizabeth Brady Rd, Hillsborough; admission free; 🕑 7am-8pm Jun & Jul, 7am-7pm Apr, May, Aug & Sep, 8am-6pm Mar & Oct, 8am-5pm Nov-Feb; ♿

North Carolina Museum of Art
An international art collection inside, a deluge of films, concerts and events outside. ☎ 919-839-6262; www.ncartmuseum.org; 2110 Blue Ridge Rd, Raleigh; museum admission free, events $3-40; 🕑 9am-5pm Tue-Sun, until 9pm Fri; ♿

Weaver Street Market
The "Weave" is not only an expansive coop, but the "town square" of Carrboro with weekly entertainment. ☎ 919-929-0010; www.weaverstreetmarket.com; 101 E Weaver St, Carrboro; 🕑 7:30am-9pm Mon-Fri, 8am-9pm Sat & Sun; ♿

EAT

518 West
Trendy Italian in the heart of Raleigh's nightlife district. ☎ 919-829-2518; www.518west.com; 518 W Jones St, Raleigh; mains $7-18; 🕑 11:30am-9:30pm Mon, to 10pm Tue-Thu, to 10:30pm Fri & Sat, 10:30am-2pm & 5:30-9pm Sun

Allen & Son Barbecue
Slow-cooked BBQ and ribs over real hickory wood with all the fixin's. ☎ 919-942-7576; 6203 Millhouse Rd, Chapel Hill; mains $4-9; 🕑 10am-5pm Tue & Wed, to 8pm Thu-Sat; ♿

Angus Barn
Special occasion steakhouse with a gift and cigar shop and a "Wild Turkey" lounge. ☎ 919-781-2444; www.angusbarn.com; 9401 Glenwood Ave, Raleigh; mains $19-51; 🕑 5:30-10:30pm Mon-Fri, 5-10:30pm Sat, 5-10pm Sun; ♿

Fearrington House Restaurant
A reclaimed village with a romantic inn, restaurant and surrounding shops and farmlands. ☎ 919-542-2121; www.fearrington.com; 2000 Fearrington Village Rd, Pittsboro; mains $18-42; 🕑 6pm-9pm Tue-Sat, to 8pm Sun

Guglhupf Bakery and Patisserie
A full selection of omelets, small plates and pastries, but the bread basket is everyone's favorite. ☎ 919-401-2600; www.guglhupf.com; 2706 Durham-Chapel Hill Rd, Durham; mains $3.50-11; 🕑 8am-6pm Tue-Fri, 8am-5pm Sat, 9am-5pm Sun; ♿

Il Palio
Upscale Italian delicacies paired with top-notch wine in an elegant setting. ☎ 919-929-4000; www.sienahotel.com/ilpalio; 1505 E Franklin St, Chapel Hill; mains $12-32; 🕑 6:30am-10am & 11:30am-2pm daily, also 5:30-9pm Sun-Wed & 5:30-10pm Thu-Sat

Krispy Kreme

Have a late-night doughnut in the state that brought the world the treat. ☎ 919-833-3682; www.krispykreme.com; 549 N Person St, Raleigh; $1; 🕒 24hr; 🕭

Lantern

Asian-Southern fusion known for its cocktails, Slow Food–inspired menus and sophisticated atmosphere. ☎ 919-969-8846; www.lanternrestaurant.com; 423 W Franklin St, Chapel Hill; mains $14-26; 🕒 5-10pm Mon-Sat, bar menu until 2am

Locopops

Beloved gourmet Mexican popsicles with shops in Chapel Hill, Raleigh, Durham and Hillsborough. ☎ 919-286-3100; www.ilovelocopops.com; 431 West Franklin, Chapel Hill; $2-3; 🕒 noon-9pm; 🕭

Magnolia Grill

An internationally award-winning neighborhood restaurant with desserts to die for. ☎ 919-286-3609; www.magnoliagrill.net; 1002 Ninth St, Durham; mains $22-31; 🕒 from 6pm Tue-Thu, 5:30pm Fri & Sat, closing around 9:30pm or 10pm

DRINK

Hell

Descend into an underworld of drinking, debauchery, trivia nights and drag bingo. ☎ 919-929-9666; www.chapelhell.com; 157 Rosemary St, Chapel Hill; drinks $2-8; 🕒 9pm-2am

SLEEP

Fearrington Inn

A reclaimed village with an inn, restaurant and surrounding shops & farmlands. ☎ 919-542-2121; www.fearrington.com; 2000 Fearrington Village Rd, Pittsboro; r $250-545

Inn at Celebrity Dairy

The most peaceful spot in the Triangle, with roaming farm animals, an inviting B&B and a third Sunday of the month supper. ☎ 919-744-5176; www.celebritydairy.com; 144 Celebrity Dairy Way, Siler City; r $90-150; 🕭

Siena Hotel

Just outside the main Franklin St strip, the Tuscan-inspired hotel has professional rooms and a *bellissimo* restaurant. ☎ 919-929-4000; www.sienahotel.com; 1505 E Franklin St, Chapel Hill; r $125-259; 🐾

Webb House B&B

The centrally located bed and breakfast offers early-19th century panache with decidedly modern amenities. ☎ 919-732-8466; www.webbhousebb.com; 117 Queen St, Hillsborough; r $95-195; 🕭

USEFUL WEBSITES

www.durhamloveyourself.com
www.visitchapelhill.org

LINK YOUR TRIP

www.lonelyplanet.com/trip-planner

University Tour of the Triangle

WHY GO Sure, Duke and University of North Carolina basketball are legendary (Michael Jordan, anyone?), but did you know the Triangle's universities are the place to go for lush gardens, groovy nightlife districts and the world's largest sanctuary of pro-simian primates?

Start in ① Raleigh at ② North Carolina State University, where football reigns supreme. Part of the Atlantic Coast Conference (ACC), NC State's team is known as the Wolfpack, a moniker assigned to rowdy student fans in 1922. Things haven't changed much, as ③ Carter-Finley Stadium, home to Wolfpack football, has one of America's great tailgating traditions. Bring your bratwurst and Nerf football and join in.

Head west on I-40 to reach ④ Durham, home to two of the largest area universities, including ⑤ North Carolina Central University. Durham was a hotbed of the intellectual African American middle class in the 1930s and 1940s and NC Central was a Southern epicenter. Zora Neale Huston spent a year teaching at the university. For an educational meal, head across the street to an impromptu alumni reunion center, ⑥ The Know Bookstore and Diner, where Bruce, the owner, has been dishing up African American–focused books and some of the area's best soul food (with a side of conspiracy theory) since 1982. Don't even consider leaving without trying the navy bean pie. On Friday nights at 7pm, The Know hosts a jazz jam popular with Durhamites from all walks of life.

Next, head to ⑦ Duke University. The sprawling campus of Gothic and Georgian architecture spills over from downtown to the east campus hospital, and includes acres of some of the finest hiking in the area, the semiprivate ⑧ Duke Forest. The favorite picnic spot of students

TIME
2 days

DISTANCE
78 miles

BEST TIME TO GO
Jan – Jun

START
Raleigh, NC

END
Chapel Hill, NC

ALSO GOOD FOR

CITY

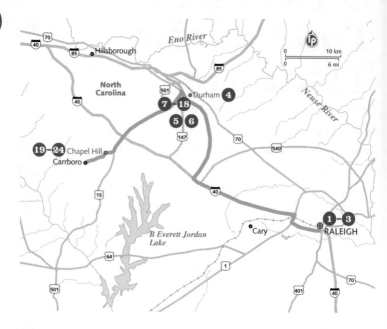

and Durham residents to stop and, well, smell the roses is the **9** **Sarah P Duke Gardens**. Just down the street is the **10** **Nasher Museum of Art**, a $24 million modernist endeavor sponsored by art collector Raymond Nasher. The collection includes a permanent collection of 13,000 pieces by artists such as Andy Warhol, John Singer Sargent, Kara Walker and Ed Ruscha, in addition to ancient Greek and Roman pieces and African art. Inside, the **11** **Nasher Museum Café** is worth a visit just for the seasonal, organic meals sourced from local farms and, especially, the scrumptious cupcakes. Or, for perhaps the most secret dining location in the entire Triangle, head to the **12** **Duke Center for Integrative Medicine** and its restaurant, **13** **The Café**, where the deliciously health-conscious lunch menu is open to all, including non-patients.

> "(It's) worth a visit just for the seasonal, organic meals."

Whether you have a five year old in tow or not, the **14** **Duke Lemur Center** is a must-see. The reservations-only guided tour takes you through outdoor enclosures and an indoor sanctuary where you can meet the real Zoboomafoo (the lemur star of the PBS kids nature show, as anyone under the age of seven will tell you). The Duke student hangout zone is the relatively tame **15** **Ninth Street**, where shops and restaurants outnumber the bars. A coffeehouse, dessert café, tapas restaurant, two bookstores and an old-fashioned soda fountain means most Durham residents end up here at least once a week. If you want to be one with the university forefathers, sleep at the **16** **Washington Duke**

Inn and Fairview Restaurant, the country inn–style hotel, restaurant and golf club where commissioned portraits of Duke family members watch over guests and dinner patrons.

Getting a ticket to Duke basketball at ❶ Cameron Indoor Stadium isn't so hard. Either sell your first-born, or earn a 3.8+ GPA in high school (extracurriculars strongly encouraged), apply to Duke, get accepted, buy a tent, find seven friends and live in it for four months at ❶ Krzyzewski-ville. Pronounced Sheshefsky-ville, the encampment is named for beloved Duke head coach Mike Krzyzewski, and pops up every January as the "Cameron crazies" student fans camp out in a highly structured bid to snap up tickets to the sought-after games, especially the annual Duke-Carolina game.

ASK A LOCAL

"Duke Gardens is one of the most soulful places in the Triangle – beauty and peace and art and nature. When you stand under the round gazebo entrance, festooned with wisteria, you're at the threshold of a magical place. I remember my wedding reception there. The "white garden" – where white roses climb all over a trellis and arbor – was the perfect place to slip away from the party with my new husband and steal a quiet kiss."

Rah Bickley, Durham, NC

Or, as it's known at ❶ University of North Carolina at Chapel Hill (usually known as UNC or Carolina), the Carolina-Duke game. UNC is the oldest public university in the USA, chartered in 1789. The Tar Heels' rivalry with the private Duke University started 90 years ago. Books have been written and families torn apart since, but as both teams are consistently ranked among the top 10 collegiate basketball teams in the country, this is a rivalry that won't be going away any time soon. If you're a sports fan, you're welcome to stop by the ❷ Dean Smith Center on nonevent days to tour its ❷ Memorabilia Room. If you're not a sports fan, you'll do just fine visiting ❷ Chapel Hill, the ultimate college town, as ❷ Franklin Street, running directly in front of campus, is the ultimate college town street. Restaurants, bars, sorority houses and shops line the street, and students in Carolina blue sweatshirts walk the off-campus corridor day and night. Bunk down for the night at the gracious ❷ Carolina Inn. Built on campus in 1924, the Antebellum hotel's front veranda, bright

DETOUR

The best hidden find on the Duke campus is the **Center for Documentary Studies**. The white house with the wraparound porch hosts films, photography shows, week-long documentary institutes and gallery events throughout the year. If you're sticking around a little longer, check out its week-long institutes and workshops on documentary film and radio.

sunroom and elegant restaurant have been pleasing returning alumni and relaxed visitors for generations, plus there's a well-loved restaurant and high tea served daily.

Alex Leviton

HISTORY & CULTURE

TRIP INFORMATION

DO

Cameron Indoor Stadium
Legendary as one of the best sporting venues in the country, home to Duke's famed Blue Devil basketball team. ☎ 919-684-8111; www.goduke.com; 301 Whitford Dr, Durham; admission times & costs vary; ♿

Carter-Finley Stadium
Join nearly 60,000 football fans for NC State Wolfpack football games. ☎ 919-865-1510; www.gopack.com; 4600 Trinity Rd, Raleigh; admission times & costs vary; ♿

Dean Smith Center and Memorabilia Room
Home to UNC Tar Heel basketball and other sports with a memorabilia room. ☎ 919-962-2296; tarheelblue.cstv.com; Skipper Bowles Dr, Chapel Hill; admission varies; ◷ 8am-5pm Mon-Fri; ♿

Duke Lemur Center
Make reservations in advance for the outdoor/indoor view into pro-simian primate life. ☎ 919-489-3364 ext 0; lemur.duke.edu; 3705 Erwin Rd, Durham; tour adult/senior & child/student $7/4/5; ◷ gift shop 8:30am-4:30pm Mon-Fri, 10am-noon Sat, call for tour times; ♿

Nasher Museum of Art and Café
Impeccable art collection and a stunningly good organic café. ☎ 919-684-5135; www.nasher.duke.edu; 2001 Campus Dr, Durham; suggested donation $3-5; ◷ 10-5pm Tue-Sat, noon-5pm Sun, to 9pm Thu

North Carolina Central University
One of the pre-eminent African American art collections in the USA. ☎ 919-530-6100; www.nccu.edu; 1801 Fayetteville Rd, Durham; admission free; ◷ tours 9am, 11am & 2pm Mon-Fri, museum 9am-5pm Tue-Fri, 2-5pm Sun

Sarah P Duke Gardens
Quiet and meditative gardens set in a quiet corner of the sprawling, leafy campus. ☎ 919-684-9368; www.hr.duke.edu/dukegardens; 426 Anderson St, Durham; admission free, parking per hr $2; ◷ 8am-dusk; ♿

EAT

The Café at Duke Center for Integrative Medicine
Even if you're not booking a massage, health coach or acupuncturist, you're still welcome to eat healthily here. ☎ 919-684-9850; www.dukeintegrativemedicine.com; Duke Center for Living Campus, 3475 Erwin Rd, Durham; mains $6-10; ◷ 10am-4pm Mon-Fri, full lunch 11:30am-2pm Mon-Sat

The Know Bookstore and Diner
Jerk chicken, mac'n'cheese and fried catfish at the diner, plus books, gifts, Friday night jazz and occasional lectures. ☎ 919-682-7223; 2520 Fayetteville Rd, Durham; mains $4-12; ◷ 11am-8pm Mon-Thu, 11am-10pm Fri & Sat; ♿

SLEEP

Carolina Inn
Historic rooms, a restaurant and high tea service in a grand campus setting. ☎ 919-933-2001; www.carolinainn.com; UNC, 201 Pittsboro St, Chapel Hill; r $160-535; ♿

Washington Duke Inn and Fairview Restaurant
Stately on-campus hotel, restaurant and golf course. ☎ 919-490-0999; www.washingtondukeinn.com; 3001 Cameron Blvd, Durham; r $139-469

USEFUL WEBSITES
www.duke.edu
www.unc.edu
www.lonelyplanet.com/trip-planner

LINK YOUR TRIP

From Dirty Dancing to Dawson's Creek

WHY GO As North Carolina is one of the top states for film production, its scenery is known to millions. Connie Nelson, co-author of "The Film Junkie's Guide to North Carolina," takes readers on a Hollywood tour through familiar territory, from the western mountains to the eastern beaches.

TIME
5 days

DISTANCE
537 miles

BEST TIME TO GO
Jun – Sep

START
Dillsboro, NC

END
Wilmington, NC

ALSO GOOD FOR

ROUTE

Start your trip in the far western part of the state in Dillsboro at the ① **Great Smoky Mountain Railroad**. Of the half-dozen films shot here, it's the train wreck scene from *The Fugitive* (still visible!) that has brought the location fame. Junior film buffs will enjoy the annual *Polar Express* train ride, and toddlers' rock star Thomas the Tank Engine often makes an appearance.

The western mountain city of ② **Asheville** has ratcheted up the most North Carolinian face time on the silver screen after Wilmington. The largest private home ever built in America, ③ **Biltmore Estate** began its starring role in films more than 60 years ago, and appears in films including *Tap Roots* (1948) and *The Swan* (starring Grace Kelly in 1956). Inside, it's no surprise that scenes from *Richie Rich* (1994) were shot in the tapestry gallery, and its 8000 acres of lush green rolling hills have served as the backdrop to *Forrest Gump* (1984), *Patch Adams* (1998) and *Last of the Mohicans* (1992), many scenes of which were shot in the adjoining Blue Ridge Parkway. If a famous person gets within 50 miles of Asheville, it seems to be a requirement to stay at the equally famed ④ **Grove Park Inn and Spa**. Photos of past guest luminaries grace the Arts and Crafts–style walls, from politicians (William Jennings Bryant spoke at the hotel's opening) to F Scott Fitzgerald. Not many hotels have their own historic walking tour; ask the concierge for a detailed map and itinerary to walk the hotel and grounds.

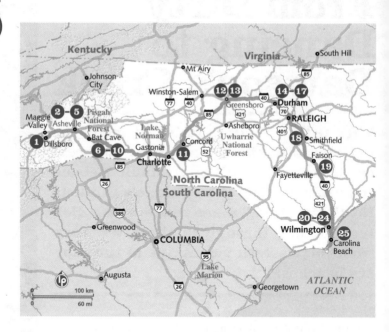

The film that is most associated with North Carolina and sports is *Bull Durham*, the 1988 Kevin Costner and Susan Sarandon baseball film. Although it was set in Durham, many scenes were filmed at historic **5** **McCormick Field** (about 1.5 miles south of I-240 off Biltmore Ave), home to the minor league baseball team, the Asheville (wait for it) Tourists. One of the oldest still standing ballparks in the country, most of the interior has been redone since it opened in 1924 but it still oozes minor-league charm.

From Asheville, take Hwy 74 southeast towards **6** **Chimney Rock State Park**. Fans of *Last of the Mohicans* (1992) will want to make sure they hit three trails: the Skyline Trail, Cliff Trail and Hickory Nut Falls (the site of the film's climactic battle). Before you reach the official town of **7** **Lake Lure**, the *Dirty Dancing* portion of your tour starts. Although the film is set in the Catskills, it was shot almost entirely on location in and around the lake. Just across from Chimney Rock is the **8** **Esmeralda Inn**, which now houses the dance floor from *Dirty Dancing*. The cozy lodge resort is outfitted in stone and natural wood with a huge wood-burning fireplace and rockers on the wraparound porch, as well as the international **9** **Prime Restaurant**.

THE BABE

McCormick Field minor league ballpark in Asheville might have hosted Kevin Costner and Susan Sarandon for a few shots in *Bull Durham*, but its claim to fame was Babe Ruth's "bellyache heard 'round the world" in an exhibition game in 1925, the same year he declared McCormick Field "A damned delightful place!"

At the lake, see the area by boat on ❿ **Lake Lure Tours**. The covered boat takes Patrick Swayze and Jennifer Grey (pre-nose job) fans around the lake, but non-fans won't be bored with the views.

The longest drive on the trip is next. Take Hwy 74E to I-85 until you hit exit 49 in Concord, home of ⓫ **Lowe's Motor Speedway**. Its first big-screen appearance was in Elvis Presley's romantic comedy *Speedway* (1968), but Will Ferrell has since brought his brand of humor to the tracks in *Talladega Nights: The Ballad of Ricky Bobby* (2006). Oh yes, and it happens to host some of the largest events in the world of NASCAR with a capacity of 167,000 fans. Stick with the sporting world when you drive through ⓬ **Greensboro** on I-70 and follow the signs for the ⓭ **War Memorial Stadium**. George Clooney sightings were a common occurrence while he was shooting his football comedy *Leatherheads* (2008). As one of the oldest minor league ballparks in the USA, the stadium didn't take much makeup to take on the look of a 1920s football stadium, as that's its original use.

"Few activities are as enjoyably American as watching mascot Wool E Bull referee fans in inflatable sumo wrestler costumes."

Take I-40 to Hwy 147, which deposits you in downtown Durham. Take Duke St north to the ⓮ **Historic Durham Bulls Athletic Park**, located in the tobacco warehouse district, where loft dwellers have replaced drying tobacco. These days, the crowds gather here mostly for the popular Durham Bulls Festival in late September and the World Beer Festival in early October. Continue north on Duke, turn right on Trinity St and continue a half mile until you reach the ⓯ **Manning House**, at 911 N Mangum St. A private home, movie fans will recognize the exterior as the home of Annie Savoy (Susan Sarandon), but architecture buffs will appreciate the preservation done in the 1990s. If you'd like to bed down for the night, the ⓰ **Old North Durham Inn** across the street offers Bulls ticket packages for the new ⓱ **Durham Bulls Athletic Park**, one mile to the south. Minor league baseball saw a nationwide upswing in popularity from *Bull Durham* and, granted, few activities are as enjoyably American as eating a hot dog in the stands on a warm summer night, watching mascot Wool E Bull referee fans in inflatable sumo wrestler costumes. Above the left-field wall is a replica of the "Hit Bull, Win Steak; Hit Grass, Win Salad" sign from the film.

The next stop on Hwy 70E past Raleigh is in Smithfield, home of the ⓲ **Ava Gardner Museum**, a tribute to a local girl who made very, very good in Hollywood. The museum was founded by a local psychologist who had received a kiss on the cheek from Ava when he was 12; as soon as she made it big with MGM Studios, he began his collection. Continuing on to the tiny town of Faison, those who loved *Divine Secrets of the Ya-Ya Sisterhood* (2002) will recognize **⑲ Buckner Hill Plantation** as the film's Pecan Grove, supposedly set in Louisiana but filmed at this impeccably preserved Antebellum mansion. Visits are by advanced reservation only.

The historic port city of **⑳ Wilmington** has hundreds of film and television credits with enough sites to fill several days. Every self-respecting film junkie should take a guided tour of **㉑ EUE Screen Gems Studios**, which is a real working studio. Recently, visitors have caught glimpses of several local films in production, including *Nights in Rodanthe* (2008), *The Secret Life of Bees* (2009) and *Bolden!* (2008), plus the sets for *One Tree Hill*, also filmed here. If you find yourself lacking background information on the filming of *Teenage Mutant Ninja Turtles* or where Katie Holmes liked to eat breakfast, look no further than the **㉒ Hollywood Location Walk**, a delightfully campy tour of dozens of film sites and star spottings in Wilmington. *Dawson's Creek* – the Warner Bros TV show that helped turn Wilmington into Hollywood East – was supposedly set in Massachusetts, but was shot at Screen Gems Studio. Dozens of Wilmington locations starred in the series, including **㉓ Water Street Restaurant** as Leery's Fresh Fish, the Dawson family's restaurant. It's also a great location for a meal with a prime spot overlooking Cape Fear River, a breezy patio and a constant stream of live entertainment. Or, grab a late-night snack or beer at **㉔ Hell's Kitchen**, which was rented by *Dawson's Creek* producers to be a set where Katie Holmes' character worked. When the show finished its sixth and final season, a local restaurateur purchased the building and turned it into a real restaurant, keeping the name and retaining 80% of the set props, including posters, tables, chairs and the bar.

Finish your journey at **㉕ Orton Plantation Gardens**. Soon after Dino De Laurentiis discovered Orton Plantation in *Southern Accents* magazine, he cast the 18th-century mansion in Stephen King's *Firestarter* (1984). With 50-plus film and TV credits, the former rice plantation overlooking Cape Fear River is now among North Carolina's most prolific locations. Orton's grounds staged weddings in *A Walk to Remember* (2002) and *One Tree Hill* (2003–8); funerals in *Dawson's Creek* (1998–2003) and *Idlewild* (2006); crime scenes in *Crimes of the Heart* (1986) and *Matlock* (1992–1995); and a hoedown in *Divine Secrets of the Ya-Ya Sisterhood* (2002).

Alex Leviton with Connie Nelson

TRIP INFORMATION

GETTING THERE

The Great Smoky Mountain Railroad is about 4½ hours west of Raleigh on I-40 and one hour west of Asheville, off Hwy 74.

DO

Ava Gardner Museum

Costumes, photos and history of the Piedmont's most beloved star of Hollywood's Golden Age. ☎ 919-934-5830; www.ava gardner.org; 325 E Market St, Smithfield; adult/child $6/4; ⊙ 9am-5pm Mon-Sat, 2-5pm Sun

Biltmore Estate

An American castle seen in the background of dozens of films. ☎ 800-411-3812; www .biltmore.com; 1 Approach Rd, Asheville; adult/child/teen $47/free/22.50 Sun-Fri, $51/free/24.50 Sat; ⊙ house 9am-5:30pm, restaurants & shops vary; ☒

Buckner Hill Plantation

A historical mansion dating back to before the Civil War. ☎ 910-293-3001; www.carolina plantation.com; 522 Taylor Town Rd, Faison; admission free; ⊙ by reservation; ☒

Chimney Rock State Park

Ask for a guide to film locations in the park at the visitors center. ☎ 800-277-9611; www .chimneyrockpark.com; Hwy 64/74A, Chimney Rock; adult/child $14/6; ⊙ 8:30am-5:30pm Mar-Nov, 8:30am-4:30pm Dec-Feb; ☒

Durham Bulls Athletic Park

In 2008, Kevin Costner returned to this iconic stadium to jam with his band. ☎ 919-956-BULL; www.durhambulls.com; 409 Blackwell St, Durham; baseball tickets $6-16; ☒

EUE Screen Gems Studio

A rare opportunity to see behind-the-scenes filming at an active studio. ☎ 910-343-3500; www.screengemsstudios.com; 1223 N 23rd St, Wilmington; adult/child/student $12/5/10; ⊙ tours noon & 2pm Sat & Sun, closed late-Dec & Jan; ☒

Great Smoky Mountains Railroad

All of the 3- to 5-hour train excursions pass by *The Fugitive*'s train wreckage. ☎ 800-872-4681; www.gsmr.com; 119 Front St, Dillsboro; high season adult/child $53/31; ⊙ departures from 8:45am-2pm, Sat & Sun only in winter; ☒

Hollywood Location Walk

Television and movie fans from young to old will get a kick out of the kitschy walking tour. ☎ 910-794-7177; www.hollywoodnc .com; gather at 1 Market St, Wilmington; adult/child $12/10; ⊙ 2pm Tue, Thu, Sat & Sun, also 10am Sat; ☒

Lowe's Motor Speedway

Catch a NASCAR or monster-truck rally where Will Ferrell was born to go fast. ☎ 704-455-3200; www.lowesmotorspeedway.com; 5555 Concord Parkway S, Concord; admission from $12; ☒

Orton Plantation Gardens

The richly landscaped gardens and the private home have hosted dozens of film crews. ☎ 910-371-6851; www.ortonplantation .com; 9419 Orton Rd SE, Winnabow; adult/child $9/3; ⊙ 8am-6pm Mar-Aug, 10am-5pm Sep-Nov, closed Dec-Feb; ☒

War Memorial Stadium

Over 90 years old, the ballpark is currently home to summer events. ☎ 800-346-8226; www.gborocollege.edu; 510 Yanceyville St, Greensboro; admission varies; ⊙ open during games & events

EAT

Hell's Kitchen

A sports pub with a juke box, live music on the weekends and a family-friendly menu. ☎ 910-763-4133; www.hellskitchenbar .com; 118 Princess St, Wilmington; mains $5-12; ⊙ 11am-2am; ☒

Prime Restaurant

Who doesn't want to try osso bucco with kumquat or ginger-beer ice cream? ☎ 828-625-2999; www.theesmeralda.com; 910 Main St, Chimney Rock; mains $21-26; ⊙ 5-9pm Wed-Sat, 11am-2pm Sun

Water Street Restaurant

Just along the waterfront with classic shrimp po'boy sandwiches and live music Thursday to Sunday. ☎ 910-343-0042; www.5southwaterstreet.com; 5 S Water St,

Wilmington; mains $7-19; ⏲ 11am-10pm Sun-Thu, to 11pm Fri & Sat; ♿

SLEEP

Esmeralda Inn

In addition to the *Dirty Dancing* dance floor (in the lobby entrance), the lodge offers impeccably decorated rooms. ☎ 828-625-2999; www.theesmeralda.com; 910 Main St, Chimney Rock; r $145-325; ♿

Grove Park Inn and Spa

A National Historic Register resort, built in 1913 with more than 500 guest rooms. ☎ 800-438-5800; www.groveparkinn.com; 290 Macon Ave, Asheville; r $200-800; ♿

Old North Durham Inn

Turn-of-the-century B&B in a historic neighborhood. ☎ 919-683-1885; www.bbonline.com/nc/oldnorth; 922 Mangum St, Durham; r $110-185; ♿

USEFUL WEBSITES

www.filmjunkiesguide.com
www.gocapefearcoast.com

LINK YOUR TRIP

www.lonelyplanet.com/trip-planner

Pirates of the Outer Banks

WHY GO From the famous black-and-white spiral Cape Hatteras Lighthouse to Ocracoke's isolated beaches, it's easy to see why Blackbeard – and millions of tourists – have chosen to make the Outer Banks their summer stomping grounds. For more pirate lore, head south to oft-missed Beaufort, home to a Blackbeard shipwreck.

TIME
4 – 5 days

DISTANCE
223 miles

BEST TIME TO GO
May – Oct

START
Corolla, NC

END
Atlantic Beach, NC

ALSO GOOD FOR

OUTDOORS

Just what the doctor ordered as an antidote to the productivity-mad American society: a day at the beach, followed by dinner at a restaurant (often featuring a cartoon mascot in a pirate outfit or a name like "Salty Sam's Seafood Sircus") and topped off by, well, another day at the beach. Throw in a few lighthouses, a shipwreck, fresh seafood and kayaking, and you've got yourself a good ol' fashioned beach vacation.

Our journey starts on Hwy 12 at the northernmost of the Outer Banks' six lighthouses, the ❶ Currituck Beach Lighthouse. The impressive all-brick sentinel has been guiding sailors since 1875. Lighthouse keepers rotated the Fresnel lens (a geometrically shaped lens lit by an enormous mineral oil lamp with 4in-thick wicks) by means of a system of weights that they had to hand-crank every 2½ hours. The grounds are free, but to appreciate the view and the loneliness of light-keeping, buy a ticket and high-tail it up the 214 steps.

For a one-of-a-kind lunch, pop across the Hwy 152 bridge to the mainland (still technically the Outer Banks) and the farm, German-inspired brewery and restaurant ❷ Weeping Radish. Plan on arriving hungry at 10:30am on Tuesdays and Thursdays for the twice-weekly three-hour farm tour and lunch. With a stomach filled with pretzel hot dogs, homemade beer and sauerkraut, sail on back to the islands to the must-see ❸ Wright Brothers Memorial. The complex covers

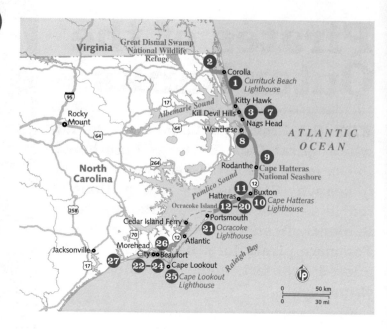

several museum spaces, a hilltop memorial and historic outbuildings and markers from the Wright Brothers' time. It spices up a beach vacation with a history lesson and, during summer, daily kid-friendly events that teach little ones about the art and science of flight.

THE CAPE HATTERAS LIGHTHOUSE

What happens when erosion and tidal movement means your 4800-ton, 1.25 million-brick lighthouse has crept to within almost 100ft of the shorelines? You pick it up and move it, of course. In 1999, after 60 years of erosion stabilization attempts, the National Park Service authorized this controversial project. Over 23 very slow days, the lighthouse was moved – safely – 2900ft from the shore, completely unscathed.

If you're not renting a vacation home, the family-owned **4 Colony IV by the Sea** motel is just down the street, loaded with fab amenities like free wi-fi and breakfast, gym privileges at the Y and beach access, and only-in-the-Outer-Banks perks like a fish-cleaning station.

Those looking to get a jump-start on counting all the grains of sand on the planet will find their bliss at **5 Jockey's Ridge**, the largest sand dune on the East Coast. In the evenings, folks often gather here to watch the sunset over the Pamlico Sound. Impress your friends with tales (and video) of your hang-gliding prowess by booking a beginner's lesson with **6 Kitty Hawk Kites**, the largest hang-gliding school in the US. Even softies would enjoy a lesson here, as safety is paramount and you're never terribly far off the ground (don't worry; we won't tell your awestruck friends).

A handful of restaurants serve up good eats without the anthropomorphic mascots, including ❼ **Basnight's Lone Cedar Café**, right on the Nags Head-Manteo Causeway. Come early to wander the fresh herb garden and pier, and then feast with a sunset backdrop on delectable seafood and vegetables. You can actually taste the commitment to sustainable farming and fishing. Bring your own freshly caught fish, and the chefs will prepare it any way you like.

The second Outer Banks lighthouse you come to is ❽ **Bodie Island Lighthouse**, on Oregon Inlet. While you can't enter the lighthouse itself, a gift shop and keeper's quarters museums will delight history and lighthouse buffs. Keep heading south on Hwy 12 to reach the ❾ **Chicamacomico Life-Saving Station**. Even with the invention of the lighthouse, more than 500 ships met their maker in the battering waves off the coast of the Outer Banks. The United States Life-Saving Service (the precursor to the Coast Guard) would risk their lives in treacherous conditions to help beleaguered sailors, and perfectly preserved rooms display their history here.

"If North Carolina ever had a different kind of secessionist movement, it would start on Ocracoke."

Keep going on Hwy 12 to reach the iconic ❿ **Cape Hatteras Lighthouse**, known as "America's Lighthouse" and with a famous black-and-white striped base. As you walk up its 248 steps to admire the breathtaking view, imagine being the lighthouse keeper back 100 years ago, carrying the 5-gallon, 40lb canister of oil on your back each day. Your last stop before catching the ferry to Ocracoke is the ⓫ **Graveyard of the Atlantic Museum**, where you can check out shipwreck artifacts dating back hundreds of years. Hint: claim a car space in the ferry line early, then walk the 200ft to the museum for a quick look-see.

If North Carolina ever had a different kind of secessionist movement, it would most likely start on ⓬ **Ocracoke**. Gone are the ubiquitous beachwear shops and BrewThru drive-through convenience stores of the Carolina coast and, in their place, handmade craft stores, organic coffee shops and hemp design boutiques. Your first stop coming from the ferry is ⓭ **Teach's Hole** store and museum. Originally a pirate-themed gift shop, it's opened a museum-quality exhibit filled with bountiful treasure like historical artifacts and a documentary about Blackbeard's life in the Outer Banks.

Laze on what's known as one of America's best beaches at ⓮ **Lifeguard Beach**, the most popular of the 16 mile white-sand-and-seashell strip of coast (there's a nude beach, as well, but we'll leave it to you to find). Head into ⓯ **Ocracoke Village** to stroll the shops or grab an ice-cream cone. But be sure to get offshore at least once during your time on the island; surfing, boating, fishing or kayaking are all options. ⓰ **Ride the Wind's** knowledgeable guides take landlubbing visitors through the reedy coast to the spot where

Blackbeard was beheaded. The locally owned surf shop also has the coolest summer camp known to kidkind: a three-day surf camp for kids aged 9 to 17 (older folk can take private lessons).

Dinners are taken very seriously on Ocracoke, almost as seriously as relaxing. For fried seafood perfection, start with the crab beignets at ⑰ **Back Porch Restaurant** and ease into the crab cake main dish, topped with a sweet red pepper sauce. Stay a second night just to dine on even more seafood at ⑱ **Café Atlantic**. Ocracoke doesn't have a single chain hotel or restaurant, and we highly recommend ⑲ **Blackbeard's Lodge**, where you and your lodgemates might tap out a sea shanty or two on the grand piano downstairs or grab one of the bicycles for a jaunt around the island. Those looking for quiet romance should check out the ⑳ **Cove B&B**. In a serene garden in the heart of the village, the well-appointed historic home comes with balconies, and the hosts greet each guest with plenty of insider information about the island and a wine reception each evening. It's not the grandest of the Outer Banks lighthouses, but the stout 1823 ㉑ **Ocracoke Lighthouse** is the second-oldest lighthouse still operating on the North Carolina coast.

For more pirate booty, take the Cedar Island Ferry from town and continue down Hwy 12 towards ㉒ **Beaufort**, home of the world-class ㉓ **North Carolina Maritime Museum**. Artifacts from 15 shipwrecks are on display, including from Blackbeard's presumed flagship, the *Queen Anne's Revenge*. To see the southernmost lighthouse in the Outer Banks, take a boat tour with the ㉔ **Outer Banks Ferry Service** to ㉕ **Cape Lookout Lighthouse**. The boat sails past Shackleford Island, home to hundreds of wild horses. You know a house is old when the "new" extension was added in 1790, like at ㉖ **Langdon House B&B**, the most historic lodging in Beaufort. For the

ASK A LOCAL

"My hypothesis as to why pirates are so fascinating is that they represent an icon of freedom; they threw off the conventions and shackles of government and did whatever they wanted. But they were also incredibly dangerous. Of the artifacts we've salvaged from Blackbeard's *Queen Anne's Revenge* here, we've discovered they were armed to the teeth, with cannonballs and more than 250,000 rounds of lead shot."

David Moore, Maritime Archaeologist, North Carolina Maritime Museum, Beaufort, NC

best of the mascot restaurants, end your vacation at ㉗ **Amos Mosquito's**. Eating sweet potato fries and s'mores in a swamp-themed restaurant known as "Skeeters" while watching dolphins swim past will remind you that, yes, you are on vacation.

Alex Leviton

TRIP INFORMATION

GETTING THERE
Part of the area's charm is that the Outer Banks isn't easy to reach from any direction. The closest interstate is I-95, 2½ hours to the west (Raleigh and I-40 are another hour away).

DO
Bodie Island Lighthouse
Visitors can't climb the lighthouse, but the museum has a good history exhibit. ☎ 252-441-5711; Bodie Island Lighthouse Rd, Bodie Island; admission free; museum 9am-5pm;

Cape Hatteras Lighthouse
Famous enough to be known as "America's Lighthouse," with a good museum and open lighthouse. ☎ 252-995-4474; www.nps .gov/caha; 46375 Lighthouse Rd, Buxton; adult/child over 42in & senior $7/3.50; 9am-5:30pm Jun-Aug, 9am-4:30pm off-season;

Chicamacomico Life-Saving Station
Join conservators Linda and James and local Coast Guard members as they re-enact historical life-saving ventures on the beach during summer; call for details. ☎ 252-987-1552; www.chicamacomico.net; NC Hwy 12, Milepost 39.5, Rodanthe; adult/child & senior $6/4; noon-5pm Mon-Fri Apr-Nov;

Currituck Beach Lighthouse
The northernmost all-brick lighthouse, surrounded by beautiful grounds. ☎ 252-453-4939; www.currituckbeachlight.com; Heritage Village Park, Corolla Village Rd, Corolla; grounds admission free, lighthouse adult/child $7/free; 9am-5pm Easter to Thanksgiving, to 8pm Thu;

Graveyard of the Atlantic Museum
A museum with 400 years of shipwreck history. ☎ 252-986-2995; www.graveyard oftheatlantic.com; ferry terminal area, Hatteras Village; admission free; 10am-4pm Mon-Fri;

Kitty Hawk Kites
Discover your adventurous side with hang-gliding lessons, kite-boarding or kayak rentals. There are other locations from Corolla to Ocracoke. ☎ 877-FLY-THIS; www.kittyhawk .com; Hwy 158, Milepost 12.5, Nags Head; 3hr beginner lesson $89; 8am-10:30pm

North Carolina Maritime Museum
More than 100 years of highlighting maritime history and, now, the archaeological remains of Blackbeard's *Queen Anne's Revenge*. ☎ 252-728-7317; www.ncmaritimemuseum .org; 315 Front St, Beaufort; admission free; 9am-5pm Mon-Fri, 10am-5pm Sat, 1-5pm Sun;

Outer Banks Ferry Service
Boat tours to Cape Lookout Lighthouse and surrounding islands. ☎ 252-728-4129; www.outerbanksferry.com; 326 Front St, Beaufort; adult $8-14, child $4-6; from 10:15am;

Ride the Wind
A surf and clothing shop that also rents kayaks, leads guided kayak tours and gives surfing lessons. ☎ 252-928-6311; www .surfocracoke.com; Hwy 12 at Silver Lake St, Ocracoke; kayak per hr $12, guided 2hr sunset or day tour $35; 10am-7pm;

Teach's Hole
Pirate-themed store with an impressive museum of pirate artifacts and lore. ☎ 252-928-1718; www.teachshole.com; Hwy 12 at West End Rd, Ocracoke; museum adult/child & senior $4/3; 10am-6:30pm daily Apr-Nov, 10am-5pm Mon-Sat Dec-Mar;

Wright Brothers Memorial
Sprawling museum with gift shop, flight demonstrations, historical buildings, replicas of the Wright Brothers' first flying machines and a hilltop memorial. ☎ 252-441-7430; www.nps.gov/wrbr; Hwy 158 Bypass Milepost 8, Kill Devil Hills; adult/child $4/free; 9am-6pm Memorial Day-Labor Day, to 5pm off-season;

EAT
Amos Mosquito's
Sure, it's a swamp-themed restaurant that sells "Skeeters" T-shirts, but isn't that all part of the fun? ☎ 252-247-6222; 703 E Fort Macon Rd, Atlantic Beach; mains $8-22; 5-10pm;

Back Porch Restaurant

Gourmet food served in an enclosed, you guessed it, back porch. ☎ 252-928-6401; 110 Back Rd, Ocracoke; mains $8-36; ☾ 5-10pm

Basnight's Lone Cedar Café

Fresh seafood caught by local fishers, vegetables grown on local farms and the on-site herb garden, with a view of the intracoastal waterway. ☎ 252-441-5405; www.lone cedarcafe.com; Nags Head-Manteo Causeway, Nags Head; mains $8-36; ☾ 11:30am-3pm Thu-Sun, 5pm to close daily; ♿

Café Atlantic

All the fried, stuffed or baked seafood one could ever want, plus a reputation as Ocracoke's best restaurant. ☎ 252-928-4861; Hwy 12, Ocracoke; mains $7-22; ☾ 5-10pm daily & 11am-3pm Sun

Weeping Radish

Tour the organic farm, or imbibe at the brewery, butcher or restaurant. There's a free brewery tour at noon on Wednesday and Saturday, and a tour and family-style meal ($20) at 10:30am Tuesday and Thursday. ☎ 252-491-5205; www.weepingradish.com; 6810 Caratoke Hwy, Jarvisburg; mains $5-13; ☾ 11am-8pm Mon-Thu, to 9pm Fri & Sat, noon-7pm Sun; ♿

SLEEP

Blackbeard's Lodge

Convivial village motel with a games room, pool and wraparound porch. ☎ 800-892-5314; www.blackbeardslodge.com; 111 Back Rd, Ocracoke Island; r $61-165, apt $115-297; ♿

Colony IV by the Sea

Family-owned beachfront motel; free internet, indoor and outdoor pools, continental breakfast and YMCA privileges. ☎ 800-848-3728; www.motelbythesea.com; Hwy 12, Milepost 8.5, Kill Devil Hills; r $80-180; ☎ 9am-5pm; ♿

Cove B&B

Quiet, historic B&B in a secluded but central location. ☎ 252-928-4192; www.thecovebb .com; 21 Loop Rd, Ocracoke Island; r $150-225; ♿

Langdon House B&B

Almost 300 years of history with hammocks, jacuzzi tubs and huge breakfasts, blocks from the water and restaurants on Front St. ☎ 252-728-5499; www.langdonhouse.com; 135 Craven St, Beaufort; r $120-220; ♿

USEFUL WEBSITES

www.historicbeaufort.com
www.outerbanks.org

LINK YOUR TRIP   www.lonelyplanet.com/trip-planner

Cape Fear & the Carolina Coast

WHY GO Wilmington is reputed to be one of America's most haunted places. But the historic district located on the Cape Fear River rivals Charleston or Savannah in its Southern grace, and surrounding white sandy beaches, statuesque gardens and oceanfront state parks allow visitors to relax after any hair-raising activities.

It's not just the Cape Fear River that gives this trip its name. Carnivorous plants, venomous snakes, poison dart frogs and haunted watering holes take up the fright factor a notch. However, loafing on the beach is also a time-honored tradition around Wilmington. Beaches dot the coast to the north, south and east and lazy gardens make for a beautiful stroll.

Start a trip to the Wilmington area with a day at ❶ **Wrightsville Beach**, just east of the city across Hwy 76. With a decidedly smaller ratio of mega-beachwear stores than its shoreline neighbors along the Crystal Coast and several isolated sandy beaches, this stretch of coast is among North Carolina's best. On the way over to loaf on the beach, pick up a few loaves at ❷ **Sweet & Savory Bakeshop and Café**. Or opt for one of the eatery's well-loved biscuits, sandwiches or soup, all homemade of course. The café is hidden behind an office building just before the Causeway, so keep an eye out.

Wilmington is the only place on the planet where you can see the carnivorous Venus flytrap plant growing in the wild. Peaceful ❸ **Airlie Gardens** features the insectivores, but it's the relaxed 0.9 mile garden tour that really impresses. The original gardens date back to a 1735 land grant from King George II, but it wasn't until the early-20th century that the half-million azaleas you see today were landscaped. Wandering

TIME
2 days

DISTANCE
48 miles

BEST TIME TO GO
Apr – Jun

START
Wilmington, NC

END
Southport, NC

ALSO GOOD FOR

CITY

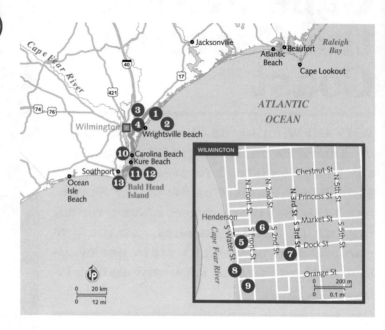

through the butterfly garden and past the swans swimming under weeping willows on the lake, you'll see why many a Southern belle chooses to get married here. If you're here on Friday night in summer, stop in for a jazz concert ($8), and don't miss the springtime azalea bloom. Just down the street is the ④ **New Hanover County Arboretum**, which has been known to house the carnivorous plants on occasion. But wandering through the manicured native plants and peaceful Japanese garden recreation is the real reason to stop in.

"For a murderously good time, head out in the evening on a Haunted Pub Crawl."

Why go with a staid daytime history lesson when you can learn about the past, see ghosts and drink beer at the same time? For a murderously good time, head out in the evening on a ⑤ **Haunted Pub Crawl**. To relax over dinner, head downtown to ⑥ **Deluxe**. Chef and Wilmington native Keith Rhodes has won the Best Dish competition at the North Carolina State Fair not once but twice for locally sourced dishes, which include the likes of North Carolina blueberry and white chocolate bread pudding or buttermilk-fried calamari with sweet and sour apricot preserves.

After all that fear, you might want to relax at the ⑦ **Graystone Inn**, a turn-of-the-century mansion turned B&B in the heart of the historic district. Fourteen-foot Corinthian columns, a mahogany library and a breezy veranda round out the romantic guestrooms.

On your second day, take a stroll along the **8** **Riverwalk** in the heart of the historic district. Within Wilmington's 300-block historic district, there are 19 mansions open to visitors. Plan on spending at least an hour at the **9** **Cape Fear Serpentarium**, an indoor reptile zoo quite unlike any other place in the world. A skull and cross-bones marks each resident's deadly rating, from 1: the beaded lizard (painful local effects) to 5: bushmaster (survival is unlikely, lasting debilitation). After reading owner Dean Ripa's harrowing description of one of his four nonfatal bushmaster bites (most people don't survive one), check out the other five-skullers, like the forest cobra and black mamba, and a 340lb anaconda that could swallow a grown person whole.

ASK A LOCAL

"Wilmington is a great place to live. Between the beach, the historic downtown and the university there is something here for everyone. But my favorite is the food. There are enough restaurants here that you would never have to learn how to cook. My favorite place is **Sweet & Savory Bakeshop and Café**. [It serves] the best sandwich in town whether it's breakfast, lunch or dinner."
Mike Polito, Wilmington, NC

Heading southeast on Hwy 421, stop in at **10** **Carolina Beach State Park** where visitors can access some of the area's best fishing, camp under giant oaks and walk along the Venus Flytrap Trail. The half-mile loop is the best place to see the flytrap in its natural habitat, and lucky visitors might find an insect in the plant's clutch. There are also examples of the two other carnivorous plants – the Bladderwort and the Pitcher Plant.

Leave the deadly flora for killer fauna at the **11** **North Carolina Aquarium at Fort Fisher**, home of sharks, poison dart frogs, alligators and various animals of mass destruction. Although the aquarium isn't vast, it's packed with information and is a great spot to picnic. It's also near the Civil War site **12** **Fort Fisher** (also supposedly haunted) and the **13** **Southport Ferry**, which transports pedestrians and road trippers to the scenic village

WILMINGTON'S FILM CENTER

Opened in 1858, **Thalian Hall** is downtown Wilmington's one-stop shop for performances, events, foreign films, city hall and, of course, ghost legends. As one of the top movie production locations in the USA, Wilmington takes its film seriously. In mid-November, Thalian Hall plays host to the Cucalorus festival and every Monday to Wednesday at 7:30pm, the Cinematique series showcases foreign, independent or notable films for the local culturati.

of historic Southport, where antiques shops, restaurants and a maritime museum provide a perfect backdrop for a lazy day of loafing.
Alex Leviton

TRIP INFORMATION

GETTING THERE
Wilmington is an easy two-hour drive east from Raleigh, just off I-40 on Hwy 17.

DO

Airlie Gardens
Historic gardens in the classic Southern tradition surrounding a picture-perfect lake. ☎ 910-798-7700; www.airliegardens.org; 300 Airlie Rd, Wilmington; adult/child $5/3; ⏰ 9am-5pm, closed Sun Jan-Mar; ♿

Cape Fear Serpentarium
More than 100 species of poisonous snakes and reptiles from around the world in various levels of deadliness. ☎ 910-762-1669; www.capefearserpentarium.com; 20 Orange St, Wilmington; admission $8; ⏰ 11am-5pm Sun-Fri, to 6pm Sat, closed Mon & Tue off-season; ♿

Haunted Pub Crawl
Those under age 21 will enjoy the other tours: ghosts, film locations and pirates. ☎ 910-794-1866; www.hauntedwilmington.com; call for meeting location, downtown Wilmington; adult $21; ⏰ 7:30pm Tue-Sat Jul, Aug & Oct, Wed-Sat Apr-Jun & Sep, Fri & Sat Mar

New Hanover County Arboretum
Demonstration garden for local plants and international flora. ☎ 910-798-7670; 6206 Oleander Dr, Wilmington; admission free; ⏰ garden dawn to dusk, gift shop 9am-4pm; ♿

North Carolina Aquarium at Fort Fisher
Scary creatures and colorful fish abound at this native aquarium, especially popular with children. ☎ 910-458-8257; www.ncaquariums.com; 900 Loggerhead Rd, Kure Beach; adult/child $8/6; ⏰ 9am-5pm, to 9pm Thu July; ♿

Southport Ferry
Runs about once an hour from Kure Beach to Southport for both cars and pedestrians. ☎ 910-457-6942; www.ncdot.org/transit/ferry; Hwy 421 S, Fort Fisher, Kure Beach; car/pedestrian $5/1; ⏰ 6:15am-7pm to Southport, 5:30am-6:15pm to Fort Fisher

EAT

Deluxe
New Southern cuisine influenced by French, Italian and Caribbean flavors with an award-winning chef. ☎ 910-251-0333; www.deluxenc.com; 114 Market St, Wilmington; mains $12-27; ⏰ 5pm until close Mon-Sat, 11am-2pm Sun

Sweet & Savory Bakeshop and Café
Locals' favorite for 120-layer croissants, omelets, local seafood and delectable pastries, on the way to Wrightsville Beach. ☎ 910-256-0115; www.sweetandsavorycafe.com; 1611 Pavilion Pl, Wilmington; mains $4-16; ⏰ 7am-9pm Mon-Sat, 8am-9pm Sun; ♿

SLEEP

Carolina Beach State Park
Shaded beachfront camping with miles of shoreline trails and a Venus flytrap trail from which to spot carnivorous plants. ☎ 910-458-8206; www.ncparks.gov; 1010 State Beach Park Rd, Carolina Beach; campsites $15; ⏰ year-round, ♿

Graystone Inn
Elegant and historic B&B central enough to get around by carriage rides. ☎ 910-763-2000; www.graystoneinn.com; 100 S 3rd St, Wilmington; r $169-379

USEFUL WEBSITES
www.capefearcoast.com
www.wilmingtondowntown.com

LINK YOUR TRIP
www.lonelyplanet.com/trip-planner

Piedmont Traditions

WHY GO This round-trip takes you through the center of North Carolina, also known as the Piedmont for its similarities to the foothill Piemonte region in Italy. A living museum, Old Salem in Winston-Salem was settled by Moravians in the 1760s, who started the craft tradition that is a mainstay of the region.

TIME
3 days

DISTANCE
190 miles

BEST TIME TO GO
Year-round

START
Charlotte, NC

END
Charlotte, NC

ALSO GOOD FOR

FOOD & DRINK

While most visitors to North Carolina stick to the edges – the eastern coast or the western Blue Ridge Mountains – many people miss out on the central foothills. The only cities in North Carolina with six-figure populations are here (Charlotte, Raleigh, Greensboro, Winston-Salem, Durham and Fayetteville), as are generations of craft traditions that have put North Carolina on the map. These days, manufacturing and crafts have given way to high-tech and biotechnology as the main exports of the state, but just a generation or two ago it was pottery, textiles and furniture.

Start your trip at the center of all things aesthetically useful in North Carolina at the **1** **Mint Museum of Craft & Design** in Charlotte. Located in the teeming part of the city amidst high-rise banks and chic coffeehouses, this is the place for aficionados of function *and* form. From giant 19th-century North Carolinian ceramic jars to ancient Peruvian textiles, if it's beautiful and serves a purpose, it can be found here.

With a menu unlike any other in the state, head out of downtown to dine at the unique **2** **Rooster's Wood-Fired Kitchen**. From downtown, wend your way south towards the South Park Mall for a gastronomic excursion unique to North Carolina. Besides being decorated almost entirely in North Carolina–made furnishings, the menu is Mediterranean tapas, Carolina style: pan-fried corn (a recipe of the owner's grandmother), duck confit BBQ, smoked charcuterie plates.

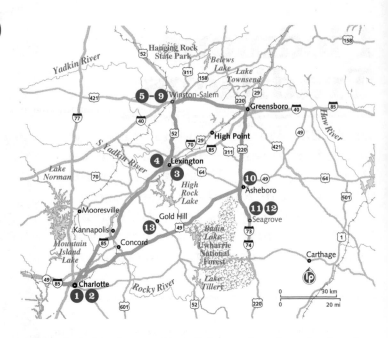

Or if you're looking for something a little more down home, head north on I-85 to exit 87, where you'll find fiery religion in a glass bottle with a screw-on red top. The most famous of the famed Lexington BBQ joints is ❸ **Lexington Barbecue #1**. Don't let the line snaking out to the parking lot scare you off, since a) it's always there and b) the joint runs like a Swiss clock. Known as the BBQ capital of the world, Lexington is famous the state – and world – over, so your booth neighbors might be Gladys from the church rectory, or Gunther,

NASCAR: BEGAT BY MOONSHINE

Before Prohibition, North Carolina had a thriving wine-growing and liquor-distilling business. Afterwards, some producers continued night deliveries, usually driving at high speeds to outrun the Feds. Certain drivers were well known for their impressive racing skills, and crowds began to gather on Sunday afternoons to watch the best bootleggers compete. Thus was born NASCAR.

who read about the legendary meal in his Berlin newspaper. Wash down the pork fat at ❹ **Childress Vineyards**, recently named one of the top wine-tasting rooms in the country. The sumptuous Italian-inspired grounds were the brainchild of NASCAR legend, Richard Childress. Sip a Syrah or a Viognier at its restaurant or wander the grounds, pretending you're at a NASCAR race in Chianti.

From the winery, take Hwy 52 into ❺ **Winston-Salem** to reach the historical village of ❻ **Old Salem**. To get to the ❼ **Old Salem Visitor's Center**, take Sprague St from the highway, then turn right on Main St until it turns into Old Salem Rd. Here, you can pick up a map of the historic district, watch a film on the earliest Moravians and buy tickets for the museums and gardens. Then, wander through this living history village, through museums and gardens, and shops selling some of the many crafts the Moravians were famed for. The only accommodations within Old Salem is the romantic **8** **Augustus T Zevely Inn**, where the furniture is authentically reproduced to mirror original pieces from early Moravian settlement. For dinner, stroll to **9** **Old Salem Tavern**, where costumed waitresses don't seem out of place serving enormously filling meals fit to nourish folks fixin' to churn pounds of butter or chop cords of wood. Two-hundred-year-old recipes for red cabbage salad and Moravian chicken pot pie have been updated with menu items like gingerbread-crusted pork over sweet potato spaetzle. Make sure you don't miss the classic Moravian gingerbread desserts.

"The sumptuous Italian-inspired grounds were the brainchild of NASCAR legend, Richard Childress."

If you want to veer away from arts and crafts, head east then south on I-74/I-73/Hwy 220 and visit the **10** **North Carolina Zoo**. The first zoo in the country to feature animals in their natural environment, it's just been named the country's number one zoo. Wear comfortable shoes, as 5 miles of shaded walking trails pass by spectacular exhibits featuring mountain gorillas, polar bears and an African plains exhibit larger than most zoos.

Keep up the artistic tradition in **11** **Seagrove**, an entire town dedicated to pottery and dating back to before the Revolutionary War. Even though the town is tiny, several families are on their ninth generation of potters, and to this day, more than 90 potters work within 20 miles of Seagrove. Get a taste of the area's artistry and pick up a travel map at the **12** **North Carolina Pottery Center**, a museum dedicated to the craft, both local and international, modern and

ASK A LOCAL

"There are more than two dozen BBQ restaurants in town, but I'll drive across town to go to the Monk. That's what locals call **Lexington Barbecue #1**, the Monk or Honey Monk. My husband Mark gets the sandwiches, and I get the plate of coarse chopped BBQ with coleslaw and hush puppies. You've got to get Cheerwine soda, made nearby in Salisbury. They only make cherry, but it's so good, Robert Redford even sells it in his Sundance catalog."
Robin & Mark Petruzzi, Lexington, NC

ancient. On the way back to Charlotte, the **13** **Bed & Bike Inn** is a mini-resort for the spiritually minded in the Uwharrie Mountains. Whether it's a drum circle around the fire pit, a walk through the meditative labyrinth, a private kayak or wine tour, or just kicking back in the log cabin, there is no shortage of things to do and see here.
Alex Leviton

HISTORY & CULTURE

TRIP INFORMATION

GETTING THERE
From Raleigh, take I-40 to Greensboro and I-85 to Charlotte, about a three-hour drive.

DO

Mint Museum of Craft and Design
The center of the Charlotte art scene, along with its sister Mint Museum of Art three blocks away. ☎ 704-337-2000; www.mint museum.org; 220 N Tryon Rd, Charlotte; adult/child $6/3; 🕙 10am-5pm Tue-Sat, noon-5pm Sun; ♿

North Carolina Pottery Center
Exhibitions of North Carolina pottery dating back to prehistoric times. ☎ 336-873-8430; www.ncpotterycenter.com; 233 East Ave, Seagrove; adult/child $2/1, guided tour & demonstration $5; 🕙 10am-4pm Tue-Sat

North Carolina Zoo
If only every zoo could aspire to the lofty heights of 5 miles of tree-draped trails winding around enclosures as large as 37 acres. ☎ 800-488-0444; www.nczoo.org; 4401 Zoo Parkway, Asheboro; adult/child $10/6; 🕙 9am-5pm Apr-Oct, to 4pm Nov-Mar

Old Salem Visitor's Center
Start a day's journey through Old Salem with a film and background on the Moravian community. ☎ 336-721-7300; www.old salem.org; 900 Old Salem Rd, Winston-Salem; adult/child $21/10; 🕙 9am-5:30pm Mon-Sat, 12:30-5:30pm Sun; ♿

EAT & DRINK

Childress Vineyards
Tuscany meets the Piedmont in this 35,000-sq-ft Italian-inspired winery and bistro.

☎ 336-236-9463; www.childress vineyards.com; 1000 Childress Vineyards Rd, Lexington; mains $7-11, tastings $10; 🕙 10am-6pm Mon-Sat, noon-6pm Sun, bistro 11am-3pm

Lexington Barbecue #1
In the center of the North Carolina barbecue city is the center of Lexington barbecue. ☎ 336-249-9814; 10 Hwy 29/70S, Lexington; mains $3-9; 🕙 10am-9:30pm Mon-Sat; ♿

Old Salem Tavern
Moravian recipes that have stood the test of time for 200 years. ☎ 336-748-8585; www .oldsalemtavern.com; 736 S Main, Winston-Salem; mains $7-24; 🕙 11.30am-2pm daily & 5-9pm Mon-Thu, to 9:30pm Fri & Sat; ♿

Rooster's Wood-Fired Kitchen
Italian, French and Southern traditions meet at the most inventive restaurant in Charlotte. ☎ 704-366-8688; www.roosterskitchen .com; 6601 Morrison Ave, Charlotte; small plates $5-18; 🕙 11am-11pm Mon-Thu, to midnight Fri & Sat, to 9:30pm Sun; ♿

SLEEP

Augustus T Zevely Inn
Soak in the 19th-century atmosphere and feast on Moravian breakfast goodies, in the center of Old Salem. ☎ 336-748-9299; www.winston-salem-inn.com; 803 S Main St, Winston-Salem; r $95-140; ♿

Bed & Bike Inn
Stay in an old tobacco barn less than an hour from Charlotte. ☎ 704-463-0768; www .bedandbikeinn.com; 15750 Matton Grove Church Rd, Gold Hill; r $79-225; ♿

USEFUL WEBSITES
www.oldsalem.org

LINK YOUR TRIP   www.lonelyplanet.com/trip-planner

Mayberry & the Yapa Valley

WHY GO The Yadkin Valley is quickly becoming North Carolina's version of Napa Valley, a Southern "Yapa" Valley. With the Blue Ridge Mountains as its backdrop, the region is anchored by Mt Airy – the real-life home of the "Andy Griffith Show" – which is as close to small-town utopia as it gets.

Anyone who watched American television in the 1960s or has seen reruns of '60s TV shows since will recognize much of Mayberry in Andy's real-life hometown of Mt Airy. You can still get a pork sandwich at Snappy Lunch or visit Mt Pilot (nearby Pilot Mountain). You might even see a glimpse of Thelma Lou from the show: actress Betty Lynn retired here in 2006.

It's rare in a travel writer's life to find a place worthy of the word "perfect," but such is ❶ **Pilot Knob Inn**, in the foothills of Pilot Mountain. The former tobacco barns-turned-guest cottages and luxurious suites cater to baby-making rather than babies (children are not allowed). Everyone can enjoy the romantic private lake, full Southern breakfast and dazzlingly cozy furnishings, but the best rooms or cabins offer two-person Jacuzzis or private hot tubs, wood-burning stoves, kitchenettes or secluded wooded decks (hint: go for cabin 1, 4 or 5). Head across the highway to ❷ **Pilot Mountain State Park** just before dusk. You can drive almost to the top, where trails lead through leafy oaks to vistas of the wineries below and the Blue Ridge Mountains to the west. If you're looking to camp in the area, this is the place. Food nearby is scarce, but as long as there's decent BBQ, who needs fancy? For six and change, try a plate of BBQ, beans (green and pinto) and hush puppies at ❸ **Aunt Bea's Barbecue** in the town of Mt Pilot. For dessert, there's an ice-cream counter.

TIME
2 days

DISTANCE
105 miles

BEST TIME TO GO
Year-round

START
Pilot Mountain, NC

END
Boonville, NC

ALSO GOOD FOR

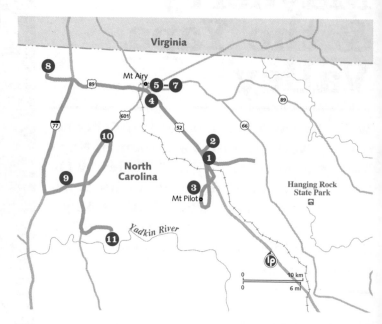

The following morning, head into Mayberry…er, Mt Airy, stopping first at the ❹ **Andy Griffith Playhouse**. A statue of Andy and Opie (a young Ron Howard) stands on the front lawn as a testament to the man who put Mayberry on the map, literally. The playhouse is the home of the Surry Arts Council, with plays, live music, the Andy Griffith museum and, starting in 2009, the Chang and Eng Bunker museum. Make sure you make it to ❺ **Snappy Lunch** before 12:30pm for its famed pork sandwiches. Opened in 1923 and the only Mt Airy business mentioned by name on the *Andy Griffith Show*, the old-school diner is where Andy bought his 10 cent hot dog during school breaks and where locals still go to get their town gossip and cheeseburgers, now a buck eighty.

> *"The old-school diner is where locals still go to get their town gossip and cheeseburgers."*

If you want a more upscale meal, try ❻ **Old North State Winery and Scuppernong's Restaurant**, where pineapple quesadilla share the menu with meatball sandwiches and fried oysters. For oenophiles, the bar offers wine tasting flights – a half-dozen samples of dry, sweet or semi-sweet wines. The only wine-tasting facilities in downtown, the winery/brewery/restaurant combo is a great place to try the native muscadine grape in red and white varietals. In the evenings, you can catch a movie at ❼ **Downtown Cinema Theater**, but it's on Saturday mornings when the place is brought to life. Old-time bluegrass radio station WPAQ 740 broadcasts its weekly live Merry-Go-Round each Saturday at 11am (arrive at 9am for the open jam session).

Before you visit the Yadkin River Valley vineyards, pick up the Visit NC Wine foldout map from any area welcome center, or order one online at www.visitncwine.com. The "Yapa Valley" now has more than 30 wineries, and **⑧ Round Peak Vineyards** is a great place to start. From Hwy 89W, take Round Peak Church Rd for 1.5 miles. The small 12-acre winery is unassuming as a tourist attraction, but notable for the production of exceptional French and Italian varietals. Take a deep breath in each glass to smell the spirit of the tobacco that once grew on this land. For a contrast, head to the most Napa of the Yapa wineries,

"Not many people realize that Mt Airy is not only the home of Andy Griffith, but where the original Siamese twins settled and raised their family. Every year, we (the descendants of Chang and Eng Bunker) all get together and have a reunion. They had 21 children, so there are a lot of us. People come in from all over the country."

Tanya Jones, descendant of Eng Bunker, Mt Airy, NC

the polished **⑨ Shelton Vineyards and Harvest Grill Restaurant**. Take Hwy 77S to exit 93 towards Dobson. Turn right on Zephyr Rd, then a right onto Twin Oaks Rd. Follow this for 2.5 miles, then take a right onto Oregon Trail Rd. Throw out your best line about "blackberry overtones with a leathery finish" at the wine-tasting facilities, tour the grounds by bicycle or arrive on a summer Saturday for a live concert. Don't miss the restaurant, with its oh-so-deliciously bastardized Southern creations, like cornbread crab cake. For more wine tasting or an off-the-beaten track winery, try **⑩ Wolf's Lair at Black Wolf Vineyards**. Continue on Oregon Trail Rd, turn right on Twin Oaks and follow the signs to Hwy 601. The restaurant makes this a must-see, with wild mushroom bruschetta and grilled elk. Sip robust Black Wolf wines and check out the upstairs for a unique mix of oenological tchotchkes and taxidermy.

For your next tasting stop, backtrack on Hwy 601 to reach **⑪ RagApple Lassie Vineyards**. Continue for 10 miles, take a left on Hwy 67 and, 3 miles later, a right on Rockford Rd. A 2006 finalist for the best new winery

WPAQ: 740 AM

If you're not in the area for the live traditional music shows on Saturday at the Downtown Cinema Theater, you can still stream it live from the web at www.wpaq740.com. The celebrated radio station first went on the air in 1948 and has played traditional music – including local boy Tommy Jarrell – along with obituaries and lost pig announcements ever since.

in the USA, the former tobacco farm named for a pet cow features unusually creative blends that would fit right in on some of the best restaurant wine lists on either coast.

Alex Leviton

TRIP
18

FOOD & DRINK

TRIP INFORMATION

GETTING THERE
From Raleigh, take the I-40 to Hwy 52 northwest out of Winston-Salem for about an hour.

DO

Andy Griffith Playhouse
Year-round live performances and home of the Andy Griffith Collection. ☎ 336-786-7998; www.surryarts.org; 218 Rockford St, Mt Airy; admission $3, performances $10; ☺ 9am-5pm Mon-Fri, 11am-4pm Sat, 1:30-4pm Sun; ♿

Downtown Cinema Theater
Live old-time music WPAQ radio broadcasts on Saturday plus second-run films daily (call for show times). ☎ 336-786-2222; 142 Main St, Mt Airy; admission $5-8, Merry-Go-Round admission free; ☺ Sat 9am jam, 11am WPAQ Merry-Go-Round; ♿

Pilot Mountain State Park
Campgrounds, hiking trails and a beautiful sunset overlooking the Yadkin River Valley. ☎ 336-325-2355; www.ncsparks.net/pmo .html; 1792 Pilot Knob Park Rd, Pinnacle; admission free; ☎ 8am-after sunset; ♿ ♿

EAT & DRINK

Aunt Bea's Barbecue
Burgers, ice cream and big plates of North Carolina BBQ. ☎ 336-368-2300; 642 S Key St, Pilot Mountain; mains $3-6; ☺ 6am-10pm; ♿

Wolf's Lair at Black Wolf Vineyards
Wine-tasting and an excellent dinner at the restaurant. ☎ 336-374-2532; www.black wolfvineyards.com; 283 Vineyard Ln, Dobson; mains $6-28; ☺ tastings 11am-2:30pm Mon-Sat, noon-4pm Sun, restaurant 11am-2:30pm Mon-Sat & 5-10pm Thu-Sat, noon-8pm Sun

Old North State Winery and Scuppernong's Restaurant
Fabulous wines and casual bistro dining downtown. ☎ 336-789-WINE; www.old

northstatewinery.com; 308 N Main St, Mt Airy; tastings premier $7, dry or sweet $4; ☺ 11am-9pm Mon-Wed, to 10pm Thu-Sat

RagApple Lassie Vineyard
Tobacco farm turned nationally acclaimed winery. ☎ 336-367-6000; www.ragapple lassie.com; Rockford Rd, Boonville; tastings $5-7; ☺ noon-6pm

Round Peak Vineyards
Italian-themed wines just outside Mayberry/Mt Airy. ☎ 336-352-5595; www.roundpeak .com; 765 Round Peak Church Rd, Mt Airy; ☺ 10am-5pm Thu-Sat & Mon, noon-5pm Sun

Shelton Vineyards and Harvest Grill Restaurant
The largest of the Yapa Valley wineries with an excellent award-winning restaurant. ☎ 336-366-4724; www.sheltonvineyards .com; 286 Cabernet Ln, Dobson; ☺ 10am-6pm Mon-Sat, noon-6pm Sun, restaurant 10am-9pm Mon-Thu, to 10pm Fri & Sat, to 6pm Sun

Snappy Lunch
The old-time diner is the only original business from the *Andy Griffith Show* and has been open since 1923. ☎ 336-786-4931; www.thesnappylunch.com; 125 N Main St, Mt Airy; mains $2-8; ☺ 6am-1:45pm Mon-Wed & Fri, to 1:15pm Thu & Sat; ♿

SLEEP

Pilot Knob Inn
Honeymooners and couples love the romantic rooms and tobacco barns, or canoeing around the private lake. ☎ 336-325-2502; www.pilotknobinn.com; 361 New Pilot Knob Ln, Pinnacle; r $99-175, tobacco barn cabins $129-199

USEFUL WEBSITES
www.visitmayberry.com

www.visitncwine.com

www.lonelyplanet.com/trip-planner

LINK YOUR TRIP
TRIP

Blue Ridge Parkway: High Country

WHY GO The Blue Ridge Parkway is the most visited area of national parkland in the USA with almost 20 million visitors a year, twice as many as any other national park. Don't be afraid to get off the Parkway, however, as many of the scenic spots are well off the main drag.

You can thank the Great Depression for the Blue Ridge Parkway. Though the idea of a scenic byway between the Shenandoah National Park and the Great Smokies had been around for a generation, Americans hadn't yet invented road-tripping as a pastime. Work on the Parkway began in earnest in 1933, when the government harnessed the strength of thousands of out-of-work mountaineers in the Civilian Conservation Corps. Yet it wasn't until the Linn Cove Viaduct – an astounding feat of bridge engineering – was completed in 1987 that the entire Parkway was finally opened to visitors. Even now, be sure to call ahead or check the website (www.blueridgeparkway.org) before you head out, as sections of the Blue Ridge Parkway are often closed after particularly nasty winters take their toll on the road's infrastructure.

With romantic rooms, a restaurant with a tailored menu of inventive fare and a wraparound porch with rockers facing a bucolic, lazy river, the only reason you might not want to start your Blue Ridge Parkway trip at ❶ **River House Country Inn and Restaurant** is that you may never want to leave. About a 20-minute drive on Hwy 16 from Milepost 258/259, this Blue Ridge Mountain inn is perhaps best known for its Sunday salons, where poets, bluegrass musicians or vintners might be plying their talent, craft or wares. Stick around for the 6pm dinner for dishes like duck confit over French lentils, bacon and braised endive or berries in a Zinfandel and honey lavender reduction.

TIME
3 days

DISTANCE
136 miles

BEST TIME TO GO
Aug – Dec

START
Grassy Creek, NC

END
Linville Falls, NC

ALSO GOOD FOR

OUTDOORS

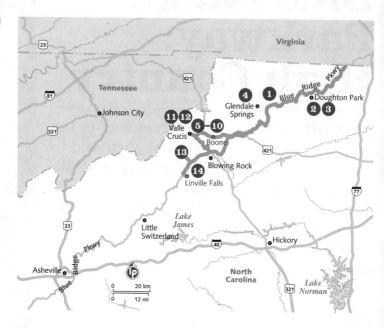

Or, if you'd prefer to start your stay on the Parkway itself, you might want to rest your head at ❷ **Bluff's Lodge**. As one of the only noncamping accommodations on the Parkway, the rooms are adequately comfortable, but it's the gobsmackingly stunning location, complete with a wraparound deck with an outdoor fireplace that practically forces one to roast s'mores while singing campfire songs or watching meteor showers. But it's the ❸ **Bluff's**

"Step inside for the best biscuits in North Carolina, nay, on Mother Earth."

Lodge Restaurant across the street that should not – under any circumstances – be missed. The "cafeteria" with easy-wipe vinyl menus and a knickknack gift store (candles! local pottery! grits!) looks like any roadside pit stop on the outside, but step inside for the best biscuits in North Carolina, nay, on Mother Earth. If you don't arrive for breakfast, you can have them served on the side for lunch or dinner, or bag them up to go (with gravy and/or jam on the side, of course). Call ahead for the fried chicken, cooked to order for 30 to 40 minutes in a cast-iron skillet, or order the BBQ, western NC-style (heavy on the tomato) served between corncakes sealed with a layer of melted cheese.

For a bit of Italia in Appalachia, head off the Parkway at Milepost 258/259 until you get to Glendale Springs and the ❹ **Holy Trinity Episcopal Church**. The fresco artist Benjamin F Long, now famed for work such as the Trans-America dome in Charlotte, started in the High Country in the late 1970s after returning from eight years apprenticing for Italian masters. Visit his

Last Supper fresco in Glendale Springs; his models for the work were local residents (the model for Thomas was Long himself).

For those with little ones in tow, a rite of passage for every North Carolinian child is the Appalachian- and Old West–themed amusement park, the **⑤ Tweetsie Railroad.** A 1917 coal-fired steam locomotive starts your journey through a gloriously campy 1950s-style Wild West show, past marauding Indians and heroic cowboys. Midway rides, Western shops selling toy guns, fudge and no-holds-barred Olde Tyme souvenirs, and family-friendly shows complete a full day's worth of innocent Americana that would make even Garrison Keillor blush.

> *"Kids will love buying a bucket of rocks and digging through it for guaranteed semiprecious gems."*

You can debate the railroad's lack of political correctness with students from nearby **⑥ Appalachian State** over dinner in **⑦ Boone,** a chilled-out university town that brings quite a bit of culture to the otherwise outdoorsy area. To check out the college town vibe and do some shopping or eating, head to **⑧ King Street.** Or to stick with the mountaineer vibe and eat one-seventh your weight in one sitting, stop in at **⑨ Daniel Boone Inn,** which has been serving up family-style meals since the 1960s, and the three-meat-and-five-veg menu hasn't changed much since then. The classic Southern/country staples are all here – green beans, country ham biscuits, stewed apples and fried chicken – and they're all here in massive quantities.

Spend a day off the Parkway after Boone. First, get your fingernails dirty at **⑩ Foggy Mountain Gem Mine.** While there are a half-dozen spots near or on the Parkway to go gem mining, many have cartoon mascots and tour-bus parking that caters to large crowds. The smaller Foggy Mountain was founded and is operated by graduate gemologists who take their craft a bit more seriously. Kids (and anyone who has ever made a mud pie) will love buying a bucket of rocks and digging through

TRADITIONAL MUSIC JAMS

There's no better area in North Carolina to hear traditional music than the hills of the High Country. This list will get you started: check with chambers of commerce, tourist offices or just about any local for more.

- Mrs Hyatt's Oprahouse, Asheville, on Thursday evenings
- Old Fort Mountain Music Jam, Rocket Building, Old Fort, on Friday evenings
- Historic Orchard at Altapass, Milepost 328, Little Switzerland, on Saturday and Sunday afternoons
- Mountain Home Music Concert Series, Blowing Rock Auditorium, Boone, on Saturday evenings (or tune in to WECR 102.3 at 8pm)
- Jim and Jennie's High Country Music Barn, Crossnore, on Saturday evenings

it for guaranteed semiprecious gems from all over the world, North Carolina included. After sifting through your rocks in a miner's flume line, you can ask the gemologists to cut and mount your hand-picked gems in any number of settings.

Continue on Hwy 105 for 1.5 miles and take a right on Broadstone Rd, reaching the **11** **Mast Farm Inn & Simplicity Restaurant**, a 200-year-old farmhouse inn and restaurant. Each guest receives a personalized menu for dinner – "Slow Chicken Nascar style but mighty low on points and Ashe County cheese trucked over by Junior Johnson" or "Hot Potato and Leek Vichyssoise buddies from West Jefferson singin' Elvis tunes while cruisin' 421 by Wilkesboro…" – so plan to stay a while. Which is a good thing, considering the rooms are as inviting as the restaurant. Sumptuous linens and claw-foot tubs in the main house might tempt you, but the front porch rockers, wood-burning stoves and an honest-to-goodness log cabin will draw most visitors to the gorgeous cottages.

> **ASK A LOCAL**
>
> "There's no place else [like North Carolina] I've been in America that reminds me so much of Europe. There's the down-home rural personality of the mountains, plus the space-age technology of the Triangle. When you're surrounded by the mountains, the coast, the Piedmont, you have a tremendous number of microcultures, much like France, or Switzerland, or Italy. Here, in the Blue Ridge Mountains, you go 10 miles between villages and each of them has a distinct character."
>
> *Henri Deschamps, owner, Mast Farm Inn*

After breakfast, head further into historic Valle Crucis to the **12** **Original Mast General Store**. The first of a band of general stores in the Blue Ridge Mountains, the original store sells much the same products as it did when it first opened in 1883. Still a gathering spot for locals and now visitors, the mercantile shop sells a dozen types of bacon, traditional handmade hard candy, games of pick-up sticks and paddle ball, signs that read "Hippies Use Side Door," and a complete selection of women's bonnets.

SECRET SITES

Those with sturdy boots might want to skip the drive up to the parking lot (and the accompanying fee) for a more adventurous climb to **Grandfather Mountain**. Park at the Boone Fork parking lot at Milepost 299.9 and take either the Profile Trail or, better yet, the Daniel Boone Scout Trail, where locals will be able to point out the way to the secret site of a small plane crash, hidden in the thick vegetation.

Head down Hwy 184 to Hwy 105 to reach **13** **Grandfather Mountain**, a Unesco biosphere reserve worthy of a day trip. On the grounds, there is a wildlife habitat with black bear, river otter and bald eagles, plus a nature preserve with miles of hiking trails, but most people come here to walk the famous mile-high swinging bridge. The 228ft bridge stretches over a precipitous chasm that exposes visitors (safely) to the full force of mountain winds and a panoramic mountain vista. On a particularly gusty day, you can hear the bridge's steel girders sing.

Follow the Parkway south to reach ⑭ **Linville Falls**. These river gorges and waterfalls are accessed by a crisscross network of trails. During the week and in the off-season months, you can find secluded spots suitable for meditating on the sheer awesomeness of a multifaceted waterfall.

Alex Leviton

ROUTE

TRIP INFORMATION

GETTING THERE

The Blue Ridge Parkway runs for 469 miles, from Virginia's Shenandoah National Park to the edge of the Great Smokies in far western North Carolina. To reach the start of the trip from Raleigh, head west on I-40 past Mount Airy to Hwy 21, about a three-hour drive.

DO

Foggy Mountain Gem Mine
Semiprecious stones guaranteed in each bucket; a gemologist on site. ☎ 828-963-4367; www .foggymountaingems.com; 4416 Hwy 105 S, Boone; buckets $15-100; ☼ 10am-6pm; ⚇

Grandfather Mountain
A Unesco biosphere reserve with hiking trails and a swinging bridge. ☎ 800-468-7325; www.grandfather.com; 2050 Blowing Rock Hwy at Hwy 221 (Milepost 305), Linville; adult/child $14/6; ☼ 8am-1hr before dusk, 9am-5pm winter; ⚇ 🐾

Holy Trinity Episcopal Church
Take an unexpected detour to see Italian-inspired frescoes. ☎ 336-982-3076; www .churchofthefrescoes.com, www.benlong frescotrail.com; 120 Glendale School Rd, Glendale Springs; admission free; ☼ 9am-5pm

Linville Falls
Hike down to a series of multilevel waterfalls. www.ncwaterfalls.com/lin1.htm; Milepost 316.3, Linville Falls; admission free; ☼ dawn-dusk; ⚇ 🐾

Original Mast General Store
More than 130 years of selling everything from cradles to caskets. ☎ 828-963-6511; www .mastgeneralstore.com; Hwy 194, Valle Crucis; ☼ 7am-6:30pm Mon-Sat, 11am-5pm Sun; ⚇

Tweetsie Railroad
A theme park based around an historic steam train. ☎ 828-264-9061; www.tweetsie.com; 300 Tweetsie Railroad Ln, Blowing Rock; adult/ child $30/22; ☼ 9am-6pm Fri-Sun Memorial Day to Labor Day, 9am-6pm daily Jun-Aug; ⚇

EAT

Bluff's Lodge Restaurant
Biscuits and fried chicken worthy of a road trip by themselves. ☎ 336-372-4499; Milepost 241, Doughton Park; mains $3-18; ☼ 8am-8pm; ⚇

Daniel Boone Inn
Family-style dining for the very, very hungry since the 1960s. ☎ 828-264-8657; www .danielbooneinn.com; 130 Hardin St, Boone; mains adult $9-16, child $4-9; ☼ 11:30am-9pm Mon-Fri, 8am-9pm Sat & Sun, closed lunch Mon-Fri winter; ⚇

SLEEP

Bluff's Lodge
Be sure to ask for a room with a view. ☎ 336-372-4499; www.blueridgeresort .com; Milepost 241.1, Doughton Park; r $85-105; ☼ late Apr-Nov; ⚇

Mast Farm Inn & Simplicity Restaurant
Inn, cabins and restaurant in buildings dating back to the late 1700s. The restaurant is open from 6pm to 8:30pm, Thursday to Saturday and for holidays. ☎ 828-963-5857; www .mastfarminn.com; 2543 Broadstone Rd, Banner Elk; r $99-269, cabins $149-459, restaurant prix fixe $38

River House Country Inn and Restaurant
More of a mountain resort retreat than a simple lodging. ☎ 336-982-2109; www .riverhousenc.com; 1896 Old Field Creek Rd, Grassy Creek; r $125-195, 2-person cabins $195-225, additional person $50 each, min 2-night stay summer; ⚇

USEFUL WEBSITES
www.blueridgeparkway.org
www.nps.gov/blri

LINK YOUR TRIP

www.lonelyplanet.com/trip-planner

48 Hours in Asheville

WHY GO Known as the Paris of the South, Freak City USA or home to the Biltmore Estate, the hippified mountain town of Asheville defies any single categorization. A mixture of Blue Ridge folk traditions, New Age healing centers and a Slow Food outpost, Asheville rightfully tops countless "Best Place to Live/Visit/ See art-deco Architecture" lists.

TIME
2 days

DISTANCE

BEST TIME TO GO
Sep – Dec

START
Asheville, NC

END
Asheville, NC

ALSO GOOD FOR

To get your bearings (and have a good laugh), start your trip with ❶ **LaZoom Tours**, a bus tour as zany as Asheville itself. The lavender biodiesel bus is run by a group of drama geeks-turned-tour guides who inform as well as they entertain. After you've driven through town, head out on foot for a walking tour. Start at ❷ **Malaprops Bookstore and Café**, the city's gathering spot for intellectual lefties where there are not only two bookcases dedicated to "Green Living" but three shelves to "*Conscious* Green Living." From the bookstore, stop in at ❸ **Tupelo Honey Cafe**, which advertises itself as a down-home Southern restaurant with an uptown twist. Be prepared to wait, as this restaurant is packed and for good reason. Sure, it's got grits, but they're basil-infused, goat cheese grits topped with fried green tomato goodness. Try them with sides like honey-pickled beet salad and candied ginger cornbread.

After lunch, head down Haywood St to ❹ **Pritchard Park**. Popular with transients most of the week, each Friday night around 7pm the park explodes with more than 100 drummers, dancers, dread-wearers, hackeysack players and those wanting to commune with the rhythmic flow of the beat. Walk down Walnut St towards ❺ **Woolworth Walk**, an art gallery housing more than 150 artists' wares. The retro soda fountain is where the old Woolworth's Luncheonette used to be, and it still serves up low-priced sandwiches, egg creams and ice-cream

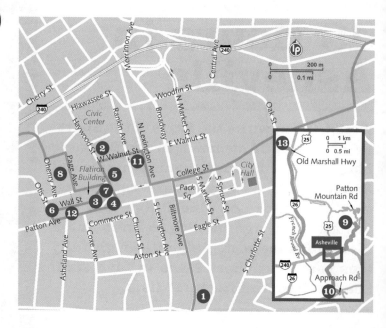

shakes. On the first Friday of the warmer months, Woolworth's is the gathering spot for the First Friday Art Walk. Head to ⑥ **Wall Street**, a bricked-over semi-pedestrianized street filled with shops and restaurants. The best of the bunch is the adorably delicious ⑦ **Early Girl Eatery**. A cross between a city diner and an organic farm restaurant, Early Girl has quickly become an institution for serving delightfully new "health" food such as biscuits with vegetarian herbed gravy alongside farmstead cheeseburgers slathered with basil mayo. Spend some time perusing the ⑧ **Grove Arcade**, the pinnacle of Asheville's art-deco architecture. Built by the Grove of the famed Grove Park Inn and Spa in 1929 but abandoned after World War II, the former public market reopened in 2002 filled with shops and restaurants, signaling the apex of Asheville's return to city-center culture.

> *"In the warmer months, it's the gathering spot for the First Friday Art Walk."*

There are dozens of B&Bs in town, but stay at ⑨ **Crooked Oak Mountain Inn** to appreciate the best of Asheville's lush surroundings only a seven-minute drive from downtown. The six-room B&B is set in a forested glen just past the Western Residence for North Carolina's governor and each room's windows look out to serene woods.

The must-see destination that put Asheville on the map is the 175,000-sq-ft ⑩ **Biltmore Estate**. The French chateau–style super-mega-mansion took six years to complete and required hundreds of artisans, craftsmen and educated professionals, many of whom made Asheville their permanent home. The Vanderbilt-Cecil family still owns the estate and, guessing by the entrance fee, the upkeep must be outrageously steep. Purchase your tickets after 3pm and you can return a second full day. In addition to the main house, four restaurants, an inn, a winery, gift shops, hiking trails, carriage rides, gardens and lakes provide a day's worth of activities.

After a day at the Biltmore, come back to town for a stroll and dinner. Stop in at ⑪ Nest Organics, the consumer culmination of Asheville's sustainability commitment. Protect the environment one hemp journal or steel sippy cup at a time. In the evening, relax at one of six local breweries, including ⑫ Jack of the Wood, which doubles as a live music venue serving casual pub fare. You can feel the connection to Asheville's original Scots-Irish settler heritage in the brew pub's camaraderie and twangy Celtic-influenced traditional music.

AMERICA'S FIRST NEW AGE TOWN

Before a family named Vanderbilt "discovered" the scenery, climate and fresh mountain air, Asheville was mostly an Appalachian livestock waystation. The 1960s town council almost razed the art-deco downtown (second only to Miami) to slap up a mall. Today, the livestock is usually found drizzled with locally grown raspberry coulis, the car repair shop is called OM (for Organic Mechanic, of course) and the neighborhood ecovillage teaches permaculture classes. Preservationists won the city center battle, and folks of all ages and hair color flock to its art, shopping and music scene.

Not a lot of cities offer a chance to sleep in the woods within a nine-minute drive of downtown. But this is Asheville, so not only can you camp nearby, you can stay in an honest-to-Mongolian-goodness yurt at ⑬ Campfire Lodgings. It blends the best of country camping (fire pits, mountain views, sweeping trees) and the city (minutes from downtown, free wi-fi, clean bathrooms). From downtown, take I-26 towards Weaverville.

Alex Leviton

CITY

TRIP INFORMATION

GETTING THERE
Asheville is a four-hour drive from Raleigh, due west through the Triad on I-40, and a little over two hours northwest of Charlotte.

DO
Biltmore Estate
An entire day's worth of architecture, history, scenery and a little 250-room summer house. ☎ 800-411-3812; www.biltmore.com; 1 Approach Rd, Asheville; adult/child/teen Sun-Fri $47/free/22.50, Sat $51/free/24.50; ☼ house 9am-5:30pm, restaurants & shops vary; ⚐

Grove Arcade
Locally made jewelry, clothes and furniture, plus restaurants, art deco architecture and a deli. ☎ 828-252-7799; www.grovearcade .com; 1 Page Ave, Asheville; ☼ core hours 10am-6pm Mon-Sat, noon-5pm Sun; ⚐

LaZoom Tours
Family friendly bio-diesel-fueled comedy tour of Asheville. ☎ 828-252-6932; www .lazoomtours.com; meets at French Broad Food Coop, 90 Biltmore Ave, Asheville; tours adult/child $22/12; ☼ 10:30am Tue, Wed & Fri; 6pm Thu & Sat May-Oct; ⚐

Malaprops Bookstore and Café
An independent bookstore with a popular café. ☎ 828-254-6734; www.malaprops .com; 55 Haywood St, Asheville; ☼ 8am-9pm Mon-Thu, to 10pm Fri & Sat, to 7pm Sun; ⚐

Nest Organics
Natural or organic bedding, towels and baby supplies. ☎ 828-258-1901; www.nest organics.com; 51 N Lexington Ave, Asheville; ☼ 11am-6pm Mon-Fri, to 7pm Sat, noon-4pm Sun; ⚐

Woolworth Walk
Start your foray into the Asheville art scene with more than 150 artists' displays in one gallery. ☎ 828-254-9234; www.woolworth walk.com; 25 Haywood St, Asheville; admission free; ☼ 11am-6pm Mon-Thu, to 7pm Fri & Sat, to 5pm Sun; ⚐

EAT & DRINK
Early Girl Eatery
Classic Southern diner fare with a farm-grown twist, especially good for breakfast. ☎ 828-259-9292; www.earlygirleatery.com; 8 Wall St, Asheville; mains $3-16; ☼ 7:30am-3pm Mon-Fri, 9am-3pm Sat & Sun, also 5-9pm Tue-Thu, 5-10pm Fri & Sat; ⚐

Jack of the Wood
Brew pub featuring local bands, pub fare and home-brewed beer. ☎ 828-252-5445; www .jackofthewood.com; 95 Patton Ave, Asheville; small plates $3.50-8.50; ☼ 11:30am-2am Mon-Sat, 3pm-close Sun

Tupelo Honey Cafe
Organic ingredients and delectable goat cheese grits; expect a wait. ☎ 828-255-4404; www.tupelohoneycafe.com; 12 College St, Asheville; mains $6.50-18; ☼ 9am-3pm Tue-Sun, also 5:30-10pm Tue-Thu, 5:30-11pm Fri & Sat; ⚐

SLEEP
Campfire Lodgings
Quiet, scenic campground with yurts, 10 minutes from downtown. ☎ 828-658-8012; www.campfirelodgings.com; 116 Appalachian Village Rd, Asheville; campsite $30-35, yurts & cabins $95-125; ⚐

Crooked Oak Mountain Inn
A peaceful retreat 3 miles from downtown. ☎ 828-252-9219; www.crookedoak mountaininn.com; 217 Patton Mountain Rd, Asheville; r $140-205

USEFUL WEBSITES
www.exploreasheville.com
www.foodtopiansociety.com

www.lonelyplanet.com/trip-planner

LINK YOUR TRIP

A Charleston Walk Back in Time

HISTORY & CULTURE

WHY GO With one of the largest historical districts in the world outside of Rome, Charleston is a city rooted in a romantic but bloody past. Civil War historian, author and tour guide Jack Thomson walks us through military forts, antebellum homes and a "new" Civil War discovery.

Few cities evoke the same storied romanticism as Charleston. While the days of hoop skirt and parasol-clad genteel Charlestonians sipping lemonade on the piazza have gone the way of the cotton gin, the magnificent city remains an elegant destination where visitors witness more than three centuries of American history.

Pipe your way into Charleston's military history on Friday afternoons at the ❶ Citadel. On most Friday afternoons during the school year, the famed military college of Charleston puts on a military dress parade, complete with a full display of its Regimental Pipe Band, open to the public. Afterwards, stop in the small ❷ museum to see 170 years of Citadel history.

Nearby is the popular ❸ Hominy Grill, which attracts mostly locals to its barn-inspired interior and relaxed back patio. Start with the popular okra and shrimp beignets with cilantro-lime salsa. Whatever main dish you get, be sure to order plenty of side "vegetables" which, in the South, means not only sweet yams and collard greens but macaroni and cheese or fried cheese grits.

Accommodations in Charleston are most definitely not cheap, so the ❹ Notso Hostel is both a rarity (a hostel! in the South!) and one of the few independent accommodations options charging less than $200 a room. Guests of all ages bunk in the back house dorm beds or the Civil War–era front house private rooms (all with shared bath), but

TIME
2 days

DISTANCE

BEST TIME TO GO
Mar – Jun, Oct & Nov

START
Charleston, SC

END
Charleston, SC

ALSO GOOD FOR

CITY

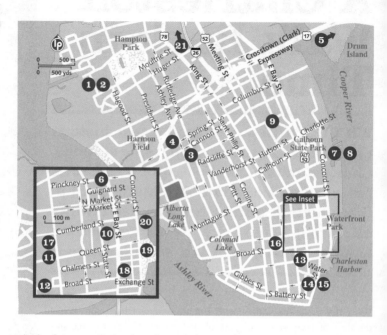

it's the front porch, free bicycles and shared continental breakfast that make this choice feel particularly homey.

Start your first morning with the Revolutionary War at **5** **Fort Moultrie**, across Hwy 17 on the Ravenel Bridge. It's named for Colonel William Moultrie who, on June 28, 1776, was the commander of this incomplete Palmetto log fort and whose flag became the South Carolina state flag. Four British frigates and a bomb ship pounded the fort for nine hours. The Patriot forces were victorious, leading to one of the first battles won by the rebels in the American Revolution. Today, the fort displays artifacts from America's seacoast defense history from the Revolutionary War to WWII.

"The days of parasol-clad genteel Charlestonians sipping lemonade have gone the way of the cotton gin."

To get a feel for the town, take a late-morning ride with **6** **Palmetto Carriage Works**. The family-run business offers tours on mule-drawn carriages out of a big red barn. The tour leaders are often young Charlestonian history majors, who bring the town to life while you and your carriage-mates (there's room for about eight to 10) go clopping through town.

See where the Civil War started at the **7** **Fort Sumter National Monument**. Stop in first at the Fort Sumter Visitor Education Center at the northern end of Concord St in Liberty Square, where you'll get an overview of the fort's history and see artifacts from its Civil War days. From there, you'll board a boat with ❽ **Fort Sumter Tours**, which will take you to the island fort. When newly elected Abraham Lincoln threatened the institution of slavery and states rights, South Carolina, which had built its rice and cotton plantation culture on the backs of West African slaves, was the first state to secede from the Union, paving the way for the Confederate States of America. After secession, Fort Sumter was in the hands of Union troops until President Lincoln sent a re-supply fleet. Confederate forces fired upon the fort in the early morning of April 12, 1861, the first event that led to the Civil War. Knowledgeable guides walk you through April 12, 1861 as you tour the well-preserved fort.

Back on the mainland, visit the impeccably preserved (not restored) ❾ **Aiken-Rhett House**, an Antebellum townhouse in the center of Charleston with a set of outbuildings, slave quarters (originally called "servants quarters") and sumptuously decorated European rooms. For the closest feel to a modern hoop skirt–and-parasol experience, dine that evening at ❿ **Magnolia's Uptown Down South**, acknowledged as kicking off the Charleston foodie revolution of the 1980s. Sure, you could go for the risotto or arugula salad, but this is the place to try classic Southern traditions – pimiento cheese and flatbread or shellfish and grits. A less-expensive lunch option offers sandwiches like fried shrimp po'boy with jalapeño peach coleslaw.

To see a different perspective of Charleston, start your second morning with a ⓫ **Civil War Walking Tour**, led by our expert author himself. Meet inside the Mills House Hotel at 9am sharp for the daily tour. A treasure-trove of living history, Jack Thomson's collection of stories, anecdotes and Civil War photography bring the subject to life for tour participants. Thomson brings along his book, *Charleston at War*, to show participants that Confederate Charleston buildings are still here. For lunch, try ⓬ **Fast & French**, also known as Gaulart et Maliclet, usually filled with more lawyers and office workers than tourists. Diners at long communal tables snack on goat cheese and black olive open-faced baguettes or escargot (vegetarian available!) in buttery garlic.

Take a walking tour of the downtown historic homes, including ⓭ **Heyward-Washington House**, known as Charleston's Revolutionary War house, as it was built in 1772 and rented to George Washington for a week in 1792. Home decor fans will appreciate some of the finest examples of colonial-era furniture in the US. Step forward in time a bit to visit ⓮ **Edmondston-Alston House**, the first house built on Charleston's High Battery, in 1825. The home still has some of its original furniture and silver. On the same lot is ⓯ **21 East Battery Bed & Breakfast**. Brick walls, low-beamed ceilings and a full selection of cheese, fruit and snacks await those looking for a romantic spot. Another historic inn nearby is ⓰ **John Rutledge House Inn**, home to

HISTORY & CULTURE

a signatory to the Constitution. George Washington wrote in his diary about eating breakfast here, and the restored rooms and elegant common space evoke the colonial time when the inn was built. Dine at ⑰ **Poogan's Porch**, home of everything good about Lowcountry cuisine – fried alligator and she-crab soup, biscuits and Kahlua pecan pie.

For some Revolutionary War history, stop in at the ⑱ **Old Exchange and Provost Dungeon**, which housed both pirates and Revolutionary War heroes in its day. Relax at ⑲ **Waterfront Park** along Concord St to picnic, swing or walk along the water (playing in the fountain is encouraged). If you haven't had enough of the view, stick around for dinner at ⑳ **Fleet Landing Restaurant**. The retired naval building dates back to the 1940s as part of the former naval yard, but now enlists diners with crab-stuffed hush puppies and fried oysters in Southern Comfort BBQ sauce.

ASK A LOCAL

"The most romantic Civil War relic ever found is the coin found in the boot of the *Hunley's* captain, George E Dixon. Dixon's girlfriend, Miss Queenie Bennett of Mobile, gave him a 20-gold piece in case he got captured. At the battle of Shiloh, Dixon was shot in the leg. However, the bullet hit his gold piece, denting the coin but saving his leg. When they found the *Hunley*, the submarine was chock full of sand, preserving everything, including the bodies. There, slipped down beneath Dixon's boot, was Queenie's gold coin, still dented, but with the inscription 'Shiloh, April 12, 1862, GED, My life preserver.'"
Jack Thomson, Civil War historian

In the morning, head up Hwy 26 to North Charleston to visit ㉑ **HL Hunley**. It's not often there's a "new" Civil War discovery, especially when it's a submarine. Yes, you heard that right. In 1861, two Confederate steam gauge manufacturers teamed up with Horace L Hunley, a Louisiana businessman, to create an underwater secret weapon. The hand-cranked craft was the only underwater vessel to sink an enemy ship up until World War I. The museum is a working archaeological site, and visitors get to peer into the 90,000-gallon tank at the *Hunley*, where eight very tightly cramped men sunk USS *Housitonic* in six minutes.
Alex Leviton

TRIP INFORMATION

GETTING THERE
From Raleigh, take I-40 to I-95 towards Benson/Fayetteville. After 194 miles on I-95, take exit 86A to I-26 east. Take exit 221B to reach the Visitors Center and the downtown area.

DO

Aiken-Rhett House
An intact example of an antebellum Charleston home. ☎ 843-723-1159; www.historiccharleston.org; 48 Elizabeth St, Charleston; adult/child $10/6; ☽ 10am-5pm Mon-Sat, 2-5pm Sun

Citadel
The South Carolina military college, founded in 1842. ☎ 843-953-6846; www.citadel.edu; 171 Moultrie St, Charleston; admission free; ☽ parades 3:45pm or 4:20pm most Fri during semester, museum 2-5pm Sun-Fri, noon-5pm Sat; ♿

Civil War Walking Tour
Time-travel back to Charleston in the 1860s with a military buff and Civil War reenactor. ☎ 843-270-2417; www.civilwarwalk.com; Mills House Hotel, cnr Meeting & Queen St, Charleston; adult/child $20/free; ☽ 9am Mar-Dec, private tours also avail; ♿

Edmondston-Alston House
A Greek Revival house from 1825, complete with period furnishings and an intact library. ☎ 843-722-7171; www.middletonplace.org; 21 E Battery St, Charleston; adult/child $10/8; ☽ 10am-4:30pm Tue-Sat, 1:30-4:30pm Sun & Mon; ♿

Fort Moultrie
Site of one of the first battles in the American Revolution, the fort was a seacoast defense outpost until WWII. ☎ 843-883-3123; www.nps.gov/fomo/home.htm; 1214 Middle St, Sullivan's Island; adult/child/family $3/free/5; ☽ 9am-5pm; ♿

Fort Sumter Tours
Tours to Fort Sumter depart from Liberty Sq in downtown Charleston, as well as the aircraft carrier in Mt Pleasant. ☎ 843-883-3123; www.spiritlinecruises.comand; 340 Concord St, Charleston; adult/child $14/8.50; ☽ 10am-5pm, seasonal variations; ♿

Heyward-Washington House
More than 200 years of history, including a stay by George Washington. ☎ 843-722-2996; www.charlestonmuseum.org; 87 Church St, Charleston; adult/child $10/5; ☽ 10am-5pm Mon-Sat, 1-5pm Sun; ♿

HL Hunley
A working underwater archaeological site of a Civil War submarine with a museum and gift shop. ☎ 877-448-6539; www.hunley.org; 1250 Supply St, N Charleston; admission $12; ☽ 10am-5pm Sat, noon-5pm Sun; ♿

Old Exchange and Provost Dungeon
Notwithstanding kid-friendly animatronic characters, adults can appreciate one of the most important Colonial buildings still standing. ☎ 843-727-2165; www.oldexchange.com; 122 E Bay St, Charleston; adult/child $7/3.50; ☽ 9am-5pm; ♿

Palmetto Carriage Works
Get a bird's-eye view of Charleston on a one-hour tour through the historic business or residential areas. ☎ 843-723-8145; www.carriagetour.com; 40 N Market St, Charleston; adult/child $20/10; ♿

EAT

Fast & French
More French than fast, the long communal table that began as an experiment is now a local favorite. ☎ 843-577-9797; www.fastandfrench.org; 98 Broad St, Charleston; snacks & light meals $4-15; ☽ 8am-4pm Mon, to 10pm Tue-Thu, to 10:30pm Fri & Sat

Fleet Landing Restaurant
Decent food but a spectacular view at this maritime-themed waterfront eatery in a former naval building. ☎ 843-722-8100; www.fleetlanding.net; 186 Concord St, Charleston; mains $7-23; ☽ 11am-10pm Mon-Thu, to 11pm Fri, 11am-3pm & 5-11pm Sat, 11am-3pm & 5-10pm Sun; ♿

Hominy Grill
Local ingredients turn inventive Southern cuisine into a destination. ☎ 843-937-0930; www.hominygrill.com; 207 Rutledge St, Charleston; mains $7-17; ☽ 7:30am-8:30pm Mon-Fri, 9am-3pm Sat & Sun; ♿

HISTORY & CULTURE

Magnolia's Uptown Down South
Casual but elegant take on Southern fare.
☎ 843-577-7771; www.magnolias-blossom
-cypress.com; 185 E Bay St, Charleston;
mains $10-36; ⏲ 11:30am-9:45pm Mon-
Thu, to 10:45pm Fri & Sat, 11am-3:45pm Sun

Poogan's Porch
Classic Southern fare in a classic Charlestonian Victorian. ☎ 843-577-2337; www
.poogansporch.com; 72 Queen St, Charleston;
mains $12-24; ⏲ 11:30am-3pm & 5-9:30pm
Mon-Sat, 9am-3pm Sun; ♿

SLEEP

21 East Battery Bed and Breakfast
Invitingly warm rooms mirror the historic Edmondston-Alston House. ☎ 843-556-0500;

www.21eastbattery.com; 21 East Battery St,
Charleston; r $250-395

John Rutledge House Inn
In a house old enough to have hosted George
Washington for breakfast, there are 19
historic rooms in an elegant setting. ☎ 843-
723-7999; www.johnrutledgehouseinn.com;
116 Broad St, Charleston; r $205-405

Notso Hostel
A little less than a mile from the historic
downtown with laundry facilities and free
wi-fi. ☎ 843-722-8383; www.notsohostel
.com; 156 Spring St, Charleston; dorms $21,
r $60

USEFUL WEBSITES
www.charlestoncvb.com

LINK YOUR TRIP
www.lonelyplanet.com/trip-planner

Ashley River Plantations

WHY GO Haven't seen an alligator in the wild yet? Want to see what plantation life was like, and hear about it from the descendants of slaves? Three historic plantations and two historic sites less than an hour from Charleston offer a fascinating glimpse into South Carolina's past.

TIME
2 days

DISTANCE
43 miles

BEST TIME TO GO
Apr – Jun

START
Ashley River Rd , SC

END
Summerville, SC

ALSO GOOD FOR

Start your tour of the historic Ashley River Rd at the site of the first successful colony in the Carolinas, the ❶ **Charles Towne Landing State Historic Site**. In 1670, the ship *Carolina* arrived from England by way of Barbados, where its passengers had learned the ins and outs of managing sugar plantations and utilizing slaves. The area they settled became the first plantation in the American South and a model for a way of life that persisted until Reconstruction. Nowadays, the site has an interactive museum, 664 acres of grounds to explore, unspoiled wetlands and a full-scale, dry-docked 18th-century trading vessel. From Charleston, take Hwy 26 to exit 216A (Cosgrove Rd), then follow signposts. *Alligator count: four adults, half a dozen babies.*

Backtrack slightly onto Old Towne Rd to Ashley River Rd for ❷ **Drayton Hall**. The genteel, stately home is the oldest preserved plantation in the US open to the public. In 2008, Drayton Hall teamed up with producers from Discovery Channel to create *The Voices of Drayton Hall*. As you tour the home and grounds of the circa 1738 home, listen to stories on a portable DVD player from former residents, descendants of the Drayton family and their slaves. Even without the DVD, the highly learned tour guides – almost all with advanced degrees in history – are fonts of information about the almost perfectly preserved structure. *Alligator count: about two dozen.*

Plan on spending the afternoon and evening at ❸ **Middleton Place**, a former plantation that's now a museum complex just north on Ashley

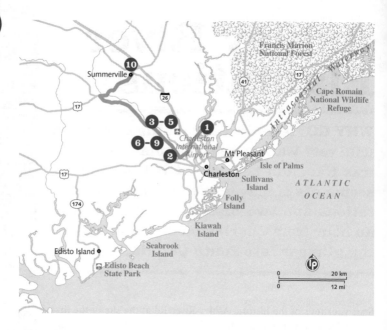

River Rd from Drayton Hall. If the name Middleton sounds familiar, you might remember that Arthur Middleton signed the Declaration of Independence. And, as invading Union troops duly noted 89 years later, Williams Middleton signed the Ordinance of Secession, which led to the creation of the Confederacy. When Charleston was ransacked in 1865, Middleton Place was burned to a crisp by the Union Army. Today, it's the guesthouse that houses the museum, but also spend a few hours strolling through the stables, where artisans in period costume show how African slaves kept the plantation running, or take a carriage ride through wild woodlands. *Alligator count: About 200.*

Feeling hungry yet? There's no need to leave for lunch or dinner, as the ❹ Restaurant at Middleton Place is on the plantation grounds, overlooking the scenic Rice Mill Pond. Delicious meals are reminiscent of Lowcountry cuisine a generation ago, but with a modern twist. Follow she-crab or okra soup with main courses such as pan-seared quail (updated with thyme and white grapes) or shrimp, crawfish and scallops with grits. You could have something besides the Carolina Gold rice pudding for dessert, but why bother? You can visit the restaurant for dinner without paying the admission fee for the plantation. Walk off your meal on your way to your hotel, the ❺ Inn at Middleton Place. Owned by the foundation that operates Middleton Place, the inn is a surprising twist of modernist architecture in a decidedly historic setting. All 52 rooms have full-length windows with, of course, plantation shutters that overlook the Ashley River. The foundation is committed to a green hotel, so each room has recycling, shower dispensers instead of travel-sized containers and locally handmade soap. There are yoga classes and a full breakfast. *Alligator count: two dozen.*

You'll need an entire day for the next destination, ❻ **Magnolia Plantation and Gardens**. Like an Antebellum Disneyland, Magnolia has dozens of "rides," activities and locations. Admission buys you entrance to the grounds, and you can then choose whether to take an additional house tour, ❼ **nature boat tour** or ❽ **nature train tour**. The grounds encompass a vast expanse of wetlands and forests, so either one of the tours can be a fabulous way to traverse a mile or two and rest your weary feet. In addition to the plantation house tour itself, the list of possibilities is endless – a biblical garden, bamboo forest, camellia maze, and a slave cabin tour. Oh, and did we also mention the zoo, Revolutionary War reenactments, never-ending gift store and tropical garden? Take a rest mid-day at the plantation's on-site restaurant, the casual, outdoor ❾ **Peacock Café**. It's suitably named, as you will be dining with the beautiful (but loud – very, very loud) creatures. Specialty sandwiches come with side salads, and there are hot dogs and PB&J sandwiches for the kids (and pecan or key lime pie for everyone). *Alligator count: more than 500.*

ASK A LOCAL

"Growing up, we listened to many stories from our grandfather, Willis Johnson, who was born a free man, son of slaves, at Drayton Hall. We finally visited with our great uncle Richmond Bowens in 1974. Can you imagine the footsteps we feel there? We feel them walking around us and we feel their presence in the cemetery. We're about to have our third reunion with the Draytons, and it will be a memorial for Richmond Bowens. We're working with Drayton Hall to enhance the African-American cemetery, which will be open so our ancestors' spirits can enter in and out freely."

Rebecca Campbell (b 1935) & Catherine Braxton (b 1937), descendants of the Bowens family

"Magnolia Plantation and Gardens… alligator count: more than 500."

That evening, stop for a picnic or a walk at ❿ **Dorchester State Historic Park**. Follow Ashley River Rd to its northern end, then bear right on Bacon's Bridge Rd. Dorchester is a lovely city park with a twist: an active archaeological dig where you might mingle with working archaeologists. Stop at the visitor's center to pick up a visitor's guide and follow the trail past remnants of the old town, including a church wall from 1719. *Alligator count: zero.*

Alex Leviton

TRIP INFORMATION

GETTING THERE
Ashley River Rd is just northwest of downtown Charleston. From I-526, take exit 11B towards Ashley River Rd/Hwy 61.

DO
Charles Towne Landing State Historic Site
Come see where it all started, way back in 1670. ☎ 843-852-4200; www.southcarolinaparks.com; 1500 Old Towne Rd, Charleston; adult/child $5/3; ☎ 9am-5pm; ♿

Dorchester State Historic Park
A city park with more than 300 years of history. ☎ 843-873-1740; www.southcarolinaparks.com; 300 State Park Rd, Summerville; adult $2; ☎ 9am-6pm; ♿

Drayton Hall
The most informative and museum-like of the three Ashley River plantations. ☎ 843-769-2600; www.draytonhall.org; 3380 Ashley River Rd, Charleston; adult/child/youth $14/6/8, DVD $7; ☎ 8:30am-5pm, to 4pm Nov-Feb; ♿

Magnolia Plantation and Gardens
The third plantation with a full day's activities. ☎ 800-367-3517; www.magnoliaplantation.com; 3550 Ashley River Rd, Charleston; adult/child $15/10, house tours $7; ☎ 8am-dusk incl holidays, shorter winter hours; ♿

Magnolia Plantation Nature Boat Tour
There's almost a guaranteed alligator spotting on each trip into the rice-growing wetlands. ☎ 800-367-3517; www.magnoliaplantation.com; 3550 Ashley River Rd, Charleston; adult & child/child under 6 $7/free; ☎ hourly from 9am Mar-Nov; ♿

Magnolia Plantation Nature Train Tour
A one-hour tour into the further reaches of the vast plantation. ☎ 800-367-3517; www.magnoliaplantation.com; 3550 Ashley River Rd, Charleston; adult/child under 6/child $7/3/5; ☎ half-hourly from 9am; ♿

Middleton Place
One of Charleston's most prominent family homes. ☎ 843-556-6020; www.middletonplace.org; 4300 Ashley River Rd; adult/child $25/5, house tours $10, carriage rides $15; ☎ 9am-5pm; ♿

EAT
Peacock Café
Outdoor casual dining at Magnolia Plantation serving breakfast, lunch and light fare. ☎ 800-367-3517; www.magnoliaplantation.com; 3550 Ashley River Rd, Charleston; mains $5-11; ☎ 8am-dusk incl holidays, shorter winter hours; ♿

Restaurant at Middleton Place
Lowcountry cuisine like mama, grandma and great-grandma used to make. ☎ 843-556-8020 ext118; www.middletonplace.org; 4300 Ashley River Rd; ☎ 11am-3pm, also 6-8pm Tue-Thu & Sun, 6-9pm Fri & Sat; ♿

SLEEP
Inn at Middleton Place
Modern structures in a historic setting, equally elegant and peaceful. ☎ 843-556-0500; www.theinnatmiddletonplace.com; 4290 Ashley River Rd; r $179-280, ste $400-500

LINK YOUR TRIP
www.lonelyplanet.com/trip-planner

South Carolina Swamps

WHY GO From the coast to Congaree National Park, this nature tour of the Palmetto State's wetlands (the politically correct term for swamp) takes you through wild bald cypress and tupelo forests and protected floodplains – seen best on naturalist-led canoe tours – with a stopover at a riverfront Trappist monastery.

TIME
3 days

DISTANCE
209 miles

BEST TIME TO GO
Feb – Jun

START
Charleston, SC

END
Santee, SC

Leave behind the urban hubbub of Charleston for the untamed backcountry of swamps and wetlands. Just before heading out of town, make your first stop on your swamp tour the ❶ **Audubon Swamp Garden** at ❷ **Magnolia Plantation**, one of the Ashley River Rd plantations. A series of boardwalks, dikes and bridges leads visitors on a self-guided tour through terrain so perfectly swampy that Wes Craven filmed a slithering Adrienne Barbeau here in *The Swamp Thing* (1982). It's still possible to see the great blue heron, river otters and alligators that brought James John Audubon on his own visit 150 years ago. Venture north on Hwy 17 for lunch at the delectable ❸ **SeeWee Restaurant**. All manner of fried seafood and shellfish are on the menu (as are grape Nehis and glass bottles of cherry Coke for the nostalgic crowd), but be sure to try the signature she-crab soup.

Whether you have a few hours or five days, hook up with ❹ **Nature Adventures Outfitters**, the modern swamp foxes of the area. If you want to float through a swamp, these are your people. The organization runs hundreds of trips throughout every inch of swamp country, from two-hour tours near Moncks Corner to overnight trips near the Santee Coastal Reserve. They're based in the ❺ **Francis Marion National Forest**, named for the Revolutionary War hero better known as the Swamp Fox, who used these 400,000 acres of wild forest to evade and outwit British troops.

BEST TRIP

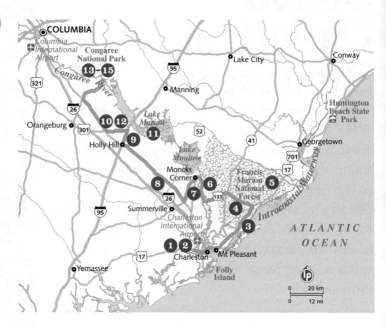

The next day, start your day at ❻ **Mepkin Abbey**, a Trappist monastery located on the Cooper River off Hwy 402 toward, coincidentally, Moncks Corner. A former plantation with roots dating back to 1681, the meditative garden is from the 1930s, when Henry and Clare Boothe Luce bought and refurbished the property. The gift shop and gardens are open daily, but plan your visit around the 11:30am monk-led tour, as participants are invited to join in prayers afterwards.

RETREAT

Mepkin Abbey invites those looking for a spiritual retreat to spend a few days in its simple lodgings. You'll share the same schedule with the monks (including 3am wake-up calls), but as only one of around 100 monasteries in the USA, it's rare to find such a relaxing spot.

Continue on Hwy 402 to Hwy 52 and follow signs for ❼ **Cypress Gardens**. Like a miniature zoo and swamp tour rolled into one, the park is especially popular with little ones. Join an hourly guided tour or take out a flat-bottom boat on your own. Either way, the low country black water swamplands are some of the most scenic in South Carolina, even with the built-up picnic areas and gift shop. Be sure to check out the butterfly house and tiny alligator zoo.

The next swamp stop is the ❽ **Audubon Center at Beidler Forest**. The Audubon society has purchased 15,000 acres of protected floodplains to study and preserve for generations to come. Miles of boardwalk crisscross the swampy plains, home to many an alligator. To see the area up close, arrive at 1pm for a guided canoe trip. For lunch, continue into Holly Hill to eat at **9** **Sweatman's Bar-b-que** and discover how good organic meat can taste. Reputed to be one of the best BBQ joints in the state, the American flag and giant pig sign lure you in to this former home where the recipes for tender and sticky ribs, cracklin' liver hash and pit-cooked pig haven't changed for a generation or two. Be warned: Sweatman's is *only* open on Friday and Saturday.

"The most politically correct of the swamps, Congaree isn't even a wetland."

Bring your fishing poles to **10** **Santee State Park**, where the expansive **11** **Lake Marion** hosts boaters and anglers year-round to catch their future campfire dinners, including catfish, bass and trout. Book in advance at the popular **12** **Cypress View Campground** on the banks of Lake Marion. For those who don't want to rough it in a tent, the yurt-like "rondettes" – several of which overlook the lake – are equipped with creature comforts like beds, heat and air conditioning, and a small kitchen. Ask at the park's tackle shop for the pontoon boat tour schedule, usually on Wednesdays and weekends, depending on the season.

Towards the center of the state is **13** **Congaree National Park**. The most politically correct of the swamps, Congaree isn't even a wetland, it's an "old-growth floodplain forest," the tallest deciduous forest east of the Mississippi with swathes of cypress, loblolly, tupelo and pine trees. The technical difference is that a swamp stays wet throughout the year but a floodplain dries up. Stop in first at the **14** **Harry Hampton Visitors Center** to pick up maps and sign up for any number of daily activities, from weekend night Owl Prowls to guided nature walks, all free courtesy of the Department of the Interior. For a guided canoe trip, call two weeks in advance for a reservation. In addition to a park policy allowing backcountry camping, Congaree has two designated **15** campgrounds. From Old Bluff Rd, turn left at the first stop sign into the After Hours Parking Lot, about 0.75

"One thing I love about working at Congaree National Park is when the fireflies synchronize their blinking for a couple of weeks in late spring. This phenomenon only happens in a few places in the whole world. Imagine being out on one of our night walks and discovering yourself surrounded by thousands of living lights all pulsating together. It's our own little firefly rave!"

Heather Schorge, park ranger, Congaree National Park, SC

miles down National Park Rd. Be prepared for a little death-defying adventure with your camping: you might have to avoid flooded campsites, fight off snakes and avoid poisonous plants. But the rewards of waking up underneath Spanish moss-draped trees is worth it.

Alex Leviton

TRIP INFORMATION

GETTING THERE

From Raleigh, take I-40 to I-95, then skirt Columbia onto Hwy 77 to exit 6.

DO

Audubon Center at Beidler Forest

A 2-mile stretch of boardwalk through 15,000 acres of swamplands. ☎ 843-462-2150; www.beidlerforest.com; 336 Sanctuary Rd, Harleyville; adult/child $7/3.50; ⏰ 9am-5pm Tue-Sun; ♿

Audubon Swamp Garden

A black water swamp with cypress gum and tupelo trees. ☎ 800-367-3517; www.magnoliaplantation.com; 3550 Ashley River Rd, Charleston; swamp tour adult/child $7/6; ⏰ 8am-5:30pm; ♿

Cypress Gardens

A family-friendly, all-in-one swamp tour destination. ☎ 843-553-0515; www.cypressgardens.info; 3030 Cypress Gardens Rd, Moncks Corner; adult/child $10/5; ⏰ 9am-5pm; ♿

Harry Hampton Visitor Center at Congaree National Park

A cadre of information about Congaree National Park leading to miles of elevated trails. ☎ 803-776-4396; www.nps.gov/cong; 100 National Park Rd, Hopkins; admission free; ⏰ 8:30am-5pm, to 7pm Fri & Sat summer; ♿

Mepkin Abbey

Walk the garden or stay for a personal retreat. ☎ 843-761-8509; www.mepkinabbey.org; 1098 Mepkin Abbey Rd, Moncks Corner; tour adult/student & child $5/free; ⏰ 9am-4:30pm Tue-Sat, 1-4:30pm Sun, docent-led tours 11:30am & 3pm Mon-Sat, 11:30am Sun; ♿

Nature Adventures Outfitters

Experience wetlands, swamps *and* floodplains on a guided tour, overnight trip or 3-day retreat. ☎ 800-673-0679; www.natureadventuresoutfitters.com; 1900 Iron Swamp Rd, Awendaw; kayak tours adult/child from $39/27; ⏰ 7am-7pm; ♿

Santee State Park

Fishing, boating, hiking and relaxing are the most popular pastimes here. ☎ 866-345-PARK; www.southcarolinaparks.com; 251 State Park Rd, Santee; admission free; ♿

EAT

SeeWee Restaurant

Over 50 years of serving up fried seafood, she-crab soup and grape Nehi sodas. ☎ 843-928-3609; www.seeweerestaurant.com; 4808 Hwy 17 N, Awendaw; mains $5-19; ⏰ 11am-9pm Mon-Thu, 11am-9:30pm Fri, 8am-9:30pm Sat, 11am-3pm Sun; ♿

Sweatman's Bar-b-que

Fall-off-the-bone good 'cue, but remember it's *only* open Friday and Saturday (plus closed for holidays in August). ☎ 803-492-7543; 1313 Gemini Blvd, Hwy 453, Holly Hill; buffet $8; ⏰ 11:30am-9pm Fri & Sat; ♿

SLEEP

Congaree National Park campgrounds

Bare-bones camping under Spanish mossed-draped cypresses. ☎ 803-776-4396; www.nps.gov/cong; 100 National Park Rd, Hopkins; campsite free; ⏰ 9am-5pm; ♿

Cypress View Campground

Reserve popular swamp-front cabins and campsites at Santee State Park far in advance. ☎ 866-345-PARK; www.southcarolinaparks.com; 251 State Park Rd, Santee; campsite $15, rondette $80-120; ♿

USEFUL WEBSITES

www.audubon.org

www.southcarolinaparks.com

www.lonelyplanet.com/trip-planner

LINK YOUR TRIP

TRIP

Myrtle Beach & the Grand Strand

WHY GO Driving the 60-mile stretch of South Carolina shore known as the Grand Strand is like taking a tour through time. On the northern end, the thumping, neon-lit nightclubs of Myrtle Beach are pure 21st-century excess. Further south, tranquil Pawleys Island and Georgetown retain their 19th-century rhythms.

Start your Grand Strand tour just over the North Carolina border in the town of ❶ Calabash, so famous for its fried seafood that "Calabash-style" dishes can be found at buffets throughout the Southeast. In a small, featureless bunker, ❷ Seafood Hut serves huge, cheap platters of briny fried oysters, popcorn shrimp and deviled crab, with dozens of crispy, sweetish hush puppies in a basket on the side. Wash it all down with some sugary tea then cruise the gift shops for starfish paperweights and ships in bottles.

A little further south, the high-rise condos of ❸ Myrtle Beach waver in the heat like mirages. Believe it or not, Myrtle Beach was once a low-key vacation spot where a working-class family could rent a cabin and spend the summer swimming, eating saltwater taffy and listening to the old band organ at the Pavilion. These days, most of the waving palmetto trees and family-run motels have been replaced by Dairy Queens and outlet malls the size of small cities. In high season, the air is thick with the smell of coconut suntan oil and cigarettes and funnel cake. Teenagers run shrieking down the boardwalk, herds of grannies troll the year-round Christmas ornament shops, grizzled bikers in leather vests cause Harley traffic jams in the middle of downtown. Everywhere you look there's a seafood buffet as long as a bowling alley, a tropical drink the color of kryptonite, a sign offering a free hermit crab with every purchase. Lose your highbrow tendencies and you're bound to have a blast.

TIME
3 – 4 days

DISTANCE
65 miles

BEST TIME TO GO
May – Sep

START
Calabash, NC

END
Georgetown, SC

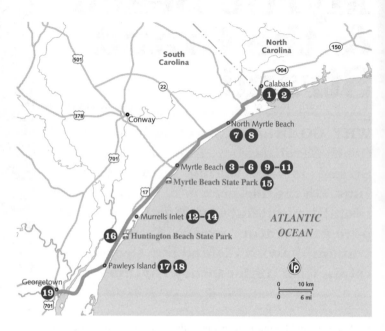

The town is easy to navigate. Kings Hwy, also known as Business 17, is the main drag, running straight through downtown parallel to the beach. Though it hardly seems like the main attraction, the **4** beach itself is lovely – wide, white and dotted with a rainbow of umbrellas. Snag a metered parking spot and head straight for the sand for an afternoon of reading cheap romance novels and floating in the warm Gulf Stream waters.

Drowsy from the sun, revive yourself with a brisk game of mini-golf, the quintessential Myrtle Beach activity. The city bills itself as the "Mini-Golf Capital of America," with a pirate-, jungle- or dinosaur-themed course every half block.

"The evening spectacular has been known to cause glitter-related blindness."

5 **Dragon's Lair Fantasy Golf**, at the 350-acre Broadway at the Beach shopping and entertainment complex, features an animatronic fire-breathing dragon. Afterwards browse the 100-plus outlet stores, grab a bucket-sized margarita, ride the carousel, sing karaoke or catch an IMAX flick, all without leaving the premises. Toss some pellets from the coin-operated fish food machines into the artificial river, and watch an army of chubby carp churn up a froth of white water and fins.

The evening spectacular at **6** **Dolly Parton's Dixie Stampede** has been known to cause glitter-related blindness. A thousand audience members dine on chicken and biscuits in an indoor arena as they watch the multi-act extravaganza on the stage floor. See stampeding buffalo, men riding ostriches, piglets dressed in red, white and blue, Southern belles "flying" from piano wires. There's simply nothing quite like it (except the other two locations, in Pigeon Forge, TN, and Branson, MO).

For nightlife without the wet T-shirt contests and Jell-O shots, backtrack a bit to the nearby town of **7** **North Myrtle Beach**, home of the shag. The dance, that is. A type of swing dance set to easygoing 1950s R&B, the shag was born here around World War II and remains massively popular. Take a free lesson on Tuesday night at **8** **Fat Harold's Beach Club**, where the spirited shaggers know all the moves – many of them have been coming here for decades. Get ready to shimmy amidst a bevy of beehived, Tom Collins-toting retirees.

Sleep in the heart of it all at the enormous **9** **Landmark Resort**, featuring its own tiki-themed water park and modern, rather tasteful rooms and efficiencies with kitchenettes. A full menu of activities, from beach kickball to tie-dying, give the place a summer-camp vibe. In the morning, grab coffee and a doughnut at one of the approximately 30,000 doughnut shops lining Kings Hwy (some are open 24 hours; you've got to love that).

> **ASK A LOCAL**
>
> "During our teenage years many of the guys and gals found summer jobs on the beaches along the eastern coast from Virginia Beach to the Carolinas: as lifeguards, working the hot dog stands, whatever they could find. These 'beach bums' didn't like the fast, jerky, jumping moves of the jitterbug and started doing the dance in a cool, slow, sexy manner. The shag is a smooth, sexy version of the old jitterbug."
>
> *Ellen Taylor, shag instructor, Myrtle Beach, SC*

10 **Myrtle Beach Water Sports** rents jet skis and pontoon boats for cruising the warm agate seas. A parasailing trip will put a smile on the most cynical of faces. Strap into the hanging seats and feel yourself lifted by the wind in your parachute, high enough above the waves to practically see into the hotel penthouse windows.

Continue the fun at **11** **Family Kingdom**, an amusement and water park. Old-fashioned rides like the Tilt-A-Whirl and Dodgem bumper cars, all lit up with neon at night, give the midway a 1950s carnival vibe. White-knuckle the rattling turns of the historic wooden Swamp Fox roller coaster, and snap a picture of the city skyline from the top of the giant Ferris wheel. The adjoining water park features flume rides and a lazy river, practically on the beach.

Though Myrtle Beach features what is possibly the highest concentration of seafood buffets in the known universe, you've got to head a little bit out of town to find quality over quantity. The nearby fishing village of **12** **Murrells Inlet**, about 17 miles to the south, has a row of popular family-run seafood restaurants, some of which have been operating for more than 50 years. At

⓭ **Russell's Seafood Grill**, in a rambling wooden building, locals hang out on the porch sipping beer while a singer-songwriter plays for tips in the corner. Stick with raw offerings and fried and true classics like popcorn shrimp.

Head down the street to sip an Inland Sunset (Smirnoff Orange, orange and grapefruit juices) in the sultry pink dusk at ⓮ **Dead Dog Saloon**. Popular with a somewhat older crew of Hawaiian shirt–wearing partiers, the Dead Dog occupies a huge building overlooking the inlet, with a big porch, hammocks and a horseshoe pit. There's live music nearly every night. Just don't forget the bug spray – mosquitoes in this neck of the woods are bigger than squirrels.

The next morning, seek refuge in nature at ⓯ **Myrtle Beach State Park**. A dim maritime forest of wax myrtles and knobby magnolias gives way to sunny, picnic-worthy fields and a wide sandy beach. Families fish off the long, worn wooden pier with bait bought at the park snack shop and pitch tents at the nearby campground. Hike the mile-long Sculpted Oak and Yaupon Trails for a bit of solitude and bird-watching.

Back to the south, ⓰ **Brookgreen Gardens** can only be described as a fairyland. Created by railroad scion Archer Huntington and his wife, sculptor Anna Vaughn Hyatt Huntington, this 9000-acre preserve sits on four former rice plantations. Wander paths abloom with honeysuckle, azalea and oleander beneath arches of ancient oaks shrouded in Spanish moss. The gardens contain the largest collection of American sculpture in the country, more than 1200 works of stone, marble and metal in all. Many works by Huntington, who specialized in equine statues, are on display. Don't miss the violent energy of her *Fighting Stallions* fountain. The on-site Lowcountry Zoo showcases the animals of the Carolina coast, with bald eagles, otters and white-tailed deer. Board a pontoon boat for a guided tour of the marshes, home to gator and waterfowl. With all that, it's a good thing admission tickets are valid for seven days.

MYRTLE BEACH BIKE WEEK

Noticing signs on hotels and restaurants saying "Bikers Welcome" or, conversely, "No Bikers"? Warm weather and lack of helmet laws have made Myrtle Beach a mecca for motorcycle enthusiasts. More than 300,000 riders vroom into town each May for **Bike Week** (www.myrtle beachbikeweek.com), an orgy of tequila, leather and blondes in bikinis. Take a deep breath and buy a beer for that scowling giant with the skull tattoo – he probably knows where all the best parties are.

Fifteen minutes down Hwy 17 is ⓱ **Pawleys Island**, a narrow four-mile strip of comfortably shabby beach cottages. Once a refuge for 18th-century rice planters who came here to escape the malaria-ridden mainland summers, Pawleys still has the laid-back vibe of an earlier era. Nothing brings you back down to earth after a few days at Myrtle Beach like an afternoon of kayaking through the coffee-colored waters of the salt marsh or climbing onto the rocky jetty to watch a summer storm over the Atlantic. Buy a bunch of chicken necks at the grocery store to use for bait and cast a crabbing line off the dock. The island has a hotel and a B&B, but the ideal way to experience Pawleys is by renting your own cottage. ⑱ **Pawleys Island Realty** rents houses and condos large and small, though you often have to book for a whole week during high season.

Finish your trip with a morning jaunt to blushingly beautiful ⑲ **Georgetown**, another 15 minutes further south. South Carolina's third-oldest town was a thriving port long before America was a country. Now faded into a pleasantly sleepy old age, Georgetown makes a nice stop for lunch and a stroll through the gardenia-scented lanes. Drive along streets shaded by massive oaks, gawking at colonnaded mansions once owned by area merchants and indigo planters. The rainbow-colored 19th-century storefronts of Front St, overlooking the bay, practically beg you to take their picture.

Emily Matchar

SEASIDE SHOPPING

The Grand Strand is a major outlet shopping destination – some visitors never even set foot on the beach. **Barefoot Landing**, in North Myrtle Beach, has shops, restaurants, clubs and more surrounding an artificial lake. **Tanger Outlets** has discount branches of higher-end shops like BCBG, Banana Republic and Ralph Lauren. **Coastal Grand Mall** is home to traditional names like Gap and Sunglass Hut, plus the 14-screen Cinemark Theater. **Broadway at the Beach** includes a NASCAR theme park and a dozen nightclubs.

TRIP INFORMATION

GETTING THERE

From Wilmington, NC, take Hwy 17 south towards Myrtle Beach. After about 40 miles, turn left at Thomasboro Rd, then right at Beach Dr into Calabash.

DO

Brookgreen Gardens

This subtropical paradise is a garden, a sculpture museum, a zoo and a nature center in one. ☎ 843-235-6000; www.brookgreen .org; 1931 Brookgreen Dr, Murrells Inlet; adult/child $12/5; ☽ 9:30am-5pm

Dolly Parton's Dixie Stampede

This dinner show involves live buffalo, trained ostriches and buckets of sequins. ☎ 800-433-4401; www.dixiestampede.com; 8901-B Hwy 17 N, Myrtle Beach; adult/child $40/20; ☽ 6pm & 8pm; ⛲

Dragon's Lair Fantasy Golf

Putt through a fake castle at this medieval-themed course, part of the massive Broadway at the Beach mall. ☎ 843-913-9301; www .broadwayatthebeach.com; 1325 Celebrity Cir, Myrtle Beach; adult/child $7.50/7; ☽ 10am-11pm

Family Kingdom

Do a surf n' turf afternoon at this two-in-one amusement and water park. ☎ 843-626-3447; www.family-kingdom.com; 300 S Ocean Blvd, Myrtle Beach; admission $32.35; ☽ hrs vary, amusement park open late in summer

Fat Harold's Beach Club

Dance the shag with graying beach bunnies to groovy 1950s "beach music." ☎ 843-249-5779; www.fatharolds.com; 212 Main St, North Myrtle Beach; ☽ 4pm-2am

Myrtle Beach Water Sports

Rent a jet ski, take a dolphin tour or go parasailing with this multi-location outfitter.

☎ 843-497-8848; www.myrtlebeachwater sports.com; 5835 Dick Pond Rd, Myrtle Beach; parasailing $60

EAT & DRINK

Dead Dog Saloon

Sip something bright pink and rum-filled or lie in the hammock of this rambling waterfront bar and grill, a favorite with bikers. ☎ 843-651-0664; www.deaddogsaloon .com; 4079 Hwy 17 Business, Murrells Inlet; mains $7-22; ☽ 11am-11pm, bar open later

Russell's Seafood Grill

A mellow crowd of regulars down oysters on the porch of this family-run seafood joint, across from the inlet. ☎ 843-651-0553; 4700 Hwy 17 Business, Murrells Inlet; mains $19-28; ☽ 4-10pm Mon-Sat

Seafood Hut

Wash down platters of fried shrimp, oysters and scallops with sweet tea at this loveably dumpy local favorite. ☎ 910-579-6723; 1125 River Rd, Calabash, NC; mains $5-12; ☽ 11am-9pm Tue-Sun

SLEEP

Landmark Resort

This vaguely Caribbean-themed behemoth has "the South's largest indoor pool complex." ☎ 800-845-0658; www.landmark resort.com; 1501 S Ocean Blvd, Myrtle Beach; r from $99

Pawleys Island Realty

Book anything from a double-wide trailer to a multistory oceanfront "cottage." Some units have one-week minimum in high season. ☎ 843-237-4257; www.pawleysisland realty.com; per night/week from $200/1000

USEFUL WEBSITES

www.discoversouthcarolina.com
www.myrtlebeach.com

www.lonelyplanet.com/trip-planner

LINK YOUR TRIP

South Carolina Upcountry

WHY GO In upcountry South Carolina, it's possible to see Vatican-worthy sacred art, maneuver around a racetrack, cuddle baby goats and watch football – all in a single day. Witness as the once-forgotten city of Greenville goes through a Southern urban revival, with your help.

Let's just get this out of the way first: this entire trip is based around corn-on-the-cob lollipops. Perhaps you think there is a better reason to travel, but you haven't tried these corn lollipops...yet.

Most of South Carolina's tourism is confined to the coastal region, but the inland farmlands and foothills can be just as stunning, plus you'll have the area practically to yourself. To boot, some of the state's quirkiest visitor attractions are hidden in these hills. The region is one of the more conservative in the USA, but you'll rarely find a friendlier set of folk.

Seeing as this is a book celebrating the American pastime of hitting the open road, start your drive with a visit to ❶ **BMW Zentrum Museum**. The only BMW manufacturing plant (and museum) in the USA is a must-see for anyone who has ever wanted to see a Z4 being made or check out dozens of classic Beemers, including an art car by Andy Warhol and a Bond car. For the particularly hard core, test your driving skills at the ❷ **BMW Performance Driving School**, where fast cars, an open track and a once-in-a-lifetime adventure meet. Burning rubber is encouraged as you slalom through the "water wall" or rev a corner.

Slow down – waaa-aaay down – in the afternoon at ❸ **Bob Jones University**. The conservative Fundamentalist college is perhaps best known for its dress code (including, for women, pantyhose on Sundays; for men, an expectation to remain clean-shaven) and controversies – interracial dating was forbidden until 2000 – but it is possible to visit

TIME
3 days

DISTANCE
131 miles

BEST TIME TO GO
Year-round

START
Greenville, SC

END
Greenville, SC

ALSO GOOD FOR

ROUTE

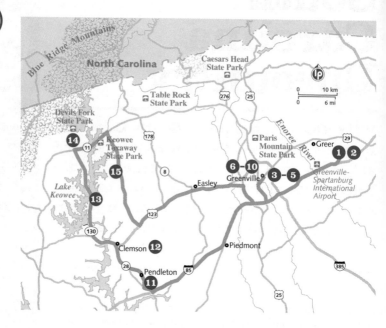

the campus (properly attired, please) to see its **4** **Old Masters Collection**. Began by Bob Jones Sr after WWII, the on-campus museum houses one of the most impressive sacred art collections in the country, including Italian baroque, 14th-century Gothic works, a Rembrandt and Russian icons. For a cheap meal, stop by the **5** **University Dining Commons**, open to visitors, between noon and 1:30pm.

"Claim the blue chair if you're feeling witty; that person is required to keep the conversation flowing."

Head into downtown **6** **Greenville**, a once down-on-its-luck Southern town. The downtown **7** **Falls Park on the Reedy River** and the surrounding **8** **River Walk** area are the epicenter of revitalization. The central park parallels the river with a series of waterfalls, floral gardens and a suspended pedestrian bridge. The neighboring pedestrianized River Walk is lined with mixed-use lofts, restaurants and shops, and the unmistakable bustle of a city rising from the ashes of postwar abandonment (bonus points if you locate the neon "free smells" sign). On Wednesday and Thursday summer evenings, you can check out a live concert at a stage set up next to the river. It's as apple pie as it gets: musicians playing, children dancing, families picnicking on the grass.

And, finally, you're here: **9** **Lazy Goat**. The Mediterranean-Southern fusion restaurant opened in 2005 and, with small plates such as braised lamb (marinated for three days) with plantain chips or fried Split Creek Farm goat cheese drizzled with honey and pistachio dust, you'll hardly have room for desserts like tiramisu poppers or churros dipped in cinnamon and pink peppercorn sugar. But it's those corn-cob lollipops – on skewers, covered with asiago and aioli – that deserve the double order. Make sure you claim the blue chair at each table if you're feeling particularly witty; that person is required to keep the meal's conversation flowing. On concert evenings, book an outdoor patio table overlooking the River Walk.

It is just a few blocks down Main St to E Washington St to arrive at ⑩ **Pettigru Place B&B**. The only historic inn in Greenville, it's set in a charming Victorian house with individual touches in each room – Jacuzzis, claw-footed tubs, a fireplace or a private porch. Each morning, guests are greeted by the epicurean equivalent of Southern hospitality – perhaps a strawberry mango Belgian waffle or eggs Florentine in ham cups.

The next stop is 25 miles south on I-85 to the aforementioned ⑪ **Split Creek Farm**. The pastoral goat dairy farm sells its award-winning goat cheese, plus goat fudge and raw goat's milk from its gift store, but the farm deserves a longer visit to commune with nature, buy local art or wander the idyllic grounds. Take exit 14 to Hwy 187 and turn right on Mt Tabor Rd and left on Centerville Rd.

Continue north on Hwy 187 toward Hwy 76 and then follow the tiger paw tracks to ⑫ **Clemson University**. Take a tour of campus, catch a football game or visit the geology museum, livestock arena and the Strom Thurmond Institute of Government and Public Affairs (he was a gradu-

MEET CHEF LINDSAY AUTRY

Lazy Goat head chef Lindsay Autry developed her fascination with food growing up on a peach farm outside of Fayetteville, NC, showing lambs and pigs as a 4H member at state fairs by age five. After a full-ride culinary scholarship at age 15 and sous-chefing her way to an *Iron Chef* knockout at 22, Autry helped open the Lazy Goat as its original head chef at the age of 24. Even if another restaurant has gobbled her up by the time you arrive, the Lazy Goat menu was entirely her creation.

ate). Continue on Hwy 130 toward Lake Keowee and ⑬ **Duke Power World of Energy**, the museum arm of the neighborhood nuclear power plant. Learn about nuclear fission and picnic on the banks of Lake Keowee, all in one afternoon. Head further north on Hwy 130 to ⑭ **Sunrise Farm B&B**, for a petting-zoo greeting and accommodations complete with a wraparound porch, private cabins and fresh-baked cookies each afternoon. On the way back to Greenville, load up on fresh fruit at ⑮ **Happy Berry Farm**, a self-pick farm filled with rows of blueberries, muscadine grapes and figs. Grazing while picking is encouraged; if you do feel guilty, feel free to drop a few coins in the "sin bucket" to atone.

Alex Leviton

TRIP INFORMATION

GETTING THERE

From Raleigh, Greensville is four hours south-west on I-40 and I-85 through Charlotte.

DO

BMW Performance Driving School

Tour participants need to be aged 12 or older and have low-heeled, closed-toed shoes. ☎ 888-345-4269; www.bmwusa.com; 1155 Hwy 101 S at I-85, Greer; classes $500-3300

BMW Zentrum Museum

Tour participants need to be aged 12 or older and have low-heeled, fully enclosed shoes. ☎ 888-TOUR-BMW; www.bmwzentrum .com; 1400 Hwy 101 S at I-85, Greer; admission free, manufacturing plant tour adult/ student $5/3.50; ☒ 9:30am-5:30pm Mon-Fri

Clemson University

A beautiful university in the classic Southern tradition, with football played in "Death Valley." ☎ 864-656-3311; www.clemson.edu; Clemson; campus tour free; ☒ tours 9:45am & 1:45pm Mon-Sat, 1:45pm Sun during semester; ♿

Duke Power World of Energy

See the lighter side of nuclear energy, on the banks of the beautiful Lake Keowee. ☎ 800-777-1004; www.duke-energy.com; 7812 Rochester Hwy, Seneca; admission free; ☒ 9am-5pm Mon-Fri, noon-5pm Sat & Sun; ♿

Old Masters Collection at Bob Jones University

One of the best collections of sacred Christian art in the USA (children under six not permitted). ☎ 864-770-1331; www.bjumg.org; 1700 Wade Hampton Rd, Greenville; adult/child/student $5/free/3; ☒ 2-5pm Tue-Sun

EAT

Happy Berry Farm

Wander through fields of blueberries, figs, muscadine grapes and strawberries for the freshest of fresh fruit. ☎ 864-868-2946; www.thehappyberry.com; 120 Kelley Creek Rd, Six Mile; self-pick per pound $1.50-2; ☒ 8am-dusk Mon-Fri, to 6pm Sat, noon-dusk Sun; ♿

Lazy Goat

Mediterranean-inspired small plates with influences of Greek, French, Italian and Southern cuisine located on the River Walk. ☎ 864-679-LAZY; www.thelazygoat.com; 170 River Pl, Greenville; plates to share $4-24; ☒ 11:30am-2:30pm Mon-Sat & 5-9:45pm Mon-Thu, 5-10:45pm Fri & Sat; ♿

Split Creek Farm

Bucolic goat dairy with a shop that sells cheese, soaps and gifts. ☎ 864-287-3921; www.splitcreek.com; 3806 Centerville Rd, Anderson; optional tour $5; ☒ 9am-6pm Mon-Sat, 1:30-5pm Sun; ♿

SLEEP

Pettigru Place B&B

Six quaintly Victorian B&B rooms, some with Jacuzzis or fireplaces, in downtown Greenville. ☎ 864-242-4529; www.pettigru place.com; 302 Pettigru St, Greenville; r $99-205; ♿

Sunrise Farm B&B

Join Muffin the pot-bellied pig, along with sheep, pygmy goats, kittens, herding dogs and acres of pastoral lands. ☎ 864-944-0121; www.bbonline.com/sc/sunrisefarm; 325 Sunrise Dr, Salem; r $107-195; ♿

USEFUL WEBSITES

www.greatergreenville.com

LINK YOUR TRIP

www.lonelyplanet.com/trip-planner

Day Trips in North Carolina & South Carolina

Journey just a few hours outside of Asheville, Raleigh or Charleston and you'll find natural beauty and outdoor adventure, towns rich in historical charm or relaxing lakes and beaches that can easily be visited in a day.

HOT SPRINGS, NC

Just 45 minutes west of Asheville is the most chilled out vacation spot for backpackers, campers or those looking to relax – the town of Hot Springs, NC. The downtown is one of the only places in the country where you can walk two city blocks of the Appalachian Trail (AT), which runs directly through town. Hundreds of section- and thru-hikers on the AT use Hot Springs as a rest stop, and its hot spring–fed private hot tubs, spa, campgrounds and organic eateries make it a good choice for "2000-milers" (those who hike the AT in one go). However, it's just as welcoming to 2-milers or even 0.2-milers. To add a bit of adventure to your hiking and relaxing, there are also opportunities to go white-water rafting on the French Broad or llama trekking. **From Asheville, take I-240 to exit 4a towards Weaverville, then head 9 miles to Hwy 19/23 North. Take the Hwy 25/70 Northwest exit towards Marshall and follow it for 26 miles, until you reach Hot Springs.**

See also **TRIPS 9, 10 & 20**

LAKE LURE, NC

The view might be best known as a stand-in for the Catskill Mountains in the film *Dirty Dancing*, but Lake Lure is a hot spot in its own right. In 1926, a local doctor realized the surrounding area was one of the most beautiful locations in all of western North Carolina and dammed the Rocky Broad River. The resulting 720-acre artificial lake has 21 miles of shoreline that winds its way through Hickory Nut Gorge, just below the equally stunning Chimney Rock State Park. To see the lake, rent a kayak or pontoon boat from the marina or take a guided tour. Dine at one of the restaurants at Lake Lure Inn, a 1927 hotel in the grand tradition which has hosted both President Roosevelt and Patrick Swayze (who stayed here during the filming of *Dirty Dancing*). Kids will love The Beach at Lake Lure, a water park on the shores of the lake. **From Asheville, take Hwy 74 east past Chimney Rock State Park. The lake is about 45 minutes east of Asheville.**

See also **TRIPS 14 & 20**

BREVARD, NC

As home to 239 mountain peaks and 250 waterfalls, Transylvania County, Pisgah National Forest and the town of Brevard make up one of North Carolina's top centers for outdoor adventure: rock climbing and mountain biking, fly fishing and inner tubing, canoeing and bird watching. Hikers have hundreds of miles of trails to choose from, but the real draw for those on foot are the Transylvania County waterfalls. The most famous and most viewed waterfall in the area is Looking Glass Falls, about 9 miles northwest of Brevard, just off Hwy 276. In the winter, the waterfall freezes on its sides, glistening in the sun like a natural looking glass. Keep heading north on Hwy 276 to reach Sliding Rock Falls where, for generations, young North Carolinians have spent warm summer days sliding down the 150ft sheer rock face. There's a pay parking lot and, during the summer, a lifeguard on duty. Brevard is known for its famous Brevard Music Center and, if you time it right, some of the best festivals in the mountains. **From Asheville, take I-26 east to exit 40 and take a right on Hwy 280 past Asheville Regional Airport. Brevard is less than an hour from Asheville.**

See also **TRIP 20**

NEW BERN, NC

Two hours east of Raleigh is the town of New Bern, the colonial heart of North Carolina and its first capital. In 1764, Royal Governor William Tryon imported his very own English architect to build a symmetrically perfect Georgian mansion and garden worthy of a London society tea party of the day. Today, costumed docents, craft demonstrations and buildings from several eras make up the Tryon Palace Historic Sites and Gardens, which is large enough to offer a two-day visitor pass. In 2010, the North Carolina History Education Center opens next door. December is the month to visit, as each house on the property splashes out in period decoration and the African-American Christmas slave tradition celebration, Jonkonnu, marches through town. If all that reveling gets you thirsty, stop in at a local pharmacy at the corner of Middle and Pollock St for "Brad's Drink." In 1895, pharmacist Caleb Bradham concocted a syrupy beverage that became so popular with his customers he eventually patented it under the name the world knows now as Pepsi-Cola. **From Raleigh, take I-440 east towards Rocky Mount, merging onto I-264 east towards Greenville. Signs will take you off the highway onto Hwy 43. Follow this for 26 miles, until you hit Hwy 17 and signs for New Bern.**

See also **TRIPS 12, 13 & 16**

PINEHURST, NC

Looking more like an upmarket New England village than a North Carolina town in the Sandhills, Pinehurst is most famous with golfing fans for its Pinehurst Resort. The resort's eight golf courses have hosted both the US Amateurs Championship and the US Open, but regular folk can play in several nearby scenic public courses throughout the year. Shop in the village, take a horse-drawn carriage ride or pick up artwork in a gallery, and be back at Raleigh by bedtime. If you'd like to spend a night or two and golf on the famous courses, check out one of the golf packages at the resort at www. pinehurst.com. **From Raleigh, take I-440 south to Hwy 1 south towards Sanford. In the town of Southern Pines, exit at Midland Rd. At the traffic circle, take the third exit, Hwy 2, west. Pinehurst is about 1½ hours from Raleigh.**

See also **TRIPS 12 & 13**

US NATIONAL WHITEWATER CENTER, CHARLOTTE, NC

Fancy an Olympic-level outdoor experience? The US National Whitewater Center (see www.usnwc.org for reservations), only 10 minutes south of uptown Charlotte, is the training center for the American canoeing and kayaking team. It's also the world's largest artificial white-water river, open to anyone who wants a unique outdoor experience. Water is diverted from the Catawba River into an upper reservoir that feeds a competition channel and a wilderness channel. At the end of your white-water kayak or rafting ride, a conveyor belt will chug you right back up to the top, ski-lift style. Watch the action from the River's Edge Bar and Grill, on a stepped hillside above the competition channel. Or choose between trying out your mountain-climbing chops on a rock-climbing wall and exploring an extensive network of mountain-biking trails. **From Raleigh, take I-85 south past Charlotte to exit 29. Take a right on Sam Wilson Rd and a left on Moores Chapel Rd. Drive for 1 mile until you reach Hawfield Rd, then follow the signs. It's about three hours from Raleigh.**

See also **TRIPS 12, 13 & 17**

AIKEN, SC

Like a miniature Charleston or Savannah, Aiken oozes historical charm. Known as Thoroughbred Country, the area surrounding Aiken provides horse racing's version of baseball spring training camp. Residents have been known to block the paving of certain roads so that equestrian traffic continues to have the right of way, and many crosswalk signals have "stop" buttons at rider's level. The sides of brick buildings are still painted with advertisements from old businesses, but the interiors have been updated with fusion restaurants and funky boutiques befitting a town that often hosts fans in town for the Triple Crown of Polo events. **From Charleston, take I-26 to exit 154A towards Orangeburg. Take Hwy 301 to Hwy 4/Surrey Race Rd and continue for 26 miles. Aiken is about two hours from Charleston.**

See also **TRIPS 21, 23 & 25**

BEAUFORT, SC

As the second-oldest city in South Carolina, Beaufort (that's pronounced *Bew-firt* as opposed to North Carolina's *Bo-furt*) is the quintessential day-trip town. A smorgasbord of outdoor activities is enough to fill an adventurous day, while historic museums and artsy shops provide for a lazy afternoon wander. Paddle across the Intracoastal Waterway for a kayak tour, visit the Lowcountry Estuarium to learn about the preserved marshlands or stroll through downtown's shops and historic architecture for a full day of sightseeing. Time your arrival for the Gullah Festival at the end of May, a three-day celebration of the art, food, culture and music of Lowcountry African Americans. To learn more about Gullah heritage, continue on Hwy 21 BR 6 miles to Dr Martin Luther King Junior Dr in St Helena, home of the Penn Center, a cultural organization with a museum and library dedicated to the traditions of the Gullah/Geechee community. **From Charleston, take Hwy 17 south to Hwy 21 south onto Boundary St into downtown. Beaufort is about 1½ hours from Charleston.**

See also **TRIPS 21 & 23**

HILTON HEAD ISLAND, SC

Make the trip from Charleston or continue on from Beaufort to reach Hilton Head Island, South Carolina's family-friendly holiday central. White sandy beaches, nature preserves, golf (miniature and full course) and more than 240 restaurants and 200 shops practically assure a day filled with vacation goodness. A list of what beach vacation activities are *not* available on the island would be shorter than the list of what *is* available. However, Hilton Head is no Myrtle Beach. Lagoons dotting the island are a feast for bird watching and turtle spotting, and it's common to see dolphins on one of the island's many guided Zodiac tours or on a self-guided kayaking expedition. **Hilton Head is just across the border from Georgia. From Charleston, drive to Beaufort and continue on Hwy 21 to Hwy 170. Merge onto Hwy 278 east towards Hilton Head (be prepared to pay the toll). Hilton Head is less than an hour from Beaufort and 2½ hours from Charleston.**

See also **TRIPS 21 & 23**

GEORGIA & ALABAMA TRIPS

Georgia and Alabama are a microcosm of the South, on one hand home to jetset cities and urban glitterati, and on the other, a slow and low lifestyle steeped in tradition and history.

Atlanta tempts visitors with its dual personality as a fast-paced metropolitan trendsetter and a leisurely metropolis. On our 48 Hours in Atlanta trip, you'll find slick design hotels, cooler-than-thou bars and restaurants, and world-class cultural attractions, all pulled off with a drawn Southern flair well-polished during Atlanta's 19th-century rise to hipdom. There's prim and proper Savannah, a gorgeous Southern belle not without its dark side, explored in depth in our eccentric Savannah tour. And outings to two coastal gems: Richly traditional Mobile in Alabama, famous for music and Mardi Gras; and Georgia's Golden Isles, a spectacular chain of barrier islands, each with its own unique character and raw natural beauty.

Though the mixed tape is a lost art, its spirit lives on with our Georgia and Alabama playlist – like the South, it reflects a multicultural potpourri of musical styles and genres, from Athens alt-rock pioneers REM to Alabama's own iconic country boy, Hank Williams.

- "Love Shack,"B-52s
- "Yeah!," Usher featuring Lil' Jon & Ludacris
- "Georgia on My Mind," Ray Charles
- "Sweet Home Alabama," Lynyrd Skynyrd
- "The One I Love," REM
- "Closer to Fine," Indigo Girls
- "Your Cheatin' Heart," Hank Williams
- "Ramblin' Man," The Allman Brothers

There is no shortage of taste bud–tempting chow along the way – Georgia peaches, tasty fried chicken, New Southern gourmet, Lowcountry cuisine and two trips planned by Southern food experts just to make sure you eat your heart out in Atlanta and leave no Georgia BBQ unturned. Spend a few weeks here and you'll leave quipping, "We'll be back now, ya'll hear?"

GEORGIA & ALABAMA'S BEST TRIPS

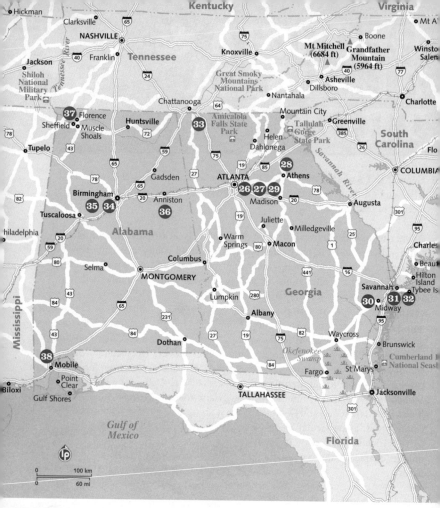

GEORGIA & ALABAMA TRIPS

48 Hours in Atlanta

WHY GO Burnt lifeless in the Civil War, Atlanta emerged from the flames a cosmopolitan juggernaut full of delectable restaurants, bohemian neighborhoods, trendy bars and world-class cultural attractions. Here's how to play, eat and drink like the locals (and sleep like a tourist) over a weekend in the sass of the South.

TIME
2 days

BEST TIME TO GO
Mar – May

START
Atlanta, GA

END
Atlanta, GA

ALSO GOOD FOR

There are two kinds of people in this world: Those who love Atlanta, and those who have only caught a fleeting glimpse on the way to Florida. If you are of the latter ilk, exit I-75/85 immediately on Williams St and start at the thriving epicenter of this booming metropolis of nearly six million, **1** **Centennial Olympic Park**. Built for the 1996 Olympic Games, this urban monument, the scene of the bombing that scarred an otherwise wonderful Olympics, is now home to two of Atlanta's most entertaining attractions, the nothing-short-of-awesome **2** **Georgia Aquarium** (the world's largest by gallon count) and the **3** **World of Coca-Cola**, where you can drink yourself silly on 60 sodas from around the world.

From the downtown epicenter, continue your tour just east across the Peters St Bridge, where trendy boutiques are popping up faster than Melrose, in Atlanta's latest gentrified historic district, **4** **Castleberry Hill**. The **5** **No Mas! Cantina** anchors the neighborhood (for now). Grab a margarita on the good-times outdoor patio here, then pop in the attached home-decor shop and do a little drunk buying. Castleberry Hill is also home to numerous art galleries and has almost single-handedly put Atlanta on the art radar as the latest place for creative talent to see and be seen. Sleeping in this area most certainly means the **6** **Glenn**, one of Atlanta's few fashion-forward boutique hotels. The rooftop bar is teeming with Beautiful People who think they are in Miami. It's right off Centennial Park.

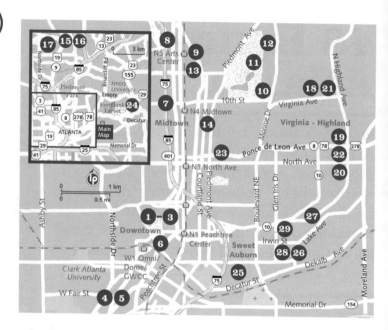

After lunch, move north to ❼ **Midtown**, the inner-city area that kicked off the city's urban renewal in the first place. One of Atlanta's unique attractions is the ❽ **Center for Puppetry Arts**. If you are towing offspring, stop here. You can browse exhibits that jar your childhood memories – Jim Henson, for instance – while your kids run around digging all the elaborate puppets. If you are towing a significant other, Atlanta's world-class ❾ **High Museum of Art** is the first museum in the world to exhibit art lent from Paris' Louvre. You could spend hours in this whitewashed multilevel space, taking in eye-catching late-19th-century furniture and countless European and American artists, Monet and Bellini among them. Two favorites: the haunting *Bust of a Man* (1525; artist unknown) and Vik Muniz's *Khyber Pass, Self-Portrait as an Oriental*, made from trash and found objects. The High Museum and its striking architecture were long ago the foundation for Midtown's renaissance.

Watch the sun go down with a microbrew in hand on the outdoor patio at ❿ **Park Tavern**, a wildly popular microbrewery on the edge of Atlanta's beautiful urban grassland, ⓫ **Piedmont Park**, Midtown's ode to Central Park. It's packed all day on weekends. Dinner must be in this area as well; it was originally restaurants that lured the Beautiful People back to the city, thanks in part to ⓬ **ONE. midtown kitchen**. It's hidden in a former warehouse – an Atlanta trend that someone should probably cry uncle on soon – on Dutch Valley Rd. A cheaper Midtown option is ⓭ **Tap** (located right on Atlanta's main thoroughfare, Peachtree St), a gastropub serving upscale bar fare to a sultry crowd sauced on microbrews. Parallel to Peachtree St on Juniper St is ⑭ **Cuerno**, an excellent Spanish tapas bar that does a wealth of interesting paellas. If you see Atlanta's finest here pouring liquor into their mouths like they are funneling a beer on Spring Break in Panama City Beach, that's just a *porron*, a Spanish wine pitcher used to drink *cava* (Spanish sparkling wine).

Further north is the notorious ⑮ **Buckhead** district, once home to so many bars and clubs, the city of Atlanta had to pull the plug on the party and rezone it residential. Essentially, it shut the bars down and turned Buckhead back into the upscale area it once was. Leading the comeback is Atlanta's most luxurious hotel (until the next one*)*, ⑯ **Mansion on Peachtree**. Opened in 2008, this well-located, lavish hotel near Lenox leaves no stone unturned. Thoughtful local touches like sweet peach tea and candied Georgia pecans served on arrival are just a few of the addictive luxuries here (the recessed TVs "hide" behind paintings).

Rounding back to the east side of the city, there's ⑰ **Virginia-Highland**, a historic district that was always home to Atlanta's more bohemian, less Brooks Brothers side. Arrive early enough to browse all the kitschy boutiques along N Highland Ave between Ponce de Leon and Morningside Dr, then dive headfirst into the city's best concentration of bars. ⑱ **Atkins Park** is the classic drinking den, but N Highland is lined with old-school taverns, outdoor patios and live music options – a perfect bar-hopping route. On the other side of Ponce is ⑲ **Manuel's Tavern**, which also packs in the hungover set on weekend mornings. Weekend brunch for those that can focus is always at ⑳ **Murphy's**, which is a little classier than Manuel's and home to scrumptious shrimp and grits and other Southern-leaning breakfast fare.

> **ASK A LOCAL**
>
> "There have been a lot of baseball parks built in that same fashion since, but when it was constructed, **Turner Field** was certainly an innovative concept – more than just a day at the ballpark. It's almost an amusement park within the stadium. A great prelude to a game is a meal at **The Varsity**. Today it's exactly how it was when I was six years old. One of best chili dogs I've ever had."
> *David Corbett, Atlanta, GA*

If you dig this area of town, ㉑ **Highland Inn** is one of Atlanta's best-value hotels, walking distance from everything on both sides of Ponce. The area is also home to Atlanta's only true traveler-friendly budget option, ㉒ **Atlanta International Hostel** (though management will hold rooms for international travelers over American ones, so it's only travel-friendly if you have flown over an ocean to get here. Yes, we're serious).

Widen the circle out to the east a bit and check out ㉓ **Decatur**, once a run-of-the-mill suburb until the vaguely bohemian and vaguely gay communities joined forces in the area to turn its small-time downtown area into a quaint little hipsterati commune. Cute boutiques and simple restaurants and coffeehouses now line Ponce de Leon Ave, including Indigo Girl Emily Salier's excellent casual Southern ㉔ **Watershed**, housed inside a former mechanic's garage. It's a favorite with Decatur lesbians, Diana Ross, Peter Gabriel and pretty much anyone in between.

> "It's a favorite with Decatur lesbians, Diana Ross, Peter Gabriel and pretty much anyone in between."

Southwest from Decatur is what is perhaps Atlanta's neighborhood *du moment* as well as its biggest urban success story. The gentrification of hip ㉕ **Inman Park** has resulted in the city's most coveted address for lovely restored Craftsman homes, design-forward lofts and countless trendsetting bars and restaurants. ㉖ **Parish**, inside a 5000-sq-ft 1890 Italianate building turned ecofriendly, New Orleans–style bistro, espresso bar and specialty organic foods market, is indicative of the area's resurgence. Another surefire option is chef Kevin Rathbun's empire to food and fun on Krog St. Rathbun consistently churns out knock-out dining experiences in industrial-hip spaces – his eponymous ㉗ **Rathbun's** offers one of Atlanta's most eclectic dining experiences inside the old Atlanta Stove Works factory.

For everything in Atlanta that is shiny and new, there's a past to the city that is less than sparkly. But the bright spot in Atlanta's role in the Civil Rights struggle is Martin Luther King, Jr, who was born and is buried here. Swing back west towards downtown to ㉘ **Sweet Auburn**, the old stomping grounds of MLK, Jr. The ㉙ **Martin Luther King, Jr National Historic Site** in this historic neighborhood – funnily enough, also beginning to see the arrival of stylish bistros and fashionable high-rise lofts – is home to the Martin Luther King, Jr Visitors Center, Ebenezer Baptist Church, and the King Center. King is buried in a dramatic overwater grave here.

MY DEAR, I DON'T GIVE A DAMN!

If you only know one thing about Georgia, it likely has to do with the 1937 Pulitzer Prize–winning novel, *Gone with the Wind*, far and away the most famous words ever written about Georgia, Atlanta and the American South during the Civil War and Reconstruction. You can tour the **Margaret Mitchell House & Museum** (www.gwtw.org), where the author lived from 1925 to 1932 and penned the romantic adventures of Rhett Butler and Scarlett O'Hara.

From Sweet Auburn, it's just a quick skip west back to Centennial Park and I-75/85. Now that you've been introduced to Atlanta, you can hop back on the interstate and head south to Florida. Frankly, we Atlantans don't give a damn.

Kevin Raub

TRIP INFORMATION

DO

Center for Puppetry Arts
This unique puppet museum is great for kids and adults (there's a *section*). Don't miss the Jim Henson exhibitions. ☎ 404-873-3391; www.puppet.org; 1404 Spring St; admission $16; ⏰ 9am-5pm Tue-Sat, 11am-5pm Sun; 🚻

Georgia Aquarium
It's crowded like Venice, but the world's largest aquarium is sensational. You can swim with the whale sharks for $250. ☎ 404-581-4000; www.georgiaaquarium.org; 225 Baker St; adult/child $29.50/22; ⏰ 9am-6pm Sun-Thu, 9am-10pm Fri, 8am-8pm Sat; 🚻

High Museum of Art
Atlanta's architecturally striking High Museum is on par with the best and features more than 11,000 permanent works in 312,000 sq ft. ☎ 404-733-4444; www.high .org; 1280 Peachtree St; adult/child $18/11; ⏰ 10am-5pm Mon, Tue, Thu & Fri, 10am-8pm Wed, noon-5pm Sun; 🚻

Martin Luther King, Jr National Historic Site
This National Park consists of the Visitors Center, MLK, Jr's birthplace, Ebenezer Baptist Church and the King Center, where he lies entombed. ☎ 404-331-5190; www.nps .gov/malu; 450 Auburn Ave, Atlanta; admission free; ⏰ 9am-6pm

World of Coca-Cola
Sipping odd-flavored sodas from around the world is the highlight at Coke's 60,000-sq-ft pat on its own back. ☎ 404-676-5151; www.worldofcoca-cola.com; 263 Blueberry Farm Rd, Richmond; adult/child $15/9; ⏰ 9am-6pm Mon-Sat, 10am-6pm Sun; 🚻

EAT

Cuerno
Upscale Spanish tapas and a head-turning crowd sipping on *cava* through hand-blown glass *porrons*. The numerous paellas are excellent. ☎ 678-904-4582; 905 Juniper St; mains $1.85-14; ⏰ 5:30-10pm Mon-Thu, 5:30-11pm Fri & Sat; 🚻

Murphy's
This people-watching brunch staple in Virginia-Highland is a longstanding favorite. Try the shrimp and grits and get there early. ☎ 404-872-0904; 997 Virginia Ave NE; mains $4-14; ⏰ 11am-10pm Mon-Thu, 11am-midnight Fri, 8am-11pm Sat, 8am-10pm Sun

No Mas! Cantina
This design-forward cantina and attached home decor hacienda is the Castleberry Hill hotspot for filling Mexican and margaritas. ☎ 404-574-5678; 180 Walker St; mains $8-28; ⏰ 11am-10pm Sun-Thu, 11am-11pm Fri & Sat; 🚻

ONE. midtown kitchen
Loud and sexy tapas-style eatery in a refurbished warehouse that oozes urban cool. Sultry cocktails and dressed-up comfort food are the icing. ☎ 404-892-4111; 559 Dutch Valley Rd; mains $7-27; ⏰ 5:30-11pm Mon-Thu, 5:30pm-midnight Fri & Sat, 5:30-10pm Sun

Parish
A speakeasy-like Cajun-Creole bistro anchored by a gorgeous walnut-and-zinc bar lit by Philippe Starck "Miss K" lamps. ☎ 404-681-4434; 240 N Highland Ave; mains $10-19; ⏰ 7am-late Mon-Fri, 8am-late Sat & Sun

Rathbun's
The hip industrial space plays second fiddle to the diverse menu — eggplant fries with confectioners sugar, crispy duck with Thai risotto — at this foodie stronghold. ☎ 404-524-8280; 112 Krog St; mains $16-40; ⏰ 5:30-10:30pm Mon-Thu, 5:30-11pm Fri & Sat

Tap
This sexy Midtown gastropub draws legions to its outdoor patio for great burgers and buffalo-fried calamari, all chased by a strong beer list. ☎ 404-347-2220; 1180 Peachtree St; mains $12-16; ⏰ 11am-midnight Mon-Thu, 11am-2am Fri & Sat, 10am-midnight Sun

Watershed
Everything at this hip regional Southern co-owned by Emily Saliers is addictive, especially the pimento and cheese. ☎ 404-378-4900; 406 W Ponce de Leon Ave, Decatur; mains $8-25; ⏰ 11am-10pm Mon-Sat, 10am-3pm Sun

DRINK

Atkins Park

It's a simple formula: hardwood booths, a long, smoky bar and a decent selection of draft beer. Try the local Sweetwater 420. ☎ 404-876-7249; 794 N Highland Ave; mains $7-24; ⏲ 11am-2:30pm Mon-Sat, 11am-midnight Sun

Manuel's Tavern

The quintessential Atlanta bar and often named one of America's best, serving suds and cheap burgers since 1956. ☎ 404-526-0733; 602 N Highland Ave; mains $6-15; ⏲ 11am-2am Mon-Sat, 11am-midnight Sun

Park Tavern

People-watch the afternoon away with a microbrew on the patio of this popular watering hole overlooking Piedmont Park. ☎ 404-249-0001; cnr 10th St & Monroe; mains $7-19; ⏲ 4:30pm-midnight Mon-Thu, 11:30am-2am Fri & Sat, 11:30am-midnight Sun

SLEEP

Atlanta International Hostel

International travelers are given priority over Americans at this hostel in a 1906 former brothel near Virginia-Highland. Sorry California backpackers! ☎ 404-875-9449; www.atlantahostel.com; 223 Ponce de Leon NE; r $24-69

Glenn

If you like your hotel lobbies doubling as painfully hip bars, the Glenn is for you, though service isn't nearly as cool as it looks. ☎ 404-521-2250; www.theglennhotel.com; 110 Marietta St NW; r $189-240

Highland Inn

Excellently located and well-priced option with a vintage upscale hostel vibe. Many of the doubles are especially roomy – almost suites. ☎ 404-874-5756; www.thehighlandinn.com; 644 N Highland Ave; r from $109

Mansion on Peachtree

A distinguished newcomer drenched in luxurious creamy earth tones and understated elegance with a stylish, wine-driven spa and NYC-transplanted Craft restaurant. ☎ 404-995-7500; www.mansiononpeachtree.com; 3376 Peachtree Rd; r $495-550

USEFUL WEBSITES

www.atlanta.citysearch.com

www.atlanta.net

LINK YOUR TRIP

www.lonelyplanet.com/trip-planner

Atlanta for Food Lovers

WHY GO Atlanta is undeniably the mecca of Southern dining. Dizzied by the myriad flavors, we teamed up with chef and author Scott Peacock of foodie favorite Watershed (co-owned by Indigo Girl Emily Saliers) to help us discover the Holy Grails of Atlanta's foodie scene.

TIME
4 days

BEST TIME TO GO
Mar – May

START
Atlanta, GA

END
Atlanta, GA

ALSO GOOD FOR

CITY

The line starts forming up to an hour before opening. There are eight stools at the counter. There is a list of 30-year-old rules. There is one woman in charge, Ms Ann, who meticulously prepares the most monstrous burger on earth – two fat, hand-slapped patties doused in paprika, deep-fried bacon, fried onions, chili, cheese, lettuce, ketchup, mustard and mayo. It takes 45 minutes to arrive. Behold: the Ghetto Burger. Welcome to ❶ **Ann's Snack Bar** on Memorial Dr, home to what more than one person has called the world's greatest burger. "I love Ms Ann," says Peacock. "I can't tell you it's the best burger ever, but it has Ms Ann. She's stern. I'm always a little nervous when I go in there – everything is on her terms. I love it when the food is an expression of someone like that." If you can actually finish this bad boy, you'll want to stop reading here.

To get a sense of Peacock's palette, a stop in his own restaurant, ❷ **Watershed**, in downtown Decatur – a hip sort of suburb of Atlanta with a small-town bohemian feel – is in order. Inside a former mechanic's garage, Peacock and Indigo Girl Emily Saliers have been serving up juiced-up versions of seasonal Southern classics since "Galileo" was on the radio. Pimento and cheese made with two-year-old Grafton cheddar is a favorite, as are the outrageously tasty sandwiches. A table on fried-chicken Tuesdays is a coveted thing indeed.

Across the street from Watershed, Peacock loves ❸ **Taqueria del Sol**, as do most Atlantans you speak to. Cheap tacos with unpredictable

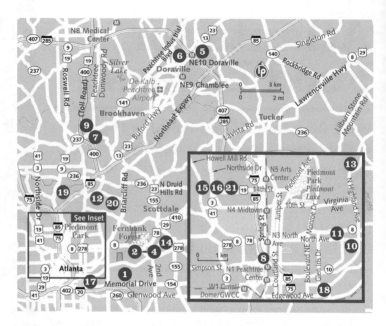

fillings (pulled pork, fried chicken, Tilapia) and a ridiculously good corn chowder with shrimp are favorites here. One of Peacock's protégés, Billy Allin, jumped shipped from Watershed to open ❹ **Cakes & Ale** down the street. No animosity here – Peacock loves the simplistic nature of the food, sourced locally wherever possible.

For goat tacos, Peacock heads straight to Buford Hwy, Atlanta's most ethnically diverse street (sometimes it feels as though you need a passport and a currency exchange to drive its length). Take your pesos to ❺ **El Cabrito** for the *chivo* (goat) – they're small, a tad greasy and taste *mucho autentico*. A few miles southwest, also on Buford Hwy, is ❻ **88 Tofu House**, an always-open Korean diner serving up succulent BBQ and various *kimchi*.

Tired of eating yet? Peacock's favorite hotel for foodies is the ❼ **Ritz-Carlton Buckhead**, though it has lost some of its previous luster in the wake of Atlanta's ever-expanding dining scene. "It's getting more and more Hiltony to me all the time, but I did used to love sitting in front of that fireplace in the wintertime, having tea with friends. I still think you can rely on it for top-end service. It's the classic hotel in Atlanta." *Atlanta* magazine recently named the restaurant at ❽ **Twelve at Centennial Park** the best new hotel restaurant in the city. This trendy option offers large, shotgun-style suites in a perfect downtown location near Centennial Park, the Georgia Aquarium and the World of Coca-Cola. An excellent Buckhead option is the newer

9 **Mansion on Peachtree**, home to NYC chef Tom Colicchio's Craft restaurant and some of the most luxurious sleeps in the city.

The size of the parking lot at **10** **Manuel's Tavern** ought to clue you in on its standing among locals – you'd think you're parking at Home Depot. It's all about weekend brunch and greasy hangover cures at this quintessential 1956 landmark. Serious breakfast folks rise and shine at breakfast-only **11** **Java Jive**. The popular gingerbread pancakes match the *Leave It to Beaver* decor – old '40s and '50s ovens and toasters fill the room like a Mayberry junkyard. Another spot stuck in time is **12** **Colonnade**, wedged between seedy adult bookstores and ethnic eateries on Cheshire Bridge Rd. "The food isn't especially great but it's such a scene," says Peacock. "It's the restaurant of this low-rent motel. In the evenings, it's 50% blue hair and 50% gay."

A healthier option Peacock raves about is the organic **13** **Morningside Market**, an artisan farmers market held every Saturday in one of Atlanta's prettiest neighborhoods. But if you would rather learn how to cook than actually eat – after all, a break is in order by this point – Peacock suggests cooking classes at **14** **Cook's Warehouse**, where you can tap into your inner chef learning everything from southern Indian to Southern fried chicken.

Some of Atlanta's best eats are found in little gourmet markets and corner groceries, places the average tourist (or local) would never think to look. Peacock counts among this breed **15** **Star Provisions** on Howell Mill Rd in booming East Atlanta. Part gourmet market, deli and kitschy homewares shop, this one is no secret – it's run by one of Atlanta's most famous kitchen teams, Anne Quatrano and Clifford Harrison. The shrimp po' boy here is sublime.

> **ASK A LOCAL**
>
> "In 1998, I took a six-month break from being an Indigo Girl, and I found myself wanting to embark upon an adventure, so my founding partners and I created **Watershed**. Sharing good food is similar to sharing music in many ways; you give something to people that makes them happy, and you partake of it yourself. It can be centered on milestones or simply a night out with friends. It comforts us in times of sadness. There are elements of a song that bring it together perfectly in its own time. It's the same with the food at Watershed; asparagus for spring, strawberries for summer, pumpkins for fall, thick stews for the cold winter months; a song for every season."
>
> *Emily Saliers, Indigo Girls*

Pork roasted in-house makes the Cuban sandwiches at **16** **Kool Korner** Atlanta's best. This small grocery-cum–food counter on 14th St is the kind of spot you would never even consider popping into for anything other than a pack of smokes or a half-pint of Jack Daniel's. Perfect pork? Who knew? Another fantastic find is the **17** **Cabbagetown Market**. "It's a little market on Carroll St," says Peacock. "They sell farm eggs and raw milk and sugar cane

Coke and they have a little lunch counter. It's so cute." The best seller here is the burger with house-made pimento cheese.

"It does delicacies for the cast-iron stomached under the menu heading 'Parts'."

Of course, Atlanta is more than capable of hosting on the high end as well. **18** **Krog Bar**, an intimate wine space in the old Atlanta Stove Works factory, is a favorite for pre-dinner wine and appetizers. There are great by-the-glass options and the wait staff is well schooled on vintages. The small plates are interesting here – try the yellowtail carpaccio with piquillo peppers and chili oil. Better yet, challenge them to pair it. Serious foodies flock to **19** **Holeman & Finch**. It does delicacies for the cast-iron stomached under the menu heading "Parts" (crisp pork ears, fatback and tails with BBQ, gratin of marrow).

Two of Atlanta's most revered tables round out this culinary crusade, both of which come back down to Quatrano and Harrison, starting with **20** **FloatAway Café**. Seasonal cuisine created with country French, Mediterranean and Italian influences and an industrial warehouse motif here are a jarring marriage at first, but service and the results of the kitchen are pure epicurean ecstasy.

"**Rathbun's** consistently delivers one of the best dining experiences in Atlanta – a cool space, great bar, flawless service…oh, and then there's the food. For a light bite, you can go with a couple of small plates, or step it up to the 'Big Plates' for a larger meal, or splurge with a 'Second Mortgage' dish (the Australian lamb chops are my favorite). Atlanta has a ton of dining options, but I'd take Rathbun's above all others."
Jason Hatfield, Atlanta, GA

No Atlanta dining debate ever concludes without mention of **21** **Bacchanalia**, consistently voted the city's top gourmand experience by nearly everyone since anyone kept track of such things. The $75 prix-fixe menu at this contemporary American mecca might include fennel soup with Maine lobster or wood-grilled California squab with glazed cippolini onions, but it changes daily and never gets tired. Speaking of which, who could use a nap?
Kevin Raub

TRIP INFORMATION

DO

Cook's Warehouse
From Indian tapas to BBQ, classes at this gourmet cooking school should set you straight in the kitchen. ☎ 404-377-4005; www.cookswarehouse.com; 180 W Ponce de Leon, Decatur; classes from $65; ☽ year-round

Morningside Market
Organic produce and artisan farmers market, in business well ahead of the curve, since 1995. ☎ 404-313-5784; www.morningsidemarket.com; 1393 N Highland Ave; ☽ 8am-11:30am Sat

EAT

88 Tofu House
All day, all night, this Korean diner does excellent Korean-marinated beef and several kimchis. You do not have to be drunk on Hite to go. ☎ 770-457-8811; 5490 Buford Hwy; mains $9-15; ☽ 24hr

Ann's Snack Bar
Get in line early. Order. Don't break the rules. Wait 45 minutes. The Ghetto Burger will emerge as the best burger in the USA. ☎ 404-687-9207; 1615 Memorial Dr SE; mains $4-9; ☽ 11:30am-7:30pm Mon-Sat, 1-5pm Sun

Bacchanalia
This New American table is consistently voted Atlanta's number one dining experience by almost everyone who ranks these sort of things. ☎ 404-365-0410; 1198 Howell Mill Rd; prix fixe $75; ☽ 6-10pm

Cabbagetown Market
This cute gourmet market on a particularly picturesque street in Cabbagetown historic district does excellent burgers with pimento cheese. ☎ 404-221-9186; 198 Carroll St; mains $2-7.50; ☽ 11am-7pm Tue-Sat, noon-6pm Sun

Cakes & Ale
Scott Peacock's protégé runs the kitchen at this minimalist Decatur newcomer focusing on simple recipes from local sources. ☎ 404-377-7994; 254 W Ponce de Leon Ave; mains $14-24; ☽ 5:30-10:30pm

Colonnade
Blue Hairs and gays tend to dominate the crowd at this Southern comfort-food throwback. ☎ 404-874-5642; 1879 Cheshire Bridge Rd; mains $9-20; ☽ 5-9pm Mon-Thu, 5-10pm Fri, noon-10pm Sat, 11:30am-9pm Sun

El Cabrito
Atmospheric Mexican restaurant (it's cuter inside than out) specializing in goat tacos. ☎ 770-300-0364; 6530 Buford Hwy NE, Doraville; mains $1.50-12; ☽ 10am-10pm Mon-Fri, 5:30-11pm Sun

FloatAway Café
Country French, Mediterranean and Italian influences tilt the menu at Bacchanalia's cheaper cousin toward mains like Amish freebird chickens or kurobata pork shanks. ☎ 404-892-1414; 1123 Zonolite Rd; mains $15-28; ☽ 6-10pm Tue-Sat

Holeman & Finch
The restaurant industry flocks to this upscale public house for pig's ear, pork belly, entrails and the like. For serious foodies only. ☎ 404-398-1175; 2277 Peachtree Rd NE; mains $7-14; ☽ 5pm-1:30am Mon-Sat, 12:30-3pm Sun

Java Jive
Gingerbread pancakes and Sante Fe scrambles rule the kitchen, kitschy '40s-era stoves and toasters rule the decor. ☎ 404-876-6161; 790 Ponce de Leon Ave NE; mains $7-9; ☽ 8am-2pm Tue-Fri, 9am-2:30pm Sat & Sun

Kool Korner
This tiny grocery store on the corner of State St sells more sandwiches than groceries. The Cuban sandwich is king. ☎ 404-892-5366; 349 14th St; mains $5; ☽ 10:30am-4:30pm Mon-Fri, 11am-4pm Sat

Star Provisions
The shrimp po' boy at this decadent gourmet market attached to Bacchanalia is a godsend, as are the desserts and trendy homewares. ☎ 404-365-0410; 1198 Howell Mill Rd; mains $8-13; ☽ 10am-10pm Mon-Sat

Taqueria del Sol
BBQ, fried chicken tacos and Atlanta's best corn chowder are highlights of this Mexican-Southern marriage. ☎ 404-377-7668; 359

W Ponce de Leon, Decatur; mains $2-11; 11am-2pm Mon-Fri, noon-3pm Sat, also 5:30-9pm Tue-Thu, 5:30-10pm Fri & Sat

Watershed

The author's regional Southern cuisine in its purest vain, co-owned by Indigo Girl Emily Saliers, in hip downtown Decatur. ☎ 404-378-4900; 406 W Ponce de Leon Ave, Decatur; mains $8-25; 11am-10pm Mon-Sat, 10am-3pm Sun

DRINK

Krog Bar

Intimate wine bar attached to Rathbun's restaurant, inside the old Atlanta Stove Works factory. Small *crudi* and *formaggi* complement the excellent by-the-glass list. ☎ 404-524-1618; 112 Krog St; mains $5-7; 4:30pm-midnight Mon-Sat

Manuel's Tavern

An Atlanta staple since 1956, this classic tavern is always packed. It serves a mean burger on toast (with greasy fries). ☎ 404-525-3447; 602 N Highland Ave; mains $6-15; 11am-2am Mon-Sat, 11am-midnight Sun

SLEEP

Mansion on Peachtree

Opened in 2008, this refined newcomer decked out in soothing earth tones and polished marble trumps the competition and is host to NYC's raved Craft restaurant. ☎ 404-995-7500; www.mansiononpeachtree.com; 3376 Peachtree Rd NE; r $495-555

Ritz-Carlton Buckhead

Atlanta's classic choice for luxe is also home to a consistently award-wining dining room, though its status has waned in recent years. ☎ 404-237-2700; www.ritzcarlton.com; 3434 Peachtree Rd NE; r from $369

Twelve at Centennial Park

Stylish shotgun-style suites clock in at 800 sq ft at this trendy newcomer, completed by a hot lobby restaurant managed by Atlanta's hippest restaurateurs. ☎ 404-418-1212; www.twelve hotels.com; 400 W Peachtree; r $229

USEFUL WEBSITES

www.atlanta.net
www.travelsouthflavours.com

LINK YOUR TRIP

www.lonelyplanet.com/trip-planner

Athens Rocks

WHY GO REM, B-52s, Pylon, Widespread Panic, Drive-By Truckers, Neutral Milk Hotel, Danger Mouse – Athens is an alternative college town with a soundtrack rivaled by none. Walk this route where the bands came, saw and shredded some guitar in Georgia's most storied musical town, often called the Liverpool of the South.

Perhaps no other college town in the USA has done more for independent music than Athens, located an hour east of Atlanta on Hwy 78 (also known as the Atlanta Hwy, name-checked in the B-52s' biggest hit, "Love Shack"). It began with REM and the B-52s in the early '80s, but has continued throughout the years across a multitude of genres: Widespread Panic (jam band), Drive-By Truckers (alt-country), Danger Mouse (hip-hop), Matthew Sweet (power pop), Neutral Milk Hotel (fuzz folk) – Athens as a breeding ground for the musical cognoscenti knows no bounds.

Of course, there was music in Athens before REM, but they put Athens on the musical map. The year was 1980 and Michael Stipe, Bill Berry, Peter Buck and Mike Mills played their first gig at ❶ **The Church**, the former St Mary's Episcopal church that had been converted into an apartment where some members of the band lived at the time. The Side Effects opened. Today, only the steeple remains. From there, a quick step over to Popular St, where the parking lot for the North Oconee River Greenways leads to a footbridge overlooking the ❷ **Murmur Trestles**. The railway trestles, built in 1880 and rescued from demolition by the city, appear on the back of REM's debut album *Murmur*.

Another REM landmark, ❸ **Weaver's D's**, lies just north at the east end of Broad St. This soul-food kitchen and the slogan of its charismatic owner, Dexter Weaver, were the inspiration for the title of the

TIME
1 – 2 days

DISTANCE
5 miles

BEST TIME TO GO
Mar – Jun

START
Athens, GA

END
Athens, GA

ALSO GOOD FOR

CITY

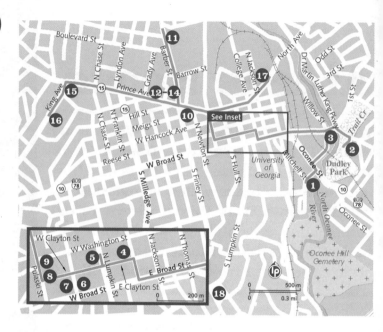

band's 1992 album, *Automatic for the People* (later revised by Barack Obama's on-campus campaigners as "Obamatic for the People" during his 2008 presidential campaign). Weaver still says "Automatic!" to this day whenever you order anything.

Moving on to downtown, **4 Wuxtry Records** has been *the* Athens indie music shop since 1975. REM's Peter Buck worked in its original location (just around the corner on College Ave). The **5 Georgia Theatre** has hosted international powerhouse acts like the Police and Dave Matthews over the years, and is where REM filmed their video for "Shiny Happy People." It still hosts legendary shows to this day. **6 Last Resort Grill**, now one of Athens' best restaurants, was once a bar so named because it was next to three finance companies. If you got turned down for a loan at all three, alcohol was your last resort. The B-52s played here in 1978. A block down at **7 250 W Clayton St** is REM's current rehearsal space, which the band used as recently as 2008's *Accelerate* tour.

> **ASK A LOCAL**
>
> "**Buck Manor** is where Peter Buck used to live and where REM made the "Nightswimming" video and also filmed a prerelease promotional video for *Out of Time*. Nirvana spent the night there when they played in town and it was the scene of many a crazy house party back in the day when it was just a rental property. There is also a photograph of the band standing in front of the house."
>
> *Paul Butchert, The Side Effects, Athens, GA*

Around Clayton St onto Pulaski St is the **8** **Caledonia Lounge,** one of a handful of local music venues, significant as one of the former sites of the famous **9** **40 Watt Club** (now around the corner on Washington St). REM filmed the video for "Turn You Inside Out" here and this location hosted legendary shows by Fugazi, Bob Mould, the Melvins and Robyn Hitchcock. The current location of the 40 Watt is still Athens' premier music venue and the place to see national acts that have no business playing a venue this small.

Heading west out of downtown on Prince Ave, you'll find a few buildings owned by Michael Stipe. In one of them, the **10** **Grit** is a hip vegetarian restaurant he frequents. A few blocks down on **11** **Barber St,** known as the "Street of Stars," is where all kinds of shenanigans took place throughout Athens' '80s heyday. Stipe and former Oh OK member Linda Hopper shared the home at **12** **169 Barber St,** while REM's Peter Buck lived with his girlfriend next door at **13** **181 Barber St.** At the corner of **14** **Barrow and Barber St,** a drunken meeting with wet cement in the early '80s resulted in Stipe's carving of his initials into the sidewalk as well as the artwork of a gaggle of groupies hanging out with the bands: REM, Love Tractor, Limbo District and Method Actors are all still visible today.

ASK A LOCAL

"The Athens music scene has grown considerably since our time. These days it's a lot more diverse, considering when Pylon was playing regularly, there were only three or four bands. Now there are close to 400! Along with that comes the good and the bad of cramming 400 bands into a small town. Sometimes I worry it will reach saturation point, but it looks like there's still room!"
Curtis Crowe, Pylon

But the most notorious address in Athens is 748 Cobb St, a Second Empire Victorian home painted 12 different colors and known as **15** **Buck Manor.** Buck lived here until his divorce from his ex-wife, Barrie, who still lives here. In that same neighborhood at 165 Hillcrest St is **16** **John Keane Studios.** The B-52s *Funplex* as well as many REM and Widespread Panic albums have been recorded in this home.

Today, the Athens music scene is as healthy as ever. Come to town, lay your head at the **17** **Foundry Park Inn** or the **18** **UGA Center for Continuing Education** and check out some live music. You never know when you might walk into a church and find sonic salvation.
Kevin Raub

HISTORY & CULTURE

TRIP INFORMATION

GETTING THERE
From Atlanta, take Hwy 78 (eastbound) to Athens.

DO
Wuxtry Records
Peter Buck worked at this indie music store, still going strong with a massive collection of new and used CDs and vinyl. ☎ 706-369-9428; www.wuxtryrecords.com; 197 E Clayton St; ☺ 10am-8pm Mon-Thu, 10am-10pm Fri & Sat, noon-6pm Sun

EAT
Grit
Meat has never been cooked in this veggie kitchen in a building owned and frequented by REM's Michael Stipe. ☎ 706-543-6592; 199 Prince Ave; mains $4-8; ☺ 11am-10pm Mon-Fri, 10am-3pm & 5-10:30pm Sat & Sun
Last Resort Grill
Athens' most creative cuisine: dig into pecan-crusted blue trout and the like. ☎ 706-549-0810; 174/184 W Clayton St; mains $10-17; ☺ 11am-3pm, also 5-10pm Mon-Thu & Sun, 5-11pm Fri & Sat
Weaver's D's
"Automatic!" soul food and the inspiration for REM's 1992 album title, *Automatic for the People*. ☎ 706-353-7797; 1016 E Broad St; mains $4-8; ☺ 11am-6pm Tue-Sat

DRINK
40 Watt Club
Athens' most legendary venue for live music. ☎ 706-549-7871; www.40watt.com; 285 W Washington St; cover $5-15; ☺ 9pm-2am

Caledonia Lounge
See up-and-coming live music from the Athens scene here before it graduates to the 40 Watt or Georgia Theatre. ☎ 802-295-4600; www.caledonialounge.com; 256 W Clayton St; cover $6; ☺ 10pm-2am
Georgia Theatre
Athens' biggest venue hosts a variety of local and national acts (but we saw Dave Matthews play a sorority gig here in the '90s!). ☎ 706-549-9918; www.georgia theatre.com; 215 N Lumpkin St; cover $5-25; ☺ 10pm-2am

SLEEP
Foundry Park Inn
Athens' nicest hotel is an 1820 replica row house that also houses a rustic pub and concert venue. ☎ 706-549-7020; www.foundryparkinn.com; 295 E Dougherty St; r $115-145; ♿ ✿
UGA Center for Continuing Education
Turn a blind eye to the old-school Victorian decor and this convenient hotel on UGA's campus is good value. ☎ 888-295-8894; www.georgiacenter.uga.edu.com; 1197 S Lumpkin St; r $99-109; ♿

SUGGESTED READS
- *Party Out Of Bounds: The B-52s, REM, and the Kids Who Rocked Athens, Georgia,* Rodger Lyle Brown
- *Adventures in Hi-Fi,* Tim Abbot & Rob Jovanovic

USEFUL WEBSITES
www.southernshelter.com
www.visitathensga.com

LINK YOUR TRIP
www.lonelyplanet.com/trip-planner

Hogs & Heifers: A Georgia BBQ Odyssey

WHY GO From North Carolina to Memphis, "Southern BBQ" is a fat-soaked umbrella encompassing smoked meat soaking in succulent sauces with countless regional variations. Georgia's BBQ is no exception. Revered Southern food historian and author John T Edge leads us on a pot-bellied journey through Georgia's pilgrimage-worthy BBQ pits.

The Deep South's contributions to the American culinary landscape are well documented – fried green tomatoes and pecan pie among them – but perhaps no food is more inherently Southern than a juicy plate of smoked meat. As we might once have overheard at a Georgia-Florida football game, "It ain't a tailgate if BBQ ain't ate."

In Georgia, the term BBQ is synonymous with chopped or pulled pork. Sure, there is chicken and beef brisket, but they play second fiddle to the hog around here. Wake up at ❶ **Highland Inn**, a bygone lodging stuck between hostel and hotel, in Atlanta's trendy Virginia-Highland neighborhood and make your way east to ❷ **Old Brick Pit** on Peachtree Rd in Chamblee. Located just outside Atlanta's city limits, a massive brick pit as old-fashioned as the barn in which it sits stands true to its name. Pulled pork doused in a vinegar-based sauce (rare in Atlanta) piled high on a sandwich with coleslaw is the big seller here.

Heading north out of Atlanta on I-75 then I-575, two dueling BBQ joints with a storied history are using pulled pork as ammunition in a culinary political war. In tiny Cherry Log, halfway between Ellijay and Blue Ridge, liberal BBQ is served up at ❸ **Holloway's Pink Pig**, a favorite of former President Jimmy Carter. About 10 miles south on Hwy 515, you can't miss ❹ **Colonel Poole's**, a right-wing roadhouse

TIME
3 days

DISTANCE
740 miles

BEST TIME TO GO
Mar – May

START
Atlanta

END
Marietta

ALSO GOOD FOR

HISTORY &
CULTURE

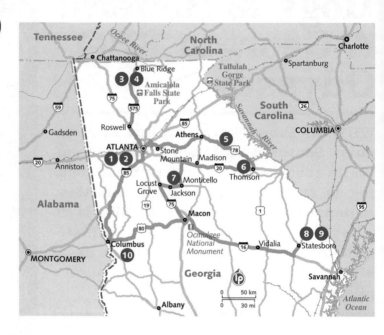

that still hangs Pat Buchanan For President signage inside – and is known as the Taj-Ma-Hog – just off the highway. Almost as interesting as the excellent pulled pork here is the Pig Hall of Fame, which looks like a folk art pet cemetery for pigs with small piglet signs dedicated to regular customers peppering the hillside like little portly headstones.

ASK A LOCAL

"I've been coming to **Fresh Air** since 1948. That's 60 years! I was a student at Mercer University in Macon and I used to hitchhike up and down Hwy 42. Then I got a car and I kept coming. I'm still coming. It's some of the best BBQ I have ever tasted. It's always excellent."

Jim A Langley, Savannah, GA

5 **Paul's** in Lexington, 16 miles or so east of Athens on Hwy 78, has been a Saturday-only affair since 1929. Jimmy Paul, a third-generation smoker, reckons he cooks 50lb to 60lb of barbecued pork on any given Saturday (about three hogs). The pulled pork is served on old-school checked tablecloths. Don't even think about showing up after noon unless you want to eat nothing but baked beans and 'slaw. Continue south on Hwy 78 to **6** **Neal's** in Thomson, where the hash (leftover pork mixed with BBQ sauce and served over rice) is every bit as important as the BBQ, still done here in a 55-gallon wash pot.

From Thomson, head down I-20 westbound to Hwy 36 south into Jackson. You can see the smoke billowing from the chimneystack as you crest the slight bend in Hwy 42 out of town: **7** **Fresh Air** beckons, the Holy Grail of

Georgia BBQ. The old, pioneer-style wooden street shack holds its ground here as if to declare, "We haven't changed a damn thing in 80 years." The outdoor seating area in front is covered in sawdust. Fresh Air only does three things: chopped pork, Brunswick Stew and coleslaw. No ribs. No shoulder. No Boston Butt (even though we are in Butts County). The hams here spend a full 24 hours in the smoker and have done so since 1929. The result is transcendent in BBQ circles. You have reached swine nirvana.

A Civil Rights case was once fought over the integration of **8** **Vandy's** in Statesboro, an institution in town since the '30s. Simplicity wins at this joint located a few hours south on I-75 and I-16 (east): its chopped pork sandwich is served with a vinegar and mustard–based sauce on two slices of Sunbeam white bread. The BBQ is smoked overnight in a massive block and brick pit out back to beat the Georgia heat. You're far east at this point, so it's a good place to crash for the night. Just around the corner from Vandy's, Blind Willie McTell was said to have written "Statesboro Blues," a song popularized by the Allman Brothers, at the historic **9** **Statesboro Inn**.

THE BBQ TIMES ARE A-CHANGIN'

Though Georgia BBQ remains fiercely traditional, an influx of immigration in the South is changing its face, according to Southern food expert John T Edge. "At Old Brick Pit BBQ in Atlanta, they still carry the wood from the pile to the pit in a liberated Winn-Dixie shopping cart. It's hyper-traditional BBQ, but reflecting the shifting demographic of Georgia everyone who works there is Mexican or Indonesian. It looks like the New South."

Directly west across the state as the crow flies, another mustard-based sauce reigns supreme in Columbus. At **10** **Smokey Pig**, the tangy, spicy, damn-near-perfect Chattahoochee-style sauce is bottled and sold. You just won't be able to resist buying some. One dousing of this miracle juice on your bite-sized pork (a unique cut designed to forgo the necessity of a knife – why that's important we're not sure, but we do not argue with anyone producing anything this good) and you'll become an addict too. Best in show.

This culinary odyssey ends in Marietta, just north of Atlanta on I-185 and I-85, at **11** **Sam & Dave's BBQ2**. For $300, you can take BBQ cooking classes here. You've had the rest, now learn to make the best.

Kevin Raub

TRIP INFORMATION

DO & EAT

Colonel Poole's
Right-wing roadside BBQ specializing in pulled pork served from the gates of its Taj-Ma-Hog. ☎ 706-635-4100; 164 Craig St, E Ellijay; mains $3.50-9.50; ☻ 11am-6pm Thu, to 8pm Fri & Sat, to 7pm Sun; ♿

Fresh Air
The Holy Grail. Since 1929, this family-owned glorified roadside shack offers Swine Heaven to all those who make the pilgrimage. ☎ 770-775-3182; 1164 Hwy 42, Jackson; mains $6-7; ☻ 8am-8pm Mon-Thu, to 9pm Fri & Sat, to 8:30pm Sun; ♿

Holloway's Pink Pig
Leftist BBQ joint favored by President Jimmy Carter; in a roadside log cabin in tiny Cherry Log, GA. ☎ 706-276-3311; 824 Cherry Log St, Cherry Log; mains $4-13; ☻ 10am-10pm Tue-Sat; ♿

Neal's
Hash is still prepared in a 55-gallon wash pot at this weekends-only joint with excellent pulled pork. ☎ 706-595-2594; 664 Augusta Hwy SE, Thomson; mains $3-7; ☻ 9am-8pm Thu, to 10pm Fri, to 9pm Sat; ♿

Old Brick Pit
The massive brick pit inside this old barn in Chamblee smokes pulled pork and ribs old school—style for nearly 24 hours. ☎ 770-986-7727; 4805 Peachtree Rd NE, Chamblee; mains $2.50-9; ☻ 11am-7pm Mon-Sat; ♿

Paul's
Third-generation smokers run this white clapboard shrine of Georgia BBQ. Get here early. ☎ 706-338-5099; Hwy 78, Main St, Lexington; mains $3-11; ☻ 9:30am-2pm Sat & July 4; ♿

Sam & Dave's BBQ2
The *Atlanta Journal-Constitution's* number one rated BBQ in Atlanta, smoked low and slow for 14 hours. Go for the pulled pork. ☎ 770-372-2272; 660 Whitlock Ave, Marietta; mains $5-13; ☻ 11am-8pm Mon-Thu, to 9pm Fri & Sat; ♿

Smokey Pig
Mustard-based Chattahoochee-style BBQ cut two ways: bite-sized and chipped. ☎ 706-327-9253; 1617 11th Ave, Columbus; mains $3-9; ☻ 10:30am-7pm Mon-Fri, to 5pm Sat; ♿

Vandy's
The sign is nearly faded away at this 60-year-old joint specializing in a mustard-based chopped pork sandwich on white bread. ☎ 912-764-2444; 22 W Vine St, Statesboro; mains $4-7; ☻ 6am-3pm Mon-Sat; ♿

SLEEP

Highland Inn
A great-value option near Virginia-Highland, one of Atlanta's most desirable urban neighborhoods. ☎ 404-874-5756; www.thehighlandinn.com; 644 N Highland Ave, Atlanta; r $109

Statesboro Inn
The homey and historic choice, walking distance from Vandy's. An Allman Brothers song was said to have been written here. ☎ 912-489-8628; www.statesboroinn.com; 106 S Main St, Statesboro; r $95-175; ♿

USEFUL WEBSITES
www.georgia.org
www.johntedge.com

LINK YOUR TRIP

www.lonelyplanet.com/trip-planner

Brunswick & the Golden Isles

WHY GO The four barrier islands that make up Georgia's Golden Isles – St Simons, Sea Island, Jekyll Island and Little St Simons Island – are a spectacular 100-mile stretch of maritime forests, wildlife-rich estuaries, blowing dunes, wild beaches and affluent coastal towns that evoke a bygone era. Georgia's best-kept secret is out.

TIME
4 days

DISTANCE
140 miles

BEST TIME TO GO
Mar – May

START
Savannah, GA

END
Brunswick, GA

Most folks who aren't from the South know very little about Georgia's fabled coast and the four barrier islands (two public, two private) that elevate it to one of America's most diverse and interesting shorelines. St Simons, Sea Island, Jekyll Island and Little St Simons Island are the jewels of the South, an affluent set of isles that offer memorable food, pristine nature, kayaking, one-third of the entire East Coast's salt marshes, preserved 18th- and 19th-century Southern architecture and, perhaps most importantly, a damn fine place to get away from it all.

The gateway to Brunswick and the Golden Isles is US-17, which rolls south from Savannah on a scenic coastal drive through several picturesque and tiny Georgia towns. Pass through the blink-and-you'll-miss-it town of Midway and take a 15-minute detour east on US-84 past Fort Morris until the road ends at ❶ **Sunbury Crab Company**, one of those truly special finds that elude most travelers these days. Here you'll find a Key West–style tree house built from rescued wood from old barns and department stores. The menu is whatever is fresh that day: blue crab caught that morning by the son; shrimp caught by the neighbor; and oysters brought in by the uncle. This is all steamed and chased by cold beer overlooking the gorgeous St Catherine's Sound.

Head back to US-17 into the small town of Darien, where fort buffs will dig ❷ **Fort King George**, a remarkably reconstructed version

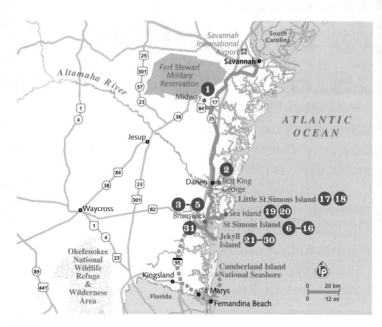

of Georgia's first fort, a British outpost dating back to 1721. The town of **3** **Brunswick** is next, well worth a stroll for its antique shops and the potpourri of architectural styles along its main drag, Newcastle St, and throughout its Old Town National Register Historic District.

True roadies with an appetite will want to head straight out MLK Blvd from downtown to **4** **Willie's Weenie Wagon**. The pork chop sandwich slathered with mustard is road food at its finest and the family folks that run the place are as friendly as spiked eggnog at Christmas – they're so confident you'll love the sandwich, they offer a $2000 reward to anyone finding a better one in Glynn County. This place is *the* reason you are on a road trip.

> *"The family folks that run the place are as friendly as spiked eggnog at Christmas."*

An interesting way to kill an afternoon here is hopping aboard a genuine shrimp trawler. The **5** **Lady Jane Shrimp Boat** takes tourists out trawling for shrimp in the St Simons Sound. Before you know it, the shrimp is peeled and served. It doesn't get any fresher than that.

Next stop: **6** **St Simons Island**. At roughly the size of Manhattan, St Simons is the largest of the Golden Isles and therefore the most developed. But it's not without its charms – namely a clutch of unconventional churches, some great watersport action and world-class golf. Follow the St Simons Torras Causeway over the Marshes of Glynn onto the island. Stop and park near the **7** **St Simons Visitors Center** (for maps and info) and stroll through the main village drag to ponder your next move over a no-frills lunch at **8** **Dressner's Village Café**, the island's requisite greasy spoon.

Great options on St Simons range from a satisfying three-hour kayak trip through the island's marshes with **9** **Southeast Adventure**; or, if you don't feel like getting in the marshes but want to knock a few balls around them, you could head over to **10** **King & Prince Golf Course** at Hampton Club, one of Georgia's finest courses; or educate yourself in a museum. There are a few here, but the **11** **Maritime Center Museum** is the most interesting, covering coastal Georgia's maritime history in a Roosevelt-era coast guard station that's on the National Register of Historic Places.

> **ASK A LOCAL**
>
> "I love to kayak through the salt marsh on Jekyll Island. In the early morning, it's still cool – you don't bake in the sun and you can see lots of animals. There are so many birds, manatees, and even an occasional sea turtle. The **Tidelands Nature Center** (www.tidelands4h.org) offers trips out there."
>
> *Alicia Marin, Jekyll Island, GA*

Settle in at the **12** **Village Inn & Pub**, a lush property with a little extra character (and a nicer price tag) than most in the area. Not as well located or as comfy but a steal for the barrier islands is the **13** **Sea Palms Inn**, located on Frederica Rd heading to the island's north side.

Being the most developed of Georgia's barrier islands, there are more nighttime distractions on St Simons than her neighbors. Stop into **14** **Blackwater Grill** for good Lowcountry/Cajun, including the area's must-try culinary creation, Brunswick Stew. The house shrimp and grits are also perfect. **15** **Gnat's Landing**, across the parking lot, is a great bar in this area – folks spill over each other on the outdoor deck here. On Sunday, it's the place to be. If you head out in the village, it's all about **16** **Rafter's**, a blues bar that is the local watering hole of choice for both St Simon socialites and the mainland khaki brigade.

The next day it's worth booking into the **17** **Lodge on Little St Simons Island**, a former hunting lodge on the private **18** **Little St Simons Island**; otherwise, take a day trip from St Simons. This unhurried, 10,000-acre island is an unspoiled jewel. Four successional stages of vegetation (dune meadow, wax myrtle and sweet grass, pine forest and climax maritime forest) make it a haven for kayaking, interpretive nature tours and birding. It's a miraculous getaway – full of European fallow deer, sea turtles and gators – that is preciously undeveloped. The Golden Isles' other private island, **19** **Sea Island**, isn't very visitor-friendly unless you're staying at **20** **Cloister Inn**, the coast's most luxurious property.

Departing St Simons, cross the sail-evoking Sydney Lanier Bridge to the Jekyll Island Causeway, the gateway to **21** **Jekyll Island**. This glorious island – 65%

undeveloped – was once the stomping ground for America's rich and famous, and it's not hard to see why: woodlands and marshlands dominate the landscape here, peppered with some of the most interesting architecture this side of Charleston. Stop at **㉒ Jekyll Island Information Center** for a wealth of information and brochures and continue down the marsh-hemmed causeway to the entrance to the island.

DETOUR

Cumberland Island, Georgia's largest and southernmost barrier island, is the belle of the ball. Isolated, rugged, and hauntingly pristine, this 57-sq-mile island is brimming with wild marshes, unspoiled beaches and a population and infrastructure lost in time amid cultural ruins and sturdy oak trees dripping in Spanish moss.

From Brunswick, it's an hour's drive south on I-95 to Fernandina Beach, FL, where ferries operated by **Greyfield Inn** (www.greyfieldinn.com) – the island's only accommodations – leave three times a day.

Sleep in a bygone era at the massive **㉓ Jekyll Island Club Hotel**, a historic Victorian monolith dating back to 1886 that once hosted folks with names like Rockefeller, Goodyear, Macy, Vanderbilt and Pulitzer. Their winter cottages are now the highlight of the **㉔ Jekyll Island National Historic Landmark District**. Built between 1884 and 1929, these historic mansions are some of the prettiest structures you ever did see. Most are closed to the public, but you can go in the **㉕ Old Infirmary**, once owned by Joseph Pulitzer and now a two-story book and gift shop that's well worth a stroll. You can see inside a few of the fancier buildings on a **㉖ Jekyll Island Museum** trolley tour. Alternatively, rent a bike from the hotel; the whole island lends itself to cycling and features more than 20 miles of bike trails.

Head across the street to Jekyll Island Club Wharf, where JP Morgan's *Corsair* and *Corsair II* once anchored. Plant yourself on the deck at **㉗ Rah Bar** and order a Lowcountry boil, the coastal *Jawga* version of a seafood platter: crab legs, shrimp, crawdaddies, corn, pork sausage and red potatoes. If you don't get too hyped on the excellent margaritas, sign up for a nighttime turtle walk at **㉘ Georgia Sea Turtle Center**, a rescue, rehabilitation and interactive research facility working to save Georgia's sea turtles.

Get up at the crack of dawn and head out to **㉙ Driftwood Beach**, an apocalyptic beach on Jekyll's northeast point that's saturated with enormous washed-up oak trees. It's magical at dawn. In fact, spend the morning lounging on any of Jekyll's 9 miles of beach. **㉚ St Andrews Beach** is another fine choice – you can see the dolphins come close to shore to feed in the early morning. On your way back to I-95, your likely exit route, don't miss the **㉛ Georgia Pig**, a petrified cedar cabin of smoked BBQ goodness near the intersection of US-17 and I-95 back in Brunswick. Definitely let some chopped pork slap you on your taste buds on your way out the door.

Kevin Raub

TRIP INFORMATION

GETTING THERE
From Atlanta, head south on I-75 to Macon, where you'll pick up I-16 east straight into Savannah. US-17 heads out of town south to Brunswick.

DO

Fort King George
An impressive reproduction of Georgia's oldest fort, a British outpost dating back to 1721. ☎ 912-437-4770; www.gastateparks .com; 1600 Wayne St, Darien; adult/child $5/2.50; ⏰ 9am-5pm Tue-Sat, 2-5:30pm Sun; ♿

Georgia Sea Turtle Center
This interactive sea turtle sanctuary and hospital is worth a visit. Don't miss the nightly turtle walks. ☎ 912-635-4444; www.georgiaseaturtlecenter.org; 214 Stable Rd, Jekyll Island; ⏰ 10am-6pm; ♿

King & Prince Golf Course
The prettiest 18 holes (6465yd, par 72) on St Simons, some on scenic marsh islands. ☎ 912-634-0255; www.kingand prince.com; 100 Tabbystone, St Simons Island; ⏰ 8am-5pm

Jekyll Island Museum
The museum preserves 34 historic structures and 53 archeological sites and offers self-guided walking and trolley tours through the Historic Landmark District. ☎ 912-635-4036; www.jekyllisland.com; 100 Stable Rd, Jekyll Island; tours adult $10-16, child $5-7; ⏰ 9am-5pm; ♿

Jekyll Island Information Center
Stop here for invaluable maps and information before crossing onto Jekyll Island. ☎ 912-635-3636; www.jekyllisland.com; 901 Jekyll Causeway, Jekyll Island; ⏰ 9am-5pm; ♿

Lady Jane Shrimp Boat
Go shrimpin' in the St Simmons Sound in this unique shrimp trawler. ☎ 912-265-5711; www.credlesadventures.com; 1200 Glynn Ave, Brunswick; adult/child $40/25; ⏰ 3:45pm Wed & Fri; ♿

Maritime Center Museum
An interesting look into the maritime history of the Georgia Coast. ☎ 912-638-4666; www.stsimonslighthouse; St Simons Island; adult/child $6/3; ⏰ 10am-5pm Mon-Sat; ♿

Old Infirmary
Eclectic bookshop and boutique inside an 1890 cottage formerly owned by Joseph Pulitzer. ☎ 912-635-3076; www.jekyllbooks .com; 101 Old Plantation Rd, Jekyll Island; ⏰ 9:30am-5pm; ♿

Southeast Adventure
The best kayak outfitter in the area. The three-hour St Simon trip winds through salt marshes and maritime forest to Sea Island. ☎ 912-638-6732; www.southeastadven ture.com; 313 Mallory St, St Simons Island; tours from $40; ⏰ 9:30am-5pm; ♿

St Simons Visitors Center
Eclectic bookshop and boutique inside an 1890 cottage formerly owned by Joseph Pulitzer. ☎ 912-638-9014; www.bgicvb .com; 530-B Beachview Dr, St Simons Island; ⏰ 9am-5pm; ♿

EAT

Blackwater Grill
This Lowcountry/Cajun place serves up the area's best Brunswick Stew. ☎ 912-634-6333; 260 Redfern Village, St Simons; mains $14-24; ⏰ 5:30-9pm Sun-Thu, to 10pm Fri & Sat

Dressner's Village Café
The island's classic joint: cheap, a little greasy and full of local color. ☎ 912-634-1217; 223 Mallory St, St Simons Island; mains $4-7.50; ⏰ 7:30am-2:30pm Mon-Fri, 8am-2:30pm Sat & Sun; ♿

Georgia Pig
Old-school open-pit BBQ in a roadside cedar cabin. A good spot to try Brunswick Stew. ☎ 912-264-6664; US-17 & I-95, Brunswick; mains $5.50-12.50; ⏰ 11am-8pm Mon-Thu, to 9pm Fri & Sat, to 7pm Sun; ♿

Rah Bar
Lowcountry boils are the main event at this casual outdoor seafooder on the Jekyll Island wharf. ☎ 912-635-3800; One Pier Rd, Jekyll Island; mains $8-21.50; ⏰ 11:30am-late Tue-Sun

Sunbury Crab Company

You can spend days sucking down fresh crab chased with suds in this Key West–style tree house on St Catherine's Sound. ☎ 912-884-8640; 541 Brigantine Dunmore Rd; mains $8-27; 🕑 5-10pm Wed-Fri, noon-10pm Sat, noon-7:30pm Sun

Willie's Weenie Wagon

The pork-chop sandwich put this family-run roadside classic on the map – there's $2000 if you find a better one in Glynn County! ☎ 912-264-1146; 3599 Althama Ave, Brunswick; mains $4.50-6; 🕑 10am-10pm Tue-Sat; 🔥

DRINK

Gnat's Landing

Charismatic spot for brews and chews with a nice outdoor patio, walking distance from Sea Palms Inn. Especially popular on Sundays. 912-638-7378; 310 Redfern Village, St Simons; mains $7-13; 🕑 11:30am-midnight

Rafter's

In the village, head to this blues and raw bar for a big ol' dose of local St Simons color...in a good way. ☎ 912-634-9755; 315 1/2 Mallory St, St Simons; 🕑 4:30pm-2am Mon-Sat

SLEEP

Cloister Inn

Horse stables, a 56,000-sq-ft spa, 54 holes of golf – no luxurious stone is left unturned at this Mediterranean-inspired resort, the Golden Isles' finest. ☎ 866-879-6238; www.seaisland.com; Sea Island; r from $650.

Lodge on Little St Simons Island

Isolated historic lodge on the pristine and private Little St Simons. Book a month ahead for day trips. ☎ 912-638-7472; www.littlessi.com; 1000 Hampton Pt, Little St Simons Island; all-inclusive r from $450; 🕑 May-Sep; 🔥

Jekyll Island Club Hotel

Sleep in a bygone era in this grand historic landmark hotel built in 1886. ☎ 912-635-2600; www.jekyllclub.com; 371 Riverview Dr, Jekyll Island; r $219-359; 🔥

Sea Palms Inn

Despite the strip-mall location, this is a steal for the price. There's even flat-panel TVs and complimentary wine and cheese from Tuesday to Thursday. ☎ 912-634-0660; www.seapalmsinn.com; 411 Longview Pl, St Simons; r from $119; 🔥 🐾

Village Inn & Pub

Great-value option with a lush pool area just steps from the village. ☎ 912-634-6056; www.villageinnandpub.org; 500 Mallory St, St Simons Island; d $160-180; 🔥

USEFUL WEBSITES

www.bgivb.com

LINK YOUR TRIP

www.lonelyplanet.com/trip-planner

Midnight in the Garden: Eccentric Savannah

WHY GO Savannah is a living museum of Southern architecture and antebellum charm, but it's also home to haunting tales of things that go bump in the night and no shortage of quirky characters that attract fans of "Midnight in the Garden of Good and Evil," the book that put Savannah on the map.

TIME
2 days

BEST TIME TO GO
Mar – May

START
Savannah, GA

END
Savannah, GA

ALSO GOOD FOR
CITY

Savannah is many things: Gorgeous, historically fascinating and full of Old South charisma. But there's a dark side to this sassy charmer. Tales of aggravated spirits, haunted homes and cemeteries, and things that go bump in the night often earns Savannah the title of America's "Most Haunted City." If that weren't enough, John Berendt's bestseller, *Midnight in the Garden of Good and Evil*, the (more or less true) tale of the murder of the town's hustler by a gay antique dealer, put the town's quirky characters and eccentric side out there for the world to see.

And visitors came in droves (tourism in Savannah multiplied tenfold after the book's publication) to see for themselves the haunted houses, the oddball characters and the peculiar tales and legends that have fueled this sultry Southern belle of the Georgia coast since 1733.

Start your tour at ❶ Clary's Café, a Savannah breakfast institution since 1903 but made infinitely more famous by "the book," as *Midnight* is referred to in these parts. Inside, it now features a stained-glass rendering of the novel's dust jacket.

North on Abercorn St you'll find one of Savannah's spooky graveyards, ❷ Colonial Park Cemetery. Notice the Masonic bricks located along the western edge of the park, one of only two places in Savannah where you'll find them. They were put there to insure whatever is down below *stays* down below (the cemetery's original boundaries extended

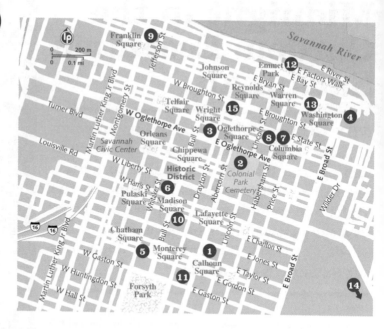

well beyond Abercorn St). A quick jaunt northwest lies ❸ **Wright Square**, one of several haunted squares. Town hangings are to blame here, and locals say it's the only square with no Spanish Moss for this very reason.

Almost every establishment in the historic district has a ghost story, but some are better documented than others. Take ❹ **Pirate's House**, for instance. Death and murder were no strangers here in the 1700s and the secret passageways and tunnels below the restaurant have been known to spawn all sort of shrieks, cries and other unexplainable racket.

> "Someone built a home on top of the unmarked graves of the 1500 dead soldiers who lost their lives there."

If you survive lunch, take in the location of another infamous homicide, the one that put Savannah on the map. The ❺ **Mercer-Williams House Museum** was purchased and restored by eccentric art dealer Jim Williams in 1969. Inside you'll find the room in which Danny Hansford was murdered under questionable circumstances in 1981. No one mentions "the Book" here.

One square north is the site of the second bloodiest battle of the Revolutionary War, the Siege of Savannah. Of course, someone built a home on top of the unmarked graves of the 1500 dead soldiers who lost their lives there. ❻ **Sorrel-Weed House**, built in 1840, has attracted everyone from the Sci-Fi channel's *Ghost Hunters* to HGTV's *If These Walls Could Talk*.

Call it a night at one of several frightening beds, such as ❼ **Kehoe House**, where twins died in the chimney and haven't vacated the premises since. Or you could risk life and limb in room 204 of ❽ **17 Hundred 90 Inn**. Poor Anna, heartbroken over a boy, leapt to her death from the window in this room. It has been called the Most Haunted Hotel in America on more than one occasion since. By now you might need a drink. Head to ❾ **Club One**, where Lady Chablis – of *Midnight* fame – still performs once a month.

Sufficiently scared and likely scarred, a little retail therapy is in order. Embrace Savannah's artistic side at ❿ **Shop SCAD**, where you'll find the eccentric wares of students from the city's well-respected College of Art & Design. Of course, it just wouldn't be right if you couldn't tote home a carry-on full of *Midnight* souvenirs. ⓫ **"The Book"** gift shop is the spot for all things good and evil. Cries of hunger should be upon you by now, but they're likely not as threatening as those coming from the cranky ap-

ASK A LOCAL

"The scariest thing in Savannah is spending a night at **Bonaventure Cemetery** when you're not supposed to be there. You're supposed to be out by 5pm. I wanted to shoot pictures late. Once it finally got dark, I noticed I couldn't get cell reception, so I couldn't call my friend to pick me up. If you don't know where to be picked up, you're stuck inside and can't get out. It's spooky, but it's probably the most beautiful place to shoot pictures in Savannah. Living here is like living in a postcard."
Bunny Ware, Savannah, GA

paritions said to be living in the attic wine cellar at the ⓬ **Shrimp Factory**, another of Savannah's possessed dining destinations.

Walk off lunch by taking a stroll past the most haunted house in America, the private ⓭ **Hampton-Lillibridge House**. During the restoration of this home, workers were freaked about all sorts of unexplainable events, so much so that many of them bailed on the job, and a priest performed an exorcism of the house. It didn't take.

Late afternoon is the best time to stroll Savannah's most eerie burial grounds, the ⓮ **Bonaventure Cemetery**, located on the outskirts of town. The grave-stones here are picturesque even for those who aren't cemetery buffs, but once you stumble upon little Gracie Watson's harrowing grave, you'll hightail it out of there so fast, you'll think twice about returning to a cemetery again. "Little Gracie" died in 1889, during Savannah's yellow fever epidemic. Her ghost is said to wander the rooms and halls at ⓯ **Marshall House**, an-other fine historic hotel in Savannah where guests report strange caresses and careless whispers. Sculpted from a photo taken shortly before her death, her gravestone depicts Gracie in her Easter finery. It looks like a cross between the long-haired silhouette in *The Ring* and every image of a ghost you've ever seen. Creepy. If I were you, I'd get out of there. The gates are snapping shut soon.
Kevin Raub

TRIP INFORMATION

GETTING THERE
From Atlanta, head south on I-75 to Macon, where you'll pick up I-16 east straight into Savannah.

DO

Mercer-Williams House Museum
This elegant mansion was the scene of the murder in *Midnight*. ☎ 912-236-6352; www.mercerhouse.com; 429 Bull St; adult/child $12.50/8; ⏱ 10:30am-4:10pm Mon-Sat, 12:30-4:10pm Sun

Shop SCAD
Savannah's most eclectic shop, full of wares from the city's art students. ☎ 912-525-5180; www.shopscadonline.com; 340 Bull St; ⏱ 9am-5:30pm Mon-Wed, 9am-8pm Thu & Fri, 10am-8pm Sat, 12-5pm Sun

Sorrel-Weed House
Tour this 1840 Greek Revival mansion featured on the Sci-Fi channel's *Ghost Hunters*. Yes, they found ghosts. ☎ 912-236-8888; www.savannahtours.net; 6 W Harris St; adult/child $15/10; ⏱ 10am-4pm; ♿

"The Book"
Your one-stop book and gift shop for all things *Midnight in the Garden of Good and Evil*. ☎ 912-233-3867; 127 E Gordon St; ⏱ 10am-6pm Mon-Sat, 11am-4:30pm Sun

EAT & DRINK

Clary's Café
Savannahians always flocked to this all-day-breakfast café; the rest of the world has only been coming since reading about it in *Midnight*. ☎ 912-233-0402; cnr Abercorn & Jones; mains $5-12; ⏱ 7am-4pm Mon-Thu, 8am-5pm Sat, 8am-4pm Sun; ♿

Club One
Lady Chablis still performs once a month at this gay cabaret bar, voted the city's best dance club since 1997. ☎ 912-232-0200; 1 Jefferson St; ⏱ 7:30am-10pm Mon-Fri, 7:30am-11pm Sat & Sun

Pirate's House
Seafaring ghosts from the 1700s loiter in the basement and secret tunnels beneath this Lowcountry staple. ☎ 912-233-5757; 20 E Broad St; mains $17-26; ⏱ 11am-9:30pm Sun-Thu, to 10pm Fri & Sat; ♿

Shrimp Factory
Servers at this coastal seafooder cringe when asked to retrieve anything from the haunted wine cellar. ☎ 912-236-4229; 313 E River St; mains $21-29; ⏱ 11am-10pm Mon-Thu, 11am-11pm Fri & Sat, noon-10pm Sun; ♿

SLEEP

17 Hundred 90 Inn
The shrieks of Anna, who plunged to her death from room 204, still linger in the night here. ☎ 912-236-7123; www.17hundred90.com; 307 E President St; r $160-215; ♿

Kehoe House
Twins died in this exquisite Queen Anne–style B&B (rooms 201 and 203 are the supernatural epicenter). ☎ 912-232-1020; www.kehoehouse.com; 123 Habersham St; r $200-400; ♿

Marshall House
Dismembered bones once occupied the basement of this former Civil War hospital, now an upscale hotel. Strange caresses in the night could be Gracie, a yellow fever victim. ☎ 912-644-7896; www.marshallhouse.com; 123 E Broughton St; r $199-249; ♿

USEFUL WEBSITES
www.savcvb.com

LINK YOUR TRIP
www.lonelyplanet.com/trip-planner

Savannah's Seafood & Soul Food

FOOD &
DRINK

WHY GO Lady & Sons might have put Savannah's culinary heritage on the foodie map, but that's merely the tip of the iceberg lettuce. From culturally unique Lowcountry boils and Southern comfort cuisine to exquisite seafood and soothing soul food, Savannah is an ideal spot to "put some South in your mouth."

TIME
3 days

BEST TIME TO GO
Mar – May

START
Savannah, GA

END
Savannah, GA

ALSO GOOD FOR

CITY

Long before literary tourism descended upon Savannah, it was gorgeous: a historic and meticulously preserved town brimming with quaint squares, antebellum mansions, tall tales, and a local population as colorful as a Rajasthani spice market. Those folks liked to eat.

Like New Orleans, the contribution of Savannah's culinary scene to the overall appeal of the town comes second to architecture and history, but also like the Big Easy, most visitors walk away with gluttonous tales of gastronomic indulgence rather than memories of the exquisite ironwork here, or the extraordinary use of primary colors in the rare 16th-century painting on display there. Refinement in Savannah is hardly unique – a bad meal, though, is much more difficult to stumble across.

For a palate-dancing introduction to Southern soul food, start your day at ❶ **Mom and Nikki's,** a working-class soul food cafeteria that is as basic as it gets. Mornings here offer grits, cheese eggs, a choice of meat (shrimp, pork, salmon, all lovingly prepared in indecipherable ways), and a fluffy buttermilk biscuit. The spicy smothered shrimp over cheese grits is the way you want to go. The staff will even call you honey.

Savannah tends to be hot and muggy most of the year, so the best time to stroll the historic district's quaint streets and picturesque squares is just after breakfast, before the paralyzing midday sun turns

BEST TRIP

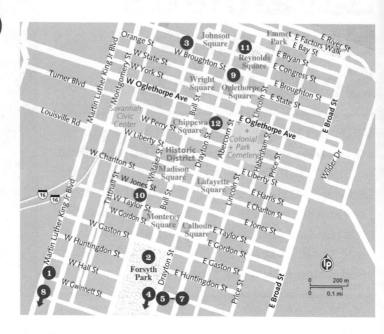

your clothes into a sweat-soaked mess. The two-tiered cast-iron fountain at ❷ **Forsyth Park** provides a quintessential Kodak moment, but Savannah's charm lurks in the more residential squares arranged through the historic district like perfectly positioned chess pieces of colonial glory. The only reason to stop wandering from one gorgeous square to the next is hunger.

No foodie pilgrimage to Savannah would be complete without popping in to Paula Deen's Southern food mecca, ❸ **Lady & Sons**, if for no other reason than to pay homage to the empress herself. Deen's restaurant is now Savannah's most-visited attraction, a two-story affair that churns out Southern fare like shrimp and grits with Tasso ham to a clientele that's no stranger to antihypertensives and Oprah-like worship.

Around dinnertime, things start to get really interesting. Do yourself a favor and walk the mile or so from the center of the historic district to the stately ❹ **Elizabeth on 37th**, a turn-of-the-century mansion that has been a Georgian culinary icon since 1981. Southern food dressed up like a debutante is the draw. Cheese drop biscuits with house-made orange marmalade start things off here, a sort of Southern gourmet chips and salsa. Seasonal gems like lacquered South Carolina quail with curried crawfish and Michelin 3-star fresh greens and herbs from the on-property garden should follow. Walk the food coma off on your way to ❺ **Mansion on Forsyth Park**, where Savannah hoity-toityness collides with contemporary abstract art at the city's swankiest hotel.

The next morning, you need not go far for your next gourmand treat. **6** **700 Drayton**, the Mansion on Forsyth Park's signature restaurant, is also home to **7** **700 Drayton Kitchen Cooking School**, where chef Darin Seh-nert runs two- to three-hour cooking classes most mornings. Join a Low-country class, the South Carolinian, Caribbean-and-African-influenced, Cajun-paralleled cuisine that char-acterizes the local food from coastal Georgia to Charleston. You'll be serv-ing up shrimp with redeye gravy or pecan praline angel food cake back in Jersey in no time.

> **ASK A LOCAL** "The crab cakes at the **River House** are excep-tional – they're made from crab, not a bunch of bread crumbs and junk. I tell people from Mary-land that! Don't overlook the **Olde Pink House**. Go downstairs and listen to Johnny Mercer–type jazz that won't give you a headache. They do a jam up good job on their duck and it's under $20, a rarity in Savannah. Also, don't miss **700 Drayton** – they do a rack of lamb that'll kill ya!"
> *Kenneth Worthy, Savannah, GA*

Escape the tourist hordes for dinner by grabbing a cab out past the gor-geous mansions along Victory Rd to where the locals eat, **8** **New South Café**. The menu here is decidedly more upscale than the atmosphere, with a focus on grown-up versions of classics: boneless Georgia peanut-crusted fried chicken, wild Georgia shrimp and Andouille grit cakes, or crab cakes with Asiago cheese dressing. For a change of scenery, lay your head at the recently renovated **9** **Marshall House**, an upscale Savannah landmark.

You'll have to work for your food the next morning. The line outside **10** **Mrs Wilkes** begins as early as 8am and extends more than a snap bean's throw down the charming street on which it sits. It's first come, first serve at this Southern comfort-food institution. Once the lunch bell rings and you are seated family-style, the kitchen unloads on you: fried chicken, beef stew, meat loaf, cheese potatoes, collard greens, black-eyed peas, mac and cheese, rutabaga, candied yams, creamed corn…and biscuits. It's like Thanksgiving, the Last Supper and a final death-row meal rolled into one massive feast, chased with sweet tea.

"It's like Thanksgiving, the Last Supper and a final death-row meal rolled into one massive feast."

Another longtime Savannahian staple beckons for dinner, the antebellum-era **11** **Olde Pink House**, located on Rey-nolds Sq. An elegant evening here should include the signa-ture crispy scored flounder or the massive braised pork shank, but everything is memorable. Of course, if all of this is just too overwhelming, you can always do-it-yourself. Savannah's squares are tailor-made for romantic picnics. Head to **12** **Parker's Market** – you'll net all the wares you'll need to lose yourself in historical gluttony.

Kevin Raub

TRIP INFORMATION

GETTING THERE
From Atlanta, head south on I-75 to Macon, where you'll pick up I-16 (eastbound) straight into Savannah.

DO

700 Drayton Kitchen Cooking School
Boil and baste your way around Lowcountry cuisine (or Italian and Latin) with chef Darin Sehnert. ☎ 912-238-5158; www.700kitchen.com; 700 Drayton St; classes from $90

Parker's Market
An upscale convenience store perfect for stocking up on gourmet goodies for a picnic in one of Savannah's postcard-perfect squares. ☎ 912-233-1000; 222 Drayton St; ⊙ 24hr

EAT & DRINK

700 Drayton
Gulf Coast grouper with Georgia shrimp and fried green tomatoes highlight offerings here. ☎ 912-238-5158; www.700kitchen.com; 700 Drayton St; mains $24-34; ⊙ 6:30am-10pm Mon-Thu, to 11pm Fri-Sun

Elizabeth on 37th
The Southern culinary empire began by James Beard Foundation Award–winning chef Elizabeth Terry is carried on inside this romantic, stately mansion by her protégé, Kelly Yambor. ☎ 912-236-5547; 105 E 37th St; mains $29-37; ⊙ 6-10pm

Lady & Sons
Paula Deen's Southern buffet, rife with fried chicken and Middle America masses. ☎ 912-233-2600; 102 W Congress St; buffet $18, mains $19-28; ⊙ 11am-3pm & 5-10pm

Mom and Nikki's
This soul food cafeteria serving up smothered shrimp and cheese grits makes for an unforgettable breakfast. ☎ 912-233-7636; 714 MLK Jr Blvd; mains $5-8.50; ⊙ 7:30am-3pm Mon-Thu, to 4pm Fri, 8am-2pm Sat

Mrs Wilkes
A Southern food institution since 1943. ☎ 912-232-5997; 107 W Jones St; mains $16; ⊙ 11am-2pm Mon-Fri

New South Café
Travel out of the historic district for New Southern delights like Georgia peanut-crusted fried chicken and fried green tomato wraps. ☎ 912-233-7568; 2601 Skidaway Rd; mains $9-28; ⊙ 11am-3pm & 5-10pm Tue-Sat

Olde Pink House
Classic Southern dining with a twist in an elegant 18th-century pink mansion on Reynolds Sq. ☎ 912-232-4286; 23 Abercorn St; mains $17-29; ⊙ 5-10:30pm Sun & Mon, 11am-10:30pm Tue-Thu, to 11pm Fri & Sat

SLEEP

Mansion on Forsyth Park
Southern touches offset abstract art at Savannah's top address, home to 700 Drayton and the cooking school of the same name. ☎ 912-238-5158; www.mansiononforsythpark.com; 700 Drayton St; r $259-399; ⊛ ⊛

Marshall House
Centrally located upscale hotel that's also home to another of Savannah's award-winning (though stuffier) restaurants, 45 Bistro. ☎ 912-644-7896; www.marshallhouse.com; 123 E Broughton St; r $199-249; ⊛

USEFUL WEBSITES
www.savcvb.com
www.travelsouthflavours.com

LINK YOUR TRIP
www.lonelyplanet.com/trip-planner

Georgia & Alabama Backroads

WHY GO What's a road trip that never leaves the Interstate? I-this and I-that. There's no "I" in adventure. True road warriors bail on the interstates occasionally, looking to uncover that off-the-radar nugget of travel gold that lies beyond the exits on the roads less traveled. In Georgia and Alabama, unearthed treasures await.

Have you ever tried to take a road trip sans interstates? It's rather difficult. When President Dwight D Eisenhower made the interstate system happen in 1956, there were probably a whole lot of lost-in-time towns and off-the-beaten-path attractions that were more than a little nervous about business moving forward. Suddenly, the traffic wasn't passing through anymore. Luckily, being located off the main thoroughfare helps keep the homegrown stuff homey, and usually insures that a Subway or McDonald's won't be popping up anytime soon (though there are a few Starbucks in oddly far-flung areas of the country).

It's pretty much impossible not to use *any* interstates. Unless you have Sal Paradise kind of time, head out of Atlanta on I-75 (northbound) to I-575 (northbound) and follow smaller state roads to ① **Carters Lake**, a lovely emerald lake nestled in the southern end of the Blue Ridge Mountains, a haven for boating, bird watching, hiking and mountain biking. There are 62 miles of shoreline here and you can access all of it for a petty day-use fee of just $4 per vehicle. Stop at the ② **Carters Lake Marina**, where you can rent a pontoon boat (no experience necessary!) or settle into one of the roomy pine log cabins with expansive decks overlooking the lake. The most popular hiking trail in the area is the ③ **Amadahy Trail** (3.5 miles, two hours round-trip) offering scenic lake views. For cyclists, the ④ **Ridgeway Mountain Bike Trail**

TIME
4 – 5 days

DISTANCE
720 miles

BEST TIME TO GO
Mar – May

START
Atlanta, GA

END
Atlanta, GA

ALSO GOOD FOR

OUTDOORS

BEST TRIP

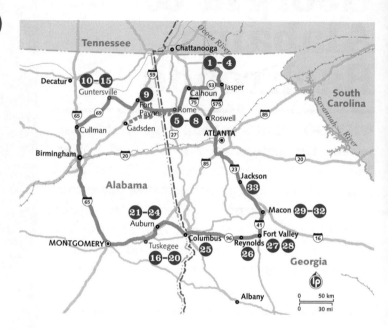

(6 miles, 40 minutes) is a mixture of single-track and narrow logging roads with creek crossings and technical downhills.

Head back to I-75 (southbound) for a few exits and take Hwy 53 to ❺ **Rome**, a small North Georgia town with a historic downtown and iconic ❻ **Clocktower** (which has told Romans the time accurately since its installation in 1872). A good place to stop for the night is ❼ **Hawthorn Suites**. Though a chain, it's located inside a 110-year-old former warehouse and still features original hardwood flooring and support beams. You can smell the history. Dinner must be at ❽ **Harvest Moon Café** which, truth be told, is a little too cool for Rome. The funky space, with its exposed brick, pop art and black-clad waiters, seems as though it was transported on a wide-load trailer straight from Midtown Atlanta.

Cross the state line into Alabama on Hwy 9 (westbound). First stop? Fort Payne, north on Hwy 35, where you'll see that Alabamians aren't afraid of a little self-love. Country music studs Alabama (the band) take musical narcissism to new heights at the ❾ **Alabama Museum**, a big ol' bear hug to themselves.

The largest lake in Alabama, ❿ **Lake Guntersville**, and its 950 miles of extensive shoreline, lie 45 miles west along Hwy 227 (westbound) just outside ⓫ **Guntersville**, a charming little shoreside resort town. The newly renovated

12 **Lodge at Lake Guntersville State Park**, about 10 miles east of town in **13** **Lake Guntersville State Park**, is the place to stay, right on the 69,000-acre reservoir. The park boasts 18 holes of golf, a small beach and 36 miles of hiking, but bass fishing is the sport that truly wets the whistles around here. **14** **Town Creek Fishing Center** on Hwy 227 can get you out on the water with boat and canoe rentals, fishing licenses, bait and tackle and supplies. Remember, as they say in Alabama, don't be a basshole on the water. **15** **Crawmama's**, in addition to sweeping the annual Best Restaurant Name Awards, is the place to feast on fresh seafood a few miles south of the main drag through town on Hwy 431.

From Guntersville, get back in touch with civilization on I-65 (southbound) through Birmingham and Montgomery to I-85 (eastbound) to **16** **Tuskegee**, located 8 miles off the interstate on Hwy 80 (take exit 32). School yourself on a little history at **17** **Tuskegee Institute National Historic Site**, which is home to the **18** **George Washington Carver Museum**, devoted to the iconic African American educator and Tuskegee University, and **19** **The Oaks**, the home of Booker T Washington, who was born into slavery but went on to become the university's first president. Both men are icons in the history of not only African Americans but also the entire US education system. Five miles outside of town, the **20** **Tuskegee Airmen National Historic Site** has been restored to its former glory as the training grounds and airfield for the first African American pilot candidates in the US military, 1941's Tuskegee Airmen. Several of the original training planes are on display here.

Head out of Tuskegee on Hwy 80 past the Tuskegee National Forest (the smallest in the USA) to **21** **Auburn**, a college town of a different ilk entirely. It's not fellowship that rules here, it's football. Here a choice must be made: to stay or not to stay? Those passing through shouldn't leave without stopping at **22** **Amsterdam Café** on Gay St, a definite don't-miss for foodies. Those who stay should dive liquor-first into the bar scene at **23** **In Italy** –

Serious river rats can paddle the Piedmont Section of the 631-mile **Alabama Scenic River Trail** (www.alabamascenicrivertrail.com), which begins at the Alabama–Georgia border and winds its way south towards Gadsden along the Upper Coosa River and its three lakes, Weiss, Logan Martin and Mitchell.

From Rome, head west on Hwy 20 to Hwy 100 (southbound). Make a right onto Black's Bluff Rd and go approximately 6 miles. Make another right onto Montgomery Landing Rd to find the boat launch at Brushy Brand Park. Give yourself several days.

with its painted concrete floors and projection TVs on silver beads – before retiring in inebriated glory to **24** **Hotel at Auburn University.**

Follow Hwy 280 out of town towards Phenix City over the Chattahoochee River into Columbus, GA, home to the fascinating **25** **National Civil War**

Naval Museum. This museum dedicated to the Confederate navy is a real surprise. Check out the CSS *Jackson*, an 1862 ironclad Confederate navy ship that was hauled up after 95 years underwater; and the stunning collection of massive mid-18th-century American and Confederate flags, unearthed from an attic in – funnily enough – Massachusetts. Skidaddle out of Columbus eastbound on Hwy 96 to Reynolds where, for $20, you can race the very vehicle you are driving in an amateur drag race on an NHRA-certified track at **26** **Silver Dollar Raceway** every Friday night. That's pure poetry.

"You can race the very vehicle you are driving in an amateur drag race on an NHRA-certified track."

Another 12 miles or so down the road, you'll enter Peach County, the peach capital of the peach state. Your nose should lead you to **27** **Lane Southern Orchards**, where you can stock up on all things peach and pecan. Peach cobbler, peach ice cream, peach BBQ sauce – embrace the peach! Hang your hat 10 minutes away at **28** **Henderson Village**, a luxurious country resort spread out over several buildings on a 3500-acre farm in Perry.

With peaches in your rearview mirror, head north to Macon on Hwy 41 and the shockingly well done **29** **Georgia Music Hall of Fame**. Otis Redding, The Allman Brothers, Ray Charles, REM, Chet Atkins, Indigo Girls, Widespread Panic, B-52s, Travis Tritt, Black Crowes, Usher – it's all here in an entertaining array of exhibits that range from a church chapel housing an ode to Georgia's gospel music to a special display dedicated to Athens, GA.

For lunch, head through the tinted door at **30** **H&H** (yes, it's open) for a whopping introduction to a traditional Southern Meat and Three. Each day, Mama Louise cooks up a collection of Southern home cookin' and soul food, and you pick out one meat (ribs, fried chicken, fried fish) and three sides (okra and tomatoes, collard greens, mac and cheese). The smoke from the kitchen nearly burns your eyes out, and the sweet tea here is sickly so, but it's an experience. A good spot to stop for the night in Macon is **31** **1842 Inn**, a museum-like B&B in the **32** **In-Town Historic District**, one of the prettiest and best preserved in the South (and one of Macon's 12 – the largest acreage of historic districts in Georgia). Pick up a self-guided walking tour map around town.

Take Hwy 23 (northbound) to Jackson on your way back to Atlanta. The best BBQ in Georgia sits in an aged roadside shack on Hwy 42 just outside town. **33** **Fresh Air** is the gospel according to pulled pork and something surely Eisenhower wasn't thinking about when he commissioned the interstates. Thank Ike for small favors.

Kevin Raub

TRIP INFORMATION

DO

Alabama Museum
This museum dedicated to one of country music's biggest bands is full of awards, guitars and personal heirlooms. ☎ 256-845-1646; 101 Glenn Blvd SW, Fort Payne, AL; adult/child $3/1.50; ☼ 9am-6pm Mon-Sat, 1-6pm Sun

Carters Lake Marina
Rent pontoon boats ($275) and spacious lakeside cabins at this marina and small supplies store run by British expats. ☎ 706-276-4891; www.carterslake.com; 575 Marina Rd, Chatsworth, GA; day use per vehicle $4, r $120-240; ☼ 10am-6pm Apr-Oct; ♿ ☺

George Washington Carver Museum
Half of this museum is devoted to Carver, the other to Tuskegee University. Check out PH Polk's old school camera! ☎ 334-727-6390; www.nps.gov/tuai; University Campus Ave, Tuskegee, AL; ☼ 9am-4:30pm

Georgia Music Hall of Fame
Shockingly well done museum full of musical memorabilia like Gregg Allman's organ and Ray Charles' silk suit. ☎ 478-751-3334; www.georgiamusic.org; 200 MLK, Jr Blvd, Macon, GA; adult/child $8/3.50; ☼ 9am-5pm Mon-Sat, 1-5pm Sun; ♿

Lake Guntersville State Park
This 6000-acre state park sits on Alabama's largest lake and offers abundant fishing, hiking, golf, camping and even a few bald eagles. ☎ 256-571-5444; www.guntersville statepark.com; 7966 Hwy 227, Guntersville, AL; admission free; ♿ ☺

Lane Southern Orchards
You can smell the sweet love from miles at this peach and pecan heaven in the heart of peach county. ☎ 800-277-3224; www .lanepacking.com; 50 Lane Rd, Fort Valley, GA; tours adult/child $5/3; ☼ 9am-7pm; ♿

National Civil War Naval Museum
A stunning mid-18th-century American and Confederate flag collection and remains of Confederate ironclads highlight this thoroughly fascinating museum. ☎ 706-327-9798; www.portcolumbus.org; 1002 Victory Dr, Columbus, GA; adult/child $6.50/5; ☼ 9am-5pm; ♿

Silver Dollar Raceway
Fancy yourself a drag racer? Prove it here on this NHRA-certified track…in your own car. ☎ 478-847-4414; www.silverdollarraceway .com; 42 Racetrack Rd, Reynolds, GA; ☼ Jan-Nov; ♿

Town Creek Fishing Center
Rents boats ($20 to $65 per day), pontoons ($250 per day) and canoes ($26 per day) as well as fishing supplies and licenses. ☎ 256-571-5440; www.silverdollarraceway.com; 2966 Hwy 227, Guntersville, AL; ☼ 7am-sunset, closed mid-Nov–mid-Mar; ♿

The Oaks
The home of Booker T Washington features an office still preserved with original everything. ☎ 334-727-6390; www.nps.gov/tuai .com; University Campus Ave, Tuskegee, AL; ☼ 9am-4:30pm

Tuskegee Airmen National Historic Site
This just-restored museum features Piper J3 Cub and PT17 Steerman biplanes flown by the first African American airmen. ☎ 334-724-0922; www.nps.gov/tuai; 1616 Chappie James Rd, Tuskegee, AL; admission free; ☼ 9am-4:30pm; ♿

EAT & DRINK

Amsterdam Café
Picasso's blue period dots the walls (it's Auburn for godsakes), an innovative menu fills your belly. Order the avocado/crab cake sandwich. ☎ 334-826-8181; 410 S Gay St, Auburn, AL; mains $7-27; ☼ 11am-9pm Sun-Thu, to 10pm Fri & Sat

Crawmama's
Giant tubs and platters of freshly steamed crab and shrimp stand out at this casual, wipe-your-mouth-with-a-paper-towel picnic-tabled joint. ☎ 256-582-0484; 5004 Webb Villa, Guntersville, AL; mains $8-21; ☼ 4:30-10pm Thu & Fri, 11:30am-10pm Sat; ♿

Fresh Air
Since 1929, this family-owned glorified roadside shack offers Swine Heaven to all

those on a BBQ pilgrimage. ☎ 770-775-3182; 1164 Hwy 42, Jackson, GA; mains $6-7; 🕑 8am-8pm Mon-Thu, to 9pm Fri & Sat, to 8:30pm Sun; 🕭

H&H

Mama Louise's traditional Meat and Three serves up traditional Southern cooking in a cafeteria-style setting. A must! ☎ 478-742-9810; 807 Forsyth St, Macon, GA; mains $9; 🕑 7:30am-4pm Mon-Sat

Harvest Moon Café

Ground zero for Rome's cool, calm and collected, serving downright homey Southern grub. ☎ 706-292-0099; 234 Broad St, Rome, GA; mains $8-26; 🕑 11am-2:30pm Mon, to 9pm Tue & Wed, to 10pm Thu-Sat, 10:30am-3pm Sun; 🕭

In Italy

Try the Watermelon Jolly Rancher cocktail at this modern monochrome bar and dance club near Auburn's campus. ☎ 334-887-5732; 145 E Magnolia Ave, Auburn, AL; 🕑 4pm-2am Mon-Sat Sep-May, 8pm-2am Jun-Aug.

SLEEP

1842 Inn

1842 antebellum-style inn in one of the South's prettiest historic districts – it's like sleeping with history (not in that way). ☎ 877-452-6599; www.1842inn.com; 353 E College St, Macon, GA; r $189-230

Hawthorn Suites

Smell the history in the 110-year-old original beams and hardwood floors in this machinery storage building turned Rome's most charming hotel. ☎ 706-378-4837; www.hawthorn.com; 100-110 W 2nd Ave, Rome, GA; r $129-239

Henderson Village

Elegant country resort featuring well-appointed 19th-century cottages close enough to peach country, you can almost smell 'em. ☎ 478-988-8696; www.hendersonvillage.com; 125 S Langston Cir, Perry, GA; r $159-225

Hotel at Auburn University

Auburn's nicest hotel is fresh off an $11 million makeover and also has a fun bar on premises. ☎ 334-821-8200; www.auhcc.com; 241 S College St, Auburn, AL; r from $129

Lodge at Lake Guntersville State Park

Fresh off a four-year, $25 million renovation, this bluffside resort boasts rooms, lakeside cottages and a 321-site campground. ☎ 256-571-5440; www.shelburnefarms.org; 1155 Lodge Dr, Guntersville, AL; r from $96, sites from $17.44; 🕭

USEFUL WEBSITES

www.800alabama.com
www.georgia.org

LINK YOUR TRIP

www.lonelyplanet.com/trip-planner

Coon Dogs & Unclaimed Baggage: Only in Alabama

WHY GO Say what you will about Alabama – many folks do – but it's nothing if not quirky. From the Unclaimed Baggage Center in Scottsboro to the Boll Weevil Monument in Enterprise, the state has more idiosyncratic ticks than a coon dog on a foxhunt. Packaged as one, it's nothing but fun.

TIME
4 days

DISTANCE
850 miles

BEST TIME TO GO
Mar – May

START
Birmingham, AL

END
Birmingham, AL

ALSO GOOD FOR

You've probably heard a lot of funny things about Alabama over the years (a few of those things aren't true, by the way. *Just a few.*). But Alabamians are a proud bunch, always quick to defend their beloved state in the wake of a little ribbing from the rest of the country (Mississippi notwithstanding). They rant and rave during college football season. They rattle and roll over the state's outstanding musical contributions. Fair enough. We all know about Bear Bryant and the Muscle Shoals Sound.

But most folks don't realize that Alabama is also one of the nation's foremost contributors to a uniquely American tradition: the roadside attraction. Americans love nothing more than driving hundreds of miles to catch a glimpse of the World's Largest this or that. If it's in the *Guinness Book of World Records*, if it contains a superlative in its name, or if it so much as hints at some magnificence currently unobtainable in their home town, Americans will put the pedal to the metal just to catch a glimpse. Alabama, dear friends, is where lots of those people are making a beeline to.

You don't have to get into the sticks, either – even cosmopolitan Birmingham isn't immune. Who's that vaguely homoerotic cast-iron dude doing overlooking the city? That's *Vulcan*, the world's largest cast-iron statue. Built in 1904 for the St Louis World's Fair, this 56ft tall, 101,200lb statue of the Roman god of forge and fire is a Birmingham

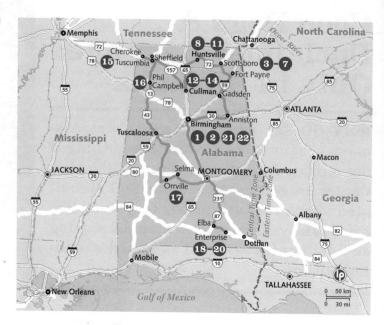

landmark, sitting in ❶ **Vulcan Park** atop Red Mountain, overlooking the city. There's a comprehensive Birmingham history museum here as well. A lookout tower under Vulcan's butt cheeks offers well-rounded views of the city. Pun intended.

Leaving Birmingham, head out on I-20 (eastbound) to Hwy 21 (northbound) to Anniston, where the ❷ **World's Largest Chair** sits in the parking lot of an office furniture store. Look closely, it's surprisingly easy to miss. Next, head north on Hwy 431 to I-59, then Hwy 35 leads you to Scottsboro where you should check into ❸ **Goose Pond Colony**, a beautiful recreational retreat on ❹ **Lake Guntersville**, Alabama's largest lake, located just outside town off Hwy 72. Grab a wonderful lakeside dinner at the ❺ **Docks**, but don't take in the longest unobstructed views of Lake Guntersville for too long; you'll need a good night's sleep for tomorrow's unconventional shopping experience.

"A lookout tower under Vulcan's butt cheeks offers well-rounded views of the city."

Head into downtown Scottsboro on Hwy 279 and follow the signs to the ❻ **Unclaimed Baggage Center**. Wait...is that your iPod? The one you left in the seat pocket on that flight from Poughkeepsie? Probably. This Macy's-sized retail space is the end of the line for the majority of unclaimed bags in the USA. After 90 days, the airlines send your lost luggage here. It takes thrift shop–level patience, but there is Tumi luggage, Kate Spade bags, Bruno Magli loafers, cameras, laptops, golf clubs, Victoria's Secret lingerie – you name it – all for a fraction of retail. Finders keepers, losers weepers!

You'll no doubt work up a hunger with all that bargain-hunting, so head down the road a few blocks to ❼ **Blue Willow Bistro**, a lovely 1890 historic home flooded with antiques – all for sale – and a wealth of made-from-scratch Southern delights. After lunch, head north on Hwy 72 to Huntsville, where the world's largest space museum is right off I-565. The ❽ **US Space & Rocket Center** is Alabama's No 1 attraction and one of the best in the USA, for that matter. TV does nothing to prepare you for the absolute awesomeness of the *Saturn V* rocket, which is so massive it looks as if the astronauts who went to the moon did so in a 30-story skyscraper.

The interiors at ❾ **Ketchup** make you feel like you're eating inside a Valentine's Day card. A Los Angeles dining transplant from the Dolce Group, it's inside the Venetian-style ❿ **Bridge Street** development just two exits from the Space Museum. It has DJs after 10pm on weekends. It's next door to the ⓫ **Westin** hotel, Alabama's only 4-star hotel and a much more comfortable option than the tired Marriott on the grounds of the Space Museum.

The next morning, pick up I-565 (westbound) to I-65 (southbound) to the ⓬ **Ave Maria Grotto** in Cullman. Located on the grounds of the only Benedictine monastery in Alabama, this amazing attraction is more or less the work of one man, Brother Joseph Zoettl, who spent the better part of 35 years hand-sculpting stone and cement miniatures of the world's most prominent religious buildings. The attention to detail and level of workmanship in the 125 pieces is incredible, regardless of your views on religion. From an art perspective, it's even more miraculous yet – after all, this was just Brother Joseph's hobby.

Cullman is located in a dry county – home to the world's only *dry* Oktoberfest, no less – so only a 12-stepper would want to sleep here. As luck would have it, the monks have a hotel (sort of). The ⓭ **St Bernard Retreat Center** is as peaceful as a prayer session. Being that cleanliness is next to godliness and all, it's clean, too. For those of you who appreciate a tipple, it's best to move on, but not before heading into town on Hwy 278 and grabbing some sickly sweet orange rolls, a syrupy treat from ⓮ **All Steak**, a restaurant located on the 4th floor of a parking deck in downtown Cullman. Don't ask.

If the idea of sleeping with the monks doesn't appeal, from East of Cullman head west on Hwy 157 to Hwy 72, then take Hwy 247 (southbound) to Tuscumbia, where you can sleep in a souped-up grain silo at ⓯ **Seven Springs Lodge**. The locals aren't sure what to make of this, but it's actually kinda nice.

About 55 minutes south of Tuscumbia is ⑯ **Dismals Canyon**, a secluded primeval forest offering hiking, camping, cabins and the strange phenomenon of dismalites, little glow-in-the-dark larvae that light up the inside of the canyon walls like an air traffic control map. This spot is the only one in the world outside New Zealand where these little suckers thrive.

Take in the countryside on the four-hour jaunt down through Tuscaloosa south to ⑰ **Old Cahawba Archeological Preserve**, a whole lot of nothing near Orrville. The former capital of Alabama is a bona fide ghost town – there's literally little here beyond a former street grid and one or two abandoned homes – and driving through beckons all sorts of mysterious questions: What happened here? Where did the people go? Were they Crimson Tide or Auburn fans?

Head to Montgomery on Hwy 80 (eastbound), then hang a right for the three-hour drive south to Enterprise. Here lies the ⑱ **Boll Weevil Monument**, perhaps the world's only monument dedicated to an agricultural pest. It's smack downtown in the middle of the street, where it has been rammed several times by drunk drivers and stolen many times by pesky vandals. (So many times, in fact, that this is a replica. The original is in a nearby museum.) But the Boll Weevil isn't the only reason to come to Enterprise. There's nothing quirky about the ⑲ **Rawls Hotel** and ⑳ **Rawls Restaurant**, but the historic hotel and dining destination are entirely too good for this town. Try the crab-stuffed salmon and ponder how a restaurant like this survives in a town that picked a farmer's nuisance as it mascot.

DETOUR More than 200 feisty coon dogs are buried in the **Coon Dog Cemetery** outside Tuscumbia, many with elaborate tombstones and even more elaborate names (Strait Talk'n Tex, Rockliffs Red Rusty). The only cemetery of its kind in the world, it all started in 1937 when racoon-huntin' hotshot Troop was buried here by his owner, Key Underwood.

From Dismals Canyon, it's a 45-minute ride north on Hwy 43 to Tuscumbia. Head out on Hwy 247 (southbound) for 12 miles and follow the signs.

Hwy 231 (northbound) then I-65 (northbound) brings you back to Birmingham, where there are yet more oddities. The courtyard at ㉑ **Garage Café** is a fine place to spend an evening tackling the sufficient beer list amid enough junk, antiques and ceramic statues to sink the *Titanic*. If you don't get lost among the clutter, call it a night at ㉒ **Redmont Hotel**, the last place Hank Williams slept in before he died – only in Alabama would anyone care about that!

Kevin Raub

TRIP INFORMATION

DO

Ave Maria Grotto
This fascinating 4-acre park features stone and cement miniatures of the world's most important religious shrines. ☎ 256-734-4110; wwwavemariagrotto.com; 1600 St Bernard Dr, Cullman; adult/child $7/4.50; ☷ 8am-6pm Apr-Sept, 8am-5pm Oct-Mar; ♿

Boll Weevil Monument
Perhaps the only monument in the world dedicated to an agricultural pest. **Main St, Enterprise**

Dismals Canyon
A primeval forest that's home to waterfalls and eerily glowing dismalites. ☎ 205-993-4559; www.dismalscanyon.com; 901 Hwy 8, Phil Campbell; adult/child $9/5.50; ☷ 10am-5pm Mon-Thu, 10am-10pm Fri, 9am-10pm Sat, 9am-5pm Sun; ♿ ⊕

Old Cahawba Archeological Preserve
Alabama's first state capital is now a spooky ghost town, interesting if for no other reason than the eerie absence of anything. ☎ 334-872-8058; 9518 Cahaba Road, Orrville; ☷ 9am-5pm

Unclaimed Baggage Center
Part pawnshop, garage sale and retail store, except everything here once belonged to someone who lost their luggage. ☎ 256-259-1525; www.unclaimedbaggage.com; 509 Willow St, Scottsboro; ☷ 9am-6pm Mon-Fri, 8am-6pm Sat; ♿

US Space & Rocket Center
The world's largest space museum houses the newly restored *Saturn V* rocket and numerous NASA attractions. ☎ 256-837-3400; www.spacecamp.com/museum; One Tranquility Base, Huntsville; adult/child $24.95/19.95; ☷ 9am-5pm; ♿

Vulcan Park
The largest cast-iron statue in the world stands proudly over Birmingham in this beautiful city park. ☎ 205-933-1409; www.vulcanpark.org; 1701 Valley View Dr, Birmingham; tower & museum adult/child $6/4; ☷ 10am-6pm Mon-Sat, 1-6pm Sun; ♿ ⊕

World's Largest Chair
This 31ft-high, 20,000lb steel office chair sitting in the parking lot of Miller's Office Furniture is a Guinness record holder. ☎ 256-237-1641; 625 Noble St, Anniston

EAT & DRINK

All Steak
Order the sweet, gooey orange rolls at this restaurant on the 4th floor of a parking deck. ☎ 256-734-4322; cnr 4th St SW & 1st Ave SW, Cullman; mains $8.50-30; ☷ 7:30am-9pm Mon-Thu, to 10pm Fri & Sat, to 3pm Sun; ♿

Blue Willow Bistro
An 1890 home brimming with antiques (all for sale) and scrumptious Southern delicacies like sweet tomato pie and fried chicken sandwiches. ☎ 256-259-3462; 303 E Willow St, Scottsboro; mains $6-15; ☷ 11am-2pm Tue-Sun, 6-8pm Fri & Sat

Docks
Good-time seafood and chop house on the edge of Lake Guntersville. Don't overdrink and fall in. ☎ 256-574-3071; 417 Hembree Dr, Scottsboro; mains $14-19; ☷ 5pm-late Tue-Sat; ♿

Garage Café
Eclectic crowds knock back myriad beer choices in a courtyard full of junk, antiques, ceramic statues and the kitchen sink. ☎ 205-322-1282; 2304 10th Ter St, Birmingham; sandwiches $5-6; ☷ 3pm-midnight Sun & Mon, 11am-2am Tue-Sat

Ketchup
Like eating inside a Valentine's Day card – this modern American LA transplant does upscale comfort food. ☎ 256-327-8390; 350 The Bridge St, Huntsville; mains $12-32; ☷ 11am-3pm & 4-10pm Sun-Thu, 11am-3pm & 4pm-2am Fri & Sat

Rawls Restaurant
Wagering this the best small-town restaurant in Alabama would net you good odds. Save room for the cheesecake. ☎ 334-308-9387; www.rawlsbandb.com; 116 S Main St, Enterprise; mains $16-24; ☷ 11am-2pm Mon-Fri & 5-9pm Mon-Sat

SLEEP

Goose Pond Colony
Recreational resort with 36 holes of golf, shoreside cabins and a great restaurant (The Docks) on Lake Guntersville, 'bama's biggest. ☎ 256-259-2884; www.goosepond.org; 417 Ed Hembree Dr, Scottsboro; r $65-170; ⛷

Rawls Hotel
This 1903 hotel has beautifully appointed rooms, shockingly so for Enterprise (though oddly, it's operated by military contractors). Don't miss the restaurant. ☎ 334-406-2817; 116 S Main St, Enterprise; r $89-149

Redmont Hotel
Not quirky itself, but this is the last place Hank Williams slept in before he died. ☎ 334-265-1010; www.theredmont.com; 205-313-2166; 2101 5th Av N, Birmingham r $139; ⛷

Seven Springs Lodge
A hunting and horse enthusiast outside Tuscumbia has turned his grain silos into well-appointed accommodations. ☎ 256-370-7218; www.sevenspringslodge.net; 1292 Mt Mills Rd, Tuscumbia; r $50-120; ☎ Feb-Oct; ⛷

St Bernard Retreat Center
Sleep like a monk in this basic but spotless hotel at Ave Maria Grotto, on the grounds of St Bernard Abbey. ☎ 256-734-3946; www.stbernardretreat.com; 1600 St Bernard Dr, Cullman; r from $40

Westin
Huntsville is hurting for some interesting accommodations, but Alabama's only four-star hotel is located at the upscale Bridge St development, right near the Space Museum. ☎ 256-420-2000; www.westin.com; 6800 Governor's West NW, Huntsville; r $199-209

USEFUL WEBSITES
www.800alabama.com
www.roadsideamerica.com

LINK YOUR TRIP
www.lonelyplanet.com/trip-planner

Thanks Hank: Hank Williams' Alabama

WHY GO From his boyhood home in Georgiana to his grave at the end of the Lost Highway in Montgomery, country icon Hank Williams left an undeniable mark on Alabama and the world. Keep Hankin' along the roads that Williams traveled on his way to becoming the undisputed Godfather of Honky Tonk.

TIME
2 days

DISTANCE
125 miles

BEST TIME TO GO
Year-round

START
Birmingham, AL

END
Montgomery, AL

ALSO GOOD FOR

What Louis Armstrong did for jazz, what Elvis Presley did for rock and roll and what Nirvana did for grunge, Hank Williams did for country music. There's no argument that holds water against him being one of the most influential musicians and songwriters of the 20th century. But both amazingly and sadly, Williams' contributions were short-lived and, like many of the greats, death knocked on his door prematurely.

If you arrive late in Birmingham, stay over at ❶ **Redmont Hotel** – the last place Williams slept in before he died. Otherwise, head south on I-65 to ❷ **Georgiana**, near where Williams was born as Hiram, not Hank, in 1929. As a young boy, Williams would belt out tunes standing on a church organ bench next to his mother, Lillie Williams. That very organ bench is on display at the large ❸ **Hank Williams Boyhood Home & Museum**, full of Williams memorabilia gathered over the years from fans. One of Hank's straightedge razors, a cowboy hat and some old dishes round out the personal items. Hank sat on the front steps here and strummed his first guitar, a gift from his mother, when he was just eight years old.

Super-keen fans will want to call ahead and make arrangements to visit the ❹ **Hank Williams Fan Club House**, across the street from the museum. Devotees from the world over gather here to shoot the breeze about all things Hank among even more trinkets. During the

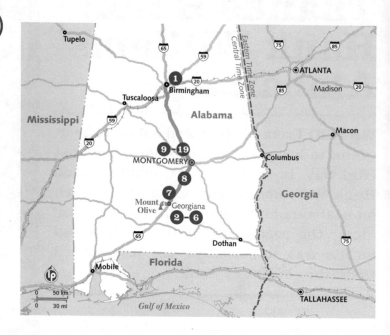

annual Hank Williams Festival, held the first Saturday of June, fans descend on the house for impromptu jam sessions and forlorn stories of Hank lore. In downtown Georgiana – if you can call it that – there's a concrete slab across from the Lowery Hardware store where once sat the **5** **Old Train Depot**. Williams shined shoes here as a boy. The **6** **Ga-Ana Theater**, across the street, is where Williams and the Drifting Cowboys played several gigs from 1939 onward. Hank was just 16 years old. It still hosts gigs today.

ASK A LOCAL "Hank would get a little bit rowdy in Chris' Hot Dogs and my dad [the owner] would say, 'Alright Hank…you gotta go. You can't be acting like that in here.' Hank would say, 'I'll take my business elsewhere then.' And my dad would say, 'Go ahead! They'll throw you out, too!' He'd be drinking beer in here at 8am when everyone else was having breakfast."

Theo Katechis, Montgomery

From Georgiana, I-65 northbound to Montgomery is now commemorated as the **7** **Hank Williams Memorial Lost Highway**. At Greenville, where Williams lived from 1934 to 1937, **8** **Hwy 31** juts slightly east into Montgomery – it was along this road that Williams found the inspiration for "I Saw the Light" when he glimpsed the nighttime beacon of Dannelly Field, Montgomery's airport. In downtown **9** Montgomery, the **10** **Jefferson Davis Hotel** on Montgomery St was once home to WFSA radio station, where Hank landed a twice-weekly gig, billed as the "Singing Kid," at merely 14 years old. Some say he saw the station's nighttime beacon as well (Williams saw a lot of lights). It's now a private building.

Within walking distance is the ⑪ **Hank Williams Museum**, an altogether more dressed-up affair than the Georgiana museum and home to his baby blue 1952 Cadillac and countless outfits and suits. Next door is the ⑫ **Hampton Inn**, in a gorgeously renovated 1920s building, and a good spot to rest up on a Montgomery Hank trip. It's hard not to imagine that more was happening in Montgomery in Hank's day as there ain't much happening now, but ⑬ **Nobles** is a good spot for a drink and live music – it sits on the former spot of the ⑭ **Elite Café**, the last place Hank performed before he died. Across the street is the former ⑮ **Empire Theater**, where Williams won $15 in a talent contest performing what was likely the first song he wrote, "WPA Blues." Ironically, it's also well known for being the spot Rosa Parks refused to give up her bus seat to a white man in 1955, and the spot is now home to the Rosa Parks Museum.

DETOUR

Hank first emptied his lungs as a young boy from an organ bench inside Mt Olive West Baptist Church in rural **Mt Olive**, a 20-minute drive from Georgiana. On the way, you'll pass the dilapidated Old Nixon House (on the corner of Nixon Rd and Hank Williams Memorial Dr) that Williams' parents moved into as newlyweds. The Red Barn at 4683 Hank Williams Memorial Dr stands on the spot where Williams was born.

From Georgiana, head on Hwy 106 (westbound) to Hank Williams Memorial Dr and turn left.

Williams would like to get to drinkin' often, and often he did so at ⑯ **Chris' Hot Dogs**, a restaurant devoted to hot dogs since 1917. The food is nothing to shake a stick at, but it's an iconic road food joint (waitress Eleanor Williams has been working there 32 years). Hard livin' and hard drinkin' did Williams in – he walked the walk he sung about – at the tender age of 29 from heart failure. His funeral, attended by over 25,000 grief-stricken fans, took place nearby at the ⑰ **City Auditorium**, now City Hall. Across the street is the small ⑱ **Hank Williams Statue** erected by Hank Williams, Jr.

"Hard livin' and hard drinkin' did Williams in – he walked the walk he sung about."

Williams is buried at the ⑲ **Hank Williams Memorial Oakwood Cemetery Annex** out on Wetumpka Rd in Montgomery, where he remains so lonesome, he could cry.

Kevin Raub

HISTORY &
CULTURE

TRIP INFORMATION

GETTING THERE
From Birmingham, take I-65 (southbound) to exit 114 for Georgiana.

DO

Ga-Ana Theater
This local theater (1939) where Hank performed at 16 with the Drifting Cowboys still hosts country gigs today. ☎ 334-376-9019; cnr E Railroad Ave & Jones St, Georgiana; cover $5-10

Hank Williams Boyhood Home & Museum
Quite the shrine to Hank, compiled from fan donations, inside the home he lived in from the age of seven to 11. ☎ 334-376-2555; 127 Rose St, Georgiana; adult/child $3/2; ☾ 10am-4pm Mon-Sat; ⚹

Hank Williams Fan Club House
More Hank memorabilia in this fan club hangout across from his boyhood home. Jam sessions and Hank powwows take place here. ☎ 334-376-9821; www.hankwilliamsinter nationalfanclub.com; Rose St, Georgiana; ☾ by appointment

Hank Williams Memorial Oakwood Cemetery Annex
Hank is buried here alongside his wife, Audrey. A sign from Hank, Jr politely asks fans not to desecrate the grave site. Upper Wetumpka Rd, Montgomery; ☾ 7am-sunset

Hank Williams Museum
More elaborate than the Georgiana museum, this all-things-Hank stop includes his 1952 baby blue Cadillac and the suit he died in. ☎ 334-262-3600; 118 Commerce St, Montgomery; adult/child $8/3; ☾ 9am-4:30pm Mon-Fri, 10am-4pm Sat, 1-4pm Sun; ⚹

EAT & DRINK

Chris' Hot Dogs
One of Hank's favorite joints, from which he was thrown out on more than one occasion. ☎ 802-295-4600; 138 Dexter Ave, Montgomery; mains $2-6; ☾ 10am-7pm Mon-Thu & Sat, to 8pm Fri; ⚹

Nobles
Once the Elite Café, the last venue Hank performed in before he died. The retro-martini vibe these days makes it a decent spot to imbibe. ☎ 334-262-3326; 129 Montgomery St, Montgomery; ☾ 11am-2pm Tue-Fri & 5pm-late Tue-Sat

SLEEP

Hampton Inn
In a 1920s building, this is not your average Hampton Inn. Next door to the Hank Williams Museum. ☎ 334-265-1010; www.hampton inn.com; 100 Commerce St, Montgomery; r $118-179; ⚹

Redmont Hotel
This historic option in downtown Birmingham was the last hotel hank Williams slept in before he died. ☎ 205-324-2101; www .theredmont.com; 2101 5th Ave N, Birmingham; r $139; ⚹

SUGGESTED READING
- *Hank Williams: Snapshots from the Lost Highway*, Colin Escott and Kira Florita
- *Hank Williams: The Biography*, Colin Escott, George Merritt and William MacEwen
- *The Life and Times of Hank Williams*, Arnold Rogers and Bruce Gidoll

USEFUL WEBSITES
www.800alabama.com
www.hankwilliamstrail.com

LINK YOUR TRIP

www.lonelyplanet.com/trip-planner

Talladega & Cheaha National Forests

WHY GO Alabama's highest point soars above the verdant Talladega National Forest in Cheaha State Park, through which scenic lookouts, unspoiled hiking trails and rustic woodsy getaways coalesce along the Talladega Scenic Byway, a 29-mile stretch of breathtaking 'Bama backdrops and pristine wilderness.

TIME
2 days

DISTANCE
45 miles

BEST TIME TO GO
Aug – Nov

START
Talladega, AL

END
Heflin, AL

It's a little known fact that the Appalachian Mountains stretch far into Northern Alabama at their southernmost point, carpeting a northwest pocket of the state with a 250,000-acre patch of protected woodland that makes for a pristine playground for nature lovers. Alabama's kin to Bobby Alison, Hank Williams and Bear Bryant are all documented – welcome to Alabama's greener side.

The logical starting point for the ❶ Talladega Scenic Byway, which cuts through the Talladega National Forest to Cheaha State Park and beyond to Heflin, is the city of Talladega, more known for NASCAR than nature. Here's where you'll want to stock up on any serious outdoor supplies (there's a Wal-Mart, at any rate) and hunker down with a meal of grilled catfish at ❷ Fincher's, an old Southern hole-in-the-wall. Heading out of Talladega to Ashland, pick up Hwy 77 (eastbound) and follow the directions to the beginning of the Hwy 281 (also known as the Byway), crossing into ❸ Talladega National Forest along the way.

Heading north, the Byway begins at the Adams Gap Trail, which connects to the 130-mile Pinhoti Trail that eventually connects up with the Appalachian Trail. Continue along quiet and winding Hwy 281 a few miles to the trailhead for the ❹ Chinnabee Silent Trail. This day hike (5 miles, 3½ hours one-way) leads to the National Forest Recreation Area at Lake Chinnabee. Along the way, you'll pass two

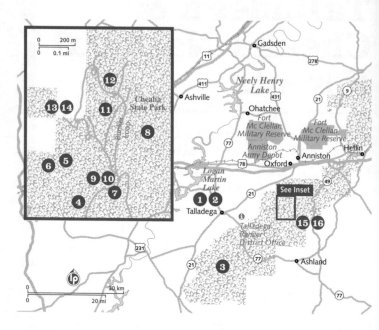

small waterfalls, Cheaha Falls and Devil's Den; the latter makes for a nice swimming hole.

Back on Hwy 281, near mile marker 474, take a left on Cheaha Rd 2 miles down to ❺ **Cheaha Lake**, a 6-acre swimming hole with a small beach. The ❻ **Cheaha State Park Improved Camping** is also here amid a slew of pine and oak trees. The best camping in the park offers electricity and old-but-clean bathrooms with hot water. On the lake, you can rent paddleboats and generally relax away the day. If you want to fish, there's bass, crappie and catfish, but you'll need a fishing license from the ❼ **Cheaha Country Store**, a few miles southeast on Hwy 281. Alabama residents pay $12 while residents of other states pay a higher rate depending on where they're from (foreigners aren't even on the radar). The store is also your last chance to grab some food and beer, and the spot where you will need to register and pay for camping inside ❽ **Cheaha State Park**. If you pay admission here, you don't need to pay again at the lake and vice versa.

> *"Alabama's kin to Bobby Alison, Hank Williams and Bear Bryant are all well documented: welcome to Alabama's greener side."*

If you're not up for camping, take a left on Bunker Loop, the small round-about road that takes in the attractions of the park, where there's the basic ❾ **Cheaha State Park Hotel**, made more appealing by a pool jutting out over a vast, scenic view of Talladega National Forest. The ❿ **Cheaha State**

Park Restaurant is also here. As it is the only eatery around, it'll have to do, but don't expect culinary wonders. Continue around the Bunker Loop to enjoy the best of the park. The high point – quite literally – is the base of the 75ft-tall ⓫ Observation Tower, which at 2407ft is the highest point in the state of Alabama. You can go up for stupendous 360-degree views.

Continuing along the one-way Bunker Loop, you'll pass the entrance for ⓬ Bald Rock Lodge on the right, a woodsy, 12-bedroom retreat with hickory headboards and slate floors that's perfect for larger groups. Rounding the loop past another improved campground is the trailhead for ⓭ Pulpit Rock Trail. This quarter-mile, 15-minute trail leads to the best view in the park at Pulpit Rock. It's also one of only two spots in the park where rock climbing and rappelling are permitted, though you must bring your own infrastructure to do so. Next door is the best place to sleep along the entire Byway, ⓮ Cheaha State Park Cabins. These semiprivate bluffside cabins are perfect for a romantic getaway, complete with fireplaces, slate floors, full kitchen, outdoor fire pits and the real coup: two wooden lounge chairs on the edge of the bluff that look out onto more or less the same view as Pulpit Rock. Divine.

ASK A LOCAL

"The best trail is to Pulpit Rock. It's the prettiest view in the whole state of Alabama. It overlooks the Talladega National Forest and the valley at the foot of the mountain. It's beautiful."
Brian Casey, Delta

Back at the country store, hop back on Hwy 281 to finish out the Byway by heading north toward Heflin. There are scenic lookouts along the way, an occasional joyriding motorcycle and not much else. The road dead-ends at the ⓯ Shoal Creek Ranger District, where you can pick up national forest and state park information if you happen to be starting your trip here. Of course, that would be quite odd considering you have followed our trip thus far, so continue onto Hwy 78 (eastbound) to Heflin, where you'll find ⓰ Pop's Charburgers, a roadside sugar shack. Skip anything savory here; instead, reward yourself with one of Northern Alabama's sweetest treats – a butterscotch milkshake. The friendly lady that runs the place might just say it: "Y'all come back now, ya hear?"
Kevin Raub

TRIP INFORMATION

GETTING THERE
From Birmingham, take I-20 (eastbound) to Hwy 77 (southbound). At Talladega, take Hwy 77 east to Ashland. Turn left at the sign for Chandler Springs on Talladega County Rd 209 and go 3.5 miles to Clay County Rd 12. Turn left. Take another left on Blue Ridge Rd and yet another on Adams Gap Rd. It dead-ends at Hwy 281, the southern start of the Talladega Scenic Byway.

DO

Cheaha Country Store
Stock up on basic supplies, park and trail maps, as well as register to camp within Cheaha State Park. ☎ 256-488-5111; **19644 Hwy 281, Delta;** ⏰ **8am-5pm**

Cheaha Lake
This 6-acre recreational lake offers swimming, fishing, paddleboats, a small beach and several campsites. Fishing license required. ☎ **256-488-5111; www.alapark .com; 19644 Hwy 281, Delta; admission $1;** ⏰ **8am-sundown;** ♿ ⛲

Cheaha State Park
Nestled in the Talladega mountain range, this trail-heavy park is home to Alabama's highest point. ☎ **256-488-5111; www.alapark .com; 19644 Hwy 281, Delta; admission $1;** ⏰ **8am-9pm;** ♿ ⛲

Shoal Creek Ranger District
Offers maps and info at the northern end of the National Scenic Byway. ☎ **256-463-2272; www.outdooralabama.com; 45 Hwy 281, Heflin;** ⏰ **7:30am-4pm**

EAT & DRINK

Cheaha State Park Restaurant
Won't jar your taste buds, but it's the only choice in the park. ☎ **256-488-5115;** 2141 Bunker Loop, Delta; mains $4.50-23; ⏰ 7:30-10:30am, 11:30am-3pm & 4:30-8pm Sun-Thu, 7:30am-9pm Fri & Sat; ♿

Fincher's
The owner says it all: "We're just a small *kountry* place with good food." Order catfish. ☎ **256-362-2174; 521 East St, Talladega; mains $4-10;** ⏰ **10am-9pm Mon-Thu, to 10pm Fri & Sat, 11am-9pm Sun;** ♿

Pop's Charburgers
A greasy burger joint (skip the food) that's famous for its butterscotch milkshakes. ☎ **256-463-5520; 1921 Almon St, Heflin; mains $3-7;** ⏰ **10am-9pm Mon-Thu, to 10pm Fri & Sat, 11am-8pm Sun;** ♿

SLEEP

Bald Rock Lodge
A 12-bedroom lodge. You have to rent the whole thing, but stuff enough people in and it makes sense. ☎ **256-488-5111; 19644 Hwy 281, Delta; lodge $2000;** ♿

Cheaha Lake Improved Camping
Thirty sites with bathrooms and electricity, and good ridge-top view in fall/winter. Register at country store. ☎ **256-488-5111; 19644 Hwy 281, Delta; campsites $17.60;** ♿ ⛲

Cheaha State Park Cabins
Semiprivate bluffside cabins with fireplaces, slate floors, full kitchens and fire pits, offering outstanding views. ☎ **256-488-5115; www.alapark.com; 2141 Bunker Loop, Delta; r $119-135;** ♿

Cheaha State Park Hotel
This basic hotel is totally average, but the pool offers magnificent views. ☎ **256-488-5115; www.alapark.com; 2141 Bunker Loop, Delta; r $76-97;** ♿

USEFUL WEBSITES
www.alapark.com
www.outdooralabama.com

LINK YOUR TRIP

www.lonelyplanet.com/trip-planner

The Shoals: Along the Tennessee River

WHY GO The quad-city region known as The Shoals has a musical secret: While the world shook, rattled and rolled in nearby Memphis, Northwest Alabama produced hit after R&B hit throughout the mid-20th century. The mighty Tennessee River felt the vibrations, making The Shoals an outdoor paradise with a soulful soundtrack to boot.

TIME
3 days

BEST TIME TO GO
May – Jun

START
Muscle Shoals, AL

END
Rogersville, AL

ALSO GOOD FOR

HISTORY & CULTURE

In Northern Alabama hill country in the 1950s, something very interesting was going on. While civil rights clashes were in full force in nearby Birmingham and Atlanta, African American recording artists and white boy record producers and studio musicians (the Muscle Shoals Rhythm Section, later dubbed the Swampers by Lynyrd Skynyrd) were getting along famously in The Shoals – the former flocking to the area for the fat-bottom baseline funk that defined the Muscle Shoals sound created by the latter. While Nashville, Memphis, Clarksdale and New Orleans received all the attention, The Shoals, made up of the quad-city region of Sheffield, Muscle Shoals, Tuscumbia and Florence, became one of the most under-the-radar hit-making hot spots in musical history. The Rolling Stones, Aretha Franklin, Wilson Pickett, the Staples Singers, Rod Stewart and others – they all flocked here to put a little junk in their musical trunks.

At ❶ FAME Studios in ❷ Muscle Shoals, classics like "Mustang Sally" by Wilson Pickett and "I Never Loved a Man the Way I Loved You" by Aretha Franklin were laid down. Up the road at ❸ Muscle Shoals Sound Studios in ❹ Sheffield, "Brown Sugar" (Rolling Stones) and "Ill Take You There" (Staples Singers) were locked in vinyl. You can tour both studios, the last of the 13 or so that were up and running during the heyday here of R&B.

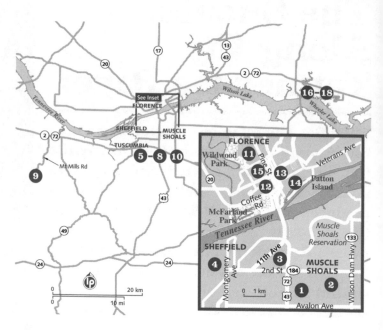

For a more in-depth look into the Muscle Shoals phenomenon, as well as all of Alabama's most prominent musical acts, the ⑤ Alabama Music Hall of Fame in ⑥ Tuscumbia does an excellent job of putting the area's musical contributions into perspective – damn near every R&B song you have ever enjoyed was recorded in this area. You can also hop onboard one of Alabama's tour buses (that's Alabama the band, not the state).

For lunch, fuel up on homey comfort food at ⑦ Claunch Café, overlooking ⑧ Spring Park in downtown Tuscumbia. At dusk, the small lake here offers a Bellagio-style fountain show set to some of the top hits recorded in the area (including "Sweet Home Alabama," of course). The most interesting place to spend the night (and load up on local atmosphere) is inside the well-appointed grain silos at ⑨ Seven Springs Lodge, about 10 miles outside Tuscumbia. Hunting and horseback riding are the big draws here.

> "Be polite while fishing, lest locals dub you a 'Basshole.'"

While tunes put The Shoals on the map, there's no shortage of other diversions in the area. The Tennessee River Valley offers pristine camping, bird-watching, hiking and plenty of world-class fishing. If you feel like getting out on the water, local guide Barry Holt of the ⑩ Tennessee River Guide Service is knowledgeable. He offers day trips out to all the lakes and rivers in the area (be polite while fishing, lest locals dub you a "Basshole").

A day on the water makes for a nice transition to ⑪ Florence, the one town in the quad-city area that falls on the north side of the Tennessee River. Florence, the most agreeable of the four towns, is where you wanna be for nightlife. The hip spot downtown is ⑫ Ricatoni's, a trendy Italian joint full of coeds and an addictive olive oil and herbs bread dip. After dinner, hop across the street to ⑬ On The Rocks, the best of the many bars offering live music nightly (read: the best bar, not necessarily the best music). For something more classic, ⑭ Dale's restaurant serves an excellent fillet mignon with a house-made seasoning famous state-wide.

A rich musical pedigree of a different kind finds its roots in Florence. The ⑮ WC Handy Museum celebrates the life of local boy WC Handy, the "father of the blues." Handy didn't invent the genre, of course, but he sophisticated it. The cabin he was born in is part of the tour. The best spot in The Shoals to sit on a porch and practice some blues of your own is ⑯ Joe Wheeler State Park in Rogersville, about 25 minutes outside Florence.

DETOUR

The Tennessee Valley is rife with outdoor recreation opportunities with fishing, bird-watching and hiking topping the list. The private, 433-acre **Cane Creek Canyon Nature Preserve** offers hiking trails, camping, waterfalls and Paleo Indian rock shelters – all for free – 10 miles outside Tuscumbia. The **Key Cave National Wildlife Refuge** is a haven for bird-watching – check those grasshopper sparrows and dickcissels – 7 miles from Florence.

At pristine Wheeler Lake, the ⑰ Joe Wheeler State Park Lodge, though aged, sits right on the lake. There is a wealth of boating, fishing and 7.5 miles of hiking around the gorgeous 2250-acre park. The ⑱ North Alabama Birding Trail rolls right through – there's a 10ft-high birding blind in the northern end, where wading birds are common in winter (and the occasional bald eagle). Listen closely – even the birds around here sing a soulful tune or two.

Kevin Raub

TRIP INFORMATION

GETTING THERE
From Birmingham, it's a two-hour drive north on I-65 (northbound) to Hwy 157, then to Hwy 72 (westbound).

DO

Alabama Music Hall of Fame
This $2.5 million exhibit hall showcases Alabama's finest. You can board one of Alabama's tour buses! ☎ 256-381-4417; www.alamhof.org; 617 Hwy 72 W, Tuscumbia; adult/child $8/7; ☾ 9am-5pm Mon-Sat, 1-5pm Sun; ♿

FAME Studios
Call ahead – if there's nobody recording, you can stand in the room "where it all started." ☎ 256-381-0801; www.fame2.com; 603 E Avalon Ave, Muscle Shoals; ☾ 9am-5pm Mon-Fri

Muscle Shoals Sound Studios
Cher put the facade on an album cover, the Rolling Stones and Stewart recorded in its hallowed halls. ☎ 256-783-2641; www .muscleshoalssound.org; 3614 Jackson Hwy, Sheffield; admission $10; ☾ noon-6pm Mon-Fri

Tennessee River Guide Service
Fishing guide Barry Holt takes anglers of all skill levels on eight-hour trips on Pickwick, Wheeler and Wilson lakes. ☎ 256-383-7481; Holt Upholstery & Audio, 1114 N Main St, Tuscumbia; ♿

WC Handy Museum
The father of the blues is memorialized in this small museum and relocated wooden cabin. ☎ 256-760-6434; www.florenceal .org; 620 W College St, Florence; adult/child $2/0.50; ☾ 10am-4pm Tue-Sat

EAT & DRINK

Claunch Café
Everything is good at this comfort-food staple overlooking Tuscumbia's pleasant Spring Park. ☎ 256-386-0222; 400 S Main St, Tuscumbia; mains $2.50-8; ☾ 11am-2pm Sun-Thu; ♿

Dale's
Small-town chophouse with a renowned steak seasoning and an oddly unrelated appetizer choice: onion soup or tomato juice? ☎ 256-766-4961; 1001 Metro Blvd, Florence; mains $16-38; ☾ 5-10pm Mon-Sat

On The Rocks
There are lots of places around The Shoals for live music nightly, but here the crowd is easier on the eyes. ☎ 256-760-2212; 110 N Court St, Florence; ☾ 11am-2am Mon-Sat

Ricatoni's
Trendy Italian hotspot with solid eats and a waitstaff of coeds from the University of North Alabama. ☎ 256-718-1002; 710 N Court St, Florence; mains $10-18; ☾ 11am-10pm Sun-Thu, to 11pm Fri & Sat

SLEEP

Joe Wheeler State Park Lodge
Fishing, bird-watching and hiking are the big draws at this lodge on picturesque Wheeler Lake. ☎ 256-247-5461; www.joe wheelerstatepark.com; 201 McLean Dr, Rogersville; camping $11-20, r $75-210; ♿ 🐾

Seven Springs Lodge
Sleep in an old grain silo at this RV-friendly hunting and horseback-riding lodge brimming with local color. ☎ 256-370-7218; www.sevenspringslodge.net; 1292 Mt Mills Rd, Tuscumbia; r $50-120; ☾ Feb-Oct; ♿

USEFUL WEBSITES
www.colbertcountytourism.org
www.visitflorenceal.com

LINK YOUR TRIP
www.lonelyplanet.com/trip-planner

TRIP

Old Mobile, Alabama

WHY GO At first glance, Mobile seems little more than a massive erector set of protruding port cranes. However, closer inspection reveals a wealth of down-home eateries, world-class war-buff attractions, decadent nightlife and a New Orleans–evoking aesthetic that weaves through the city's eight historic districts – the shining star of Alabama's Gulf Coast.

Mobile is one of the South's most polarizing towns: talk to someone from Montgomery, and they'll fire off a list of must-eats and must-dos; hit up someone from Atlanta and they'll tell you to skip it and go straight to the Gulf shores…or New Orleans. Let them go. Mobile – the true mouth of the South – is best enjoyed for what it is: less grimy and less crowded than New Orleans, this former French colony of Louisiana (founded in 1702) grew up on a completely different path to its French-leaning cousin two hours to the west.

Driving through Mobile leaves something to be desired, but off the exit ramps there are clandestine pockets of pure architectural joy. Mobile's eight National Register Historic Districts pepper the city like little goldmines of 18th- and 19th-century life. The *Mobile Historic District Driving Tour* map is an invaluable tool available at the welcome center at ❶ **Fort Condé**, a reconstructed 1723 fort that houses a fascinating array of antebellum weaponry and some great old photographs of Mobile. Before setting off for the historic districts, take a peek also into the ❷ **Museum of Mobile** across the street, one of the South's better city museums. The Human Cargo slave exhibit here is absolutely harrowing…check out the Mardi Gras history to lighten things up.

Most of the historic districts in Mobile rub up against each other like prepubescent Mobilians against the debutantes at a Mardi Gras

TIME
2 days

BEST TIME TO GO
Oct – Mar

START
Mobile, AL

END
Mobile, AL

ALSO GOOD FOR

CITY

HISTORY & CULTURE

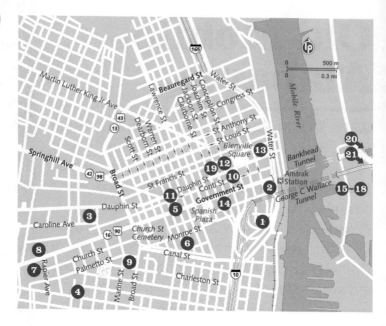

ball. If you have the time, walking the driving tour is preferable as you will have more time to read about each address. The neighborhoods of ❸ **Old Dauphin Way** (notable for its fine collection of bungalows), ❹ **Oakleigh Garden** (characterized by looming mansions next door to humble shotgun-style homes and smaller cottages), ❺ **Lower Dauphin** (where brick has been the required building material since 1839) and ❻ **Church Street East** (full of churches and beautiful civic buildings) make for a convenient four-point stroll. Highlights along the way include ❼ **The Lott House**, an imposing classic revival home in Oakleigh, and ❽ **1216 Government Street**, an elaborate Queen Anne home on Old Dauphin Way. Lunch could be nowhere else: ❾ **Callaghan's Irish Social Club** in Oakleigh that dates back to 1946. The burgers here would do just fine as a last meal.

"From Southern rock to boogie-woogie jazz, Mobile turns musical after sundown."

For all its historic glory, Mobile also knows how to get down. From Southern rock to boogie-woogie jazz, Mobile turns musical after sundown. All the action is centered on Dauphin St – like a distant cousin to Bourbon St that can hold its liquor, keep its shirt on and manage to avoid arrest. Almost all the bars here – nicely positioned between art galleries and antique shops – offer live music. Nothing gets going until after 11pm, so a good early evening stop is ❿ **Hurricane Brewing**, where patrons put up with mediocre pub fare for the excellent microbrews, all the while keeping an eye on the inhouse hurricane tracking map, or the bar at ⑪ Winchell's Oyster House, also the spot for superb fresh oysters and a healthy shovelin' of traditional Mobile culture. It opened with a six-stool oyster bar in 1938.

Membership cards are required at most late-night bars (and when we say late night, we really mean sunrise). The particulars are handled at the door. ⑫ Boo Radley's is a good choice that skews a little more preppy, a little less cheesy (though wandering up and down Dauphin to make a choice is half the fun). It's open until 7am, so there's no need for a hotel! If you do want to lay your weary head, the ⑬ Battle House, on the site of Andrew Jackson's former military headquarters, is well located only steps from Dauphin on Royal St. The remarkable stained-glass, domed lobby dates back to 1908. ⑭ Malaga Inn, not far away on Church St, offers more history, though less services. The twin town houses that make up the historic portion of the hotel date back to 1862 and open up onto a lovely interior courtyard.

Having slept off the night before, you could spend an entire day exploring ⑮ USS Alabama Battleship Memorial Park. Regardless of personal war views, it's hard not to be awed by the impressive display of military might here. Highlights include the massive ⑯ USS Alabama battleship, the claustrophobic ⑰ USS Drum submarine, and the totally menacing ⑱ SR-71, a stealth black Mach 3 reconnaissance aircraft that looks scarily ahead of its time.

'NAWLINS AIN'T GOT NUTHIN' ON US

Though New Orleans snags all the glory, America's first Mardi Gras celebration was actually in Mobile in 1703. Its history is best detailed in the wonderful **Mobile Carnival Museum** (www.mobilecarnivalmuseum.com), which offers a fascinating look into the mystic societies that rule the celebrations here as well as a close-up look at the elaborate trains (some costing upwards of $45,000) from several past queens.

Running around the 165-acre park will elicit overheating in the muggy Mobile sun, so try ⑲ Spot of Tea, back on Dauphin, for a strawberry sweet tea that's an Alabama bragging point in Deep South circles. It's a strange place – one part Hallmark store, one part Victorian tearoom – but the food is undeniably special.

To complete your Mobile visit, head out onto the swamps. ⑳ Five Rivers Delta Safaris offers 20-mile pontoon safaris on five different rivers in the ㉑ Mobile-Tensaw Delta, the second-largest river delta in the USA. It's a haven for canoeists and kayakers as well. Abundant birdlife and surprising wildlife dominate the area (alligators, red-bellied turtles, wild boar and the occasional black bear). Don't fall in – lest you ate one of those Callaghan burgers for lunch.

Kevin Raub

HISTORY & CULTURE

TRIP INFORMATION

GETTING THERE
From Birmingham, it's a four-hour straight shot south on I-65 (southbound).

DO

Five Rivers Delta Safaris
Pontoon safaris deep into the Mobile-Tensaw Delta. ☎ 251-259-8531; www.hovercraft safaris.com; 30945 Five Rivers Rd, Spanish Fort; tours adult/child from $20/12; ⏱ 2pm Wed-Sun, 11am & 2pm Sat; ♿

Fort Condé
Reconstructed 18th-century French brick fort with an impressive assortment of antebellum weaponry. ☎ 251-208-7503; 150 Royal St; ⏱ 8am-5pm; ♿

Museum of Mobile
One of the South's most interesting history museums, chronicling Mobile past and present. ☎ 802-223-5200; www.museumof mobile.com; 111 S Royal St; adult/child $5/3; ⏱ 9am-5pm Mon-Sat, 1-5pm Sun; ♿

USS Alabama Battleship Memorial Park
Impressive military park home to decommissioned USS *Alabama* battleship and various other war machines. ☎ 251-433-2703; www .ussalabama.com; 2703 Battleship Park; adult/ child $12/6, parking $2; ⏱ 8am-7pm; ♿

EAT

Callaghan's Irish Social Club
Mobile's best burgers and consistently voted one of America's best bars. This ramshackle place in the Oakleigh district is unmissable. ☎ 251-433-9374; cnr Marine & Charleston; mains $7-9; ⏱ 11am-midnight

Spot of Tea
The atmosphere evokes grandma's post-haircut lunch, but the sandwiches are killer

and the strawberry tea famous statewide. ☎ 251-433-9009; 310 Dauphin St; sandwiches $8-9.50; ⏱ 7am-2pm; ♿

Winchell's Oyster House
Mobile classic since 1938 serving up tasty oysters numerous ways and plenty of other tremendous seafood. 'Bama truths line the walls. ☎ 251-432-4605; 605 Dauphin St; mains $7-23; ⏱ 11am-10pm Sun-Thu, to 11pm Fri & Sat; ♿

DRINK

Boo Radley's
One of the better live music bars on Dauphin. Free crawfish on Wednesdays in crawfish season! ☎ 251-432-1996; 276 Dauphin St; ⏱ 8pm-7am Thu-Sat; 8pm-7am Wed only Mar-Jul

Hurricane Brewing
Nobody raves about the food at this micro-brewery, but the suds are solid. Long wooden picnic tables facilitate interesting encounters. ☎ 251-445-2544; 225 Dauphin St; mains $7-11; ⏱ 11am-11pm Mon-Thu, to 2am Fri & Sat

SLEEP

Battle House
1908 hotel turned upscale Renaissance with a gorgeous domed glass lobby. ☎ 251-338-2000; www.rsabattlehouse.com; 26 N Royal St; r $119-249; ♿

Malaga Inn
These two restored town houses open onto an interior garden. It's worth the extra money for the 1862 rooms, which are larger and more authentic. ☎ 251-438-4701; www.malagainn.com; 359 Church St; r $94-129

USEFUL WEBSITES
www.mobile.org

LINK YOUR TRIP

www.lonelyplanet.com/trip-planner

Day Trips in North & South Georgia

DAY TRIPS

Atlanta and Savannah provide enough amusement to hold your attention for weeks, but why not live a little and get out into the surrounding mountains, waterways and national parks that pepper the countryside outside these two Southern belles? Within an hour or two of both, there's no shortage of distractions.

LAKE LANIER

Georgia's most visited lake is a 39,000-acre aquatic playground under the verdant gaze of the North Georgia Mountains. Atlantans flock here in the summer, content to get out on the water and bask in the sweltering Georgia heat. Diversions in the area include lakeside cottages, camping, boat rentals (from Harbor Landing), and two award-wining golf courses, Emerald Pointe and Pinelsle. In summer, the beach and water park open for business; from mid-November through December, the world's largest animated holiday light extravaganza, the Magical Nights of Light, illuminates the lake. Drought threatened the lake in 2007, resulting in a 15ft drop in water levels, but that didn't stop Atlantans from enjoying 692 miles of shoreline: they were just extra careful where they dove! **North of downtown Atlanta, take I-85 (northbound) to I-985 (northbound) to exit 8 (Friendship Rd). Follow the signs to Lake Lanier.**

HELEN

Popping up out of the Blue Ridge Mountains like Bavaria's Schloss Neuschwanstein, two hours north of Atlanta, is a charming little piece of Germany – no passport required. Helen is modeled after an Alpine village, right down to the *bier*, *brats* and lederhosen. Narrow cobblestone alleys, old-world towers and balconies, German-spiced restaurants and bakeries and specialty shops are tucked along the *Straßes* and *Platzes* that line Chattahoochee River through this mountain town. One of the country's most popular Oktoberfests is here, as is a wealth of outdoor adventures, including Anna Ruby Falls, a 150ft double waterfall, and hiking, biking and fishing in the area. Tubing in the Chattahoochee is one of the most popular ways to kill an afternoon.

From Atlanta, take I-85 (northbound) for 31 miles to I-985/Lanier Parkway/exit 113 (signs for Gainesville/I-985 North/Lanier Parkway) and follow Lanier Parkway 32 miles to Hwy 23 (northbound). Take a left on Duncan Bridge Rd/Hwy 384. Take a right on Hwy 75 into town.

TALLULAH GORGE STATE PARK

Two miles long and 1000ft deep, Tallulah Gorge (www.gastateparks.org/info/tallulah) is one of the most spectacular swaths of cut canyon this side of the Mississippi River and is considered the first tourist attraction in north Georgia, designated as such as far back as the 19th century. A 90-minute drive northeast of Atlanta puts you in one of Georgia's prettiest parks, Tallulah Gorge State Park, home to rim trails to several outlooks as well as a trail to the canyon floor (leave your flip-flops and Crocs at home, a permit is required, and those don't make the cut). The Tallulah River and Falls are best viewed from the 80ft suspension bridge dangling above the rocky canyon bottom. Rock climbing is popular on the Main Wall on the North Rim. Though the river has been tamed by a series of Georgia Power hydroelectric dams, you can beef up on its once-mighty history and the biology of the area at the Jane Hurt Yarn Interpretive Center. From Atlanta, take I-85 (northbound) for 31 miles to I-985/Lanier Parkway/exit 113 (signs for Gainesville/I-985 North/Lanier Parkway) to Cornelia Hwy/Hwy 23 North and follow Hwy 23 for another 32 miles. Turn right on Jane Hurt Yarn Rd into the park.

See also **TRIPS 34 & 35**

OKEFENOKEE NATIONAL WILDLIFE REFUGE

Established in 1937, the Okefenokee Swamp is a national gem, encompassing 396,000 acres of bog in a giant saucer-shaped depression that was once part of the ocean floor. The swamp is home to an estimated 9000 to 15,000 alligators, 234 bird species, 49 types of mammal and 60 amphibian species. The Okefenokee Swamp Park (www.okeswamp.com) has captive bears and gators on-site, or you can explore the swamp in a canoe or on a boat tour. The ultimate experience is a multiday canoe trip on the swamp's 120 miles of waterways. Call the US Fish and Wildlife Service's Okefenokee National Wildlife Refuge Wilderness Canoe Guide (www.fws.gov/okefenokee) if you're considering a trip. Guided boat trips are also available. Warning: the water level in 2006 and '07 was so low that water trips from the park were suspended indefinitely. From Savannah, take I-95 (southbound) to exit 29 (S Georgia Parkway, Hwy 82). Turn right on S Georgia Parkway, Hwy 82 (westbound). Stay straight onto Hwy 82 West/Hwy 520/Corridor Z/S Georgia Parkway for approximately 40 miles. Turn left onto Hwy 177 and follow for about 6 miles (you will cross Hwy 1 at the entrance to the park).

MISSISSIPPI, LOUISIANA & ARKANSAS TRIPS

Venture into these three distinct, alluring states, and you may just fall in love.

Arkansas flaunts granite bluffs, scenic rivers and tasty barbecue. The Ozarks are laced with winding roads, quirky towns and narrow trails that lead to the edge of heaven. And don't sleep on Little Rock. It's a small but charming city seasoned with a sweet River Front District and a whole lot of Clinton.

Sultry Mississippi will lavish entrancing blues and seductive history upon you. Juke joints hum until the wee hours in delta blues country. Historic Oxford is the kind of fun-yet-refined college town that reels you in, and the Natchez Trace Parkway is simply the most beautiful highway in the South.

Then let Louisiana satiate you with the naughty flavor of New Orleans. Though beaten and bruised, the Crescent City remains a gorgeous goddess, showing off diverse cuisine and architecture, and an infinite river of free, live music. Outside the city limits explore a fertile maze of plantations, misty bayous and swamps, and tasty Cajun towns.

 PLAYLIST From Robert Johnson to Louis Armstrong and BB King, America's musical roots run deep in this particular swath of Southern soil. Car dancing required.

- "Cross Road Blues," Robert Johnson
- "Make Me a Pallet on Your Floor," Mississippi John Hurt
- "One Bourbon, One Scotch, One Beer," John Lee Hooker
- "Got My Mojo Working," Muddy Waters
- "Shake for Me," Howlin' Wolf
- "Hound Dog," Big Mama Thornton
- "Lucille," BB King
- "Hot Venom," Rebirth Brass Band
- "Really the Blues," Panorama Jazz Band
- "Wonderful World," Louis Armstrong

And feel free to share your love. We won't make you choose between them.

 MISSISSIPPI, LOUISIANA & ARKANSAS' BEST TRIPS

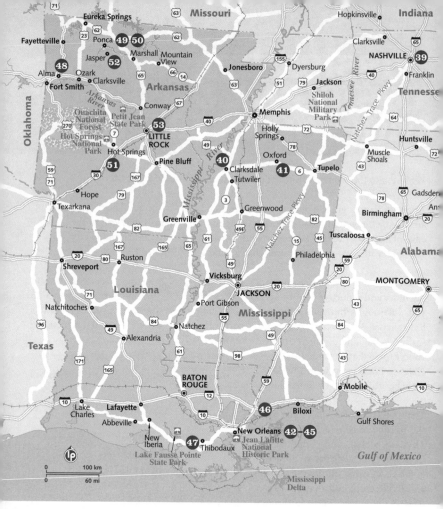

MISSISSIPPI, LOUISIANA & ARKANSAS TRIPS

Driving the Natchez Trace Parkway

WHY GO With emerald mounds, jade swamps, hiking trails, opulent mansions, riverside saloons, and layer upon layer of American history, the Natchez Trace Parkway is the richest drive in the South. It winds 442 gorgeously wooded miles from Nashville all the way to Natchez in southern Mississippi.

America grew from infancy to childhood then adolescence in the late 18th and 19th centuries. That's when we explored and expanded, traded and clashed with Native Americans, and eventually confronted our own shadow during the Civil War. Evidence of this drama can be found along the Natchez Trace, but before you begin, enjoy a little night music.

You'll begin in ❶ Nashville, where amateur musicians descend in the hopes of becoming country music stars. There are boot-stomping honky-tonks, the country music hall of fame and a sweet historic district to explore. Don't miss ❷ Bluebird Cafe, tucked away in a suburban strip mall. This is a singer-songwriter haven. While you eat and sip cocktails, souls will be bared on the tiny stage. No mid-show chitchat, mind, or you will get bounced.

If you'd like to enjoy a less controlled musical environment, head over to ❸ Tootsie's Orchid Lounge. In 1960, when Hattie "Tootsie" Bess bought the joint, she began nurturing up-and-coming country stars like Waylon Jennings and Faron Young on two stages. It remains a glorious dive smothered with old photographs and handbills from the Nashville Sound glory days, while the music (still country) has evolved with the times.

Grab dinner at ❹ Swett's, a family-owned, cafeteria-style Nashville institution that's been around for 53 years. It's all about Southern food

TIME
3 days

DISTANCE
442 miles

BEST TIME TO GO
**Apr – Jun &
Sep – Nov**

START
Nashville, TN

END
Natchez, MS

ALSO GOOD FOR

HISTORY &
CULTURE

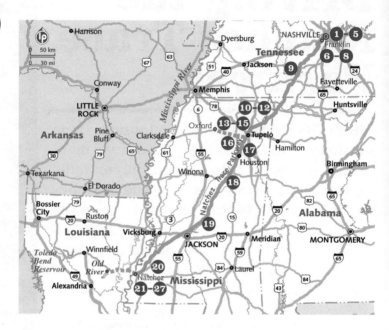

here, covering everything from BBQ chicken and pig's feet to turnip greens and baked apples. Snooze at the ❺ Union Station Hotel on Broadway. If the 65ft vaulted lobby and 100-year-old timetables remind you of a train station, that's because this was the Nashville rail depot once upon a time.

"It remains a glorious dive smothered with old photographs and handbills from the Nashville Sound glory days."

The next day head south, and you will traverse the Double-Arch Bridge, 155ft above the valley, before settling in for a pleasant country drive. You'll notice dense woods encroaching and arching elegantly over the smooth highway for the next 442 miles.

Although it's just 10 miles outside of Nashville, it's worth stopping in the tiny historic hamlet of ❻ Franklin. The Victorian-era downtown is charming and the nearby artsy enclave of Leiper's Fork is fun and eclectic. But you're in the area to check out one of the Civil War's bloodiest battlefields. On November 30, 1864, 37,000 men (20,000 Confederates and 17,000 Union soldiers) fought over a 2-mile stretch of Franklin's outskirts. Nashville's sprawl has turned much of the battlefield into suburbs, but the ❼ Carter House property is a preserved 8-acre chunk of the Battle of Franklin. The house is still riddled with 1000 bullet holes.

At mile-marker 403.7 (don't mind the "backward" mile-markers, we think a north–south route works best), you'll find the first of several sections of the

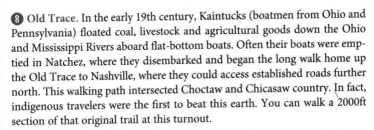

8 Old Trace. In the early 19th century, Kaintucks (boatmen from Ohio and Pennsylvania) floated coal, livestock and agricultural goods down the Ohio and Mississippi Rivers aboard flat-bottom boats. Often their boats were emptied in Natchez, where they disembarked and began the long walk home up the Old Trace to Nashville, where they could access established roads further north. This walking path intersected Choctaw and Chicasaw country. In fact, indigenous travelers were the first to beat this earth. You can walk a 2000ft section of that original trail at this turnout.

Just under 20 miles later, at mile-marker 385.9, you'll come to the **9** Meriwether Lewis Site, where the famed explorer and first governor of the Louisiana territory died of mysterious gunshot wounds at nearby Grinders Inn. Lewis' good friend, Thomas Jefferson, was convinced it was suicide, though his family begged to differ. Continue on and you will

DETOUR If you plan on driving the entire Natchez Trace from Nashville to Natchez, you may want to detour at Tupelo along Hwy 6 to **Oxford**, Mississippi (about 50 miles), a town rich in culture and history. This is Faulkner country, and Oxford is a thriving university town with terrific restaurants and bars. Don't miss the catfish dinner at Taylor Grocery, 15 minutes south of Oxford.

cross into Alabama at mile-marker 341.8, and Mississippi at mile-marker 308.8 where you'll also find **10** Bear Creek Mound, an ancient indigenous ceremonial site built between 1200 and 1400.

The highway bisects **11** Tishomingo State Park at mile-marker 304.5. If you're taking it slow, you may want to camp here among the sandstone cliffs, fern gullies and waterfalls of Bear Creek canyon. Hiking trails abound and canoes are available for rent. The **12** Phar Mounds, a 2000-year-old, 90-acre complex of eight indigenous burial sites, are worth braking for at mile-marker 286.7, and at mile-marker 269.4 you'll contemplate the Civil War once again, this time at the **13** Confederate Gravesites for 13 unknown soldiers.

At mile-marker 266 you'll roll into Tupelo and the **14** Natchez Trace Parkway Visitors Center. Peruse natural and American history displays, grab maps and pick the brains of local rangers behind the counter. While you're in town consider visiting the **15** Elvis Presley Birthplace. The original structure has a new roof and furniture, but Elvis grew up, learned to play the guitar and dreamed big in these humble rooms.

South from Tupelo, the Trace winds past **16** Chicasaw Village, where displays document how the Chicasaw lived, and the 2100-year-old **17** Bynum Mounds, before reaching **18** French Camp. If you plan on driving the trace in two days, you should overnight here in log cabins on the site of a former French pioneer settlement. You can tour a cute antebellum two-story home, built by Revolutionary War veteran Colonel James Drane. The table is set for dinner, aged leather journals are arranged on the desk and Drane's original US flag is in an upstairs bedroom along with a cool antique loom.

At mile-marker 122, tour the **⑲ Tupelo-Baldcypress Swamp**. The 20-minute trail snakes through an abandoned channel and continues on a boardwalk over the milky green swamp shaded by water tupelo and bald cypresses. Look for turtles on the rocks and gators in the water.

At mile-marker 10.3 is **⑳ Emerald Mound**, the best of the indigenous mound sites. Using stone tools, pre-Columbian ancestors to the Natchez Indians graded this 8-acre mountain into a flat-topped pyramid. It is now the second-largest mound in America. There are shady, creekside picnic spots here too.

KAYAKING THE OLD RIVER

According to Keith Benoist, a photographer, landscaper and co-founder of the **Phatwater Challenge** marathon kayak race, the Mississippi has more navigable river miles than any other state in the union. Natchez-born Benoist trains for his 44-mile race by paddling 10 miles of the Old River, an abandoned section of the Mississippi fringed with cypress and teeming with gators. If you're lucky enough to meet him at Under the Hill, he may just take you with him.

When the woods part, revealing historic antebellum mansions, you have reached **㉑ Natchez**, Mississippi. In the 1840s, Natchez had more millionaires per capita than any city in the world (because the plantation owners didn't pay their staff). Yes, old cotton money built these homes with slave labor, but they are graced all the same with an opulent, *Gone With the Wind* charm. "Pilgrimage season" is in the spring and fall, when the mansions open for tours, though some are open year-round. The redbrick **㉒ Auburn Mansion** is famous for its freestanding spiral staircase. Built in 1812, the architecture here – a pediment roof supported by thick columns – influenced countless mansions throughout the South.

Care to taste mansion life? **㉓ Monmouth Plantation** will do just fine. This 26-acre mansion property has 30 guest rooms within the mansion and in outlying buildings, done up with old Southern antiques. There are original Waterford chandeliers and luxurious canopy beds. Service and food are impeccable, as well. **㉔ The Castle**, a restaurant set at Dunleith mansion (also turned B&B), is widely considered the best in town, while **㉕ Magnolia Grill** is a casual spot for tasty salads and grilled fish, shrimp and steaks.

Natchez has dirt under its fingernails too. When Mark Twain came through town, he crashed in a room above the local saloon. **㉖ Under the Hill Saloon** remains the best bar in town, with terrific (and free) live music on weekends. And you can still crash upstairs at **㉗ Mark Twain Guesthouse**, where rooms on the riverside have a balcony overlooking the Mississippi River.

Adam Skolnick

TRIP INFORMATION

GETTING THERE
Catch the Natchez Trace Parkway in Nashville and follow it 442 miles until it ends in Natchez. Or vice versa.

DO

Auburn Mansion
An antebellum Natchez mansion open for year-round tours. ☎ 800-647-6742; www.natchezpilgrimage.com; Duncan Park, Natchez; ☻ 11am-3pm Tue-Sat, last tour departs 2:30pm; ⓖ

Bear Creek Mound
One of several ceremonial mounds along the Natchez Trace Parkway. ☎ 800-305-7417; www.nps.gov/natr; mile-marker 341.8 Natchez Trace Parkway; ⓖ ☙

Bluebird Cafe
Obscure talents come to this suburban strip-mall café hoping to be discovered. ☎ 615-383-1461; www.bluebirdcafe.com; 4104 Hillsboro Rd, Nashville; admission free-$15; ☻ early/late shows 6pm/9:30pm most nights

Bynum Mounds
Another interesting mound site with information detailing native life. ☎ 800-305-7417; www.nps.gov/natr; mile-marker 232.4 Natchez Trace Parkway; ⓖ ☙

Carter House
A preserved, 8-acre swath of the Franklin Battlefield. ☎ 615-791-1861; www.carter-house.org; 1140 Columbia Ave, Franklin; adult/senior/child $8/7/4; ☻ 9am-5pm Mon-Sat, 1-5pm Sun; ⓖ ☙

Chicasaw Village
An old indigenous village site just off the Trace. ☎ 800-305-7417; www.nps.gov/natr; mile-marker 261.8 Natchez Trace Parkway; ⓖ ☙

Confederate Gravesites
Thirteen unidentified Confederate soldiers were buried here just off the parkway. ☎ 800-305-7417; www.nps.gov/natr; mile-marker 269.4 Natchez Trace Parkway; ⓖ ☙

Elvis Presley Birthplace
Elvis freaks descend to see where the king learned to walk then play guitar then thrust his pelvis. ☎ 662-841-1245; www.elvispresleybirthplace.com; 306 Elvis Presley Dr, Tupelo; adult/child $10/5; ☻ 9am-5pm Mon-Sat, 1-5pm Sun, closed Thanksgiving & Christmas; ⓖ

Emerald Mound
These two massive grassy pyramids still buzz with ancient energy. ☎ 800-305-7417; www.nps.gov/natr; mile-marker 10.3 Natchez Trace Parkway; ⓖ ☙

Meriwether Lewis Site
The legendary explorer Lewis died in these woods from mysterious gunshot wounds. ☎ 800-305-7417; www.nps.gov/natr; mile-marker 385.9 Natchez Trace Parkway; ⓖ ☙

Natchez Trace Parkway Visitor Center
The parkway visitors center is just outside Tupelo. ☎ 800-305-7417; www.nps.gov/natr; mile-marker 286.7 Natchez Trace Parkway; ☻ 8am-5pm, closed Christmas; ⓖ ☙

Old Trace
Remnants of the Old Trace walking trail are preserved at various points in the woods along the parkway. ☎ 800-305-7417; www.nps.gov/natr; mile-marker 403.7 Natchez Trace Parkway; ⓖ ☙

Phar Mounds
This 2000-year-old complex includes eight mound sites scattered over 90 acres. ☎ 800-305-7417; www.nps.gov/natr; mile-marker 286.7 Natchez Trace Parkway; ⓖ ☙

Tootsie's Orchid Lounge
This purple glazed honky-tonk has hosted good live country music since 1960. ☎ 615-726-7937; www.tootsies.net; 422 Broadway, Nashville; admission free; ☻ 10am-late

Tupelo-Baldcypress Swamp
This 20-minute walk around a gorgeous jade swamp is an ideal stretch break. ☎ 800-305-7417; www.nps.gov/natr; mile-marker 122 Natchez Trace Parkway; ⓖ ☙

Under The Hill Saloon
Historic bar that was once a favorite haunt of Mark Twain. ☎ 601-446-8023; www.underthehillsaloon.com; 25 Silver St, Natchez; ☻ 9am-late

EAT

Castle
Upscale continental cuisine served on the sensational Dunleith Plantation. ☎ 601-446-8500; www.dunleith.com; 84 Homochitto St, Natchez; mains $18-34; ⏰ 7:30-10am, 11am-2pm & 6-9pm Mon-Thu, to 10pm Fri & Sat

Magnolia Grill
Delicious, fresh, grilled fare served with fabulous Mississippi River views. ☎ 601-446-7670; www.magnoliagrill.com; 49 Silver St, Natchez; mains $13-29; ⏰ 11am-9pm, to 10pm Fri & Sat; ♿

Swett's
Tasty traditional Southern cooking has been served up cafeteria-style at this Nashville institution since 1954. ☎ 615-329-4418; www.swettsrestaurant.com; 2725 Clifton Ave, Nashville; mains $9; ⏰ 11am-8pm; ♿

SLEEP

French Camp B&B
Stay the night in a log cabin built on a former French pioneer site that was further developed by a Revolutionary War hero. ☎ 662-547-6835; www.frenchcamp.org; mile-marker 180.7 Natchez Trace Parkway; r $75; ♿

Mark Twain Guesthouse
Riverboat captain Samuel Clemens used to drink till late at the saloon and pass out in one of three upstairs bedrooms (room 1 and has the best view). Can be noisy until after 2am. ☎ 601-446-8023; www.underthehill saloon.com; 25 Silver St, Natchez; r from $85

Monmouth Plantation
If you've ever wanted to make like Scarlett O'Hara and collapse into the luxurious shade of your verandah, you can do so at this historic plantation turned boutique hotel and divine restaurant. ☎ 800-828-4531; www .monmouthplantation.com; 36 Melrose Ave, Natchez; r from $199

Tishomingo State Park
Campers can rent canoes and paddle Bear Creek. ☎ 662-438-6914; www.mississippi stateparks.reserveamerica.com; mile-marker 304.5 Natchez Trace Parkway, Tishomingo; campsite $16; ♿ 🅿

Union Station Hotel
Once the Nashville train station and now a grand and elegant modern hotel. ☎ 615-726-1001; www.unionstationhotelnashville .com; 1001 Broadway, Nashville; r from $159; ♿

USEFUL WEBSITES
www.scenictrace.com

LINK YOUR TRIP
www.lonelyplanet.com/trip-planner

The Blues Highway

WHY GO To listen to living blues legends howl their sad enlightenment into a microphone, shrouded in a smoky red glow. And to pay homage to Mississippi Delta Hwy 61, the birthplace of the blues music that has saturated Northern Mississippi for almost 100 years, and just so happens to be the origin of rock and roll.

In the flat land that stretches out on either side of Hwy 61, American music took root. It came from Africa in the souls of slaves, morphed into field songs, then found its way into the brain of a mythical sharecropping troubadour waiting for a train. ❶ Clarksdale is the hub of delta blues country. It was here, at the crossroads of Hwys 61 and 49, that Robert Johnson made a deal with the devil and became America's first guitar hero. And it's here where live music and blues history are most accessible.

Clarksdale is a useful base for your exploration of the Blues Highway. Stay at ❷ Shack Up Inn, a B&B (that's bed & beer in this case) and an antique-kitsch paradise. Another option, the ❸ Riverside Hotel, lacks style points but it has history, with Sonny Boy Williamson and Ike Turner having stayed here. ❹ Ground Zero, Morgan Freeman's blues club, also rents smart furnished rooms on the floors above the club.

Delta blues territory is all about the nights, but there are plenty of daytime sights and excursions. Have breakfast at ❺ The Crossroads. Peeking out above the trees on the northeast corner of Hwys 61 and 49 is the landmark with three blue guitars interlocking like a weather vane, and just behind it is ❻ Delta Donuts, a greasy Mississippi dive, with an ancient coffee maker on permanent percolate and cases of delectably warm doughnuts stuffed with chocolate and vanilla cream.

TIME
3 days

DISTANCE
319 miles

BEST TIME TO GO
June

START
Clarksdale, MS

END
Bentonia, MS

ALSO GOOD FOR

OUTDOORS

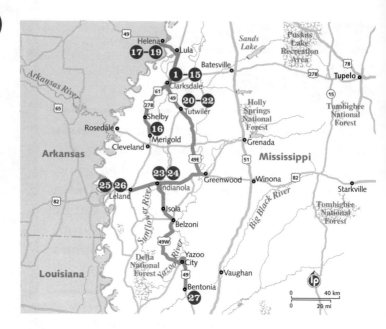

All the refurbished buildings downtown support and honor Clarksdale's blues tradition. **7** **The Delta Blues Museum**, set in the city's old train depot, has arguably the best collection of blues memorabilia in the delta, including Muddy Waters' reconstructed Mississippi cabin. The creative, multimedia exhibits also honor BB King, John Lee Hooker, Big Mama Thornton and WC Handy. The **8** **Rock and Roll & Blues Heritage Museum** is a private enterprise launched by a Dutch expat who over the years amassed an incredible record and memorabilia collection, then bought a defunct Clarksdale movie theater in order to show it off.

9 **Cat Head** makes for some interesting shopping and up-to-the-minute live music tips. If you want to know who's playing where in the delta, come see Roger behind the counter. He also sells a good range of blues CDs, books and some sensational folk art.

"Wednesday through Saturday live music sweeps through Clarksdale like a summer storm."

Clarksdale has a number of tasty dining rooms (none serve health food). **10** **Sarah's Kitchen** is the juke joint of restaurants. It's only open for lunch Thursday to Saturday, and there's no menu, but you will love Sarah's ample portions of soul food. **11** **Ramon** serves terrific, golden fried shrimp in a family-owned, candlelit diner. And **12** **Abe's** has been nestled just off the crossroads since 1924. The ribs are sensational, but the BBQ beef, pork and ham sandwiches are popular, too.

When Morgan Freeman built Ground Zero, he also launched a buttoned-up New York City-esque bistro, ⑬ **Madidi**. Prices are high and reservations required, but the food has a terrific reputation. ⑭ **Rust** is the newest restaurant in town. It attracts well-to-do families and has a fashionable eco-decor with mirrors framed in recycled wood, and hammered brass tables. The tender shrimp and creamy grits come in a peppery gumbo broth.

Wednesday through Saturday live music sweeps through Clarksdale like a summer storm. Ground Zero has the most professional bandstand and sound system, a huge room with dining and pool tables, and a consistent lineup. But it will never compare to ⑮ **Red's**, a funky, smoky, red-lit, beat-up, leaky juke joint run with in-your-face charm by Red himself. He has live music nearly every Friday and Saturday night. Sometimes he brings in legends, and he'll fire up his enormous grill outside on special occasions.

⑯ **Po Monkeys** is hidden down a country road 30 miles south of town. This is a real-deal country juke joint. It only has live music about once a month, but there's sweet trouble to be found here on Mondays when Shack Dancers prowl, and on Thursdays when college kids dance to DJ sets till the wee hours.

AND THE WOLFMAN PLAYS ON

There's nothing like seeing Robert "Wolfman" Belfour, 72, solo on electric guitar at Red's. He doesn't play music. It pours through him, as he wails and roars like a witch doctor, like a prophet. Soon all of us are swallowed by the music, enraptured in the one soul, as he mines light from his darkest moments. Red keeps shouting, "Go Wolf. You're evil, man!" But he isn't. He's simply a master.

⑰ **Helena**, Arkansas, a depressed mill town 32 miles north and across the Mississippi River from Clarksdale, was once the home of Sonny Boy Williamson. He was a regular on *King Biscuit Time,* America's original blues radio show. BB King recalls listening to the lunch-hour program as a young buck, and being influenced by Sonny Boy. The radio show, which begins weekdays at 12:15pm, is still running, and has been hosted by Sunshine Sonny Payne since 1951. It broadcasts out of the ⑱ **Delta Cultural Center**. Down the street you'll find the delta's best record store, ⑲ **Bubba's Blues Corner**, a regular stop on Robert Plant's personal blues pilgrimage.

You can hit several historic blues sites by driving a loop south from Clarksdale to Tutwiler, Indianola and Leland, and returning to Clarksdale via Hwy 61. Sleepy ⑳ **Tutwiler** is where WC Handy heard that ragged guitar man in 1903. Handy, known as the "father of the blues," was inspired to write the original popular blues song, in 12 bars with a three chord progression and AAB verse pattern, in 1912. That divine encounter, which birthed blues and jazz, is memorialized along the ㉑ **Tutwiler Tracks**, where the train station used to be. The mural also reveals the directions to ㉒ **Sonny Boy Williamson's**

Grave. He's buried amid a broken-down jumble of gravestones. Williamson's headstone is set back in the trees. Rusted harmonicas, candles and half-empty whiskey bottles have been left here out of respect.

㉓ Indianola spawned BB King. The old train depot was being transformed into the BB King Blues Museum at the time of research, so check when you come through. The corner of Church and 2nd Sts is where BB used to strum his beloved guitar, Lucille, for passers-by. King returns once a year for Indianola's Blues Festival, and now owns ㉔ Club Ebony, the club that gave him his first steady work. A fixture on the "chitlin' circuit," BB, Howlin' Wolf, Muddy Waters, Count Basie and James Brown all played here. King plays a free annual show for locals right after his Homecoming Blues Festival in June.

FAVORITE BLUES FESTS

To make the most of your music-loving dollar, hit the Delta during one of its many blues festivals. Rooms can be scarce. Book in advance.

- Juke Joint Festival Clarksdale, mid-April
- Mississippi Delta Blues & Heritage Festival, Greenville, mid-May
- BB King Homecoming, Indianola, early June
- Highway 61 Blues Festival, Leland, early June
- Bentonia Blues Festival, Bentonia, mid-June
- Sunflower River Blues & Gospel Festival, Clarksdale, August

From Indianola, go west on Hwy 82 to ㉕ Leland, a much less prosperous town, but with a terrific blues festival. The ㉖ Hwy 61 Blues Museum is also worth a peek. It's dustier and has less funding than others in the region, but offers more details on local folks like Ruby Edwards and David "Honeyboy" Edwards.

Bentonia, once a thriving farming community, now has fewer than 100 people and the downtown is gutted, but it's still home to one of Mississippi's most historic juke joints. The Holmes family opened ㉗ The Blue Front during the Jim Crow period, when blacks weren't even allowed to sip Coca-Cola. They sold homemade corn liquor (to blacks and whites) during Prohibition and welcomed all the delta blues artists of the day: Sonny Boy, Percy Smith and Jack Owens among them. The joint still opens in the evenings, but live blues only blooms during Bentonia's annual festival when the town comes back to life, ever so briefly.
Adam Skolnick

TRIP INFORMATION

GETTING THERE
Follow Hwy 61 south from Memphis to
Clarksdale. Take Hwy 49 south to Greenwood
and Bentonia. Double back to Hwy 82W to
Indianola and Leland, and then head north
up Hwy 61.

DO
Blue Front
Bentonia's heyday has long since passed, but
this blues institution is still alive. ☎ 662-
755-2278; www.bentoniablues.com; downtown Bentonia; ☾ hours vary, call ahead

Bubba's Blues Corner
Many music legends have perused these
stacks for vinyl gems. Pick up your essential Sonny Boy here. ☎ 870-338-3501;
105 Cherry St, Helena, AR; admission free;
☾ 9am-5pm Tue-Sat; ♿

Cat Head
Owner/operator Roger Stolle, who doubles as
Ground Zero's booking agent, has the last word
on who's playing where and when. ☎ 662-
624-5992; www.cathead.biz; 252 Delta Ave,
Clarksdale; ☾ 10am-5pm Mon-Sat; ♿

Club Ebony
This historic club nurtured the careers of
countless legends, including Count Basie, Ray
Charles, Howlin' Wolf and current owner, BB
King. ☎ 662-887-3086; www.clubebony
.biz; 404 Hannah St, Indianola; no cover;
☾ noon-late daily, live music 6-10pm Sun

Delta Blues Museum
The best of the delta's many blues museums
will soon unveil the long awaited "Muddy
Wing." ☎ 662-627-6820; www.deltablues
museum.org; 1 Blues Alley, Clarksdale;
adult/child $7/5; ☾ 9am-5pm Mon-Sat; ♿

Delta Cultural Center
Helena's musical past is distilled to an annual
blues festival and this fine museum, which
doubles as the home for *King Biscuit Time*,
the longest-running blues show on earth.
☎ 870-338-4350; www.deltaculturalcenter
.com; 141 Cherry St, Helena, AR; admission
free; ☾ 9am-5pm Tue-Sat; ♿

Ground Zero
Morgan Freeman's take on an old juke joint
hosts live blues four nights weekly. Also rents
nice furnished rooms. Freeman stays here
from time to time. ☎ 662-621-9009; www
.groundzerobluesclub.com; 0 Blues Alley,
Clarksdale; ☾ 11am-2pm Mon-Tue, to 11pm
Wed & Thu, to 1am Fri & Sat

Hwy 61 Blues Museum
Set in the Old Temple Theater. This dusty
museum honors Leland's local legends.
☎ 662-686-7646; www.highway61blues
.com; 400 N Broad St, Leland; admission $7;
☾ 10am-4pm Mon-Sat; ♿

Po Monkeys
An authentic country juke joint. There's live
music here once a month. Off Pemble Rd,
Merigold; cover $5; ☾ 9pm-late Mon & Thu

Red's
Its dark, somewhat ramshackle environs may
intimidate, but you're welcome here. If the
grill is smokin', order a plate of whatever's
cookin'. ☎ 662-627-3166; 395 Sunflower
Ave, Clarksdale; cover $5; ☾ 9pm-late Fri
& Sat

Rock & Roll & Blues Heritage
Museum
This collection includes early blues vinyl,
pressed as Race Records, the Beach Boys'
stage-prop surf boards, and original art
by John Lennon. ☎ 901-605-8662; www
.rockmuseum.biz; 113 E 2nd St, Clarksdale;
donation $5; ☾ 11am-5pm Fri & Sat, by
appointment Thu & Sun; ♿

Sonny Boy Williamson's Grave
Amid a huddle of humble headstones off the
highway is Sonny Boy's honored grave. Off
Hwy 49, Tutwiler; ♿ ◉

The Crossroads
This strip-mall infested intersection was
the setting of the blues' greatest legend.
Hwy 61 & Hwy 49, Clarksdale; admission
free; ♿ ◉

Tutwiler Tracks
These overgrown tracks witnessed WC
Handy's cathartic encounter with a country
troubadour. Off Hwy 49, Tutwiler; ♿

EAT

Abe's
The slow-burning tamales and melt-off-the-bone ribs are dynamite. ☎ 662-624-9947; 616 State St, Clarksdale; mains $3-12; ✲ 10am-9pm Mon-Thu, to 10pm Fri & Sat, 11am-2pm Sun; ♿

Delta Donuts
Forget calories, just eat. ☎ 662-627-9094; 610 N State St, Clarksdale; doughnuts $2; ✲ 6am-11am; ♿

Madidi
Clarksdale's upscale eatery has a menu (and prices) straight out of New York. ☎ 662-624-9947; 616 State St, Clarksdale; mains $3-12; ✲ 10am-9pm Mon-Thu, to 10pm Fri & Sat, 11am-2pm Sun

Ramon's
Another local fave; this family-owned, candle-lit diner has tablecloths and sensational fried shrimp. ☎ 662-624-9230; 535 Oakhurst Ave, Clarksdale; mains $8-16; ✲ 11am-2pm Thu-Sat; ♿

Rust
The decor is eco-chic, and the menu is Southern fine dining. ☎ 662-624-4784; 218 Delta Ave, Clarksdale; mains $11-25; ✲ 10am-9pm Mon-Thu, to 10pm Fri & Sat, 11am-2pm Sun

Sarah's Kitchen
This soul food kitchen is a local favorite. ☎ 662-627-3239; 278 Sunflower Ave, Clarksdale; mains $7-12; ✲ 11am-2pm Thu-Sat

SLEEP

Riverside Hotel
An aging hotel with a bluesy backstory. ☎ 662-624-9163; 615 Sunflower Ave, Clarksdale; r from $75; ♿

Shack Up Inn
Snooze in an old sharecropper shack done up retro-chic. Fantastic! ☎ 662-624-8329; www.shackupinn.com; 1 Commissary Circle, off Hwy 49, Clarksdale; r from $75; ♿

USEFUL WEBSITES
www.cathead.biz
www.msbluestrail.org

LINK YOUR TRIP
www.lonelyplanet.com/trip-planner

Oxford, Mississippi

WHY GO Don't be surprised if after two days of hanging out on the quaint yet hip Square, and wandering through Oxford's lush residential streets, shaded with majestic oaks, sprinkled with antebellum homes and a whole lot of Faulkner, you utter: "I could live here."

TIME
3 days

BEST TIME TO GO
Sep – Nov

START
Oxford, MS

END
Oxford, MS

Oxford has history, including a once-torched town square and some Civil War burial ground. It has cultural gravitas, and we're not just talking Faulkner. There's chic shopping, cool bars and wonderful food. Which is why long after you leave town, Oxford somehow never quite leaves you.

Oxford's beating heart is ❶ **Courthouse Square**, simply known as the Square. Most of the original buildings surrounding the throwback, whitewashed courthouse went the way of the Union torch, when it was invaded and devastated in 1864. But the layout remains the same as it did in 1841 after the newly christened city of Oxford welcomed Mississippi's first university. Today, Oxford appears to be in the midst of its salad days. With dozens of bars, restaurants, boutiques and a world-class bookstore it's all sipping, snacking, shopping and smiling on the Square.

❷ **Square Books** is one of the country's great, and still-thriving, independent bookstores. Visiting authors read from their newly published works weekly. Autographed copies of hot novels abound, and upstairs, next to the cozy café, is a terrific Faulkner section. As there should be.

Speaking of Billy F, he lived here, often hiding out at ❸ **Rowan Oak** – his gorgeous 33-acre estate that was something of a muse for this quirky, hard drinking genius. Ninety percent of his furnishings have

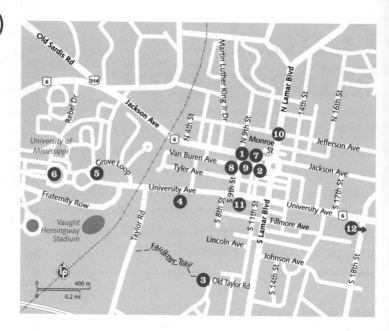

been preserved. Look for his typewriter in the study, an outline for a future fable scrawled on the walls, and his final (and half-slurped) bottle of Jack in the kitchen, before wandering beneath the massive cypress and oak trees in the garden.

HISTORIC WALKS

One of the best ways to absorb Oxford's genteel charms is by walking its lush, residential streets. The Oxford Convention & Visitors Bureau publishes a terrific brochure outlining four walking tours that take in Oxford's antebellum landmarks. The 1.4-mile North of Square route leads you past the regal yet seemingly abandoned **Ammadelle**, an Italianate villa designed by architect Calvert Vaux in 1859. It was nearly burned in the 1864 Union raid, around the same time Vaux was maneuvering to co-design Central Park in New York City.

A trail leads from Rowan Oak through the woods to the ❹ University of Mississippi Museum, where you'll find a collection of early astronomical marvels, Choctaw lacrosse sticks, Confederate soldier gear and original Man Ray and Georgia O'Keefe canvasses.

While on campus, be sure to swing by ❺ The Grove, one of those shady green spaces that's an oasis of cool on even the most sweltering days. During football season the tailgating here is sensational. It's football madness meets debutante ball. Blues and Southern culture buffs will want to stop by the ❻ Blues Archive & Center for Southern Culture at the campus library. The blues archive has over 50,000 sound and video recordings, including some pre-blues field songs recorded on wax cylinders. Faulkner is the star of the Center of Southern Culture, where his 1950 Nobel Prize is on permanent display. It's a charming campus, but don't forget that John F Kennedy had to order the National Guard to protect James Meredith when he became the school's first African American student in 1962.

When you're ready to eat, it's time to head back to the Square. **7** Ajax Diner's menu is like some funky New Orleans echo. There are sensational andouille sausage po'boys, savory crawfish étouffée, and the bar is ringed with colorful lights and dangles with African gourd lanterns. **8** City Grocery, a restaurant and bar on the south end of the Square, is the class of Oxford. The Creole-spiced lamb meatloaf and the Southern classic shrimp and grits are both exceptional. And the upstairs bar is where Oxford's literary lions, like Larry Brown and Tom Franklin, sip happy-hour cocktails. In a town where last call comes before midnight (during the week), happy hour is a big deal. Several Oxford bars (from sports bars to artsy pubs) buzz on either side of sunset, crawl the square (and its outlaying arteries) and you'll find a scene that suits you.

"And the upstairs bar is where Oxford's literary lions sip happy-hour cocktails."

Oxford, however, is definitely not a breakfast town. Most restaurants don't open until lunch, but the **9** Bottletree Bakery bucks the trend. Its founding baker trained at Los Angeles' famed La Brea bakery, before trucking her considerable gifts to this funky old diner with a rusted lunch counter and found art on the walls. There are ginger scones, fruit and cream filled brioche, bagels made the old-school way – hand-rolled and boiled in molasses – and air-roasted coffee from Portland.

Nest near the Square, too, where all the nocturnal action sizzles. The closest option, **10** Downtown Oxford Inn & Suites, is not going to win any design awards, but like an indie version of the Courtyard Marriott, rooms are clean, the suites have plenty of space and swift wireless internet for a reasonable price. **11** Puddin' Place, a cozy B&B set in a turn-of-the-century home filled with antiques, is far more charming. Think four-post beds and claw-foot bathtubs. Reserve ahead and ask for a cottage if you don't want to share a bathroom.

Before you leave Oxford, there is one can't-miss meal nestled in the countryside 15 minutes from downtown Taylor. **12** Taylor Grocery, established in 1889, is a local favorite – which is why you'll be waiting up to an hour for a table – serving up perfectly tender and fresh grilled and fried catfish platters. Bring your own booze. Disguise it in a paper bag, and everything will be kosher. If you're lucky you'll dine to live bluegrass, and depart with some down-home Mississippi memories.

Adam Skolnick

TRIP INFORMATION

GETTING THERE
Fly into Memphis and take I-40E to I-240S.
Continue on I-55S to Hwy 278E. Exit Lamar
Blvd and turn left toward the Square.

DO

Blues Archive & Center for Southern Culture
It's two archives-in-one on the top floor of
the University of Mississippi's JD Williams
library. ☎ 662-915-5855; 1 Library Loop;
admission free; ⏲ 8am-9pm Mon-Thu, to
4pm Fri, to 5pm Sat, 1-5pm Sun; ♿

Rowan Oak
The graceful 1840s home of William Faulkner.
He lived here from 1930 until he died in
1962. ☎ 662-234-3284; Old Taylor Rd;
adult/child & student $5/free; ⏲ 10am-4pm
Tue-Sat, 1-4pm Sun; ♿

Square Books
An indie bookstore that has the power
to inspire someone to become an author.
☎ 662-236-2262; www.squarebooks.com;
111 Courthouse Sq; ⏲ 9am-9pm Mon-Thu,
to 10pm Fri & Sat; ♿

The Grove
A verdant campus hangout that spills from
the steps of the student union. University
Ave; admission free; ♿

University of Mississippi Museum
History, science and art are on display at
this small but interesting campus collection.
☎ 662-915-7073; University Ave at 5th St;
admission free; ⏲ 9:30am-4:30pm Tue-Sat,
1:30-4:30pm Sun; ♿

EAT

Ajax Diner
This Southern nouveau diner is consistently
good and packed with locals. ☎ 662-232-
8880; 118 Courthouse Sq; mains $7-12;
⏲ 11am-9pm; ♿

Bottletree Bakery
Bakery cases overflow with gourmet pastries
and fresh-baked bread. ☎ 662-236-5000;
www.thebottletreebakery.com; 923 Van
Buren Ave; pastries $2-5; ⏲ 7am-4pm Tue-
Fri, 9am-4pm Sat, 9am-2pm Sun; ♿

City Grocery
Chef John Currence cooks up eclectic Southern cuisine on the south side of the Square.
☎ 662-232-8080; www.citygroceryonline
.com; 152 Courthouse Sq; mains $10-25;
⏲ 10am-2pm & 6-10pm Mon-Sat

Taylor Grocery
Order the catfish, blackened and grilled.
☎ 662-236-1716; www.taylorgrocery.com;
Old Taylor Rd, Taylor; mains $7-14; ⏲ 5-
10pm Thu-Sat, 5-9pm Sun; ♿

SLEEP

Downtown Oxford Inn & Suites
Simple, practical and spacious, this business-
style motor hotel won't change your life, but
the location rocks. ☎ 662-234-3031; www
.downtownoxfordinnandsuites.com; 400 N
Lamar Blvd; r from $99; ♿

Puddin' Place
A historical B&B within walking distance of
the Square. Reserve ahead! ☎ 662-234-
1250; 1008 University Ave; r from $145; ♿

USEFUL WEBSITES
www.oxfordcvb.com

LINK YOUR TRIP
TRIP

7 Southern Gothic Literary Tour p83
40 The Blues Highway p269
56 Memphis Music Tour p351

www.lonelyplanet.com/trip-planner

OUTDOORS

Gulf Coast Volunteering

WHY GO Because when Katrina and Rita descended with category-5 fury, their winds and subsequent floods impacted 80% of New Orleans, flattened parts of Biloxi, and tore through Mother Nature's original storm buffer, the gorgeous Gulf Coast marshes. You can help heal those wounds by volunteering on the Gulf Coast.

TIME
5 days

DISTANCE
298 miles

BEST TIME TO GO
Feb – May

START
New Orleans, LA

END
Grand Isle, LA

Ever since the storms hit, nonprofit organizations and compassionate volunteers have been helping to pick up the pieces. Join them by planting trees and community gardens, rebuilding entire neighborhoods and restoring Louisiana's estuaries – the state's most critical habitat.

No single organization has done more for hurricane victims than Habitat for Humanity (HFH). Their presence in ❶ New Orleans alone continues to be heroic, and one of the secrets of their success is that they have worked here for 25 years. Their inroads with community and political leaders enabled them to carve out a large stake in the rebuilding effort. The ❷ Musicians' Village, set on 8 acres in the Upper Ninth Ward, is their most famous project. This development, conceived by Harry Connick Jr and Branford Marsalis, will eventually consist of 72 single-family homes, to be sold to local New Orleans musicians at low cost and enabling them to make music full-time with less financial burden. Included in the attractive new neighborhood, which gleams compared to the older blocks on the Village's outskirts, is the Ellis Marsalis Center for Music, an education and social development center for residents.

If you wish to help build houses in the Musicians Village or on one of ❸ New Orleans Area HFH's other 160 housing projects, contact its volunteer office. All they ask is for volunteers to work at least one full day (7:30am to 3pm). No experience is necessary, but if you have carpentry or other construction skills let the volunteer coordinator know.

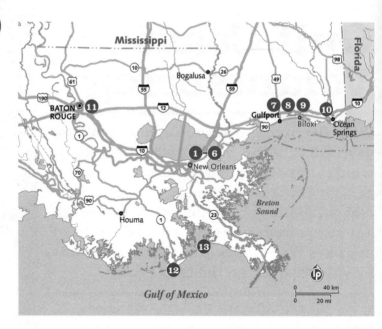

4 **Parkway Partners** sponsors tree plantings and builds community gardens in New Orleans. According to Parkway, 75% of the city's tree canopy and all of its urban gardens were damaged or destroyed by Hurricane Katrina. To date, Parkway have planted 3000 trees and rebuilt 25 of 54 former vegetable gardens, which provide food to needy neighborhood families. Volunteers are welcome between September and June: call ahead and let them know you're coming.

During your lunch break, make sure to grab a roast duck po'boy at 5 **Crabby Jacks**, the best po'boy haunt in the city. It's tender, rich and smothered in gravy, so a half-sandwich will do. Habitat does offer cheap, basic housing for volunteers, but you might also choose to bed down in the French Quarter at the traditional 6 **Andrew Jackson Hotel**. Ask for one of the front 2nd-floor rooms with access to the veranda.

Katrina carnage extended far beyond New Orleans, so consider lending a hand at one of the 17 Habitat for Humanity affiliates rebuilding homes throughout the Gulf Coast. 7 **HFH Mississippi Gulf Coast**, based in 8 **Biloxi**, is active in building small, single-family homes, which are sold to displaced residents for no profit. During our research, HFH had already begun or completed 200 homes and their goal is to build 800 homes along the Gulf Coast by 2012.

Volunteers are welcome to stay at 9 **Habitat Village** in East Biloxi. There are four bunkhouses and a lounge with computers, wireless internet, a dining area, TV and pool table. The Salvation Army provides three meals a day for volunteers. But after a hard day's work, you just might need the kind of satisfaction only a Mississippi BBQ can provide. Check out the ❿ **Shed**, a downhome barbecue joint and live blues venue in Ocean Springs, just 16 miles from Biloxi.

Hurricanes and storm surges are practically an annual occurrence down here. Once upon a time the coast was ringed with thick swaths of brackish marshland, which absorbed the saltwater and prevented flooding further inland. Even the mighty Mississippi was once buffered with swamps and marsh. But a combination of overdevelopment, tragically poor engineering and natural subsidence had weakened and endangered Louisiana's marsh long before Katrina arrived. When that storm blew through, there wasn't enough intact acreage left to withstand the surge and the remaining wetlands were severely damaged. With all the talk of rising seas and eroding coastline in Louisiana, your time may be best spent restoring this vital ecosystem.

"Consider lending a hand at one of the 17 Habitat for Humanity affiliates rebuilding homes."

⓫ **Americas Wetland Conservation Corps** organizes volunteer-driven marsh grass and tree plantings, beach sweeps, and provides habitat for the threatened wood duck by installing wood duck boxes in areas where trees have been damaged by Katrina and Rita. They work throughout coastal Louisiana, but if you call the Baton Rouge headquarters you'll hear about upcoming volunteer events.

The ⓬ **Barataria-Terrebonne National Estuary Program** also leads volunteer-driven beach clean-ups and marsh grass plantings. They work in the Fourchon and Grand Isle areas, which encompass some of the most beautiful wetlands in America. Much was destroyed during Katrina when the sea surged through abandoned oil exploration canals and poisoned the usually brackish estuary with too much saltwater. In addition to wetlands restoration and oil exploration, this slice of the Gulf Coast is home to Louisiana's best beach and fishing resort, Grand Isle. You can rent a condo or stilted house on the beach or camp at beautiful ⓭ **Grand Isle State Park**, where the wetlands end, the golden beach begins and the warm Gulf of Mexico rolls in from the equator

GLOBAL GREEN IN NEW ORLEANS

Just blocks from a levee that held in the Lower Ninth Ward, Global Green's fully sustainable eco-home is part of a larger-scale development called the **Holy Cross Project**. The first home, a model open for tours, was completed in 2008. Four additional homes are under construction, along with an 18-unit apartment and community center. Take the Global Green tour and see high design and sustainability in perfect balance. For more information about its efforts to green New Orleans, visit www.globalgreen.org.

Adam Skolnick

TRIP INFORMATION

GETTING THERE
Fly into New Orleans and take I-10E to Hwy 605S to Biloxi. Or take I-10W to the 90W to 308S to Hwy 1 for Grand Isle.

DO

America's Wetland Conservation Corps
A volunteer and community-driven wetland restoration group that works in 22 locations. Call for a listing of volunteer events when you're in town. ☎ 225-578-4514; www.lsuagcenter/awcc; project sites vary; free; ⏱ 9am-5pm; ♿ ⬜

Barataria-Terrebonne National Estuary Program
Join twice-monthly beach clean-up, mangrove seed collection and marsh grass planting events near Grand Isle. ☎ 985-447-0836; www.btnep.org; Nicholls State University, Thibodaux; ⏱ 9am-5pm, call ahead for volunteer opportunities; ♿ ⬜

Mississippi Gulf Coast HFH
Help rebuild 800 homes by 2012. ☎ 228-314-0011; www.habitat.org; 1636 Popps Ferry Rd, Biloxi; ⏱ 7:30am-3pm; ♿

Musicians' Village
Jazz royalty and Habitat for Humanity have turned this devastated 'hood into a haven. ☎ 504-861-4121; www.habitat.org; 4000 Roman St, New Orleans; ♿

New Orleans Area Habitat for Humanity
Habitat has 160 residential projects in five parishes. ☎ 504-861-4121; www.habitat.org; ⏱ 7:30am-3pm Tue-Sat; ♿

Parkway Partners
Plant trees or build and tend community gardens in underserved urban neighborhoods. ☎ 504-620-2224; http://parkwaypartners nola.org; 1137 Baronne St, New Orleans; per 2hr $15; ⏱ call for volunteer appointment, no projects Jul & Aug; ♿ ⬜

EAT

Crabby Jacks
Has tasty salads and fish tacos, but you're here for the po'boys. ☎ 504-833-2722; 428 Jefferson Hwy, New Orleans; mains $6-12; ⏱ 10am-5pm Mon-Fri, 11am-4pm Sat, closed Sun; ♿

Shed
A mythic BBQ and blues joint. ☎ 228-875-9590; www.theshedbbq.com; 7501 Hwy 57, Ocean Springs; mains $13-22; ⏱ 11am-9pm, to 10pm Fri & Sat

SLEEP

Andrew Jackson Hotel
A boutique hotel in the French Quarter. ☎ 504-561-5881; www.frenchquarterinns.com; 919 Royal St, New Orleans; r from $100

Grand Isle State Park
Camp on Louisiana's most beautiful beach. ☎ 985-787-2559; www.crt.state.la.us; Admiral Craik Dr, Grand Isle; campsite per night $18, day use $1; ♿ ⬜

Habitat Village
It's basic but it has a lounge with TV, pool table and wireless internet. ☎ 228-314-0011; www.habitat.org; 1636 Popps Ferry Rd, Biloxi; registration fee $100, then lodging free for volunteers; ♿

USEFUL WEBSITES
www.volunteerlouisiana.gov

LINK YOUR TRIP
www.lonelyplanet.com/trip-planner

48 Hours in New Orleans

WHY GO Few destinations have as many sensational ways to kill time as the Crescent City. Its history runs deep, the colonial architecture is exquisite, there's mouthwatering Cajun and Creole food, historic dive bars, a gorgeous countryside, and lashings of great free live music.

The Vieux Carre, or **①** **French Quarter**, is a good place to start your trip. At first it was just a tiny settlement on the river, surrounded by swamps and plantations. After the Louisiana Purchase prompted an influx of Anglo Americans, the French Quarter remained the heart of the Creole city, while white Americans settled Uptown. By the early 20th century the Quarter was a run-down working-class neighborhood and home to 12,000 people. But a 1930s preservation movement polished the old town houses and saved it from demolition. About 5000 people live here today.

Navigation remains a snap even though the grid was laid out in 1722. The narrow streets are lined with 19th-century Creole town houses and Victorian-era shotgun houses. You'll see wooden shutters, ornate cast-iron balconies and courtyards as you explore an endless lineup of appealing restaurants, bars, shops and galleries.

Begin your Nawlins adventure with a tipple at **②** **Lafitte's Blacksmith Shop**, set in one of the few 18th-century cottages to survive the French Quarter fires during the Spanish era. This candlelit hole-in-the-wall is purported to have been smuggler Jean Laffite's workshop and French Quarter hideout. In the 20th century it became the favored watering hole of Tennessee Williams. Dine at **③** **Felix's Restaurant & Oyster Bar**. It's been serving fresh-shucked oysters and boiled crawfish (in season) for 55 years. Or head to **④** **Coops**, a Decatur St bar serving fantastic Cajun and Creole dishes. The fried chicken is particularly good.

TIME
2 days

BEST TIME TO GO
Feb – May

START
New Orleans, LA

END
New Orleans, LA

ALSO GOOD FOR

BEST TRIP

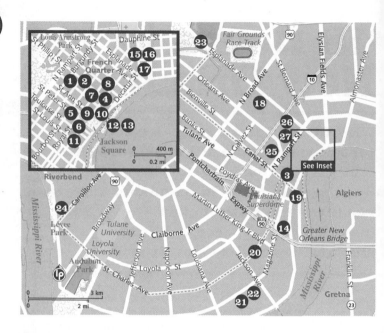

Take 30 minutes and experience the cheesy go-go bars and mid-grade meat market scene that have colonized Bourbon St, one of the oldest streets in town. Then quickly seek some cleansing night music. ❺ **Preservation Hall** is the place to hear authentic New Orleans jazz played by local masters. The hall is cramped and sweaty, plus there's no bathroom, booze or snacks, so you'll likely just take in one of the three 50-minute nightly sets. But when the seven-piece band blows, the roof rocks and the crowd goes wild. ❻ **One Eyed Jacks** offers a hip, local scene attracting bands that vary from punk to gypsy jazz. The front bar room is swanky, but the main theater is absolutely stunning with early-20th-century chandeliers, an oval bar and tables topped with miniature lamps. It's the perfect setting for the venue's burlesque shows.

Bed down at the traditional ❼ **Andrew Jackson Hotel**, set on the same property of the former courthouse where the beloved general and future president, who saved the city from British invaders during the War of 1812, was famously held in contempt of court in 1815. You'll love the 18th-century courtyard, furnishings and gas lamp courtyard. Ask for one of the front 2nd-floor rooms with access to the verandah. It's next to the Cornstalk Hotel, so you'll hear horses trot by on occasion, which just adds to the charm.

In the morning swing by ❽ **Croissant D'Or** for a breakfast of exquisite fresh-baked pastries. This is another locals' joint hidden in plain sight and the perfect place to recalibrate after a long New Orleans evening. Then stroll over to **9** **Jackson Square**, where you'll see a garden surrounding a monument to Andrew Jackson, the hero of the Battle of New Orleans, and the seventh president of the USA. But the real stars are the magnificent St Louis Cathedral and **10** **Presbytere**, designed in 1791 as the cathedral's rectory. It now holds a permanent exhibit of vibrant masks and costumes, parade floats and historic photos called "Mardi Gras: It's Carnival Time in New Orleans."

Royal St is a fun scene on Saturdays, when motorized traffic is blocked and pedestrians rule. In addition to the weekly influx of street musicians, magicians and puppeteers there are elegant antique shops, art galleries and vintage dress and hat boutiques. Chartres St is another great shopping lane for ladies looking for dresses and another pair of heels. **11** **Napoleon House** makes for a cozy lunch spot. Rumor has it that after Napoleon was banished to St Helena a band of New Orleans loyalists plotted to snatch him and set him up on the 3rd floor here (didn't happen). An attractive bar set in a courtyard building erected in 1797, it has a back patio, crumbling stucco walls and extraordinary service.

After lunch walk to the **12** **French Market**. New Orleanians have been trading goods for over 200 years from this spot on the Mississippi's riverbanks. In addition to **13** **Café Du Monde** (famous for serving beignets 24 hours a day for decades), where you can snack on fried and sugared beignets, there's a flea market, permanent gift stalls geared to tourists and a produce market. Dine on spectacular Cajun fare at **14** **Cochon** in the Warehouse District, owned and operated by the reigning James Beard Southern Chef of the year (at the time of research), Donald Link. He serves a spectacular oyster roast and tasty *cochon* (Cajun spiced rice and sausage balls).

When darkness deepens, head to Frenchman St in the Faubourg Marigny District. This is where the

ART ANYONE?

New Orleans' Warehouse District, once a 19th-century industrial district where grain, coffee and produce were stored, fell into disrepair in the mid-20th century. But in 1976 the **Contemporary Arts Center** opened and launched a neighborhood revival. Artists rented lofts on the cheap, dozens of galleries sprang up, and the Warehouse District became known as the Arts District. Care to explore? Join the well-lubricated herd on Julia St for a district art walk on the first Saturday of every month.

locals party, and if you are staying in the Quarter, you can easily walk here. **15** **Snug Harbor Bistro** offers nightly live jazz. Sometimes it's an authentic brass band augmented with West African drummers, but you'll also find funky acid jazz and straight-ahead bop. The bar has an incredible selection of bourbon, tequila and rum. The **16** **Spotted Cat** is famous for "gypsy jazz": electric guitar, clarinet and a rhythm section. If you're lucky you'll see some hot local dancers swing. If you crave a late-night meal, order the pulled pork po'boy at **17** **13 Monaghan**. It's not just an extraordinary sandwich, but an effective hangover vaccine.

If you feel like a new place to rest your head, consider the **18 Degas House** on Esplanade Ridge. When Edgar Degas lived here he also produced the city's most famous painting, *The Cotton Exchange In New Orleans*. The **19 W New Orleans** in the Central Business District (CBD) is another fine choice. It's modern and stylish, walking distance to countless restaurants and art galleries in the CBD, and just a streetcar ride away from the Garden District.

The **20 St Charles streetcar** will take you up and down this famous avenue, through the CBD, to the Garden District and Uptown mansions. Peer through the gates on Prytania and Coliseum Sts (you'll like Anne Rice's house on First St) before walking up and down Magazine St. There are tremendous snacking and shopping opportunities here. **21 Agora Galleries** has a sexy collection of retro-1940s inspired dresses and jewelry. **22 Parasol's**, a neighborhood bar in the Garden District, has terrific roast beef po'boys.

If you make it all the way to Uptown, you can peruse the **23 New Orleans Museum of Art & Besthoff Sculpture Gardens**, which has a permanent collection of over 40,000 pieces (paintings, sculpture, photography) from France, Africa, Japan and, of course, New Orleans, as well as edgy rotating exhibits and films, or just stroll beneath the old, mossy oaks in City Park.

THE TRAGIC TOUR

It's impossible to come to New Orleans without remembering Katrina and those caught in the floods. If you want a deeper view, take Grayline's Hurricane Katrina tour. You'll explore the vital Port of New Orleans, see the "breached" levee, and roll through the devastated Lower Ninth Ward. But you can also tour these neighborhoods by car on your own, or get a feel for ongoing reconstruction by visiting Habitat for Humanity's Musicians Village and Global Green's Eco Home.

Before heading back to the CBD, stop into **24 Jacque Imos Café**, one of the best-loved Creole and Cajun kitchens in the city.

You can also hop the Cemeteries streetcar from the CBD and take it to the above-ground tombs at the end of Canal St. The oldest, most famous and easiest to find is **25 St Louis Cemetery #1**. But if it's Sunday consider brunch at **26 Lil Dizzy's**, a laidback neighborhood soul food joint where you'll find delicious waffles, buttery biscuits, savory shrimp omelettes and spicy hot sausage, in the working-class, predominantly African American Tremé District, which was hit hard by the Katrina floods. Nearby the **27 Backstreet Cultural Museum** documents African American cultural traditions such as Mardi Gras Indians, Jazz Funerals and Social Aid & Pleasure Clubs; you can find out where that Sunday's Second Line Parade (Mardi Gras–style marching bands) might be. Or you may discover it in full bloom as you stroll through gritty Tremé.
Adam Skolnick

TRIP INFORMATION

GETTING THERE
From Mississippi take Hwy 61 to the I-10. From the east take I-20 to I-59 to New Orleans.

DO

Agora Galleries
An elegant, fun and rambling antiques showroom. ☎ 504-525-2240; 2240 Magazine St; ⏱ 11am-6pm

Backstreet Cultural Museum
This private, nonprofit museum in the Tremé District documents New Orleans African American cultural traditions. www.back streetmuseum.org; 1116 St Claude Ave; admission by donation; ♿

New Orleans Museum of Art & Besthoff Sculpture Gardens
The city's preeminent museum. The sculpture garden is free. ☎ 504-658-4100; www.noma .org; 1 Collins Dibol Circle; adult/senior/child $8/7/3; ⏱ 10am-5pm Thu-Sun, noon-8pm Wed, closed Mon & Tue; ♿

One Eyed Jacks
One of the Quarter's younger, hipper scenes presents everything from burlesque theater to punk rock bands. ☎ 504-569-8361; www .oneeyedjacks.net; 615 Toulouse St; cover $5-15; ⏱ 2pm-6am

Presbytere
The old St Louis rectory houses a terrific Mardi Gras museum. ☎ 504-568-6968; 751 Chartres St; adult/senior & student/child under 12yr $6/5/free; ⏱ 9am-5pm Tue-Sun; ♿

Preservation Hall
Traditional, and consistently great, live New Orleans jazz in a cramped, sweaty music hall in the Quarter. ☎ 504-522-2841; www .preservationhall.com; 726 St Peter St; admission $10; ⏱ 8am-11pm; ♿

Snug Harbor Bistro
At the time of writing, this was the best jazz club on Frenchman. And that's saying something. ☎ 504-949-0696; www.snugjazz .com; 626 Frenchman St; cover $5-25; ⏱ 5pm-3am

Spotted Cat
The early-days jazz always delivers, and it's free. ☎ 504-943-3887; 623 Frenchman St; ⏱ 4pm-late

St Louis Cemetery #1
New Orleans' oldest cemetery is where all the city's original luminaries, like Marie Laveau, are buried. *Easy Rider*'s acid trip was shot here. Basin St; admission free; ⏱ 8am-3pm; ♿

Trashy Diva
The rebellious name doesn't do these retro-designer dresses justice. ☎ 504-299-3939; www.trashydiva.com; 2048 Magazine St; ⏱ noon-6pm Mon-Sat, 1-5pm Sun

EAT & DRINK

Café Du Monde
The floors are coated with powdered sugar from the famous beignets at this 24-hour French Quarter café. ☎ 504-525-4544; www .cafedumonde.com; 800 Decatur St, New Orleans, LA; beignets $1.75; ⏱ 24hr

Cochon
This James Beard–approved hot spot serves up succulent Cajun cuisine. The *cochon* (fried rice balls mixed with sausage) and the wood-fired oysters rock! ☎ 504-588-2123; www .cochonrestaurant.com; 930 Tchoupitoulas St; dishes $7-22; ⏱ 11am-10pm Mon-Fri, 5:30-10pm Sat; ♿

Coops
Insanely good regional pub grub. The fried chicken and redfish dinners with red beans and rice are fantastic. ☎ 504-525-9053; www.coopsplace.net; 1109 Decatur St; mains $10-15; ⏱ 11am-late

Croissant D'Or
A quiet French-run patisserie with wonderful stuffed croissants (sweet and savory) and exquisite quiche. ☎ 504-524-4663; 617 Ur-sulines Ave; pastries $2-5; ⏱ 7am-5pm; ♿

Felix's Restaurant & Oyster Bar
Has the best freshly shucked oysters in the Quarter. ☎ 504-522-4440; www.felixs.com; 739 Iberville St; mains $12-20; ⏱ 10am-10pm Mon-Thu, to midnight Fri & Sat, to 9pm Sun; ♿

Jacque Imos Café
Superb Creole and Cajun cooking in Uptown. The steaks are exceptional, and enjoy the deep-fried po'boy if you dare. ☎ 504-861-0886; www.jacqueimoscafe.com; 8324 Oak St; mains $15-29; ⏱ 5:30-10pm Mon-Thu, to 10:30pm Fri & Sat, closed Sun

Lafitte's Blacksmith Shop
Bourbon St's most historic and soulful watering hole. ☎ 504-523-0066; 941 Bourbon St; ⏱ noon-late

Lil Dizzy's
This classic New Orleans soul food haunt is famous for its lunch buffets and Sunday brunch. ☎ 504-569-8997; 1500 Esplanade Ave; mains $12; ⏱ 7am-2pm; ♿

Napoleon House
Wonderfully timeworn French Quarter institution just off Jackson Sq. ☎ 504-524-9752; 500 Chartres St; mains $9-15; ⏱ 11am-5pm Mon, to midnight Tue-Thu, to 1am Fri & Sat, to 7pm Sun

Parasol's
This neighborhood bar and eatery in the Garden District has a dozen po'boys on the menu. Order the roast beef. ☎ 504-897-5413; www.parasols.com; 2533 Constance St; po'boys $6-9; ⏱ 11am-late; ♿

SLEEP

Andrew Jackson Hotel
A comfortable hotel in the Quarter. Rooms on the 2nd floor with balcony access are best. ☎ 504-561-5881; www.frenchquarterinns.com; 919 Royal St; r from $100; ♿

Degas House
The famous French artist lived here in the 1870s. Rooms are older but large and comfortable, and suites have fireplaces and balconies. ☎ 504-821-5009; www.degashouse.com; 2306 Esplanade Ave; r from $125; ♿

W New Orleans
Rooms on the upper reaches and the rooftop pool have insane Mississippi River views. ☎ 504-525-9444; www.whotels.com; 333 Poydras St; d from $210

USEFUL WEBSITES
www.experienceneworleans.com

LINK YOUR TRIP
www.lonelyplanet.com/trip-planner

New Orleans Perfect Po'boy Quest

FOOD & DRINK

WHY GO You are about to embark on a mission that is absurdly high both in flavor and cholesterol. It will involve hot sausage, fresh oysters, pulled pork and slow roasted duck. Whole sandwiches will be deep-fried in your honor as you scour New Orleans in search of po'boy perfection.

TIME
2 days

BEST TIME TO GO
Feb – May

START
New Orleans, LA

END
New Orleans, LA

ALSO GOOD FOR

For the next few days, the only vegetables that matter will be iceberg lettuce, beefsteak tomato and mayonnaise (it is too a vegetable!). And you will not chastise yourself nor will you feel an ounce of guilt for indulging in a diet that is oddly both life affirming and, well, the opposite of good for you.

And so, what if it is? With all the carb-hating, calorie-counting, raw food-dieting agendas swirling on the information superhighway, someone has to take a stand in defense of the po'boy. The most versatile sandwich in the gastronomical universe has sustained the working people of New Orleans for centuries. Back in the day, baguettes were hollowed and filled with cheap ingredients like potatoes and brown gravy, and served, almost exclusively, to "poor boys." Today, po'boys are the indigenous fast food of Louisiana, served in bars, delis, sit-down restaurants and roadside mini-marts, and will fill your days and nights with tender, spicy, crunchy goodness.

The best part of this po'boy hunt is that it will take you through nearly every neighborhood in the city. Too often, visitors remain in the pedestrian-friendly confines of the French Quarter. But to truly know New Orleans you must venture out to the leafy, mansion-strewn Garden District, the artsy Warehouse District, City Park and Mid-City, and to Uptown and the Riverbend. Your taste buds will lead you there.

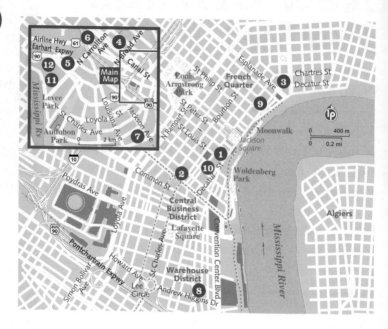

It all starts with the bread. New Orleans' hot, swampy climate co-mingles with yeast to deliver a unique French baguette that cannot be duplicated outside of the city. It's crunchy and hard on the outside, while moist and light on the inside. Have your baguette stuffed with smoked andouille sausage, fried shrimp and catfish, roast beef and gravy, soft-shell crab and crawfish. When you order a po'boy, your server will ask if you want it "dressed," meaning with mayo, shredded iceberg lettuce and tomato. A simple yes will do.

① **Johnny's Po-boys**, with its checkered tablecloths and headshots on the wall, is a French Quarter institution. The shrimp and catfish come pre-fried, but the deli case is filled with fresh meat, including smoked andouille and a superb hot patty sausage. It absolutely snaps with garlicky spice; each bite morphs into the next, and it is impossible to put down. It won't take long to taste why Johnny's has been here since 1950. **②** **Acme Oyster House** is another French Quarter favorite. Yes, it's a small, local chain, but it does have wonderful fresh oysters year-round, which means the fried oyster po'boy shouldn't be passed by. Once shucked, the oysters are battered and deep-fried until they're golden, which (attention oyster haters) takes the controversial texture issue out of the equation. The best offering here is the delicious Peacemaker – seasoned and fried oysters and shrimp dressed with Tabasco-infused mayo.

> *"New Orleans' hot, swampy climate co-mingles with the yeast to deliver a unique French baguette."*

Your work in the French Quarter is now done, so seek out some of the best po'boys in town on Frenchman St, a short walk into the Faubourg Marigny District. Frenchman is currently New Orleans' choice nightlife district with incredible free live music, and ample beer and liquor selections at 10 bars and venues within two blocks. ❸ **13 Monaghan**, a casual bar and restaurant, is hidden in the thrum, and is best known among locals as a place to enjoy decent late-night eats served by a rather grumpy bartender, not as a po'boy goldmine. But forget what they tell you – 13 Monaghan's pulled pork po'boy is stunning. Imagine a toasted baguette stuffed to the limit with tender and juicy pulled pork, dressed with spring greens, topped with pickled red cabbage and served with tater tots. Napoleon Dynamite would be stoked! Granted, its garnish won't please some po'boy purists, but it is so tasty even the most ardent traditionalists will become converts.

Near oak-studded City Park, in Mid-City, you'll find the ❹ **Parkway Bakery & Tavern**, a sports bar with a po'boy Jones. This is a good place to order the fried catfish po'boy. Get it dressed sans mayo and instead ask for a side of tartar, dash it with Tabasco and cocktail sauce, and smother the fish. Now that's a fish sandwich worth writing about.

Speaking of bars that are famous for po'boys, there are two more to consider. ❺ **Ye Olde College Inn**, also in Mid-City, is the brainchild of Johnny Blanchard. He's something of New Orleans royalty, considering his dad launched and still runs the ❻ **Rock n' Bowl**, probably the best live music/bowling scene in the world. He presents incredible jazz, R&B and zydeco bands that play to a consistently full house of dancing fools. After learning the ropes, Blanchard, an LSU baseball player turned chef, opened his own place, a sports bar that recalls Sam Malone's *Cheers,* with its large and loyal customer base. This might have something to do with the fact that after Katrina flooded their neighborhood, and gutted both the Rock n' Bowl and Ye Olde College Inn, the Blanchards didn't evacuate. Instead, they went to work and rebuilt both places within two months. At times theirs were the only electric lights for over 20 city blocks. Or maybe it's because this is just a comfortable, polished neighborhood bar and grill with damn good food.

Blanchard won the top prize at the 2008 Po'Boy Preservation Festival for his shrimp rémoulade po'boy. If you've had your fill of fried fish or roast meat, this is a nice departure. Rémoulade is a local cold shrimp salad dressed with a spicy take on Thousand Island dressing. Blanchard places it on a warm baguette, and it delivers big time. If you're tiring of the dive bar scene, you'll appreciate this tavern.

Not that there's anything wrong with dive bars. Some of us love them, and there's a good one in the lower Garden District. ❼ **Parasol's** is part neighborhood bar, part fast-food joint. If you're traveling with your young brood, you'll have to sit in the garishly lit restaurant side. If it's an adult trip, belly up in the narrow sports bar and eat there. Either way your roast beef po'boy, and that's the one you'll order, will be made by two capable chefs in the open kitchen. It's not pretty, but they do phenomenal work. The proof is in the shredded roast beef slathered in thick, savory gravy scooped inside a light and crunchy roll. At first glance, the bread doesn't look like it will hold, but this sandwich has integrity. And it's one of the best in all of New Orleans. Walk it off with a Garden District walking tour. You'll hear the clatter of horse-drawn carts and see swank old-world mansions shaded by centuries-old oak trees.

Tired of po'boys yet? Then eat some sensational Cajun cooking at ⑧ **Cochon**, in the artsy Warehouse District. The chef, Donald Link, is the owner of Herbsaint, and at research time was the reigning James Beard Foundation's Best Chef of the South. Which is why his modern dining room is always packed.

HOW KATRINA SAVED THE PO'BOY

In the months before Katrina hit New Orleans, the po'boy had its lowest ever approval rating. Sandwich shops complained of an eroding customer base while Subway franchises experienced a surge in popularity because po'boys were more expensive (to make and buy) than Subway sandwiches. Then Katrina happened and the only restaurants open during the early days of reconstruction were Subways. When the po'boy shops finally reopened months later, customers flocked in droves. It seems folks were starving for the stability of tradition.

Everything here, from the oysters to the gator (yes, they serve it up) to the *cochon* (a Cajun rice and sausage ball) is terrific. We especially loved the wood-fired oyster roast. If you time it right, you can eat here just before or after the New Orleans "art walks" held in the Warehouse District on the first Saturday of every month.

For an alternative break from po'boys, try ⑨ **Coops**, a neighborhood bar in the Quarter that is on the shortlist for best pub grub in the universe. All dark wood and brick walls, Coops serves a tremendous blackened redfish, insanely tender and moist Cajun-spiced fried chicken, and the red beans and rice come with a little ham hock thrown in. If you must shirk tradition, try the smoked duck quesadillas (the bomb!). If you are craving an upscale experience, the W's new restaurant at their quarter hotel, ⑩ **Bacco**, is the latest addition to the Ralph Brennan empire. Think of it as New Orleans fusion. You'll love the crawfish tail ravioli drizzled in sweet and smoky Creole sauce. And the 10-cent martinis (only available at lunch) are always nice.

Cajun food is also on the menu at ⑪ **Jacque Imos Café**, in Uptown, which has been around a lot longer than Cochon, and still has a line out the door almost every night. Chef Leonardi, who trained under Paul Prudhome, broils tender steaks and chops and barbecues shrimp and blackened redfish to perfection. He also gets creative with traditional ingredients: he stuffs acorn squash with curried mussels, tops fired oysters with a tangy plum sauce, and his po'boy is ridiculous. Best shared, this is an appetizer on steroids, a concoction of roast beef and gravy, pepper jack cheese, pickles and green pepper layered on French bread then deep-fried. The peppers give it an Italian flare, and the bread is so flush with oil it's frighteningly addictive.

But Leonardi's best po'boy work can be found at his sandwich shop, ⑫ Crabby Jacks, in an industrial corner of New Orleans. This is hands down the best po'boy haunt we experienced. There are a dozen varieties on offer here, but we suggest the slow-cooked duck. It's the only duck po'boy in the city, and like the roast beef it comes smothered in gravy. It is tender and rich and somehow not overwhelming. Crabby Jacks also has terrific salads, so if you get half a sandwich and a salad, you may be able to convince yourself, or your doubting partner, that you're eating healthy. Sure, it's a stretch but if it gets you another bite at Crabby Jacks, it's worth a shot. Get yours to go, find a quiet bench, and munch and contemplate on the banks of the Mississippi River.

Adam Skolnick

TRIP INFORMATION

GETTING THERE
From Mississippi take Hwy 61 to the I-10. From the east take I-20 to I-59 to New Orleans.

DO
Rock n'Bowl
Some of the best live music in town can be found at this Mid-City bowling alley. ☎ 504-482-3133; www.rockandbowl.com; 4133 S Carrollton Ave; cover $10; 🕑 5pm-late Tue-Sat; ♿

EAT
13 Monaghan
Surly barkeeps serve pulled-pork enlightenment in the heart of Frenchman's live music district. ☎ 504-942-1345; www.13monaghan.com; 517 Frenchman St; po'boys $8; 🕑 10am-3am

Acme Oyster House
Known for fresh, roasted and fried oysters. The po'boy works too. ☎ 504-522-5973; www.acmeoyster.com; 724 Iberville St; mains $7-10; 🕑 11am-10pm, to 11pm Fri & Sat; ♿

Bacco
Ralph Brennan serves fancy Nawlins fusion at the French Quarter W hotel. ☎ 504-522-2426; www.bacco.com; 310 Chartres St; mains $13-34; 🕑 lunch 11:30am-2:30pm daily, dinner 6-9:30pm Sun-Thu, to 10pm Fri & Sat

Cochon
This James Beard–approved hot spot serves up sensational Cajun cuisine. ☎ 504-588-2123; www.cochonrestaurant.com; 930 Tchoupitoulas St; dishes $7-22; 🕑 11am-10pm Mon-Fri & 5:30-10pm Sat; ♿

Coops
Insanely good regional pub grub. ☎ 504-525-9053; www.coopsplace.net; 1109 Decatur St; mains $10-15; 🕑 11am-late, kitchen closes at midnight

Crabby Jacks
Has salads and fish tacos, but you're here for the roast duck po'boy. Divine! ☎ 504-833-2722; 428 Jefferson Hwy; mains $6-12; 🕑 10am-5pm Mon-Fri, 11am-4pm Sat, closed Sun; ♿

Jacque Imos Café
Superb Creole and Cajun cooking, and home of the deep-fried po'boy. ☎ 504-861-0886; www.jacqueimoscafe.com; 8324 Oak St; mains $15-29; 🕑 5:30-10pm Mon-Thu, to 10:30pm Fri & Sat, closed Sun

Johnny's Po-boys
An old-school po'boy deli in the Quarter. ☎ 504-524-8129; www.johnnyspoboy.com; 511 St Louis St; mains $6-10; 🕑 9am-3pm Mon-Fri, 8am-4pm Sat & Sun; ♿

Parasol's
This neighborhood bar has a dozen po'boys on the menu. Order the roast beef. ☎ 504-897-5413; www.parasols.com; 2533 Constance St; po'boys $6-9; 🕑 11am-late, kitchen closes 10pm; ♿

Parkway Bakery & Tavern
A Mid-City sports bar with terrific seafood po'boys. ☎ 504-482-3047; 538 Hagan St; po'boys $3.50-7; 🕑 11am-11pm

Ye Olde College Inn
This beloved, well-scrubbed neighborhood tavern was the reigning local po'boy champ at the time of research thanks to its exquisite shrimp remoulade. ☎ 504-866-3683; www.collegeinn1933.com; 3000 S Carrollton Ave; mains $6.50-14.50; 🕑 4-11pm Tue-Sat

USEFUL WEBSITES
www.gumbopages.com/food/po-boys.html

LINK YOUR TRIP
www.lonelyplanet.com/trip-planner

Voodoo Tour of New Orleans

WHY GO Voodoo is that mysterious ingredient in the cultural gumbo of New Orleans. Part medicine, part religion, it once nourished the souls of slaves in Congo Sq and famously healed local children suffering from yellow fever in 1853. Yet, even though voodoo is intertwined with the city's soul, it's often misunderstood.

TIME
2 days

BEST TIME TO GO
Feb – May

START
New Orleans, LA

END
New Orleans, LA

ALSO GOOD FOR

Voodoo is a drumbeat, a flickering candle, a collection of hexes, potions and spells, and animal sacrifice. But mostly it is, as it always has been, a way for millions to commune with the divine, feel alive in the moment and spiritually nourished in this life. With some supernatural mixed it.

Voodoo came to the New World from the French colony of St Domingue (Haiti), where slaves from West Africa used Catholic saints and rituals to cloak their gods and religious traditions. This allowed the slaves to worship without Church interference, even as members of dozens of African tribal traditions contributed various spiritual practices – including ancestor worship and animal sacrifices to deities called *loas*. In the late 18th century, Haitian *vodoun* cults became revolutionary militias and *vodoun* priests recruited freedom fighters who donned charms for protection. In the aftermath of Haiti's successful revolt, many French landowners settled with their slaves in New Orleans.

There was already a similar spiritual stew bubbling in New Orleans when the refugees infused it with Haitian *vodoun* spice. Over the next century, New Orleans voodoo continued to evolve into the unique practice that is still alive today.

The wafting candles, African and Haitian masks, human bones, jars of snakes and Yoruba drumbeats streaming through the funky halls of the ❶ **National Historic Voodoo Museum** will get you in the mood.

HISTORY & CULTURE

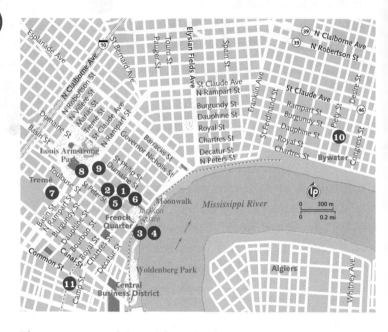

The Marie Laveau exhibit and shrine details the exploits of the original Queen of New Orleans Voodoo. Born free of mixed black and white ancestry in 1794, Laveau was a great beauty and her charisma allowed her to cross racial lines. She rubbed shoulders with the likes of Andrew Jackson, Marquis de Lafayette and Queen Victoria. By the 1830s she was the city's preeminent voodoo queen. She helped reel in wayward husbands, and presided over fire-lit night rituals in Congo Sq and at Lake Pontchartrain. Her crowning achievement came in 1853 during a brutal yellow fever epidemic. Medical doctors were powerless to stem the disease, which claimed 8000 lives (nearly 10% of the city's population at the time). Laveau stepped in and saved lives with voodoo medicine.

> "By the 1830s Marie Laveau was the city's preeminent voodoo queen."

Even 120 years after her death Laveau remains synonymous with New Orleans. That's not always a good thing. ❷ **Marie Laveau's House of Voodoo**, for instance, is pure capitalism. You could also call it voodoo kitsch where the dolls, masks and books hint at this thing called voodoo and readings are offered, but it doesn't feel like the real deal. ❸ **Marie Laveau's Voodoo Bar** likewise is trading on its famous namesake. Though the voodoo dolls, masks and alligator heads do make for some evocative cocktail scenery, and you can buy a voodoo doll to cast your own drunken spells on the one who's done you wrong, there's no actual historical connection to Laveau. However, it is attached to the ❹ **Historic French Market Inn**, built in the early 19th century. You'll love the Decatur St location and the inn's palpable history. But choose rooms wisely; some are quite small and others have beautiful exposed brick walls.

5 **Reverend Zombie's House of Voodoo** in the French Quarter is stuffed with dolls and old African masks, though it is a little geared toward tourists. If you're looking to self-ritualize the better bet is **6** **Voodoo Authentica**. It sells Voodoo Ritual Kits, which include a doll, candle, potion, gris-gris bag (small cloth bags stuffed with stones, salts, herbs etc), parchment paper and Louisiana black moss, all of which may help you cultivate money, health, peace or protection.

Now that you're armed with voodoo gear, you need to find the proper ritual setting. Some choose to light their candles at Marie Laveau's tomb in **7** **St Louis Cemetery #1**, just outside the quarter. But **8** **Congo Square** is more ideal. This shaded plaza in Louis Armstrong Park is where slaves, free blacks and some white folks converged on Sundays to drum, dance, chat and trade. Laveau conducted public ceremonies here in the mid-19th century.

MUSICAL VOODOO

The Voodoo Experience, a lesser-known New Orleans music fest, launched in 1998 when Wyclef Jean, Ben Folds and Dr John headlined a modest one-day jam. The next year Eminem headlined. Since then it has attracted the Red Hot Chili Peppers, Green Day, 50 Cent and the Beastie Boys along with legendary New Orleans bands. In 2005 it was held just two months after Katrina, and musicians performed for volunteers and first responders. It takes place on six stages in City Park.

If you are really intent on mingling with the divine, you should consider seeking professional help. Across the street from Congo Sq you'll find the **9** **Voodoo Spiritual Temple**, run by Priestess Miriam Williams. This dimly lit temple is packed with strange altars to various deities replete with offerings of money, cigarettes and liquor. Priestess Miriam has live snakes and a pantry stuffed with herbs and spices that she uses to prepare gris-gris bags, but once you chat with her, voodoo doesn't feel so exotic or threatening. To her, it's all about universal love.

Sallie Ann Glassman is another voodoo master for hire. She was ordained as a priestess in Port-au-Prince and has a great reputation among locals for delivering authentic rituals (care to see her bite off a chicken's head?). Glassman's shop, **10** **Island of Salvation Botanica**, is a voodoo apothecary with handmade candles, incense, oils, tinctures, soaps and salts. She also caters to tourists through the **11** **International House Hotel**'s Sanctuary of Love Package. Glassman will come to your hotel room and perform a "sensual ritual" that is intended to link you with your lover for eternity. Or at least set the tone for some red-hot voodoo romancing.

Adam Skolnick

HISTORY & CULTURE

TRIP INFORMATION

GETTING THERE
From Mississippi take Hwy 61 to the I-10. From the east take I-20 to I-59 to New Orleans.

DO

Congo Square
The plaza at Louis Armstrong Park has been a gathering place for centuries. Rampart St; ♿

Island of Salvation Botanica
Priestess Sallie Ann Glassman's apothecary. She's available for consultation by appointment. ☎ 504-948-9961; www.feyvoudo .com; 835 Piety St; ☾ 10:30am-5pm Wed-Sat; ♿

Marie Laveau's House of Voodoo
It's got the dolls and masks, but it feels a little too touristy. ☎ 504-581-3751; 739 Bourbon St; ☾ 10am-11:30pm Sun-Thu, to1:30am Fri & Sat; ♿

National Historic Voodoo Museum
Exhibits are enthralling and mysterious – look for the multi-headed totem in the back room. ☎ 504-523-7685; 724 Dumaine St; ☾ 11am-5pm; ♿

Reverend Zombie's House of Voodoo
Voodoo-themed gifts (including fantastic hand-carved masks) are here for the taking. ☎ 504-486-6366; 723 St Peter St; ☾ 10am-11:30pm Sun-Thu, to 1:30am Fri & Sat; ♿

St Louis Cemetery #1
The whitewashed tombs at New Orleans' oldest cemetery (established 1789) are crum-bling at the corner, which gives it a dated beauty. **Cnr Conti & Basin;** ☾ 8am-3pm; ♿

Voodoo Authentica
Don't mind the New Age trappings, this is arguably the most authentic of all the voodoo shops. ☎ 504-522-2111; 612 Dumaine St; ☾ 11am-7pm; ♿

Voodoo Spiritual Temple
Voodoo is a gentle practice of universal love in the hands of Priestess Miriam. ☎ 504-522-9627; 828 N Rampart St; ☾ 10:30am-5pm Mon-Fri; ♿

DRINK

Marie Laveau's Voodoo Bar
You've seen the preserved reptiles, now order an Embalming Fluid cocktail; there's no food to speak of, but it does have voodoo dolls for sale. ☎ 504-522-7225; 501 Decatur St; drinks $2-12; ☾ 11am-3am

SLEEP

Historic French Market Inn
Attached to Marie Laveau's voodoo bar, this early-19th-century inn is right in the thick of the Decatur St scrum. ☎ 504-561-5621; www.neworleansfinehotels.com; 501 Deca-tur St; r $120; ♿

International House Hotel
This luxe, hip hotel in the CBD offers Sallie Ann Glassman's Sanctuary of Love Voodoo package. ☎ 504-553-9550; www.ihhotel .com; 221 Camp St; r $210; ♿

USEFUL WEBSITES
www.neworleansvoodoocrossroads.com

LINK YOUR TRIP
www.lonelyplanet.com/trip-planner

Gator Watching in South Louisiana

WHY GO Because nothing quiets the mind like the profile of a half-submerged gator in a Louisiana swamp shaded by moss-draped cypress. And nothing is quite as alarming as the sight of said gator edging ever closer as you snap fear-tinged photos and prepare to run for your life.

TIME
1 – 3 days

DISTANCE
40 – 189 miles

BEST TIME TO GO
Apr – Jun & Sep – Nov

START
New Orleans, LA

END
Lafayette, LA

ALSO GOOD FOR

ROUTE

It almost certainly will not come to that. But the fact remains that you will be nearly nose-to-nose with huge American alligators without a fence or a weapon, and with nothing but thick bayou air between you. And that is exhilarating. You can spot gators from the deck of a flat-bottomed boat, from a kayak or canoe, from a table in a suburban restaurant, from a country road or a park trail. And spot them you will, because gators thoroughly patrol the bayous and backwaters of Louisiana. This is one ubiquitous reptile, so get your cameras ready.

You don't even have to leave New Orleans' city limits to get to gator country. ❶ **Bayou Sauvage National Wildlife Refuge** protects 23,000 acres of pristine marshland that buffers both Lake Pontchartrain and Bayou Sauvage. It's a beautiful slice of wetlands with huge numbers of resident and migratory birds (hawks circle during the day while owls patrol the night sky) as well as rabbit, raccoon, osprey, deer and wild hogs, and, of course, large American gators. Most folks go for the soft adventure of a two-hour tour aboard a covered flat-bottom boat, but canoe rentals and private wildlife tours are available.

Well within an hour's drive of New Orleans is the 20,000-acre ❷ **Barataria Preserve**, part of the Jean Lafitte National Historic Park. There are over 300 species of bird in these marshes, as well as a handful of large resident gators that cruise the bayous and swamps. Canoes and kayaks are available for rent nearby by at ❸ **Bayou Barn**, on the Bayou de Familles, and the preserve's friendly rangers guide guests

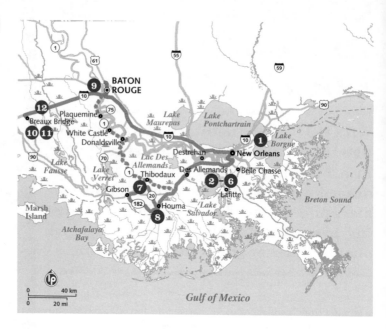

on moonlit paddles, which are a great way to see the park. If you're short on time, you can also stroll the flat trails to get a feel for the marsh and see some lazy gators cooling off. The park is named for the hero of the Battle of New Orleans, Jean Lafitte, a pirate and smuggler who, along with his international band of ne'er-do-wells, helped Andrew Jackson defeat the British on the **4** **Chalmette Battlefield**. This park endured some Katrina damage, but it's making a comeback and all the trails should be open when you visit.

> *"You'll be able to watch some large gators sunning themselves while you munch soft-shell crab."*

Stop for lunch at **5** **Restaurant de Familles**, behind Bayou Barn near the Barataria Preserve. The dining room overlooks the bayou, which means you'll be able to watch some rather large gators sunning themselves on the banks while you munch soft-shell crab (the seasonal house specialty). If you'd rather spend the night in bayou country, consider the **6** **Jean Lafitte Inn**, with modern cabins on the preserve's doorstep. It rents canoes and offers drop-off and pick-up services if you plan on paddling into the park. Rustic Earl's Bar, next door, is a great place to grab a beer and troll for loony gator stories.

Southwest of New Orleans is a maze of swamps and bayous that arches toward Lafayette. This is where the Cajuns first settled, and although assimilation has dulled their cultural edge, there are still a handful of old-timers who speak nothing but French and fish these gator-infested waterways. If you're interested in Cajun culture, don't miss the **7** **Wetlands Cajun Cultural Center**. Cajun musicians jam here every Monday night between 5pm and 7pm. After your cultural fix head to **8** **Annie Miller's Son's Swamp & Marsh Tours** in Houma. Run by the son of Alligator Annie, a swamp tour legend, this family has been feeding chickens to alligators so long that the gators perk up and snap whenever they hear that familiar motor hum.

You can get even cozier with gators at the **9** **Alligator Bayou**, just 15 minutes from Baton Rouge in the Spanish Lake basin. Its 90-minute alligator swamp tour includes a cruise through moss-draped cypress trees that are hundreds of years old and you'll see plenty of gators in the water, sunning on logs, and even feel their breath in the alligator eco-habitat, where you'll walk on a boardwalk above the swamp and your guides will feed the gators right in front of you. Um, those are some big jaws!

> **DETOUR**
>
> If you plan on making the drive to Lake Martin, consider stopping over in historic **Donaldsonville**. Located just off the River Rd, this is the heart of Louisiana plantation country. **Grapevine Café** has some incredible regional cuisine and a dynamite brunch, and the **River Road African American Museum** is also worth a peek. Strangely, the plantation tours rarely mention the regional African American history. But you'll get the scoop on everything from slave revolts to the Underground Railroad in here.

You can also spot gators in and around **10** **Lake Martin**, a gorgeous fishing lake and bird rookery just outside of Lafayette. This is the heart of Cajun Country, with plenty of tasty food and music to nourish your soul. They don't specialize in gator tours out here, but if you look close, you'll find them. Stay at **11** **Maison Madeleine**, a lovingly restored 1840 Creole cottage converted into a B&B. Gators are often cooling in the swamps and can be seen from the dirt road. Or walk the 7-mile trail around the lake and you are guaranteed a sighting. Hundreds of gators nest here. Dine at **12** **Pat's Fisherman's Wharf**, serving boiled crawfish, fried gator tail (it really does taste like chicken), and terrific étouffée and gumbo.

Adam Skolnick

TRIP INFORMATION

GETTING THERE

For the Barataria Preserve take the Westbank Expressway to Barataria Blvd. For Houma take Hwy 90W to Hwy 311S. For Alligator Bayou take the I-10 to the Highland Rd exit, and for Lake Martin take the I-10 to Breaux Bridge and Lake Martin Rd.

DO

Alligator Bayou

Has an alligator habitat on land, where you'll get dangerously close to the beasts, and offers wonderful tours of the cypress-sprinkled Spanish Lake. ☎ 225-677-8297; www .alligatorbayou.com; 35019 Alligator Bayou Rd, Prairieville; tours adult/child $27/22; ⊙ 8am-6pm, reservations required; 🚻 🐾

Annie Miller's Son's Swamp & Marsh Tours

A classic two-hour Cajun gator tour. ☎ 985-868-2732; www.annie-miller.com; 3718 Southdown Mandalay Rd, Houma; ⊙ seasonal hrs, call ahead; 🚻

Bayou Sauvage National Wildlife Refuge

Gator-watching trips within spitting distance of New Orleans. ☎ 985-882-2000; www.fws .gov/bayousauvage; Lake Pontchartrain; trips free; 🚻 🐾

Barataria Preserve

Another great option for a gator-watching day trip. ☎ 504-589-2330; www.nps.gov /jela; Barataria Blvd, Chalmette; trips free; ⊙ 9am-5pm, closed Christmas & Mardi Gras; 🚻 🐾

Bayou Barn

Rent canoes from this shack on the Bayou de Familles. ☎ 504-689-2663; Bayou de Familles, Chalmette; per 2hr $15; ⊙ 9am-5pm Thu-Sun; 🚻 🐾

Chalmette Battlefield

Where Jean Lafitte was transformed from an outlaw smuggler into an American hero. ☎ 504-281-0511; www.nps.gov/jela; 8606 West St Bernard Hwy, Chalmette; admission free; ⊙ 9am-4:30pm Thu-Sun; 🚻 🐾

Wetlands Cajun Cultural Center

A national park-run center with ranger-guided boat tours of the Bayou Lafourche. ☎ 985-448-1375; www.nps.gov/jela; 314 St Mary St, Thibodaux; tours free; ⊙ 9am-8pm Mon, to 6pm Tue-Thu, to 5pm Fri & Sat, closed Sun Jun-Aug, plus Christmas & Mardi Gras; 🚻 🐾

EAT

Pat's Fisherman's Wharf

Authentic Cajun seafood joint perched on the levee above the river. Fantastic! ☎ 337-228-7512; www.patsfishermanswharf.com; Hwy 352, Henderson; mains $13-22; ⊙ 11am-10pm; 🚻

Restaurant de Familles

Nestled behind Bayou Barn, with gator views. ☎ 504-689-7834; Bayou de Familles, Chalmette; mains $8-17; ⊙ noon-8pm Wed-Sun; 🚻

SLEEP

Jean Lafitte Inn

Cabins and canoes are yours just outside the entrance to Barataria Preserve. ☎ 504-689-3271; cnr Hwys 45 & 3134, Chalmette; cabins $75-90; 🚻 🐾

Maison Madeleine

Overnight in this gorgeous, historic B&B just up the dirt road from Lake Martin. ☎ 337-332-4555; www.maisonmadeleine.com; 1015 John D Hebert Dr, Breaux Bridge; r $120

USEFUL WEBSITES

www.thewildones.org

LINK YOUR TRIP

www.lonelyplanet.com/trip-planner

Cajun Country Road Trip

HISTORY &
CULTURE

WHY GO Hidden in the maze of bayous, lakes, swamps and prairies that unfurl south and west of New Orleans is a wild and jubilant French-speaking culture punctuated by crawfish boils, all-night jam sessions and dance parties. You'll enjoy a small taste by looping through Cajun Country to Lafayette and back.

TIME
4 days

DISTANCE
370 miles

BEST TIME TO GO
**Mar – Jun &
Sep – Nov**

Most folks view Louisiana through a prism called New Orleans, but to experience Cajun Country is to know another side of one of America's most fun, and funky, states. In the South eras, cultures and fortunes collide, overlap and intermingle. Which is why in addition to legendary music halls and Cajun kitchens you'll also experience Louisiana's Creole culture and plantation history as you make this glorious trek.

Depart New Orleans on Hwy 90 through Westwego, then detour on Hwy 1 north to Thibodaux, where you'll find the **❶ Wetlands Cajun Cultural Center**. Take a boat tour through the bayous and swamps with rangers who will detail Cajun history and discuss their traditional lifestyle. You'll learn that Cajuns came from rural France and settled in the Acadie region of Nova Scotia. When Great Britain took over, the Acadians refused to swear allegiance to the crown. Tempers flared until the British forcibly removed Acadians from their land in the mid-18th century. Many came to these wetlands in South Louisiana. Most hunted, fished and trapped, while others moved to the prairies to grow rice and beef. Over time their dialect crystallized, and so did their music and food, but they remained true to their own French heritage. If you're lucky you'll land here during a boat-building demonstration, or better yet, on a Monday evening when Cajun musicians jam (5pm to 7pm).

Next double back to Hwy 90W and go south on Hwy 182, the Old Spanish Missionary Trail, to **❷ Houma**, the economic hub of the

START
New Orleans, LA

END
New Orleans, LA

ALSO GOOD FOR

FOOD &
DRINK

BEST TRIP

303

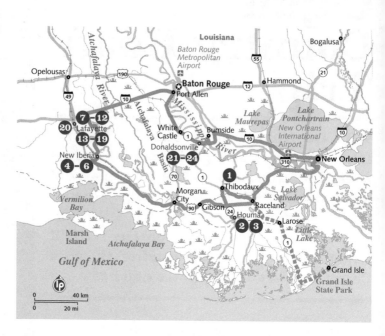

Cajun Wetlands. Like many towns and counties in the USA, it was named for the Native Americans whom the white settlers replaced. Carved by bayous, channels and waterways, you can understand their self-anointed title "Venice of America." But this isn't a tourist town, so you'll likely just pass through on your way to ③ **Annie Miller's Son's Swamp & Marsh Tours**. Take an entertaining two-hour tour aboard a flat-bottom boat to see swamp life, plus some massive gators.

> *"Carved by bayous, channels and waterways, you can understand their self-anointed title 'Venice of America.'"*

Follow Hwy 182 to Gibson, where you'll link back onto Hwy 90W, Cajun Country's commercial lifeline. You'll roll past too many swamps, bayous, rivers and lakes to count, and eventually you'll reach ④ **New Iberia**, a plantation town founded in 1779 on sugar and slaves, on Bayou Teche. Echoes of its plantation past are still on display. ⑤ **Shadows on the Teche** is a palatial Greek-revival mansion with gorgeous grounds. Massive oaks drip with Spanish moss and a dark green lawn rolls to the brown banks of the bayou. Order a traditional Creole plate lunch at ⑥ **Brenda's Diner**. The menu rotates, but there's always a selection of meats (such as smothered liver, fried pork chops, turkey wings and meatloaf) and sides (do not sleep on the creamy, tangy mustard greens).

Next turn onto Hwy 31, a two-lane country road that leads to ⑦ **Breaux Bridge**, a charming small country town outside of Lafayette. If you are in the area on a Saturday do not miss the zydeco brunch at ❽ **Café Des Amis**. From 8:30am some of the best zydeco bands in Louisiana jam as guests dance like mad. Stay the night nearby at ❾ **Maison Madeleine**, an 1830s Creole cottage set on a dirt road just off Lake Martin. The lake is known as the biggest white ibis rookery on earth. When dinner calls, head to ❿ **Pat's Fisherman's Wharf**, just 15 minutes away by car. It's a legendary Cajun seafood house built on a levee above the river and serving up boiled crawfish, fried gator tail and terrific crawfish and lump crab étouffée.

On Sunday afternoon, ⓫ **Angelle's Whiskey River** rocks to zydeco and Cajun tunes. It's a small house, and it gets packed. Locals dance on tables, on the bar and in the water. If you want to really experience a night or two on the water, rent a houseboat at ⓬ **Cypress Cove**. You don't even have to drive it. They'll pilot the boat out into the middle of Lake Henderson and lend you a little johnboat to get back to land for more beer.

⓭ **Lafayette** is the grooviest town in Cajun Country. It's home of the University of Louisiana, full of beautiful people, tasty Cajun cuisine and an abundance of live music. If you're looking for a young scene, check into the ⓮ **Blue Moon Guesthouse**. Part outdoor saloon, part hostel, you will not be bored, but don't expect early shuteye. Crave more sophisticated sleep? Check into ⓯ **La Maison de Belle B&B**, a converted 1898 house with a lavish downstairs suite (including its own parlor and sitting room), and a rustic cabin out back where John Kennedy Toole penned Confederacy of Dunces, adjacent to the park.

On Wednesday mornings stop by ⓰ **Dwyer's** for a breakfast biscuit and listen in as old Cajun codgers hold court in their local French patois. The best plate lunches in town can be found at ⓱ **Antlers**, an old pool hall turned

TERRANCE SIMIEN'S LAFAYETTE

Louisiana-based musician Terrance Simien is considered a master of the zydeco genre and proud ambassador of Creole culture. Here are some of his favorite Lafayette haunts.

- Blue Moon Saloon (www.bluemoon presents.com) "It's a real down-home place where local people go to hear local music," says Terrance of the roots, honky-tonk, Creole and Cajun music bar nestled on the back porch of the Blue Moon Guesthouse. "It's about good times, good people coming together, dancing and having a good time."

- McGee's Café & Bar (www.mcgees landing.com) "It's right on the banks of the Atchafalaya Basin, so you have a beautiful view while you eat your meal," Terrance says of the family-owned marina restaurant renowned for some of the city's most authentic Cajun cooking. "They have real great crawfish, everything you order is done great."

- Old Tyme Grocery (www.oldetymegrocery .com) Terrance loves bringing out-of-towners to this old-fashioned white-and-red shack, which serves up some of Louisiana's finest po'boys. "They're some of the best I've ever had," he raves. "My favorite is the half-shrimp, half-oyster; they do these jumbo shrimps and huge oysters, and the bread is baked fresh in a local bakery."

Interview by Simona Rabinovitch

Cajun rice and gravy lunch counter, dishing up stuffed and smothered pork chops, terrific stewed chicken and rice, and killer soft-shell crab po'boys. Dinner at ⑱ **Don's Café**, a legendary local seafood house, is always tasty. The crawfish bisque is superb and comes with the heads stuffed with breadcrumbs and ground crawfish.

DETOUR

Once you are in Lafayette, detour northwest to **Eunice** (46 miles) and you'll land in Cajun music central. Musician Mark Savoy builds accordions at his **Savoy Music Center**, where you can also pluck some CDs and catch a Saturday morning jam session. Saturday night means the Rendez-Vous Cajuns are playing the **Liberty Theater**, which is just two blocks from the **Cajun Music Hall of Fame & Museum**.

If you're looking for something regional yet upscale, sample the Cajun fusion at ⑲ **Charley G's**. All ingredients come from local fishermen and farmers, and their smoked duck and andouille gumbo, and bluepoint crab cakes come highly recommended. If you're hungry for Cajun snack food between meals, take the short drive west to Scott and pick up some *boudin* (pork, rice, gravy and green onions) sausage from the ⑳ **Best Stop**, a third-generation Cajun butcher. Eat it with cracklin' (fried pork fat sprinkled with salt and pepper). When the moon shines, patrol the many buzzing bars on Jefferson Ave in Lafayette or head over to Blue Moon Saloon (attached to the guesthouse) for some live and local Cajun music.

You'll take the I-10 back to New Orleans, but make sure to turn off on Hwy 70 to historic ㉑ **Donaldsonville**. Although 632 buildings were burned and bombed during the Civil War, there remain dozens of antebellum homes in the area. But one of the city's most interesting attractions is the ㉒ **River Road African American Museum**, a private museum that tells the story of local African Americans from slave ships to the vicious toils and abuse of slavery to slave revolts and the Underground Railroad, to freedom and Jim Crow. This is a place to learn about African American Louisiana's unsung heroes and pioneers.

DETOUR

While you are in Thibodaux consider heading further south on Hwy 1 before heading toward Houma. You'll roll along the bayou through traditional shrimp fishing towns before the wetlands unfurl and roll onto **Grand Isle State Park** and the Gulf of Mexico. There's oil production (and oil money) here, but it's still a beautiful stretch of coastline, and has long been Louisiana's favored beach destination. Jean Lafitte and his crew once set up camp on the golden sand.

Hit ㉓ **Grapevine Café** for lunch or dinner, or for a dynamite Sunday brunch. It's owned by one of the founders of Café Des Amis in Breaux Bridge. Bed down in one of the large suites at ㉔ **Cabahanosse B&B**, which open onto a 2nd-story verandah shaded by an oak canopy. From here, return to the I-10 and follow it back to Nawlins.
Adam Skolnick

TRIP INFORMATION

GETTING THERE
Take Hwy 90W from New Orleans to Hwy 1 and Thibodaux. Double-back to Hwy 90W, turn onto Hwy 182S to Houma. Back on the 90W stop in New Iberia, take Hwy 31 to Breaux Bridge and I-10 to Lafayette.

DO

Angelle's Whiskey River
Get wild on Sunday evenings at this long-beloved Cajun juke joint. Bar- and table-dancing is recommended. ☎ 337-228-8567; 1006 Earlene Dr, Breaux Bridge; cover varies; ☾ call for hrs

Annie Miller's Son's Swamp & Marsh Tours
A classic two-hour Cajun gator tour. ☎ 985-868-2732; www.annie-miller.com; 3718 Southdown Mandalay Rd, Houma; ☾ seasonal hrs, call ahead; ⓐ

Cypress Cove
Rent a houseboat and cruise beautiful Lake Henderson. ☎ 337-228-7484; www.houseboat-adventures.com; 1399 Henderson Levee, Henderson; houseboat per day from $135; ☾ 8am-5pm Mon-Sat; ⓐ ⓔ

River Road African American Museum
Details the harsh reality, and the heroes and triumphs of Louisiana's African American history. ☎ 225-474-5553; www.africanamericanmuseum.org; 406 Charles St, Donaldsonville; admission $4; ☾ 10am-5pm Wed-Sat, 1-5pm Sun; ⓐ

Shadows on the Teche
New Iberia's most famous and accessible antebellum plantation home. Stroll the grounds and watch gentle Bayou Teche roll by. ☎ 337-365-5213; www.shadowsontheteche.org; 317 E Main St, New Iberia; adult/senior/student $10/8/6.50; ☾ 9am-4:30pm Mon-Sat, noon-4:30pm Sun; ⓐ

Wetlands Cajun Cultural Center
Enjoy ranger-guided boat tours of Bayou Lafourche where you'll learn about the natural and cultural history of Cajun Country. Has live Cajun music every Monday night. ☎ 985-448-1375; www.nps.gov/jela; 314 St Mary St, Thibodaux; admission free; ☾ 9am-8pm Mon, to 6pm Tue-Thu, to 5pm Fri & Sat, closed Sun Jun-Aug, plus Christmas & Mardi Gras; ⓐ ⓔ

EAT

Antlers
Hands-down the best plate lunch in Lafayette. ☎ 337-234-8877; 555 Jefferson St, Lafayette; mains $7-15; ☾ 11am-2pm; ⓐ

Best Stop
It's worth a drive from Lafayette just for the smoked boudin, a Cajun pork, rice and gravy sausage. ☎ 337-233-5805; www.thebeststopsupermarket.com; Hwy 93, Scott; boudin $4; ☾ 6am-3pm Tue-Fri; ⓐ

Brenda's Diner
Brenda serves heaping portions of delicious soul food. ☎ 337-367-0868; 409 W Pershing St, New Iberia; mains $6-12, plate lunches $8; ☾ 6:30am-3pm Mon-Fri, closed Sat & Sun; ⓐ

Café Des Amis
The Creole and Cajun menu is good, but the real hit is the live zydeco breakfast every Saturday morning. ☎ 337-332-5273; www.cafedesamis.com; 140 E Bridge St, Breaux Bridge; mains $12-22; ☾ 11am-2pm Tue, to 9pm Wed & Thu, 7:30am-9:30pm Fri & Sat, 8am-2:30pm Sun; ⓐ

Charley G's
This popular dining room serves upscale Cajun fusion. ☎ 337-981-0108; www.charleygs.com; 3809 Ambassador Caffrey Parkway, Lafayette; mains $10-39; ☾ 11:30am-2pm & 5:30-9pm Mon-Thu, to 10pm Fri, 5:30-10pm Sat, closed Sun

Don's Café
A vintage seafood and steak house in downtown Lafayette. Don't miss the crawfish bisque. ☎ 337-235-3551; 301 E Vermilion St, Lafayette; mains $12-25; ☾ 11am-9pm Sun-Thu, to 10pm Fri & Sat; ⓐ

Dwyer's
This family-owned joint is especially fun on Wednesday mornings when local Cajuns shoot the breeze in their old-school French dialect. ☎ 337-235-9364; 323 Jefferson St, Lafayette; mains $5-12; ☾ 7am-3pm; ⓐ

HISTORY & CULTURE

Grapevine Café
The former owner of Café Des Amis serves up scrumptious Creole and Cajun dishes. The brunch is spectacular. ☎ 225-473-8463; www.grapevinecafeandgallery.com; 211 Railroad Ave, Donaldsonville; mains $7-27; 11am-2:30pm & 5-9pm Tue-Thu, to 9:30pm Fri & Sat, 11am-2:30pm Sun;

Pat's Fisherman's Wharf
A delicious and authentic Cajun seafood joint perched above the river. ☎ 337-228-7512; www.patsfishermanswharf.com; Hwy 352, Henderson; mains $13-22; 11am-10pm;

SLEEP

Blue Moon Guesthouse
There's a backyard nightclub and hostel environs (dorms and with some private rooms) in this tidy old Lafayette home. ☎ 337-234-2422; www.bluemoonguesthouse.com; 215 E Convent St; Breaux Bridge; dm $18, r $70-90

Cabahanosse B&B
The four suites are large and comfortable with a fantastic 2nd-floor verandah, claw-foot bathtubs and a grill out back. ☎ 225-474-5050; 602 Railroad Ave, Donaldsonville; r $159;

La Maison de Belle B&B
Overnight where John Kennedy Toole dreamed up *Confederacy of Dunces*. The grounds and adjacent park are lovely. ☎ 337-235-2520; 608 Girard Park Dr, Lafayette; r $110-150

Maison Madeleine
Overnight in this gorgeous, historic Creole cottage surrounded by luscious gardens, just up the dirt road from Lake Martin. ☎ 337-332-4555; www.maisonmadeleine.com; 1015 John D Hebert Rd, Breaux Bridge; r $120

USEFUL WEBSITES
www.epiculinary.com
www.theind.com

LINK YOUR TRIP   www.lonelyplanet.com/trip-planner
TRIP

Best State Park Picks

WHY GO To experience the pristine and rugged Arkansas wilderness, absorb the history and languid beauty of Mississippi and taste Louisiana's delicious, gator-infested Cajun Country in a single four-day road trip that winds from Devil's Den in Northwest Arkansas to Grand Isle and the Gulf of Mexico.

TIME
4 days

DISTANCE
977 miles

BEST TIME TO GO
Apr – Nov

START
Fayetteville, AR

END
Grand Isle, LA

Technically, it's not impossible to see every park listed here in a long weekend, but your journey will be far more enjoyable if you pick and choose. Fly into Fayetteville, and take Hwy 540S to ❶ **Devil's Den State Park**. You're here for two reasons: to hike or to go caving. The park's best trek is the 15-mile Butterfield Trail, but the wet slog up the fern-fringed Lee Creek is also a treat. Backpackers can camp in one of two backcountry camping sites and free backcountry permits (available at the visitors center) are compulsory for all hikers, whether or not you plan on sleeping in the bush. But the trails aren't Devil's Den's chief attraction. Most people come here to explore the park's deep, dark caves.

Bring a flashlight and enjoy Devil's Den Cave that penetrates 550ft deep into the sandstone cliff. You can also explore Farmer's Cave, a smaller, and gated, limestone cave. Check in at the visitors center to receive a free permit for Farmer's. It's rare to find limestone and sandstone caves in one location, so be sure to take a look and discover their differences. Camping options are available here, but if you only wish to see the caves and run, take Hwy 540S to I-40E and follow the signs to ❷ **Mt Magazine State Park**.

❸ **Mt Magazine**, at 2753ft, is Arkansas' highest peak. It's also a 6-mile-long by 1-mile-wide plateau that overlooks the misty Petit Jean and Arkansas River Valleys. There are plenty of short hikes perfect for

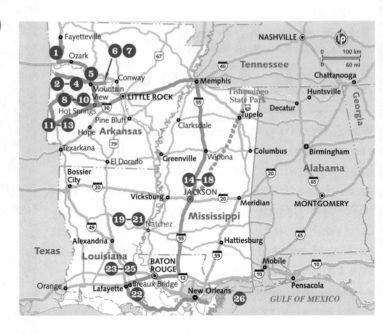

young children. Rock climbers love the park's sheer rock faces, while mountain bikers will be tempted to bomb the 34-mile multi-use trail that snakes down the mountain and into the Ozark National Forest. You'll also see hang gliders soar. Camping is available, but if you prefer a bed, check out ❹ **The Lodge**, which has a decent restaurant, a pool and rooms with views.

DETOUR Located about 120 miles away from Devil's Den State Park, **Mountain View**, a northwest Arkansas mountain town, is famous for its blacksmiths, fiddle makers, and its nightly folk/country/bluegrass jam sessions at the **Ozark Folk Center State Park**. Listen to men play dulcimers, jugs and banjos for adoring crowds, and you'll understand why Mountain View is considered by some (mainly its own residents) to be the "Folk Music Capital of the World."

If you really only have four days, you'll have to choose between Mt Magazine, ❺ **Mt Nebo State Park** and Petit Jean State Park. Though it's a relatively small hill, 1850ft-high Mt Nebo does have sweeping views of the Arkansas River Valley. There are plenty of campsites to choose from and rustic cabins for rent. Fourteen miles of trails wrap around the mountain and young grommet mountain bikers will love the 4.5-mile Bench Trail that circles the peak. If the winds are right you'll see hang gliders ride the thermals while you pedal and sweat. You can rent bikes at the visitors center.

Nice as it is, you'll be tempted to bypass Nebo for the spectacular ❻ **Petit Jean State Park**. It's named for a female French explorer (Little Jean) who posed as a man so she could accompany her lover to the New World, and eventually settled here – she could have done much worse. Hit the 20-plus miles of hiking trails and you'll see sandstone caves, limestone bluffs, old growth hardwood forest and gushing waterfalls. Stay in one of the 24 guest rooms or 20 rustic cabins available at **7** **Mather Lodge**. The cabins have kitchens for self-catering, fireplaces and hot tubs.

Head south along the insanely gorgeous Hwy 7, which traverses the rolling Ozarks all the way to **8** **Hot Springs**. If you're planning an autumn trip, the fall color will rival that of New England. If you're tired of state park food, and you probably will be, make your way to **9** **McClard's**, Bill Clinton's favorite rib shack. The ribs, glazed in McClard's signature sweet and spicy sauce, are otherworldly, but don't miss the tamales – buried in Fritos, and smothered in chopped beef, beans, cheese, onions and barbecue sauce. Pitch a tent at **10** **Gulpha Gorge Campground**, 2 miles north of town off Hwy 70B.

When you get to Jackson, consider following the Natchez Trace parkway north past Tupelo to **Tishomingo State Park** at mile-marker 304.5 (about 232 miles from Jackson). Named for an old Choctaw chief, this park is Mississippi's finest. You'll especially love the sandstone cliffs, fern gullies and waterfalls of Bear Creek canyon. There are plenty of campsites, hiking trails abound and canoes are available for rent.

Wake up early and drive 60 miles from Hot Springs to **11** **Crater of Diamonds State Park**, the world's only public diamond mine. Old mining equipment and mine shafts remain, but you're here for the white, brown and yellow diamonds that mingle with semiprecious stones including amethyst, agate and garnet. Finders keepers!

After rummaging for diamonds you can travel back to 1824. **12** **Historic Washington State Park** is Arkansas' answer to colonial Williamsburg. The leafy town was founded on George Washington's birthday and has never been paved. There are wooden sidewalks, dirt roads rutted by horse-drawn carriages, and 30 19th-century structures meticulously restored and with displays of early American knives and guns. Tour guides are costumed in period attire and a Southern country lunch is served in **13** **Williams Tavern**, circa 1832.

From Washington, take Hwy 82E to Hwy 49S to **14** **Jackson**, Mississippi's state capital. Stop for a lakeside stroll, or play nine holes at the leafy **15** **Lefluer's Bluff State Park**, in the center of town. Then dine on heavenly tamales at **16** **Walker's Drive-In**, and bed down at the cozy **17** **Old Capitol Inn**. You'll enjoy the rooftop hot tub and full country breakfast.

Pick up the scenic **18** **Natchez Trace Parkway** in Jackson and follow it all the way to **19** **Natchez**, Mississippi, an antebellum town on the Mississippi

River. If you have the extra cash, keep your tent in the truck and sample the old South at **20 Monmouth Plantation**, a 26-acre mansion property with 30 guest rooms sprinkled with antiques. Need a beer? Head to the historic **21 Under the Hill Saloon**, one of Mark Twain's old haunts.

Cross the Louisiana state line and Hwy 61 bleeds into the 110S, which merges with I-10 in Baton Rouge. Take the I-10W to West Atchafalaya Levee Rd and **22 Lake Fausse Point State Park** in St Martinsville. This is the heart of Cajun Country. Rent a canoe or kayak to skirt the banks crowded with old cypress trees dripping with Spanish moss, and you'll spot some gators. But keep your distance just to be safe. Mosquitoes can be rough here, so overnight at lovely **23 Maison Madeleine**, an 1830s Creole cottage set on a dirt road just off nearby Lake Martin. If you haven't seen gators yet, stroll the flat 7-mile trail around the lake, and you will.

When dinner calls, head to **24 Pat's Fisherman's Wharf**, a legendary Cajun seafood house just 15 minutes from Lake Martin. If you land in the area on Sunday afternoon, head to **25 Angelle's Whiskey River**, just down the levee road from Pat's. It's a small club that rocks to local zydeco and Cajun bands. It gets so packed you may have to make like the locals and dance on the bar.

> *"You'll camp in the park, where the sound of the rolling surf will lull you into a deep sleep."*

When you've had your fill of Cajun fun, head east on Hwy 90 past too many swamps, bayous, rivers and lakes to count. Eventually you'll intersect with Hwy 1. Head south along the bayou, through traditional shrimp fishing towns, before wetlands unfurl like an out-of-control shag carpet that rolls into the Gulf of Mexico. That's where you'll find the beach resort of Grand Isle and **26 Grand Isle State Park**. Yes, there's oil production here, but it's still a beautiful stretch of shore. Jean Lafitte and his crew once set up camp on the golden sand, which is now patrolled by vacationing families who descend to lounge and fish the estuaries and the deep sea. You'll camp in the park, just off the beach where the sound of the rolling surf will lull you into a deep sleep.

Adam Skolnick

TRIP INFORMATION

GETTING THERE

Fly into Fayetteville, take I-540S to I-40E to Hwy 7S to I-30S to Hwy 82E to Hwy 49S to the Natchez Trace Parkway to Hwy 61S to I-110S to I-10W to 90E to Hwy 1S to Grand Isle.

DO

Angelle's Whiskey River

Get wild on Sunday evenings at this Cajun juke joint. You may be encouraged to dance on the bar. Don't ask questions. Just do it. ☎ 337-228-8567; 1006 Earlene Dr, Breaux Bridge; cover varies; ☽ call for hrs

Crater of Diamonds State Park

Dig for "free" diamonds 60 miles from Hot Springs. Finders keepers. Seriously. No kidding. ☎ 870-285-3113; www.craterof diamondsstatepark.com; 209 State Park Rd, Murfreesboro; adult/child $6.50/3.50; ♿

Devil's Den State Park

Explore sandstone and limestone caves in one stop. Camping and cabins available. ☎ 479-761-3325; www.arkansasstateparks .com/devilsden; 11333 West Arkansas Hwy 74, West Fork; hiking permit free; ♿ 🐾

Grand Isle State Park

See where the vast south Louisiana wetlands meet the Gulf of Mexico. ☎ 985-787-2559; www.crt.state.la.us/parks; Admiral Craik Dr, Grand Isle; admission per person $1, campsites $18; ♿ 🐾

Historic Washington State Park

Journey to the 19th century in this preserved frontier town. ☎ 870-983-2684; www .historicwashingtonstatepark.com; Washington; adult/child $8/4; ☽ 8am-5pm, closed holidays; ♿ 🐾

Lake Fausse Pointe State Park

Paddle among the cypress trees and resident gators of Cajun Country. ☎ 337-229-4764; www.crt.state.la.us/parks; 5400 Petit Levee Rd, St Martinsville; canoe & kayak per hr $5; ♿ 🐾

Lefluer's Bluff State Park

Jackson's rambling city park has a Natural Science Museum, a nine-hole golf course and camping. ☎ 601-987-3923; www.mississippi stateparks.reserveamerica.com; 2140 Riverside Dr, Jackson; admission free; ♿ 🐾

Mt Magazine State Park

Explore Arkansas' highest mountain, which is really just one wide table top, on foot, bike or from the sky (bring your own hang glider). ☎ 479-963-8502; www.mountmagazine statepark.com; 16878 Hwy 309S, Paris; admission free; ♿ 🐾

Mt Nebo State Park

A gorgeous slice of wilderness overlooking the Arkansas River Valley. Camping available. ☎ 479-229-3655; www.arkansasstateparks .com/mountnebo; 16728 Hwy 155W, Dardanelle; hiking permit free; ♿ 🐾

Petit Jean State Park

It's just a stone's throw from Little Rock, and when the waterfalls gush, Arkansas does not get any better. ☎ 501-727-5541; www .petitjeanstatepark.com; 1285 Petit Jean Mountain Rd, Morrilton; hiking permit free; ♿ 🐾

EAT & DRINK

McClard's

Slow-cooked meat melts off ribs, and the outrageous tamale spreads (Fritos are involved) are tasty too. ☎ 501-623-9665; www.mcclards.com; 505 Albert Pike, Hot Springs; mains $5-11; ☽ 11am-8pm Tue-Sat; ♿

Pat's Fisherman's Wharf

An authentic Cajun seafood joint stilted over the water. Dine on gator and crawfish. ☎ 337-228-7512; www.patsfishermans wharf.com; Hwy 352, Henderson; mains $13-22; ☽ 11am-10pm; ♿

Under The Hill Saloon

An historic bar and favored haunt of Mark Twain. Live music most weekends. ☎ 601-446-8023; www.underthehillsaloon.com; 25 Silver St, Natchez; ☽ 9am-late

Walker's Drive-In

Traditional Mississippi cooking never tasted so good. If you come for lunch, it's all about the tamales. ☎ 601-982-2633; www .walkersdrivein.com; 3016 N State St, Jackson; mains $24-32; ☽ 11am-2pm Mon-Fri & 5:30-11pm Tue-Sat; ♿

Williams Tavern

Devour a traditional Southern country lunch in the early-19th century. Consider it a lucid past-life regression. ☎ 870-983-2898; Historic Washington State Park, Washington; mains $12-25; 🕑 11am-3pm; 🚹

SLEEP

Gulpha Gorge Campground

Pitch a tent in the shade next to a gurgling creek at the national park campsite. ☎ 501-624-3383; off Hwy 70B, Hot Springs; campsites $10; 🚹 🐾

Lodge

Nest on the highest mountain in Arkansas. Has the views to prove it. ☎ 877-665-6343; www.mountmagazinestatepark.com; 16878 Hwy 309S, Paris; r $84-204, cabins $169-439; 🚹 🐾

Maison Madeleine

Overnight in this gorgeous, historic Creole cottage surrounded by luscious gardens, just up the dirt road from Lake Martin. ☎ 337-332-4555; www.maisonmadeleine.com; 1015 John D Hebert Rd, Breaux Bridge; r $120

Mather Lodge

This massive log lodge was built in the 1930s. ☎ 877-665-6343; www.petitjeanstatepark.com/lodge; 1285 Petit Jean Mountain Rd, Morrilton; r $65-70, cabins $100-175; 🚹 🐾

Monmouth Plantation

Make like Scarlett O'Hara and collapse into old Southern luxury. ☎ 800-828-4531; www.monmouthplantation.com; 36 Melrose Ave, Natchez; r from $199

Old Capitol Inn

The best B&B you've never been to. The Southern breakfast is legendary. ☎ 601-359-9000; www.oldcapitolinn.com; 226 N State St, Jackson; r from $95

LINK YOUR TRIP

www.lonelyplanet.com/trip-planner

Paddling the Buffalo

WHY GO "It begins life bubbling from moss-covered springs deep in the Ozarks. Countless streams tumbling down thousands of boulders until they merge and meander and grow into one crystalline 135-mile river that carves some of the most beautiful country in mid-America," says Mike Mills, the longest-tenured outfitter on the Buffalo River, Arkansas.

In an era where grand rivers all over the world are overdeveloped, diverted and dammed, the Buffalo flows freely, flanked by federally protected wilderness, from the tiny mountain hamlet of Boxley until it spills into the White River. No wonder the Buffalo was the first National River in American history. "And you don't need a guide to experience it," Mills says. Aside from its rugged class IV headwaters, only passable for a handful of weeks every year, amateurs can self-navigate the class I-II rapids. You may not stay dry, but you'll avoid danger as you paddle into some serious bliss.

Start in ① **Ponca**, an early-20th-century mining camp turned ranch town. Remember to buy your beer in Little Rock, because Ponca is in a dry county. Ponca's nicest digs belong to Mills' ② **River Wind Lodge & Cabins**. The former state minister of tourism under Governor Bill Clinton built the log cabins, which sleep up to eight people, by hand. They have outrageous mountain and valley views. Budgeters should pitch a tent at ③ **Lost Valley Canoe**, River Wind's humbler, barefoot, hippie neighbor, and still well-located for a good Buffalo paddle.

There are no restaurants in Ponca, so self-cater or drive 15 miles to ④ **Jasper**, a rustic town with two good restaurants. ⑤ **Boardwalk Café** is the healthy choice. It sources local, organic meat and produce and prepares delicious New Orleans and Cajun food along with terrific

TIME
2 – 10 days

DISTANCE
285 miles

BEST TIME TO GO
Apr – Jun

START
Ponca, AR

END
White River, AR

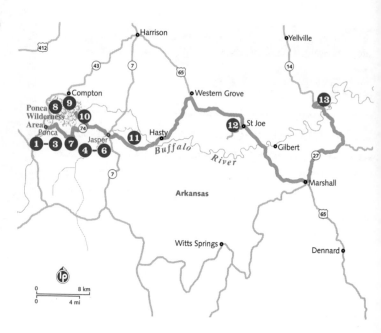

elk burgers, chili and steaks. A few doors down is the town's landmark diner, the **6** **Ozark Café**. It's a tasty greasy spoon established in 1909 with black-and-white homesteader photos on the old stonewall to prove it.

Now it's time to paddle. When *National Geographic*'s team of photographers documented this great river, they came to Mills for advice. "They came back with 60,000 slides and published just 13 photographs," he says. "Nine of them were taken between Ponca and Pruitt – the most spectacular two-day, 24-mile stretch of the Buffalo." Rent canoes or kayaks from Lost Valley Canoe or from Mills at **7** **Buffalo Outdoor Center** (BOC) in Ponca, which has been run by Mills since 1974, along with 18 cabins on 1000-plus acres. Both Lost Valley Canoe and BOC will shuttle your car to your landing spot.

The river snakes between multicolored granite bluffs. Usually they are as high as 200ft, but the cliffs at Big Bluff are a mind-boggling 525ft, the highest rock faces in mid-America. "Once you pass them, the river makes a 90-degree bend to the right, where you'll find a thumb. Pull into it," advises Mills, "and head up hill to link into the **8** **Goat Trail** (you'll find it on the left bank)." The trail leads to a sublime lookout 350ft above the river. A few miles downstream, three bluffs after the well-marked Jim's Bluff, the river makes a hard right. "Stay on the left bank," Mills says, "and stop on the gravel bar in the center of that curve. Follow the unmarked spur trail to **9** **Hemmed-in-Hollow**, the Ozarks' tallest waterfall, 200ft of water falling and splashing against a colorful limestone backdrop. Paddle on to Kyle's Landing, a campground 10 miles downstream from Ponca. If you are only looking for a day trip, this is where you'll pull out. If you are forging on, don't camp here. You can overnight among much more secluded environs along the river."

From the Kyle's Landing campground take the marked trail to the mouth of ⑩ **Indian Creek**. Bring a flashlight and sturdy shoes, because you are going to hike and boulder-hop up this strange and gorgeous creek that snakes through caves, beneath a natural rock bridge, and eventually into a box canyon. "You'll see dozens of waterfalls in the canyon, but that's a five-hour hike, one-way, so most turn around at the bridge, which is only three-hours round-trip."

"The cliffs at Big Bluff rise a mind-boggling 525ft, the highest rock faces in mid-America."

After two days and 24 soggy miles you'll be glad to see the old iron bridge at Pruitt. Most folks take out here. The Little Buffalo joins with the Big Buffalo about 4 miles below Pruitt. ⑪ **John Eddings Cave** is set between two bluffs on the right-hand side (the best landmark is a huge gravel bar on the left – when you spot it, pull over to the right). It's about 1 mile upstream from Carver campground.

Keep paddling and you'll move through rapid after rapid, and eventually come to the Lower Buffalo River, which begins at the Hwy 65 bridge in Gilbert. Water conditions provide year-round paddling for the remaining 58 miles. "The gravel bars are long and lush here," says Mills, "but the corridors between bluffs stretch from a few hundred yards in Ponca to a few miles in the lower stretch." It's still gorgeous, and a great paddling option in Ponca's off-season. ⑫ **Buffalo River Outfitters** rents canoes and cabins in St Joe in the middle river. ⑬ **Wild Bill's** in Buffalo Point is the best lower river outfitter. It is 10 miles upriver from the old ghost town of Rush, which makes for an eerie day trip. Unfortunately, in this life even beautiful things fade away, and 125 miles downstream from Ponca, the Buffalo disappears into the cold, crystalline White River.

Adam Skolnick

TRIP INFORMATION

GETTING THERE
From Little Rock Take I-40 West to exit 64 at Lamar. Go west on Hwy 64, 9 miles to Ark Hwy 21 North and go 50 miles to Boxley. Then turn right onto Hwy 43 North to Ponca.

DO

Buffalo Outdoor Center
The most senior outfitter on the Buffalo offers canoes and kayaks in terrific condition. ☎ 800-221-5514; www.buffaloriver.com; cnr Hwys 43 & 74, Ponca; kayak/canoe per day $45/50, car shuttle available; ⊗ 8am-5pm; ♿ 🐾

Buffalo River Outfitters
The best canoe operator on the middle river. ☎ 870-439-2244; www.buffaloriveroutfitters.com; Hwy 65, St Joe; kayak/canoe per day $35/45, passenger pick-up per person $6; ⊗ 8am-5pm; ♿ 🐾

Goat Trail
A strenuous but short hike offering one of the best views on the Buffalo. ☎ 870-741-5443; www.nps.gov/buff; Upper Buffalo River; ♿ 🐾

Hemmed-in-Hollow
The trail can be tough to find, but it leads to the highest waterfall in mid-America. So look for it. ☎ 870-741-5443; www.nps.gov/buff; Upper Buffalo River; ♿ 🐾

Indian Creek
Terrain seldom gets stranger or more beautiful. ☎ 870-741-5443; www.nps.gov/buff; Upper Buffalo River; ♿ 🐾

John Eddings Cave
The National Park Service closes the cave to visitors in the high season, but it's still worth walking to its mouth. ☎ 870-741-5443; www.nps.gov/buff; Middle Buffalo River; ♿ 🐾

Lost Valley Canoe
Ponca's barefoot, shirtless outfitter; budget travelers will save a few bucks here. It's a younger outfitter which offers good canoes and car shuttles. ☎ 870-861-5522; www.lostvalleycanoe.com; cnr Hwys 43 & 74, Ponca; canoe per day $40, car shuttle $25, pick-up per person $10; ⊗ 8am-5pm; ♿ 🐾

Wild Bill's
If you plan on paddling when autumn color pops in the off-season, you'll need to explore the Lower Buffalo. ☎ 870-449-6235; www.ozark-float.com; 23 Hwy 268E, Yellville; kayak & canoe per day $40, passenger pick-up per person $3; ⊗ 8am-5pm; ♿ 🐾

EAT

Boardwalk Café
Get a warm, organic meal here after a soggy day. ☎ 870-446-5900; www.theark house.com; Court St, Jasper; mains $7-23; ⊗ 11am-7pm Sun-Tue & Thu, to 9pm Fri & Sat, closed Wed; ♿

Ozark Café
The funky environs go well with the all-American diner fare. ☎ 870-446-2976; www.thefrontporchinn.net; 107 E Court St, Jasper; mains $3-17; ⊗ 6:30am-8pm; ♿

SLEEP

Lost Valley Canoe
Pitch a tent in the leafy campground, or rent one of the affordable, rustic cabins. ☎ 870-861-5522; www.lostvalleycanoe.com; cnr Hwys 43 & 74, Ponca; campsites $10, cabins $80; ♿ 🐾

River Wind Lodge & Cabins
Choose from among 18 immaculate, well-appointed log cabins. ☎ 800-221-5514; www.buffaloriver.com; cnr Hwys 43 & 74, Ponca; cabins $139-279; ♿ 🐾

LINK YOUR TRIP

www.lonelyplanet.com/trip-planner

Exploring the Ozarks

WHY GO Hiking trails wind through lush hardwood forests to granite overhangs, misty meadows and waterfalls. Backroads wander through funky mountain communities with unique folk music traditions and exquisite Victorian-era architecture. You are in the Ozarks, trekking and driving through a meandering mid-American wilderness.

Fly into Fayetteville, and drive to ❶ Ponca, Arkansas, where you can access a series of day hikes to some of the Ozarks' signature photo ops or hump the sensational ❷ Buffalo River Trail. This 36.5-mile trail skirts the bluffs that run parallel to the Upper Buffalo River. It makes for a perfect five-day backpacking trip, as the National Park Service (NPS) permits backcountry camping throughout the Buffalo Wilderness. There's loads of wildlife here, including elk, bear, lynx and Florida panther. May is the birding month in the Ozarks. Species include red-tailed hawks, Baltimore orioles and resident blue herons.

If you prefer campsites with amenities, there are NPS campsites every 6 or 7 miles when the trail spurs to trailheads off winding country roads. ❸ Kyle's Landing Campground is a drive-in campground with showers, toilets and grills, right on the Buffalo River 20 minutes from Ponca.

The ❹ Buffalo Outdoor Center in Ponca sells trail maps and doles out handy driving directions and hiking tips. Staff here know the Buffalo Wilderness better than anyone.

For a shorter day hike in the Buffalo Wilderness, take Hwy 43 past the Hwy 21 turnoff. You will go over two small bridges, and just before the third bridge make a right up a graded dirt road. In 6 miles, just

TIME
3 days

DISTANCE
326 miles

BEST TIME TO GO
Apr – Nov

START
Fayetteville, AR

END
Eureka Springs, AR

ALSO GOOD FOR

HISTORY & CULTURE

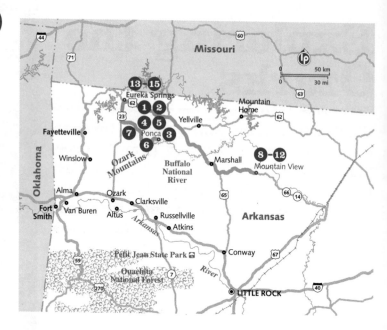

past Cave Mountain Church, you'll find the trailhead to **5** Whitaker Point – the Ozark's most photographed location. The easy 3-mile round-trip leads past cascading creeks and old hardwood stands to a granite table top jutting out from streaked bluffs that drain rainwater 500ft above the lush river valley. Pristine, verdant ridges roll to the horizon in all directions. It's simply spectacular. Bring a big picnic, because you'll want to stay awhile. The 2.3-mile **6** Lost Valley Trail is a great hike for kids. Wildflowers bloom in the spring, fall color is gorgeous. Plus, you'll love Eden Falls and Cobb Cave, a hollowed-out bluff once home to early Native Americans.

"The culture of the Ozarks is also worth experiencing."

If you're looking for a day hike in the Ozarks, the **7** Ozark Highlands Trail offers plenty of options. The trail, which links to the Buffalo River Trail, is akin to the John Muir Trail in the Sierra Nevada. It crosses more than 60 creeks, streams and rivers, and hundreds of waterfalls, bluffs and caves as it traverses 165 miles from Lake Fort Smith to the Buffalo River. The trail was built and is maintained entirely by volunteers. There are spring wildflowers, fall leaves turn orange, red and gold, and in the winter ice formations cling to the bluffs. Although backcountry camping is recommended the trail does pass through 18 well-maintained campgrounds and spurs to 50 trailheads and highways.

The culture of the Ozarks is also worth experiencing. **8** Mountain View, accessed via US65 or Hwy 5, is famous for its wacky mix of old-school crafts (such as blacksmiths and fiddle makers) and music traditions. Nightly folk/country/bluegrass jam sessions at the ⑨ **Ozark Folk Center State Park** have earned it the self-anointed title, "Folk Music Capital of the World." And when old men play dulcimers, jugs and banjos for adoring crowds, who can argue? Unfortunately, there aren't any young bucks waiting in the wings, and these crafts and song traditions could be on their last legs. So get here soon. Thankfully, Southern cooking will never go out of style. ⑩ **Jo Jo's Catfish Wharf**, overlooking the river 6 miles north of town, serves up tasty fried catfish with hushpuppies and pickled green tomatoes.

The ⑪ **Blanchard Springs Caverns** make for a mind-bending day trip. Just 15 miles northwest of Mountain View, these extensive caverns carved by an underground river rival those at Carlsbad. The Forest Service runs guided tours that range from wheelchair accessible to hardcore spelunking. Lack of experience isn't a problem, so go for the real thing. Then bed down at ⑫ **Country Oaks B&B** in one of two converted turn-of-the-century homes on 69 acres, where you'll have access to a private 7-acre lake and breathtaking valley views.

⑬ **Eureka Springs** is a progressive, artsy haven and one of the few nooks in Arkansas where you'll see a thriving, openly gay community. It's also a tourist town thanks to its pedestrian-friendly, Victorian-era historic district crowded with restaurants and art galleries, and studded with restored turn-of-the-century homes. The majestic ⑭ **Crescent Hotel & Spa**, established in 1886, is set on a hill along the historic loop. The in-house New Moon Spa offers a range of massage techniques (including reflexology and hot stone), facials, body polishes and wraps. It's a long and lovely walk or short drive from downtown, and is a pleasant place for a quiet sundowner. Rooms are furnished with antiques and have great views from the upper reaches. Nearby, ⑮ **Ermilio's** is a cute bistro set in a converted home and renowned locally for authentic Italian country cooking. And there are plenty more gems in Eureka Springs: bakeries, creameries, live music venues, plus the artesian (cold-water) springs that attracted Native Americans and pioneers for their healing powers.

Adam Skolnick

PALACE BATH HOUSE

Back in the Victorian age, hotels often doubled as bordellos. Which is why when the **Palace Bath House** and hotel opened in 1901, the first neon west of the Mississippi illuminated a giant penis. Girls cleansed their filthy, tense clientele with piped and heated artesian water from nearby Harding Spring before they got busy. Today, you can once again bathe and steam at the Palace.

TRIP INFORMATION

GETTING THERE
From Fayetteville take I71N to Hwy 180N. Merge onto Hwy 412E which becomes Hwy 68. Turn right on Hwy 21 which becomes Hwy 74. Turn left on Hwy 43 to Ponca. From Ponca double back to Hwy 74 and head west. Turn left on Hwy 123, right on Hwy 65 and left on Hwy 66 to Hwy 14 in Mountain View. Swing back to Hwy 65N to Hwy 62W to Eureka Springs.

DO

Blanchard Springs Caverns
Take a mellow stroll, or spelunk deep into a glittering underground maze. ☎ 888-757-2246; off Hwy 14, Mountain View; guided tours adult/child $10/5, spelunking $75; ⊙ last tour 4pm, spelunking by reservation only; ♿ ⛹

Buffalo Outdoor Center
Come here for spot-on advice about the best hiking trails in the Buffalo Wilderness. It has maps and directions on hand, as well. ☎ 800-221-5514; www.buffaloriver.com; cnr Hwys 43 & 74, Ponca; ⊙ 8am-5pm; ♿ ⛹

Buffalo River Trail
This 36.5-mile slice of the Ozarks is the most spectacular. Trailheads span from Boxley Valley to Pruitt Ranger Station. ☎ 870-741-5443; www.nps.gov/archive; ♿ ⛹

Lost Valley Trail
There's great diversity in the terrain on this short hike that's ideal for young children. The trailhead is off of Hwy 74, Ponca. ☎ 870-741-5443; www.ozarkmountains.org; ♿ ⛹

Ozark Folk Center State Park
Hosts ongoing craft demonstrations and nightly jam sessions that lure older musicians. ☎ 870-269-3851; www.ozarkfolkcenter.com; Hwy 382, Mountain View; admission crafts or music/both $10/17.50; ⊙ crafts 10am-5pm, performance 7:30pm; ♿ ⛹

LINK YOUR TRIP

Ozark Highlands Trail
This volunteer built and maintained network of gorgeous backcountry singletrack spans the entire mountain range. ☎ 870-861-5536; www.hikearkansas.com; headquarters, Pettigrew; ♿ ⛹

Whitaker Point
A 3-mile round-trip hike that leads to one of the most sensational cliffs in the Ozark range. The trailhead is off Hwy 43, Ponca. ☎ 870-741-5443; www.ozarkmountains.org; ♿ ⛹

EAT

Ermilio's
Eureka Springs locals swear by Ermilio's rustic Italian food. ☎ 479-253-8806; www.ermilios.com; 26 White St, Eureka Springs; mains $11-19; ⊙ 5-9pm; ♿

Jo Jo's Catfish Wharf
A riverside catfish joint that always satisfies. ☎ 870-585-2121; Hwy 5, Mountain View; mains $7-13; ⊙ 11am-8pm, until 9pm Fri & Sat; ♿

SLEEP

Country Oaks B&B
This sweet country B&B has eight rooms in two houses. There's ample outdoor space including a 7-acre lake. ☎ 870-269-2704; www.countryoaksbb.com; 17221 Hwy 9, Mountain View; s/d $65/110

Crescent Hotel & Spa
A grand, hilltop relic with some of the best views in Eureka Springs. ☎ 877-342-9766; www.crescent-hotel.com; 75 Prospect Ave, Eureka Springs; s/d $119/329

Kyle's Landing Campground
A full-service campground with 33 sites. www.nps.gov/buff; off Hwy 43, near Ponca; $10 Mar-Nov, free Nov-Mar; ♿ ⛹

USEFUL WEBSITES
www.ozarkmountains.org

www.lonelyplanet.com/trip-planner

HISTORY & CULTURE

Hot Springs National Park

WHY GO Icons like "Scarface" Al Capone, Lucky Luciano, Hank Williams and Tony Bennett once graced this mountain resort. What drew them here was the water that also lured Native Americans and French pioneers. And it will soothe you, too. So dip into Hot Springs, and soak up some history.

TIME
2 days

DISTANCE
175 miles

BEST TIME TO GO
Apr – Jun

START
Hot Springs, AR

END
Hot Springs, AR

ALSO GOOD FOR

OUTDOORS

Coursing beneath the lush Zig Zag Mountains that horseshoe the city of Hot Springs and encapsulate Hot Springs National Park are geothermal veins of healing mineral water. They surface from 47 natural springs, most of which are piped for public consumption. The first public bathhouses opened in the 1880s, but the town came into prominence in the 1920s and 1930s when gangsters like Al Capone, who often came to Arkansas to fetch forbidden whiskey, flocked here to gamble, hit the cathouses and dip into the healing waters.

In 1967 Governor Rockefeller shut down the casinos, and the local economy. So don't be surprised that the town looks like it's stuck in a 1960s time warp: like *Dirty Dancing* in the South. If you're gunning for full kitsch, check into the ❶ **Arlington Hotel & Spa** on Central Ave. This art-deco monolith is perfectly positioned along Hot Springs' main drag, has one of the nicest and oldest spas in town, and is where Al Capone would nest when he retreated to Hot Springs. On weekends their local big band (decked out in white dinner jackets) brings the bop. If you're looking for more Mother Nature, less Father Time, pitch a tent beneath the oaks at ❷ **Gulpha Gorge Campground**, 2 miles northeast of town off Hwy 70B.

Now it's time to stroll to the national park visitors center, in the ❸ **Fordyce Bathhouse** on Bathhouse Row, to grab maps and literature detailing the history and science of the local hot water and

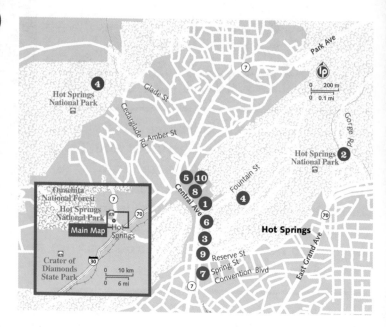

all it has wrought. It's also a museum. You'll notice Victorian-style stained-glass ceilings in the lounges, marble benches and chunky, gleaming old steam works in the bath areas. The marble steam cabinets look like some kind of sweaty, wellness stockade. In the basement you can watch the water gurgle from the Fordyce Spring into old cast-iron water tanks.

ART ANYONE?

Hot Springs isn't all about mid-century glory and hot water; there's also a thriving art scene, with 20 art galleries in downtown Hot Springs, many of which are artist-owned. Our favorite is **Blue Moon Gallery**, a brick loft with old wood floors owned by a lifelong Hot Springs resident. She features the very best of Arkansas' artists. As many as 500 people gather, sip wine and stroll through all the galleries during Art Walks, held the first Friday of every month.

Behind Bathhouse Row are the low-lying mountains where rain and groundwater trickles down through increasingly warm layers of rock before gushing to the surface. The mountains are draped in hardwoods, mostly oak and hickory. Twenty-six miles of ❹ national park trails wind through the hills. The longest trail in the park – Sunset Trail – connects the busier North Mountain with West Mountain and Music Mountain, the park's highest point (1405ft). If you're looking for a shorter walk, Goat Rock Trail has some pretty views. Wildflowers bloom from rocks, ferns sprout from the bluffs and the verdant hills roll all the way to the horizon. It's fun to imagine what the French trappers and American explorers (sent by Thomas Jefferson) might have thought when they trekked these same ridge lines.

Before night falls visit the ❺ **Gangster Museum of America** where you'll hear the sordid history of Hot Springs' gangster past. The Cotton Club's Owney Madden, Lucky Luciano and Al Capone are featured thugs. They and their entourages often moved from casinos to their hotel via underground tunnels.

The former Ohio Club, the 1930s' hippest joint, is now ❻ **Capone's.** Belly up to the mahogany bar, lit by antique-ish fixtures, for some tasty pub grub, occasional live music and a tremendous bourbon selection. This remains the coolest spot in town. If you're looking for something louder, head to ❼ **Maxine's Bordello.** The infamous cathouse turned live music venue regularly hosts bands out of Austin. It caters to a younger crowd. Before the bars, you will want to visit one of the tastiest restaurants in town: ❽ **Rolando's** serves South American cuisine with a touch of earthy elegance.

After too much bourbon or too much Maxine, you'll need to clear your head on Bathhouse Row. At the time of research, only ❾ **Buckstaff Bathhouse** was open for business (although Quapaw was expected to reopen as a full-service spa in late 2008). It doesn't take appointments, but come early, and you won't have to wait long. Your gruff but knowledgeable bath attendant will lead you to huge, steaming, gleaming white tubs outfitted with a blender-like jet system. You'll also visit the steam chamber and get mummified in piping-hot towels. Massages are available, but the bath experience is supercharged, so you can pass.

DETOUR Down on blood diamonds? Then drive 60 miles from Hot Springs to Murfreesboro and **Crater of Diamonds State Park**, the world's only public diamond mine. The farmer who owned this land in 1906 discovered the first diamonds and started the Arkansas mining rush. Old mining equipment and mine shafts remain, but you're here for the white, brown and yellow diamonds that mingle with semiprecious stones including amethyst and garnet. You'll love the park policy: "Finders Keepers!"

Perhaps the best part of living in the American past are the old-school diners, and Hot Springs has its share. After your bath, step in to the ❿ **Colonial Pancake & Waffle House** and feast on buttermilk or buckwheat pancakes topped with fruit, or a malted pecan waffle. Then feel free to drive back into the 21st century.

Adam Skolnick

TRIP INFORMATION

GETTING THERE
From Little Rock take I-30W to US-70W. Exit on Convention Blvd. Follow it to Central Ave in downtown Hot Springs.

DO

Buckstaff Bathhouse
Sample the magic water that made this town. ☎ 501-623-2308; www.buckstaff baths.com; 509 Central Ave; thermal bath/ with 20min massage $22/46; ☸ 7-11:45am & 1:30-3pm Mon-Sat, 8-11:45am Sun, closed Sun Dec-Feb

Fordyce Bathhouse
The national park visitors center is set in this historic Victorian bathhouse that doubles as a museum. ☎ 501-620-3715; www.nps .gov/hosp; 369 Central Ave; admission free; ☸ 9am-5pm; ⬤

Gangster Museum of America
Get your underworld primer during a guided tour of privately owned gangster memorabilia. ☎ 501-545-0700; www.tgmoa.com; 113 Central Ave; adult/senior/child $8/7/3; ☸ 10am-10pm; ⬤

National Park Trails
Although not particularly challenging, these trails are quite beautiful with plenty of shade, flowers, ferns and birds to entrance you. ☎ 501-624-2701; www.nps .gov/hosp; 369 Central Ave; admission free; ⬤

EAT & DRINK

Capone's
One of the Gangster crowd's favorite gambling and music haunts, it remains the best bar in town. ☎ 501-627-0702; 336 Central Ave; mains $6-20; ☸ noon-late

Colonial Pancake & Waffle House
A greasy spoon diner that has breakfast down to a science. It should, it's been here for decades. ☎ 501-624-9273; 111 Central Ave; mains $4-7; ☸ 6:30am-2:30pm

Maxine's Bordello
Rock to local and visiting bands from Austin. ☎ 501-321-0909; www.myspace.com /maxineslive; 700 Central Ave; Fri, Sat & special events $5; ☸ 4pm-2am

Rolando's
Brings global chic to Hot Springs. And the food rocks! ☎ 501-318-6054; www.rolandos restaurante.com; 210 Central Ave; mains $11-18; ☸ 11am-10pm

SLEEP

Arlington Hotel & Spa
The lobby and spa still flash some dusty glamour and attract a big weekend crowd, even if the rooms are a tad aged. ☎ 501-623-7771; www.arlingtonhotel.com; 239 Central Ave; r $80-175

Gulpha Gorge Campground
Pitch a tent in the shade next to a gurgling creek at the national park campsite. ☎ 501-624-3383; off Hwy 70B; sites $10

USEFUL WEBSITES
www.hotsprings.org

LINK YOUR TRIP
www.lonelyplanet.com/trip-planner

Hwy 7 & Little Rock

WHY GO Hwy 7 is an unforgettable drive. It skirts Ozark ridge lines, penetrates lush hardwood forests and frames some glorious horse country. It also happens to link dry Harrison to Altus' quirky wine country, and when you've had your fill there, you'll veer toward ever-charming Little Rock. This is Arkansas.

Your journey begins in ① **Harrison**, the heart of Arkansas' Bible Belt. Churches of every ilk rise among the lovely horse ranches that surround this otherwise charmless town. There are old sensible brick ones, the shabby, peeling whitewashed variety, Jehovah's Witness yurt churches, and in Harrison proper you'll see a massive arena-style evangelical church surrounded by acres of athletic fields. Good luck buying booze in this end of Arkansas. Although rumor has it that there are backyard brewers hidden in the hills, Harrison is the virtuous heart of a dry county.

Cute ② **Jasper** is just up the road. You can't buy beer here either, but you will love the charming town square, antique shops and its landmark diner, the ③ **Ozark Café**, a tasty greasy spoon established in 1909, when beer was still legal.

After Jasper, the two-lane Hwy 7 becomes curvy and gorgeous. This is when you turn up the radio and roll past acres of ranch-land carved by countless streams, and linked by intact hardwood forests home to deer, bear and hundreds of bird species. In less than three hours you'll descend from the mountains, merge onto busy I-40W, then veer onto Hwy 64 in the Arkansas River Valley for 14 miles before landing in ④ **Altus**, a quaint winemaking town that doubled as the quirky setting for the first season of *The Simple Life*, where Paris and Nicole proved that the shallow can be misconstrued as charming.

TIME
2 – 3 days

DISTANCE
292 miles

BEST TIME TO GO
Apr – Nov

START
Harrison, AR

END
Little Rock, AR

ALSO GOOD FOR

ROUTE

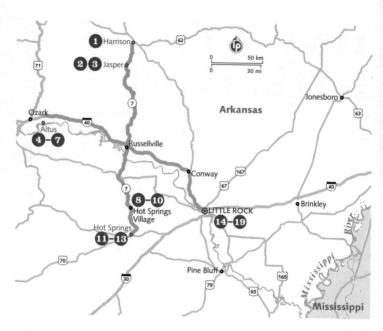

While Italians were busy planting vineyards in northern California, Swiss and German immigrants brought wine to Altus in 1880. Their wine leaned toward the sweet, with grapes, berries and wild plums all part of the equation. ❺ **Mount Bethel Winery**, family owned and operated for more than 100 years, is the oldest and largest winery in the region. It offers regular tours. The folks at ❻ **Altus City Hall**, in the small town square, will be happy to point you toward other wineries in the area.

> *"Come in the fall, and you'll see color here that rivals New England on its best autumn afternoon."*

Don't leave town until you've dined at ❼ **Kelt's**, a self-declared "guilt-free zone." This excellent pub, with a full line of rich beers, has a spoken menu of, among other things, home-cooked rib eye steaks with three delectable sauces, shrimp *en croute*, and chocolate crepes. When local bands play, the joint rocks.

Next, backtrack to Hwy 7, and you'll drive south past the wide Arkansas River, into the mountains, and through the stunning ❽ **Ouachita National Forest**. This 60-mile stretch has been designated a National Scenic Byway. Come in the fall, and you'll see color here that rivals New England on its best autumn afternoon. You can hike or mountain bike into the backcountry on the ❾ **Ouachita National Recreation Trail**, 192 miles of unspoiled single track that links Oklahoma to the wild western edge of Little Rock. The trail rises from 600ft to over 2600ft as it crosses pure streams, climbs peaks and bisects breathtaking valleys. Camp in the backcountry or at ⑩ **Iron Springs Campground**, a developed site with bathrooms, grills and picnic tables, just off Hwy 7.

Soon after Iron Springs, Hwy 7 winds through the Zig Zag Mountains and into ⑪ **Hot Springs**, America's original spa resort destination where hot water is piped from 47 natural springs into public bathhouses. Most of these Victorian-era spas opened in the 1880s, but only a few remain. One of the best is ⑫ **Buckstaff Bathhouse**. You'll enjoy soaking in the swirling mineral water before stepping into the antiquated steam chamber to sweat out residual stress. Follow up with a stack of pancakes (or a damn good waffle) at charming Hot Springs classic, the ⑬ **Colonial Pancake & Waffle House**.

Bid adieu to sweet Hwy 7, take Hwy 70E to Hwy 30, and roll into ⑭ **Little Rock**. This emerging city feels like a small town, with friendly locals and a River Market District that bustles day and night, thanks to the ⑮ **Clinton Presidential Library**. Before the library opened, this warehouse zone, which flanks the Arkansas River, was a good example of urban blight. But the library, with its modern edge, optimistic multimedia displays on the Clinton era, and steady tourist traf-

CENTRAL HIGH

1957 was to be Little Rock's year of school desegregation, but on September 3, the first day of school, Arkansas Governor Orval Faubus called in the Arkansas National Guard to prevent black students from attending Central High. On September 18, a federal judge outlawed the use of troops to prevent integration. Finally, on September 25, nine black students endured an angry mob shouting hateful threats and slurs and entered the school under the protection of the US Army.

fic, changed all that. Today, small businesses are opening their doors with the support of tax breaks and grants, and riverside Little Rock is thriving. ⑯ **Ottenheimer Market Hall**, on President Clinton Ave, is packed with stalls selling everything from fresh fruit to BBQ to homemade chocolate. For an inexpensive and delicious seafood dinner, head up the street to ⑰ **Flying Fish** for grilled rainbow trout. Afterward peruse the bustling strip's sports bars and nightclubs, some of which offer weekly live music.

Tuck into Little Rock's best bed at the ⑱ **Capital Hotel**, within walking distance of the Clinton Library and River Market District. Rooms are spacious and furnished with antiques, and the service is superb. In the morning walk a few blocks to the ⑲ **Old Statehouse**, a museum that details the state's political history and you'll learn that Arkansas, a beautiful state nestled in the center of the continental USA, was once its wild frontier.

Adam Skolnick

TRIP INFORMATION

GETTING THERE
Take Hwy 71N to Hwy 412N, turn right on Hwy 65S and follow it to Harrison. Pick up Hwy 7 in Harrison and follow it to Hot Springs. In Hot Springs take I-70E to I-30 to Little Rock.

DO

Altus City Hall
The friendly folks representing Altus will be glad to direct you to some of the sweetest wineries in America. ☎ 479-468-4191; 125 W Main St, Altus; admission free; ♿

Buckstaff Bathhouse
Sample the magic water that made Hot Springs famous. ☎ 501-623-2308; www .buckstaffbaths.com; 509 Central Ave, Hot Springs; thermal bath/with 20min massage $22/46; ⏰ 7-11:45am & 1:30-3pm Mon-Sat, 8-11:45am Sun, closed Sun Dec-Feb

Clinton Presidential Library
Clinton-lovers will enjoy the multimedia memories and the replica of the Oval Office. ☎ 501-370-8000; www.clintonpresidential center.org; 1200 President Clinton Ave, Little Rock; adult/student/child $7/5/3; ⏰ 9am-5pm Mon-Sat, 1-5pm Sun

Mount Bethel Winery
Visit the vineyards and sip the sweet stuff at this pioneering, family-owned winery. ☎ 479-468-2444; www.mountbethel .com; 5014 Mount Bethel, Altus; tours free; ⏰ 8:30am-6pm Mon-Sat, noon-5pm Sun

Old Statehouse
This handsome, whitewashed relic was the first state government building in Arkansas. ☎ 501-324-9685; www.oldstatehouse.org; 300 W Markham, Little Rock; admission free; ⏰ 9am-5pm Mon-Sat, 1-5pm Sun

Ouachita National Recreation Trail
Walk 190 miles of single-track bliss, linking Oklahoma and Arkansas. ☎ 501-321-5202; www.aokforests.com; Hwy 7, Jessieville; admission free; ♿ 🐾

EAT & DRINK

Colonial Pancake & Waffle House
Everything you've ever wanted in a greasy spoon breakfast. ☎ 501-624-9273; 111 Central Ave, Hot Springs; mains $4-7; ⏰ 6:30am-2:30pm

Flying Fish
It's laid-back, funky and serves some dynamite fresh grilled and fried seafood meals. ☎ 501-375-3474; 511 President Clinton Ave, Little Rock; mains $5-15; ⏰ 11am-10pm

Kelt's
Altus' shockingly gourmet pub. ☎ 479-468-2413; 119 W Main St, Altus; mains $7-15; ⏰ 11am-10pm Mon-Sat, noon-3:30pm Sun

Ozark Café
The funky, antiquated environs go well with the all-American diner fare. The exposed, original stonewall is particularly cool. ☎ 870-446-2976; www.thefrontporchinn .net/ozarkcafe; 107 E Court St, Jasper; mains $3-17; ⏰ 6:30am-8pm; ♿

SLEEP

Capital Hotel
The best bed in Little Rock can be found at this recently renovated historic hotel. ☎ 501-374-7474; www.capitalhotel.com; cnr Markham & Louisiana, Little Rock; r $199-229

Iron Springs Campground
Just off Hwy 7 and in the heart of the beautiful Ouachita National Forest. ☎ 501-984-5313; Hwy 7, Jessieville; campsites $7; ♿ 🐾

LINK YOUR TRIP
www.lonelyplanet.com/trip-planner

The Billgrimage

WHY GO Bill Clinton confidant and local boy, Jordan Johnson, met Mr President in the oval office mere days after graduating from college. And he wants you to follow in Clinton's footsteps to learn how an ambitious, barbecue-munching, self-professed lefty rose from humble roots to become what some argue was one of the world's most beloved and visionary leaders.

Start in ❶ Little Rock where the ❷ Clinton Presidential Library will help you flashback onto those innocent years when the internet was an infant, the economy was rocking, and Clinton was a global, political superstar. Stroll minimalist halls, peruse multimedia displays, and you'll learn that, at 32, Bill became the youngest governor in American history. You'll read that during his 12 years in office he overhauled the state's education system and led the nation in job growth, sparking a surge of popularity that eventually propelled him to Washington.

The display commemorating his unlikely victorious 1992 presidential campaign includes a video clip from the famous debate when Clinton defended his wife's good name after Jerry Brown attacked Hillary and her law firm's work on Whitewater on a nationally televised debate. But what is more likely to stick with you is how his optimistic cries for change echo the 2008 campaign of Hillary's democratic opponent, Barack Obama.

On the 3rd floor, you can peruse gifts presented by diplomats, and signed memorabilia from legendary athletes. The enormous Crystal Tree of Light resembles an avant-garde bong, and was the centerpiece of the Clintons' 1999 New Year's bash. But the building exists to frame Bill's legacy, including displays on his work to curb poverty, expand health care and bolster international relations. In hindsight you'll be swayed by his thoughtful policies and passion to be a force of good in the world.

TIME
3 days

DISTANCE
142 miles

BEST TIME TO GO
Apr – Jun

START
Little Rock, AR

END
Hope, AR

ALSO GOOD FOR

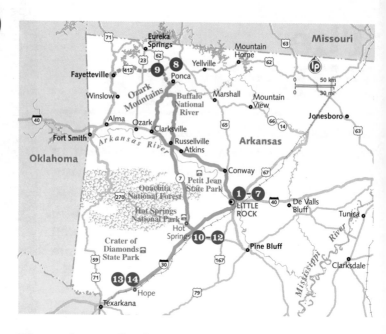

When you leave, you'll walk past the perfectly rusted Rock Island Railroad bridge, through the 30-acre Clinton Presidential Park and the thriving River Market District, which was a great example of urban blight prior to the library's opening, to the **3** **Old Statehouse**. Ensconced in the sweet shade of Southern live oaks, this is where Bill announced his 1992 presidential campaign, and delivered his acceptance speeches in 1992 and 1996.

Speaking of that elegant 1992 campaign, according to Johnson, its unofficial headquarters was **4** **Doe's Eat Place**. "Clinton, [campaign manager, James] Carville, and the team would eat chili-smothered tamales and porterhouse steaks in the back room at least once a week," says Johnson. "Clinton still orders out tamales when he's in town." There's nothing fancy about it, but the steaks are world-class, which explains why Doe's goes through over 700lb of beef in one weekend.

"You'll also notice young, dapper Bill gazing down from his canvas in the domed atrium."

Bill was never a health nut, but he did jog. His favorite route led 0.9 miles, from the **5** **Governor's Mansion** to the two-story McDonald's on Broadway, where he pressed flesh and refueled. "You might remember that this 'exercise' routine was made famous by Phil Hartman on *Saturday Night Live*," adds Johnson.

From here it's a short jaunt to the **6** **Arkansas State Capitol**. Guests are free to roam the marble halls and duck into state offices. The open vibe hints at Bill's best-kept secret. He was a profound beneficiary of big fish–small pond politics. There are less than 3 million people in Arkansas. He worked his way to the top, and won sustained popular support, which he parlayed into party seniority and federal power. "If you visit you'll see that Arkansas [politics] is still wide-open," says Johnson. "Our state is really just a small town." You'll also notice young, dapper Bill gazing down from his canvas in the domed atrium. Sleep off your first day on the Billgrimage at the historic **7** Capital Hotel.

From Little Rock, head to the Ozarks, via Hwy 65, and bed down in the **8** President's Cabin in Ponca. This is where the Clintons bunked when they retreated to the lush Buffalo Wilderness, and one of their skeletons is hidden in these same mountains. In Kingston, a short ride down Hwy 21 from Ponca is where you'll find a quaint country bank with a past. In the 1980s **9** Kingston Bank was the Madison Bank & Trust Company and the Whitewater Development Corporation. Kenneth Starr's investigation into Clinton's Whitewater investment gave us Monica and her dress.

10 Hot Springs was Bill's childhood home. It was here where he played sax in his high school marching band and had his junior and senior proms, held at the **11** Arlington Hotel, an aging art-deco monolith where you'll bed down. **12** McClard's remains Bill's favorite rib shack. Its sauce is sold in his honor at the state capitol, and at the Clinton Museum Store in Little Rock. But he also adored the tamales, buried in Fritos, and smothered in chopped beef, beans, cheese, onions and BBQ sauce. They're tasty, but with such lifelong dining habits the whole open-heart surgery episode makes a lot more sense.

DETOUR From 1973 to 1976 Bill was a law professor at the University of Arkansas in Fayetteville. His Yale sweetheart, Hillary, joined him on their faculty in 1974, and in holy matrimony at their first home on October 11, 1975. The 1930s bungalow is now the **Clinton House Museum**. Photos, vintage campaign materials, and Hillary's wedding gown are on display. Before heading to Hot Springs and Hope, consider looping through Fayetteville, Arkansas' biggest city.

There is one Hot Springs moment you can't relive. Before Bill left for Georgetown in 1964, he watched Martin Luther King Jr deliver his "I Have A Dream" speech from his Hot Springs living room. Catharsis struck, and an ambitious Arkansas boy became The Man.

But, like he said many times on the stump, it all started in a place called **13** Hope. **14** President Bill Clinton's 1st Home Museum is where he and his widowed mother, Virginia, lived with her parents until she remarried. If you're looking for Bill's baby pictures, you've come to the right place...a place called Hope.

Adam Skolnick

TRIP INFORMATION

GETTING THERE
Take 1-40W to Hwy 64W. Go 9 miles to Hwy 21. Head north on Hwy 21 to Boxley where you'll turn right onto Hwy 43 into Ponca. Then retrace your steps to Hwy 21. Stop in Kingston and make your way back east on Hwy 64 to I-40E to Hwy 70 to Hot Springs. From Hot Springs take I-30 South to a place called Hope.

DO
Arkansas State Capitol
Looming from all corners of town, this white domed monument with marble halls is open to visitors. ☎ 501-682-5080; www.state.ar.us; Woodlane & Capitol Ave, Little Rock; admission free; ☺ 7am-5pm Mon-Fri, 10am-5pm Sat & Sun

Clinton Presidential Library
Clinton-lovers will enjoy the multimedia memories. ☎ 501-370-8000; www.clinton presidentialcenter.org; 1200 President Clinton Ave, Little Rock; adult/student/child $7/5/3; ☺ 9am-5pm Mon-Sat, 1-5pm Sun

Governor's Mansion
Bill's old brick mansion is set in a regular Little Rock neighborhood. ☎ 501-324-9805; www.arkansasgovernormansion.com; 1800 Center St, Little Rock; admission free; ☺ 10-11:30am Tue, 1-2:30pm Thu

Kingston Bank
Know that this innocent pink-washed hunk of bricks helped get Clinton impeached...for something that had nothing to do with banking. intersection Hwys 21 & 74, Kingston; admission free; ☺ 9am-4pm Mon-Fri

Old Statehouse
This handsome, whitewashed relic was the first state government building in Arkansas. ☎ 501-324-9685; www.oldstatehouse.org; 300 W Markham, Little Rock; admission free; ☺ 9am-5pm Mon-Sat, 1-5pm Sun

President Bill Clinton's 1st Home Museum
This home-turned-museum includes the pleasantly blooming memorial garden for Billy's mom. ☎ 870-777-4455; www.clintonbirth place.com; 117 S Hervey St, Hope; adult/senior/child $5/4/3; ☺ 10am-5pm Mon-Sat

EAT
Doe's Eat Place
The chili tamales are a scintillating start, but you'll also want a steak. Medium-rare means bloody. ☎ 501-376-1195; www.doeseat place.com; 1023 W Markham St, Little Rock; mains $15-30; ☺ 11am-2pm & 5:30-9:30pm Mon-Thu, 11am-2pm & 5:30-10pm Fri & Sat

McClard's
The tangy, tender baked beans simmer. Slow-cooked meat melts off ribs, tamale spreads are as delicious as they are intimidating. And the BBQ sauce kills. ☎ 501-623-9665; www.mcclards.com; 505 Albert Pike, Hot Springs; mains $5-11; ☺ 11am-8pm Tue-Sat

SLEEP
Arlington Hotel & Spa
Its aging art-deco bones ooze kitschy charm. ☎ 800-643-1502; www.arlingtonhotel.com; 239 Central Ave, Hot Springs; r $80-175

Capital Hotel
The best bed in Little Rock can be found at this recently renovated historic hotel. ☎ 501-374-7474; www.capitalhotel.com; cnr Markham & Louisiana, Little Rock; r $199-229

USEFUL WEBSITES
www.clintonfoundation.org

LINK YOUR TRIP
TRIP

www.lonelyplanet.com/trip-planner

Day Trips in Mississippi, Louisiana & Arkansas

DAY TRIPS

Leave these bustling, modernizing Southern cities in the rearview mirror for a day and traverse national scenic roads, take in quirky Ozark mountain towns, tour antebellum mansions, and get lost in swampy, gator-infested backwaters.

VICKSBURG

This city was the backdrop for a tide-turning Civil War battle in 1843, when Ulysses S Grant led a 47-day siege to overtake a Confederate stronghold on the bluffs high above the Mississippi River. Tens of thousands of soldiers lost their lives, but when it was over the Union owned the Big Muddy. Take the 16-mile scenic drive through the National Military Park and you'll see monuments, statues, battle trenches, Union and Confederate graves. Civil War reenactments are held here in May and June. Later head downtown to stroll cobblestone Washington St and the Garden District, which is crowded with historic homes-turned-museums. **Take the simple if not quite scenic drive from I-20W from Jackson to Vicksburg. Signs on the freeway lead to the National Military Park and downtown.**

See also **TRIP 11**

PORT GIBSON & THE NATCHEZ TRACE

From Mississippi's state capital you can drive north or south on the national scenic Natchez Trace Parkway and enjoy some of the most beautiful countryside in Mississippi. North of Jackson is French Camp, an original pioneer settlement that was taken over by Revolutionary War Colonel James Drane. His antebellum home is open for tours. South of Jackson, you'll find Port Gibson. Like Natchez, its antebellum homes are the main attraction here. Majestic, ancient oaks arc the parkway, but they are endangered of being destroyed if the state extends a planned four-lane highway through sleepy Port Gibson. So come soon. **Hop on the Natchez Trace Parkway in Jackson and travel north to French Camp at Mile 180.7, and/or drive south to Port Gibson at Mile 40, 72.4 miles south of Jackson.**

See also **TRIP 39**

BARATARIA PRESERVE

Well within an hour's drive south of New Orleans is the 20,000-acre Barataria Preserve. Scan the marshes and swamps for 300 bird species, or better yet, search for the American alligator. Large resident gators cruise the bayous and swamps, and you can rent a canoe or kayak to find them on the water, or slowly stroll the trails and turn a keen eye to the bayou. You'll often see these prehistoric beasts half-submerged, skimming through the murky green water like another log drifting in a slow-motion current. You can rent canoes at Bayou Barn, and Restaurant de Familles serves a mean soft-shell crab with bayou (and gator) views. **From New Orleans, take the Westbank Expressway to Barataria Blvd, and look for the sign on the right. If you get to the town of Lafitte, you've gone just a bit too far.**

VENICE & THE MISSISSIPPI DELTA

Seventy miles from Louisiana, Venice, a town laced with bayous, canals and fed by a steady diet of oil and sport fishing, is worth the drive. This is the mouth of the Mississippi and you'll see the river spread into rivulets that flood a vast estuary protected by the Fish and Wildlife Service as the Delta National Wildlife Refuge. Sport fishermen troll the estuaries for redfish (a Cajun staple) and speckled trout, and motor into the deep sea to hook tarpon, snapper and grouper in the warm waters of the Gulf of Mexico. If you really want a surreal fishing experience, hire a boat to a defunct oil platform and cast off. **Merge onto the 90W and take exit 9A onto the Terry Parkway. Turn left on Hwy 23S (the River Rd) and follow it to Venice.**

See also **TRIP 34**

DONALDSONVILLE

Perfectly situated halfway between New Orleans and Baton Rouge, but still off the beaten track, is historic Donaldsonville. Most come to see the dozens of antebellum mansions off the Great River Rd, but unlike Natchez, which remains largely intact, the Union army torched and bombed 632 buildings here during the Civil War; what remains is just an echo of its architectural history. Still, thanks to a surge in restoration and investment by folks as diverse as the co-founder of Café Des Amis (in Breaux Bridge) and a current NFL star, this town is on the rise. Aside from the mansions, one of the most interesting attractions is the River Road African American Museum. Grapevine Café serves an exceptional Creole and Cajun brunch, and if you linger after the sun drops, take in some live jazz or blues at Hambonz. **From New Orleans take I-10W to Hwy 22S. Turn left onto Hwy 70, right onto Hwy 3120, and left on Hwy 18 into Donaldsonville. From Baton Rouge take I-10E to Hwy 44S to Hwy 70, and then follow the directions above.**

LONGLEAF SCENIC BYWAY

Get your road bikes ready and pedal through a gorgeous 17-mile stretch of the 600,000-acre Kisatchie National Forest. It's a rolling, winding road that borders the 8700-acre Kisatchie Hills Wilderness, crosses the Kisatchie Bayou and skirts a section of the Old River – an abandoned stretch of the Mississippi. You'll see deer and wild turkey and if you'd rather drive and hike, seek out the backbone trail that traverses the hardwood forests, sandstone bluffs and flat-top mesas of the Kisatchie Hills, Louisiana's signature mountain range. **Take I-10W to Hwy 167N. Make a left on Hwy 112, a right on Hwy 165, a left on Hwy 112 which merges into Hwy 121, turn left on the Alexandria Hwy and take another left on Hwy 171 where the scenic byway begins.**

PETIT JEAN STATE PARK

Spectacular Petit Jean State Park, nestled just an hour northwest of Little Rock, is named for a female French explorer (Little Jean) who posed as a man so she could accompany her lover to the New World and eventually settled here. There are sandstone caves, soaring limestone bluffs and old growth hardwood forests that shade 20-plus miles of hiking trails. Campsites are available and Mather Lodge has a restaurant and guest rooms, but if you come for the day, take a day hike to gushing waterfalls and picnic in the Arkansas wilderness. **From Little Rock take I-40W to Hwy 65N to Hwy 9. Make a left on Hwy 9 and a right on Hwy 154 to Petit Jean State Park.**

EUREKA SPRINGS

Escape the Wal-Mart capital of the world and find soothing Eureka Springs, a progressive, artsy Ozark mountain town. Streets are pedestrian friendly – especially the Victorian-era historic district crowded with bakeries, cream-eries, bars and art galleries, and studded with restored turn-of-the-century homes. The historic loop leads up the winding roads past the giant neon penis to the majestic Crescent Hotel, established in 1886 and set on a hill above downtown (along the historic loop). It's a fine place for a quiet sun-downer. If you decide to stay for dinner, there's Ermilio's, a cute bistro set in a converted home, and a local favorite for the authentic Italian country cooking. **From Fayetteville take Hwy 71N to Hwy 45E. Make a left on Hwy 412 and a right on Hwy 45, a right on Hwy 12 and a right on Hwy 127. Make a left on Hwy 23 to get to Eureka Springs.**

OUACHITA NATIONAL FOREST

A vast swath of hardwood forest drapes the hills that rise to the west, north and south of Little Rock. This is the beautiful Ouachita National Forest. Lake Ouachita, on the slopes of Mt Ida, is the closest destination to Little Rock. Weekenders descend to boat, fish and camp on the riverbanks. Others park here and trek the area's 16.5 miles of steep mountain trails. If you're look-ing for a day's drive that will give you a taste of the Ouachita, take I-40W to Hwy 7S. Hwy 7 is one of Arkansas' most beautiful roads, and that's say-ing something. You'll roll up and down endless hills on the two-lane coun-try drive until you reach Hot Springs, which is just a short drive on the interstate back to Little Rock. **From Little Rock take Hwy 70W to Hwy 270W to Mt Ida and the Ouachita National Forest. Or take Hwy 40W to Hwy 7 and drive south.**

See also TRIP 52

VAN BUREN

Historic Van Buren makes for a perfect afternoon excursion from nearby Fayetteville. It has a six-block historic district, comprising Victorian-era brick buildings with verandahs overlooking the street, just off the Arkansas River. Most stop by the Drennan-Scott House, once owned by Revolutionary War hero John Drennan and later linked to the Underground Railroad, and if you time it right you can see a show at the King Opera House on Main St. And make sure to board the Ozark Scenic Railway. The train rumbles 70 miles over trestles and through tunnels to Winslow and back, just like it did during the Roaring Twenties. **From Fayetteville take I-540S to Hwy 71S to Hwy 64W. Continue on Hwy 59 to Van Buren.**

TENNESSEE & KENTUCKY TRIPS

Tennessee and Kentucky, part of the geographic region known as the Upland South, reward road trippers with an accessible mix of pastoral countryside and quirky midsize cities.

Tennessee has three distinct regions, represented by the three stars on the state flag. In the east you'll hike through the heather-colored Great Smokies exalted in Dolly Parton ballads. In the middle of the state you'll check out the glittering honky-tonks of Nashville and ride horses through the lush farmland outside Shelbyville. In the Delta lowlands of the west, you'll dig barbecue and blues in soulful Memphis.

Kentucky's exquisite countryside makes it a prime road trip state. If there's an afterlife, it might well look like the emerald hills of Horse Country, with poplar-shaded lanes and tall grasses swaying calmly in the wind. In Kentucky you'll follow the Bourbon Trail, check out the million dollar thoroughbreds of Lexington and spelunk in the cool gloom of Mammoth Cave. The state has more than its fair share of American icons: Buy a Slugger in Louisville, eat some finger lickin' chicken in Corbin and watch a Corvette coming off the line in Bowling Green.

PLAYLIST ♫

Tennessee and Kentucky provided the fertile soil for the country's richest homegrown musical genres. Check out these all-American country, blues and bluegrass classics:

- "Blue Moon of Kentucky," Bill Monroe
- "Coal Miner's Daughter," Loretta Lynn
- "Foggy Mountain Breakdown," Flatt and Scruggs
- "Kentucky Rain," Elvis Presley
- "Mountain Dew," Grandpa Jones
- "My Tennessee Mountain Home," Dolly Parton
- "Rocky Top," Osborne Brothers
- "Tennessee Blues," Steve Earle

TENNESSEE & KENTUCKY'S BEST TRIPS

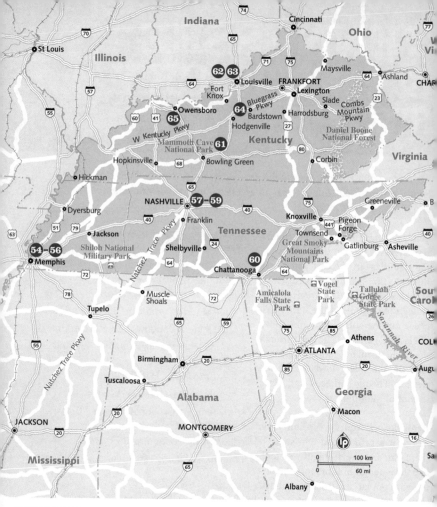

TENNESSEE & KENTUCKY TRIPS

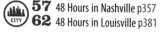

FOOD &
DRINK

Pulled Pork & Butt Rubs: Eating in Memphis

WHY GO Memphians love their barbecue and will fight tooth and nail over which pit master reigns supreme. Truth is, it's hard to find truly bad pig in this town. Tour the city's shabby-but-fabulous barbecue shacks, strolling its quirky, colorful streets between meals to work up your appetite for more.

In Memphis, barbecue means two things: pork ribs or pulled-pork sandwiches. The ribs – mahogany-tinted and the size of a keyboard – can be dry (rubbed with a dry mixture that usually includes paprika, brown sugar, salt, pepper and garlic, maybe some cumin) or wet (basted in a sweet, tangy sauce). Pulled pork means soft shoulder meat mixed with crispy charred bits and doused in sweetish tomato-based sauce.

For a Southern breakfast, you can't beat sunny ❶ Bryant's Bar-B-Q & Breakfast, in a corner storefront of a Midtown strip-mall. On Saturday morning, the line snakes out the door, and the red and yellow tables are full of young couples, yuppie families and John Deere hat-wearing grandpas chowing down on biscuits with sorghum syrup, greasy omelets, grits and country ham. On a weekday morning, swing by for one of its famous fried fruit pies and a cup of coffee to go, or stop in at lunch for a dirt-cheap BBQ bologna sandwich.

If you're lucky enough to be in Memphis on the third weekend of the month, head to the ❷ flea market in the Mid-South Coliseum on Central Ave and Early Maxwell Blvd. Here, you can walk off breakfast by perusing the tables and blankets stacked high with glorious junk – doll furniture, discontinued brands of sunscreen, old Dr Pepper signs, panty girdles and mannequin feet. Nearby, ❸ Overton Park is another good place to work up your appetite for lunch, with walking trails meandering through forests of gnarled hardwood trees.

TIME
3 days

BEST TIME TO GO
Apr – Jun

START
Memphis, TN

END
Memphis, TN

ALSO GOOD FOR

CITY

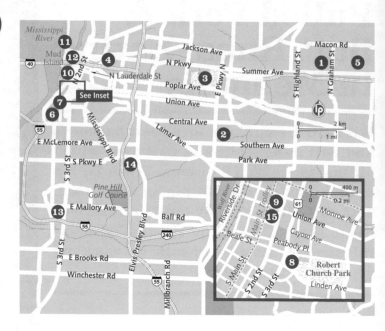

❹ **Cozy Corner**, on a rather bleak stretch of North Parkway, is a serious don't-miss. More dumpy than cozy, with wood-paneled walls and shredded vinyl booths, this family-run place is rightfully renowned for its barbecued Cornish hen. Tear the little bird apart with your hands and suck every bit of sauce off its tiny wings – it's not considered bad manners here. Cozy Corner also does barbecue turkey and a mean rack of ribs.

About 5 miles to the southeast is ❺ **Central BBQ**, with massive rib platters and cheap, smoky pulled-pork, chicken or brisket sandwiches served at long tables in a sunroom-like space. There's even a vegetarian option – a portabella mushroom sandwich – rarer than hen's teeth in carnivorous Memphis. If the dense, moist caramel cake with crunchy brown-sugar icing is on the dessert menu, consider it your lucky day.

Afterwards, take a walk in Midtown's arty Cooper-Young neighborhood, named for its cross streets. There are several good bookstores, bistros and boutiques, as well as a number of funky antique/junk warehouses. A little to the southeast, the Central Gardens neighborhood blooms with crepe myrtle and heirloom roses. A streetcar suburb in the early-20th century, it's now a showcase for Memphis's eclectic architectural styles – Craftsman bungalows sit next to Queen Anne and Tudor Revival mansions. The annual Home and Garden Tour, held in September, is like stepping into the pages of *Southern Living* magazine.

Another good place for eatin' and strollin' is the up-and-coming South Main Historic Arts District, where art galleries and pricy, jewel box-like boutiques sit cheek-to-jowl with grimy sports bars and abandoned hotels. The neighborhood, an easy walk from busy Beale St, is home to several worthy restaurants. The **6 Arcade**, open since 1919, is the oldest restaurant in Memphis and its ultra-retro interior has appeared in a number of movies, including *Great Balls of Fire* and *The Client*. Elvis used to eat here, and the Arcade still has a fried peanut butter and banana sandwich in his honor. Have breakfast – country ham and eggs, sweet-potato pancakes, or biscuits with cream gravy – at the counter, or grab a quick lunch in one of the aqua-and-teal booths before the 3pm closing time. The Arcade is still run by the family of founder Speros Zepatos, whose Greek heritage is reflected in the feta salad and Greek-style pizza.

Over on Front St, **7 Gus's World Famous Fried Chicken** has been written up in *Vogue* and named by *GQ* as one of 10 meals in the world worth flying in for. *GQ*'s right. Gus's golden chicken skin is shatteringly crisp, yet melts in your mouth with a burst of spice; the meat beneath is fall-of-the-bone moist. You could easily eat a whole chicken's worth, happily ignoring the dreary tile walls and concrete floor of the dim space. The original Gus's is in nearby Mason, TN, and the owner still sends buckets of batter daily to the Front St location rather than put the recipe in another pair of hands.

MEMPHIS IN MAY

The month-long **Memphis in May** festival (www.memphisinmay.org) is held in Tom Lee Park overlooking the river downtown. First comes the **Memphis Music Festival**, when 100,000 visitors show up for a rollicking weekend to watch big-name acts from Aretha Franklin to Cat Power. Next is **International Week**, a food and culture celebration dedicated to a different country each year. Then there's the **World Championship Barbecue Cooking Contest**, where hundreds of teams compete in three categories: pork ribs, pork shoulder and whole hog.

Downtown by the Mississippi, the air is always perfumed with the scent of stale beer and fry grease. The Delta blues were born here on Beale St, now a pedestrian thoroughfare lined with crowded juke joints and Southern-themed souvenir shops. By day the street has a carnival ambience, complete with funnel cakes and bright, plastic yard glasses of daiquiris. More often than not, nice weather brings outdoor mini-fairs of various stripes to the plaza at the corner of Beale and 4th St, with corn dogs, knock-off purses and incense vendors.

On Beale, the place for late-night, post-bar grub is **8 Dyer's**, home of the deep-fried hamburger. Dyer's claims its "ageless cooking grease" – oil that has been continuously strained and added to since 1912 – is the secret to the burgers' succulence. When Dyer's changed locations in the 1990s, the magic grease was transported in a locked box under police escort. Though the patties are not noticeably greasy, they are thin, so go for a triple. Though the restaurant itself is new, it maintains a bright, retro-style ambience, with booths and snappy service. After eating, you'll be ready to put in another round at the clubs – many are open until 3am or later on weekends.

For another time-honored Memphis meal, find your way to **9 Charlie Vergos' Rendezvous**. In a back alley off Third St and down a flight of stairs, just getting to the Rendezvous seems a bit illicit, like you're on your way to a speakeasy. This cavernous cellar, made cozy with red-and-white checked tablecloths and all sorts of historical memorabilia on the walls, has been serving the quintessential dry-rub ribs since 1948. Gnawing every bit of succulent meat off the bones is a primal experience. Expect big crowds.

> *"Just getting to the Rendezvous seems a bit illicit, like you're on your way to a speakeasy."*

At lunchtime, old-fashioned **10 Leonard's** on Main is always full of downtown working stiffs filling up at the lunch buffet, which offers pork barbecue along with yummy Southern sides like turnip greens, maple peaches and banana pudding. Leonard's mascot, a pig in a top hat and tails, is nicknamed Mr Brown – a reference to the Memphis tradition of mixing in the burnt bits (Mr Brown) from the outside of the pork shoulder with the lighter inside meat (Miss White). The original 1922 Leonard's is still operating on the far southeast side of town.

While downtown, stroll the aerial walkway over to **11 Mud Island**, a small raft of land in the middle of the great, brown Mississippi. It's all about scale models here – wade through a five-block long topographic replica of the lower Mississippi, paddle around in a 1-acre enclosed "Gulf of Mexico," stroll the deck of a model 19th-century packet boat in the museum. When you're done, take the monorail back and snap some pictures of the city skyline, including the 32-story silver **12 Pyramid Arena** on the waterfront.

ASK A LOCAL

"Great barbecue is cooked low and slow. The meat should appear pink to red down to the arm bone. It should be pulled, not chopped – this is when the meat is hand pulled and served without ever taking a knife to the meat. And there should be a crust on the meat. That's where the cook applies a glaze and cooks further to form a tasty bark."

Mary Horner, judge, Memphis in May Barbecue Cooking Competition

If you're headed to Graceland, about 8 miles south of downtown, there are two barbecue joints worth a stop along the way (they're worth a stop even if you're not headed to Graceland, for that matter). **13 Jim Neely's Interstate Bar-B-Que** is a classic, run by ex-insurance agent Jim Neely in an old grocery store since 1979. This is the place to try a Memphis-only oddity – barbecue spaghetti. It's exactly what it sounds like – chopped spaghetti, cooked to near-mush, mixed with pulled pork in a smoky barbecue sauce. Though reminiscent of an elementary school cafeteria "lunch special," it's strangely tasty. But if that's not your speed, the pulled-pork sandwiches, with crunchy bits of well-done outer meat mixed with soft, tender white meat, are tops. ⑭ **Payne's Bar-B-Q**, in an old storefront up the street from Graceland, is the place to stop for

a sandwich when on the trail of the King. Order a sloppy sandwich at the scuffed counter and listen to locals shooting the breeze.

Is there anything more indulgent than getting an order of ribs and a slice of pie to go and taking it back to your hotel, to consume sitting cross-legged on top of the bedspread while watching HBO? Do it at the ⑮ **Talbot**

About 40 miles across the Mississippi state line, the town of **Tunica** (www.tunicamiss.com) has styled itself as a Southern Las Vegas. Even if blackjack's not your thing, the glittery casinos host some marquee-name Southern acts like Merle Haggard, Gladys Knight and BB King. Make a night of it with dinner at the Paula Deen Buffet at Harrah's Casino.

Heirs, where studio suites have kitchen tables, and fridges for leftovers. The tiny brownstone hotel has an offbeat charm, with brightly painted contemporary rooms. Best of all, it's within walking distance of the downtown eats.

Emily Matchar

FOOD & DRINK

TRIP INFORMATION

GETTING THERE

From Nashville, take I-40 W about 200 miles, take exit 10B, then exit 1A onto Second St.

EAT

Arcade

Memphis's oldest restaurant does diner-style eggs, sandwiches and salad, in a retro setting. ☎ 901-526-5757; www.arcaderestaurant.com; 540 S Main St, Memphis; mains $6-8; 7am-3pm, dinner on Fri;

Bryant's Bar-B-Q & Breakfast

Lines snake out the door on Saturday morning – load up on grits and country ham. ☎ 901-324-7494; www.bryantsbreakfast.com; 3965 Summer Ave, Memphis; mains $2-9; 5am-1pm Mon-Sat;

Central BBQ

Come for the hefty racks of ribs, stay for the teeth-achingly sweet Southern desserts. ☎ 901-767-4672; www.cbqmemphis.com; 4375 Summer Ave, Memphis; mains $4-22; 11am-9pm Sun-Thu, to 10pm Fri & Sat;

Charlie Vergos' Rendezvous

Dry-rubbed ribs are the thing at this always-crowded subterranean institution. ☎ 901-523-2746; www.hogsfly.com; in alley off Second St btw Union & Monroe, Memphis; mains $7-18; 4:30pm-10:30pm Tue-Thu, 11am-11pm Fri & Sat

Cozy Corner

Order the barbecued Cornish game hen at this no-frills spot. ☎ 901-527-9158; 745 N Parkway, Memphis; mains $5-16; 10:30am-5pm Tue-Sat, later in summer;

Dyer's

"Triple with cheese" is exactly what you need when starving on Beale at 3am. ☎ 901-527-3937; www.dyersonbeale.com; 205 Beale St, Memphis; meals $4-9; 11am-1am Sun-Thu, to 5am Fri & Sat

Gus's World Famous Fried Chicken

This concrete bunker is home to some of the best fried chicken in the universe. ☎ 901-527-4877; 310 S Front St, Memphis; mains $5-9; 11am-9pm Sun-Thu, to 10pm Fri & Sat;

Jim Neely's Interstate Bar-B-Que

Try the oddball barbecue spaghetti at this homey "pork house". ☎ 901-775-1045; www.interstatebarbecue.com; 2265 S Third St, Memphis; mains $5-9; 11am-11pm Mon-Thu, to midnight weekends;

Leonard's

Hungry downtown office workers fill up at the plentiful buffet at Leonard's. ☎ 901-528-0875; www.leonardsbbqdowntown.com; 103 N Main St, Memphis; mains $4-19; 11am-8pm Sun-Thu, to 9pm Fri & Sat;

Payne's Bar-B-Q

This south Memphis storefront is your place for post-Graceland pork sandwiches. ☎ 901-942-7433; 1393 Elvis Presley Blvd, Memphis; mains $4-6; 11am-6:30pm Mon-Sat;

SLEEP

Talbot Heirs

Each suite in this small brownstone hotel has its own personality, plus a full kitchen. ☎ 901-527-9772; www.talbothouse.com; 99 S Second St, Memphis; r $130-275

USEFUL WEBSITES

www.memphisflyer.com
www.memphistravel.com

LINK YOUR TRIP

www.lonelyplanet.com/trip-planner

TRIP
1 A Taste of the South p37
56 Memphis Music Tour p351

Going to Graceland: Touring the Shrine of Elvis

WHY GO When Elvis wiggled his hips, women fainted, preachers screamed hellfire and damnation, and the National Guard had to storm in to keep the peace. Come on down to Memphis to visit the King's home, his studio, even his favorite diner, and find out what the madness was all about.

Elvis Aaron Presley lived most of his life in Memphis – this sultry, gritty city on the banks of the Mississippi River. He was raised here on the hallelujahs of Pentecostal Holiness choirs and the rhythms of the blues singers in the ❶ Beale St clubs, sounds that would later inform his genre-bending rock 'n' roll.

❷ Graceland Mansion lies about 7 miles south of downtown on Elvis Presley Blvd, a seedy thoroughfare of fast-food restaurants and cash-checking agencies. The white-columned Colonial-style mansion – smaller than one might have imagined – sees 600,000 visitors a year. A then-22-year-old Elvis bought it for about $100,000 in 1957, the year after his self-titled debut record was released by RCA.

Press play on the free audio tour and enter. Graceland, as you'll see, is as much a shrine to ostentatious 1970s decorating as it is to Elvis. Highlights include a hideous wood-paneled kitchen where housekeepers once fixed vats of banana pudding; a stairwell covered entirely – ceiling included – in pea-green shag carpet; and, of course, the tiki-styled Jungle Room, with its faux waterfall and leopard-print furniture.

Out back, you'll find the movie memorabilia-filled Trophy Room, the racquetball court, and Elvis' old office. The Platinum admission includes tours of Elvis' private planes, the Elvis jumpsuit collection and the ❸ Graceland Automobile Museum.

TIME
2 days

BEST TIME TO GO
Apr – Jun

START
Memphis, TN

END
Memphis, TN

ALSO GOOD FOR

HISTORY & CULTURE

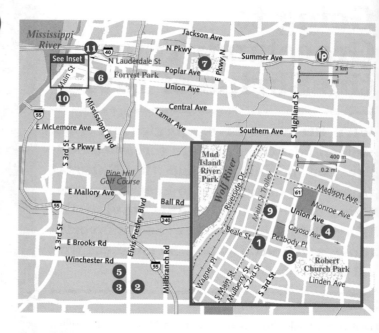

If you feel like the tour's over rather quickly, it may be because you can't go upstairs. Elvis always greeted visitors on the 1st floor, keeping the upper bedrooms his private space. Priscilla and Lisa Marie have left it that way (plus, the volume of visitors means the estate would have to knock a hole in the wall for an exit staircase, potentially angering the King's ghost).

THE KING IS DEAD

During **Elvis Week** (www.elvisweek.com) in mid-August, tens of thousands of shiny eyed pilgrims descend on Memphis to honor the King's death, with seven days of concerts, auto shows and memorabilia sales. Attend an International Elvis Fan Club charity dinner one night and get up early for a Hunka Hunka Burnin' Peppers sale at the Memphis Farmers Market the next day. The whole thing culminates in a spooky, solemn candlelight march to his grave. *This* is Weird America.

Elvis died here, face down in the bathroom, on August 16, 1977, felled by heart failure likely brought on by chronic drug abuse. He was 42. He's buried out back with his parents and grandmother in the Meditation Gardens, next to the kidney bean-shaped pool. There's a grave marker here for Jesse Garon, Elvis' stillborn twin brother, though his body is buried some 100 miles away in Tupelo, Mississippi.

If you're short on time, try ④ **Blues City Tours.** The seven-hour bus trip includes a stop at Graceland, lunch and a tour of various Elvis-themed sites throughout the city. See Sun Studio, the Mississippi River and the rather unimposing Elvis statue on Beale St.

Sleep at – you guessed it – **5** Heartbreak Hotel. Across the street from Graceland (on Lonely St), it has ordinary (even tasteful) doubles, and four themed suites. The Graceland Suite has its own miniature Jungle Room and the Burning Love Suite is straight out of the red velvet-draped 1970s honeymoon of your nightmares.

In the morning, hop on the free minibus to Union Ave, home of the venerable **6** Sun Studio. An 18-year-old Elvis reportedly walked in here and, when asked what famous musician he most sounded like, replied, "I don't sound like nobody." The best part of the fact-filled tour is the old studio itself, where you can pose for pictures on an "X" marking the spot where Elvis stood while recording his breakout single, "That's all Right."

In leafy Midtown Memphis, **7** Overton Park has the band shell where Elvis played his first stage show in 1954. The once-decayed shell was narrowly saved from demolition and reopened as Levitt Shell in 2008, with a full concert schedule.

Part of downtown's massive FedExForum, the **8** Memphis Rock 'n' Soul Museum explains how Elvis practically invented youth culture as we know it today. Hear low, sweet Delta blues and the skit-skat of early rock 'n' roll on the song-packed audio tour. Nearby, the posh **9** Lansky Brothers department store once supplied Elvis with his Hi-Boy collar shirts and gold lamé suits. Buy your own pink- and black-striped "speedway" shirt, sequined button-up, or Humes High School (Elvis' alma mater) tee.

> **DETOUR** Two hours southeast of Memphis in **Tupelo, MS** is Elvis' childhood home. The humble, white shotgun shack is now the **Elvis Birthplace Museum**. Fervent fans can visit the hardware store where he got his first guitar, the courthouse where he performed his first live radio show and the drive-in where he chowed down on cheeseburgers.

In downtown's arty South Main district you'll find the **10** Arcade, Memphis's oldest restaurant and one of Elvis' favorites. The vinyl-and-Formica decor is straight out of the 1940s and the menu includes the infamous fried peanut-butter-and-banana sandwich. Fans who reserve well in advance can sleep in Elvis' actual bedroom at **11** Lauderdale Courts, a Depression-era public housing complex where the Presley family lived at number 328 from 1949 through 1953. The Elvis Suite is preserved with period furnishings, including a vintage Frigidaire and reproduction family photos.

As you leave the city, ponder what Elvis said at the end of a concert during what would prove to be his final tour: "Til we meet you again, may God bless you. Adios."

Emily Matchar

TRIP
55

OFFBEAT

TRIP INFORMATION

GETTING THERE
From Nashville, take I-40 West about 200 miles to exit 10A towards Jackson, MS, then take exit 5B toward Elvis Presley Blvd.

DO
Blues City Tours
A bus will pick you up at your hotel for a daylong tour of Graceland and the King's favorite city sights. ☎ 901-522-9229; www .bluescitytours.com; 325 Union Ave, Memphis; adult/child $70/51; ⏰ 10am; ♿

Graceland Automobile Museum
Across the street from the mansion, see 33 of Elvis' own vehicles, including a pink Cadillac. ☎ 901-332-3322; www.elvis.com; 3765 Elvis Presley Blvd, Memphis; Graceland admission plus museum adult/child $29/15; ⏰ 9am-5pm summer, 10am-4pm winter; ♿

Graceland Mansion
Poke your nose into Elvis' private home, viewing his kitchen, TV room, racquetball courts, and poolside gravesite. ☎ 901-332-3322; www.elvis.com; 3765 Elvis Presley Blvd, Memphis; adult/child $27/24; ⏰ 9am-5pm daily summer, 10am-4pm Wed-Mon winter; ♿

Lansky Brothers
This upscale department store, formerly "Clothier to the King," sells a line of Elvis-themed duds. ☎ 901-529-9070; www .lanskybros.com; 149 Union Ave, Memphis; ⏰ 9am-6pm Sun-Wed, to 9pm Thu-Sat

Memphis Rock 'n' Soul Museum
This Smithsonian-affiliated music museum has plenty of info on Elvis among its exhibits tracing the history of music in the Mississippi Delta. ☎ 901-205-2533; www.memphis rocknsoul.org; 191 Beale St, Memphis; adult/child $10/7; ⏰ 10am-7pm

Overton Park
See bands play at the band shell in this Midtown city park, where Elvis first shook his hips. ☎ 901-272-5159; www.levittshell.org; park btw Poplar Ave & N McLean Blvd, shell is west side; admission free; ⏰ park 6am-6pm, to 8pm summer

Sun Studio
Knowledgeable guides lead tours of the studio where Elvis, Johnny Cash and Roy Orbison were discovered. ☎ 901-521-0664; www .sunstudio.com; 706 Union Ave, Memphis; adult/child $10/free; ⏰ 10am-6pm

EAT & SLEEP
Arcade
Memphis's oldest restaurant has the King's favorite peanut butter and banana sandwich. ☎ 901-526-5757; www.arcaderestaurant .com; 540 S Main St, Memphis; mains $6-8; ⏰ 7am-3pm daily, dinner Fri

Heartbreak Hotel
Every room has a framed picture of Elvis at this theme hotel across the street from Graceland. ☎ 901-332-1000; www.heartbreak hotel.net; 3677 Elvis Presley Blvd, Memphis; r from $125

Lauderdale Courts
Sleep in the Elvis Suite in the apartment complex where the Presley family once lived. ☎ 901-523-8662; www.lauderdalecourts .com; 252 North Lauderdale St, Memphis; Elvis Suite $250

USEFUL WEBSITES
www.elvis.com
www.memphistravel.com

LINK YOUR TRIP

www.lonelyplanet.com/trip-planner

Memphis Music Tour

WHY GO Memphis's founders had high hopes when they named their city after the capital of ancient Egypt. Memphis lived up to its legacy with music, bringing forth blues, soul and rock 'n' roll. The beat lives on, pulsating out of sweltering juke joints and baroque concert halls. Come hear.

TIME
3 days

BEST TIME TO GO
Apr – Jul

START
Memphis, TN

END
Memphis, TN

ALSO GOOD FOR

CITY

To understand Memphis's music scene, you have to understand the 2-mile stretch of downtown pavement that is ❶ Beale St. It all started here, just after the Civil War, when freed slaves began to move to the riverfront area and build the foundations for a vibrant African American community. Black doctors, lawyers and store owners set up shop and traveling musicians performed on the corners and in the bars.

In 1909, a young Beale St band leader named WC Handy was commissioned to write a campaign song for mayoral candidate EH Crump. The song, later titled "Memphis Blues," was one of the first published songs in the emerging genre known as the "blues" – a guitar-based mixture of old slave "field hollers," church music and African call-and-response songs. You can see Handy's old shotgun shack, now the ❷ WC Handy House Museum, at the corner of Beale and 4th.

In the 1920s and '30s, Beale St was sin central, lined with whorehouses, juke joints and pool halls. It was here, in the 1940s, that a teenage Elvis used to come to listen to the sounds of African American blues masters like BB King and Little Junior Parker. White country met black blues, and the result made music history. Snap your picture with the ❸ Elvis statue on Beale between Main and 2nd Sts.

These days Beale St, now partially a pedestrian thoroughfare, is like a giant fraternity party and street carnival. Revelers of all ages roam

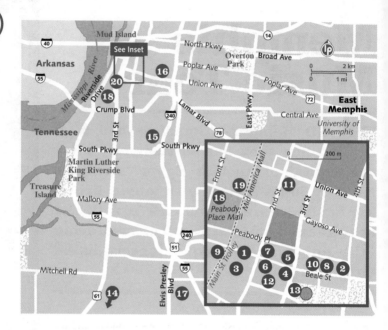

the street day and night, eating corn dogs and ordering Jell-O shots from walkup windows. If it sounds trashy, it sure is, but it can also be a lot of fun. When things are hoppin', the clubs stay open as late as 5am. Most clubs don't charge covers, so skip your way down the block until you find the right vibe.

On the corner of Beale and South 3rd, ❹ Silky O'Sullivan's is an enormous, Irish-Caribbean–themed drunk-making factory whose gimmick is keeping several goats in a pen on the patio. Barbara Blue, the middle-aged human jukebox who performs here five evenings a week, is a trip. Opposite Silky's is ❺ Rum Boogie, a Cajun-spiced restaurant and dance hall. The brick walls are hung with music memorabilia, including some 200 guitars autographed by the likes of Sting and Billy Joel. Down the block is ❻ Black Diamond, a cozy dive hidden in plain sight in the middle of Beale, a chill option for those looking to sit back with a beer and watch some quality blues. For weekend after-hours action, try ❼ Blues City Cafe, with a late-night menu and jumpin' jazz, funk and rockabilly acts.

MEMPHIS ROCK 'N' ROLL TOURS

For those without a car or short on time, **Memphis Rock 'n' Roll Tours** (www.memphis rocktour.com) will take you on a 90-minute create-your-own trip of sights both famous (Graceland, Beale St) and obscure (Carl Perkins's tomb, hole-in-the-wall BBQ joints). Local guides love to show you the weird side of town. Tours will pick you up at any area hotel.

A little further east on Beale is the **8** New Daisy Theater, where you can see kickboxing, Elvis impersonators, up-and-coming rock, metal, and rap acts, and the occasional star performer. To the west, at the corner of Beale and South Main, is **9** The Orpheum, with its glittering red-and-gold marquee. This opulent 1928 theater, originally built for vaudeville, now hosts traveling Broadway musicals and big-name musicians and comedians. It's even got its own ghost – little pigtailed Mary, killed by a downtown trolley, is sometimes seen enjoying the shows from C-5, Box 5.

All 3am cravings can be satisfied at **10** Dyer's, a Beale diner specializing in deep-fried hamburgers cooked in the same constantly replenished batch of grease since 1912. After eating, spend the night near the action at the handsome **11** Peabody Hotel, where a flock of ducks is marched from the penthouse to the marble lobby fountain every morning at 11am.

The **12** Gibson Beale Street Showcase, not on Beale St proper, offers a 30-minute tour of the factory where the iconic guitars are crafted. The lounge has food and live music. If you're short on time, peer at the workshop from the oversized street-level window.

PLAYLIST From blues to soul to rock 'n' roll, here are some of the best Memphis songs:

- "Beale Street Blues," WC Handy
- "Blue Suede Shoes," Elvis Presley
- "Down in the Alley," Memphis Minnie
- "Great Balls of Fire," Jerry Lee Lewis
- "Green Onions," Booker T & the MGs
- "Matchbox," Carl Perkins
- "Soul Man," Sam & Dave
- "The Thrill is Gone," BB King

Around the corner is the Smithsonian-affiliated **13** Memphis Rock 'n' Soul Museum, a must-see overview of the music of the Mississippi Delta. Exhibits and audiovisual programs show how this gritty riverside city crossed racial divides to revolutionize American music. The audio tour has more than 100 songs spanning the history of Memphis Sound.

If you're in Memphis on a Sunday, don't even think about missing church. The Church of the Reverend Al Green, that is. The soul superstar is the pastor of the **14** Full Gospel Tabernacle Church in a quiet, wooded area of south Memphis, where a robed choir belts out window-rattling hallelujahs and the Reverend Green breaks into songs of praise mid-sermon. Visitors are quite welcome, though you will be asked to tithe. No torn jeans, please.

Next, head directly to Soulsville USA. This historically black neighborhood was once the epicenter of Southern soul music, where local studios launched the careers of Al Green, Booker T & the MGs, and Otis Redding, among others. The centerpiece of a neighborhood revitalization project is the **15** Stax Museum of American Soul Music, housed in a replica of the old Stax

Records building. Here, you can step into a rebuilt 100-year-old Mississippi Delta church and get funky on the Soul Train dance floor.

For that true, flesh-tingling "it all happened here" feeling, head to **16** **Sun Studio**, the centerpiece of any musical Memphis trip. Here, in a shabby semi-industrial area not far from downtown, Sun Records founder Sam Phillips took a chance on a series of scrawny nobodies barely out of their teens (ever heard of Elvis, Johnny Cash or Roy Orbison?). Tours are led by enthusiastic guides, many of them country singers themselves. Descriptions of the studio's history are interspersed with loudspeaker clips, like Elvis' first recording. Pose with the old-school mic in the recording studio and buy a CD of the "Million Dollar Quartet," a 1956 spur-of-the-moment jam session between Elvis, Johnny Cash, Carl Perkins and Jerry Lee Lewis. Man, to have been a fly on the acoustic tile *that* day.

"At the upstairs bar, grizzled Nate serves warm beer beneath a flickering blue light"

A few miles south of town, Elvis Presley's beloved **17** **Graceland Mansion** is a marvel of 1970s bad taste. Peering into the King's wood-paneled kitchen and watching his TVs is fascinating and kind of sad. For an extra fee you can tour his private jet and visit the jumpsuit museum.

For funkier, more adult nightlife than the Beale St offerings, try the South Main area. A spooky brothel-turned-bar, **18** **Earnestine & Hazel's** is named after its late madams. Order a "soul burger" at the dusty, dim bar then poke around the old boudoirs with their rusty bedsprings and claw-footed tubs.

ASK A LOCAL

"Most locals don't go to Beale. If I do, I go to **Silky O'Sullivan's**, where my friend plays piano. He'll play anything you yell at him. **Young Avenue Deli**, in the Cooper-Young neighborhood, is the hipster mecca of Memphis. They have two really good jukeboxes. I like **Murphy's**, a little hole-in-the-wall, and the **Hi-Tone**, for the *That Thing You Do* feel – the drums are all from the 1960s."

David Brookings, musician & Sun Studio tour guide, Memphis

At the upstairs bar (if you can call a plywood counter and a plastic cooler a bar), grizzled Nate serves warm beer beneath a flickering blue light. He's been off the sauce for years, he says, but seems to have a soft spot for sorry drunks. The place heats up late, with occasional live music. Also check out the schedule at the **19** **Center for Southern Folklore** on S Main St, with live blues in an intimate café setting. In a nearby concrete bunker, **20** **Gus's World Famous Fried Chicken** lives up to the hype. Have a spicy battered wing and thigh, and finish with the Caribbean caramel cake.

Emily Matchar

TRIP INFORMATION

GETTING THERE

From Nashville, take I-40 W about 200 miles, take exit 10B, then exit 1A onto Second St.

DO

Center for Southern Folklore

This storefront cultural center has live blues and regional music, and art books. ☎ 901-525-3655 www.southernfolklore.com; 119 S Main St, Memphis; show times vary

Full Gospel Tabernacle Church

Listen to the Reverend Al Green and his potent-voiced choir praise Jesus during their regular Sunday service. ☎ 901-396-9192; www.algreenmusic.com/fullgospel tabernacle.html; 787 Hale Rd, Memphis; tithe per person minimum $1; ☽ 11:30am Sun

Gibson Beale Street Showcase

See the factory where the legendary guitars are made, or hear live music in the lounge. ☎ 901-544-7998; www.gibsonshowcase .com; 145 Lt George W Lee Ave, Memphis; admission $10; ☽ 11am-4pm

Graceland Mansion

It's forever 1970 in Elvis' old house; the King himself is buried by the pool. ☎ 901-332-3322; www.elvis.com; 3765 Elvis Presley Blvd, Memphis; adult/child $27/24; ☽ 9am-5pm daily summer, 10am-4pm Wed-Mon winter

Memphis Rock 'n' Soul Museum

This Smithsonian-affiliated museum traces the history of Mississippi Delta music. ☎ 901-205-2533; www.memphisrocknsoul .org; 191 Beale St, Memphis; adult/child $10-7; ☽ 10am-7pm

New Daisy Theater

This Beale venue has everything from soul music to rap to boxing. ☎ 901-525-8979; www.newdaisy.com; 330 Beale St, Memphis; prices & times vary

Orpheum

This old Vaudeville palace now hosts Broadway shows and big-name musicians. ☎ 901-525-7800; www.orpheum-memphis .com; 203 S Main St, Memphis; prices & times vary

Stax Museum of American Soul Music

See Isaac Hayes' Superfly Cadillac and other soul-music artifacts on the site of the old Stax recording studio. ☎ 901-946-2535; www.staxmuseum.com; 926 E McLemore Ave, Memphis; adult/child $10/7; ☽ 9am-4pm Mon-Sat, from 1pm Sun; ♿

Sun Studio

Elvis, Roy Orbison and others got their start at this tiny studio. Tours are run every hour on the half-hour. ☎ 901-521-0664; www .sunstudio.com; 706 Union Ave, Memphis; adult/child $10/free; ☽ 10am-6pm

WC Handy House Museum

Visit the shotgun shack home of the "Father of the Blues." ☎ 901-522-1556; 352 Beale St, Memphis; adult/child $3/2; ☽ 11am-4pm Tue-Sat, later in summer

DRINK

Black Diamond

Hidden in plain sight in the middle of Beale, this cozy pub has cold beer and hoppin' live music. ☎ 901-521-0800; 153 Beale St, Memphis; ☽ 6pm-late

Earnestine & Hazel's

This brothel-turned-bar is filthy, dark and totally awesome. Have a "soul burger" and a warm Miller and put some coins in the jukebox. ☎ 901-523-9754; 531 S Main St, Memphis; ☽ 5pm-late

Rum Boogie

Get your party on at this noisy Cajun-themed restaurant and nightclub. ☎ 901-528-0150; www.rumboogie.com; 182 Beale St, Memphis; ☽ 11am-2am

Silky O'Sullivans

This huge tavern specializes in bucket-sized cocktails called "Divers." ☎ 901-522-9596; www.silkyosullivans.com; 183 Beale St, Memphis; ☽ 11am-late Tue-Sun, from 4pm Mon

EAT & SLEEP

Blues City Cafe

The late night grub and music at this casual joint is popular with off-work Beale St waiters and bartenders. ☎ 901-526-3637;

www.bluescitycafe.com; 138 Beale St, Memphis; mains $8-20; ⏰ 11am-3am

Dyer's
Chow down on post-bar cheeseburgers, deep-fried in century-old cooking grease. ☎ 901-527-3937; www.dyersonbeale .com; 205 Beale St, Memphis; mains $4-9; ⏰ 11am-1am Sun-Thu, to 5am Fri & Sat

Gus's World Famous Fried Chicken
This dumpy fried-chicken joint is straight-up addictive. ☎ 901-527-4877; 310 S Front St,

Memphis; mains $5-9; ⏰ 11am-9pm Sun-Thu, to 10pm Fri & Sat; ♿

Peabody Hotel
This grand downtown hotel has well-appointed rooms, a classy bar and a flock of pet ducks. ☎ 901-529-4000; www.peabodymemphis .com; 149 Union Ave, Memphis; r from $240

USEFUL WEBSITES
www.memphisflyer.com
www.memphistravel.com

LINK YOUR TRIP
www.lonelyplanet.com/trip-planner

48 Hours in Nashville

WHY GO With the grinning, irascible charm of the high-school bad boy (or girl), Nashville will spin you around and leave your ears ringing with the sound of steel guitar. But the city's got its brainy side too, with great museums, grand old government buildings and a diverse university community.

TIME
2 days

BEST TIME TO GO
Mar – Jun

START
Nashville, TN

END
Nashville, TN

ALSO GOOD FOR

HISTORY & CULTURE

Nashville has been the center of the country music industry since the 1920s, attracting countless young musicians hoping to be discovered at an open-mic night and cut a deal in the studios out on Music Row. Head directly to downtown's ❶ Country Music Hall of Fame & Museum, a must-see, where artifacts like Elvis' gold Cadillac and Johnny Cash's guitar are enshrined like religious relics. Written exhibits trace country's roots from the banjo-pickin' "old time" hillbillies of the early-20th century through to the tattooed and pierced alt-country stars of today. Walk-in listening booths give you access to the Country Music Foundation's vast archives. When you're done, catch the shuttle to Studio B to tour the historic RCA studio on Music Row, birthplace of the slick, highly produced Nashville Sound of the 1960s. Elvis recorded "Are You Lonesome Tonight" here, the Everly Brothers cut "When Will I be Loved," and Roy Orbison warbled "Only the Lonely" and "Crying."

Next, visit the District, the area of Lower Broadway and Second Ave. It's famous for beer- and guitar-fueled nightlife, rib joints, dusty vintage guitar shops and record stores staffed by mad-eyed clerks who can recite the Top 40 hits from the first week in July, 1962. And yes, there's a Hard Rock Café and a Hooters as well. Take in the neon-lit honky-tonks, the crowds of tourists in painfully new cowboy boots, and the kid on the corner singing his heart out on a battered Dreadnaught guitar.

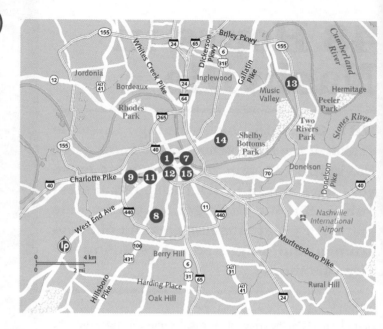

Cobblestone-paved ❷ **Printer's Alley**, now lined with bars and restaurants, used to be home to the city's thriving printing industry. Beginning in the early 1800s, horse carts carried paper and ink to the alley's publishing houses, many of which printed religious literature. The printing of Christian hymnals gave way to secular music publishing, which helped attract large record labels to town in the 1940s and '50s.

Two blocks over on Fifth Ave North, take a look at the 1849 ❸ **Downtown Presbyterian Church**, one of the best examples of Egyptian Revival Architecture in the country – you can pop inside during daylight hours to see the towering painted columns and winged-sun and lotus-leaf carvings.

Down the steep steps behind the capital building is the ❹ **Nashville Farmers Market**, running alongside Bicentennial Park. Here, government employees chow on sloppy gyros and jerk chicken in the indoor food hall. The line is always long at Swetts, the farmers market outpost of the popular Clifton Ave soul-food café. Try the squash casserole and peach cobbler. Though the market is large – 16 acres of plants, fruits and vegetables, specialty markets and a weekend flea market – it still feels like a bit of a secret. Just browsing the covered plant stands is a nice respite from downtown crowds, especially when it's hot.

Down along the banks of the Cumberland River, ❺ **Fort Nashborough** is a reconstruction of the late-18th-century wooden fort of the settlement that later became Nashville. The surrounding waterfront park is a pleasant place to sit for a spell.

Though most of the downtown shops are souvenir junk, there are a few gems: if it's cowboy boots you're looking for, try Boot Corral off I-65 a little north of town – no atmosphere, but a great selection and a heck of a lot cheaper.

6 Hatch Show Print is one of the oldest letter-print shops in the country, printing promotional posters since the early days of vaudeville. Their very first commission was a handbill announcing an appearance of Reverend Henry Ward Beecher, brother of Harriet Beecher Stowe, the author of the history-changing anti-slavery novel *Uncle Tom's Cabin*. Here, you can pick up old-fashioned cut-block prints advertising long-dead country stars for as little as $10. They also do custom orders, in case you've got a big gig coming up.

NASHVILLE ON FILM

Like Hollywood, Nashville symbolizes the hope for a magical future. Filmmakers have been capturing the city's glittery lure for decades. Here are some of our favorite Nashville films:

- *Nashville* – This 1975 Robert Altman masterpiece casts a jaundiced eye at the winners and losers in the country music biz
- *The Thing Called Love* – Samantha Mathis and River Phoenix portray aspiring singer-songwriters at the legendary Bluebird Café
- *Coalminer's Daughter* – Sissy Spacek's Loretta Lynn goes from Appalachian poverty to the Grand Ole Opry

Feel the hush descend as you step into the palatial, vaulted lobby of the **7** Hermitage Hotel, Nashville's first luxury hotel. Tallulah Bankhead, Al Capone and JFK stayed here, and legendary pool shark Minnesota Fats used to challenge guests at his own table on the mezzanine. Rooms have mahogany fixtures and deep, marble soaking tubs.

Hungry the next morning? Find out why there's always a line outside **8** Pancake Pantry, a well-loved West Nashville breakfast joint that serves up all kinds of flapjacks – sweet potato, buttermilk, chocolate chip – with a variety of sweet, gooey toppings like cinnamon syrup and raspberry cream.

Cross Vanderbilt University campus to Centennial Park, where you can gawk at a full-sized plaster model of the Athenian **9** Parthenon. This spectacular feat of kitsch was originally built for the 1897 Tennessee Centennial Exposition, and rebuilt in 1930 due to popular demand. It now houses a small art museum, but unless you've got time to kill, you should probably stick to snapping a picture outside so you can tell your friends you went to Greece.

Down the block is a strip of cafés, boutiques and music venues called Elliston Place, a favorite hangout of Vandy students and punk-rock teenagers. Check out **10** Elder's Bookstore, where Randy Elder still runs the store his father, Charlie, opened in the early 1930s. The dusty stacks are the go-to source for

Southern literature, and books on Nashville history and the Civil War. It's the kind of place where you can walk in looking for a novel and walk out three hours later with three hardcover histories on 19th-century guitar-making, an invitation to dinner at the house of a man known only as "the Professor," and a profound new understanding of speculative metaphysics.

LOCAL TREAT: GOO GOO CLUSTER

Take heart: this chocolate-coated clump of peanuts, marshmallow and caramel bears an unfortunate resemblance to a cow patty, but Nashville's favorite sweet tastes better than it looks. The Goo Goo was America's first combination candy bar, invented in 1912 at the Standard Candy Company on First Ave. Goo Goos, the unofficial candy of the Grand Ole Opry, are given away upon check-in at downtown's Millennium Maxwell House hotel.

Just off Elliston Place in a sprawling old mansion, ⓫ Cafe Coco has pie, veggie quesadillas and free wi-fi all day, every day. Watch live music and drink cheap longnecks at the back bar or shoot the breeze with the purple-haired philosophy majors chain-smoking on the patio at 4am.

Head back downtown and have a spiritual experience at ⓬ Ryman Auditorium, the former Union Gospel Tabernacle-turned-"Mother Church of Country Music." The soaring Gothic Revival building was commissioned in the late 1800s by crusty old riverboat captain Thomas Ryman, after his soul was saved by a popular Christian evangelist. These days, the 2000-seat Ryman hosts distinctly secular acts such as Lou Reed and cross-dressing comedian Eddie Izzard, as well as serving as the occasional home to the Grand Ole Opry. Check out the calendar in advance and catch a show here if you can. If not, the tour is neat for architecture and music history aficionados.

Speaking of the Opry, the venerable country music variety show's current HQ is a vast modern brick complex some 10 miles northeast of downtown. This area, known as Music Valley, is a sprawling suburban landscape of chain restaurants, themed budget motels and souvenir stores – if you need a Confederate flag shot glass, commemorative Dolly Parton T-shirt or banjo-shaped ashtray, this is the place.

"The walls of the theatrically grimy dive are paved with old photographs and handbills."

Since so little of downtown is actually on the water, it's easy to forget that Nashville is a riverfront city. Remedy that with a ride on the ⓭ General Jackson Showboat. Day and evening cruises on the 300ft paddlewheel riverboat can include everything from breakfast buffets to glittery music and dance extravaganzas. Sure, it's gaudy. But it's a theatrical good time and offers amazing views of the Nashville skyline (the pointy eared "bat building" dominating the horizon is the BellSouth tower). Tours depart from the Opryland complex in Music Valley.

For dinner, skip over to the up-and-coming East Side, where **14** Margot Cafe has become a favorite with local foodies for its creative touch with rustic French and Italian dishes. Think shad roe and Parmesan polenta, veal chops with morel risotto, and Riesling ice cream. The cozy space, with its low light and exposed brick walls, is an oasis in what's still a rather gritty area.

By evening time, you can just wander up and down Broadway, pausing outside any bar to listen to whoever's on the early stage. Don't like what you hear? Just move along; on any given evening you've got your pick of dozens of acts – most places start with the up-and-comers in the late afternoon and move on to bigger names as the night goes on. But whatever you do, you should not miss spending an hour or two at **15** Tootsie's Orchid Lounge, the purple-painted queen of downtown nightlife. Hattie "Tootsie" Bess bought the joint, then called Mom's, in 1960 and began a long career of nurturing up-and-coming country stars like Waylon Jennings and Faron Young, calling them her "chill'un" and letting them pay for their beer in IOUs. The walls of the theatrically grimy dive are paved with old photographs and handbills from the glory days of the Nashville Sound, but the music on Tootsie's two stages is as fresh as ever.

> **DETOUR**
>
> The 444-mile scenic **Natchez Trace Parkway** starts about 25 miles southwest of Nashville, just off Hwy 100. Drive under a canopy of hickory trees as you wind your way through the sun-dappled limestone hills. Originally a footpath for Ohio River boatmen returning home after delivering goods to Natchez, Mississippi, the Trace passes through old Choctaw and Chickasaw territory. There are three campsites (no cost) along the way, as well as a number of bike and hiking trails.

Emily Matchar

TRIP INFORMATION

GETTING THERE

From Memphis, take I-40 E for about 200 miles, exiting at 86 B onto I-24 E towards Chattanooga. Take exit 48 towards State Capital.

DO

Country Music Hall of Fame & Museum

This shrine to the most American of musical genres was designed to look like a piano. ☎ 615-416-2001; www.countrymusichalloffame.com; 222 5th Ave S, Nashville; adult/child $18/10; ☽ 9am-5pm

Elder's Bookstore

Find books on Southern history and more at this Elliston Place institution. ☎ 615-327-1867; www.eldersbookstore.com; 2115 Elliston Pl, Nashville; ☽ 10am-4:30pm Mon-Sat

General Jackson Showboat

Choose from a variety of Cumberland cruises on this old-fashioned paddleboat. ☎ 615-458-3900; www.generaljackson.com; 2812 Opryland Dr, Nashville; adult/child from $18/13

Hatch Show Print

Buy vintage music posters at this old-school printer, around since the late 1800s. ☎ 615-256-2805; www.hatchshowprint.com; 316 Broadway, Nashville; ☽ 9:30am-5:30pm

Ryman Auditorium

Once a church, this towering brick tabernacle is now one of America's most-loved music venues. ☎ 615-458-8700; www.ryman.com; 116 5th Ave N, Nashville; tours adult/child $13/6; ☽ 8am-4pm

Tootsie's Orchid Lounge

This two-story purple building is the queen of the Broadway honky-tonks. ☎ 615-726-7937; www.tootsies.net; 422 Broadway, Nashville; no cover; ☽ 10am-late

EAT & SLEEP

Cafe Coco

This 24-hour cafe is like the perfect college dorm, with munchies, wi-fi, music and easy conversation. ☎ 615-321-2626; www.cafecoco.com; 210 Louise Ave, Nashville; mains $6-10; ☽ 24hr

Hermitage Hotel

Luxuriate in the ornate, high-ceilinged lobby, plush rooms and an oak-paneled bar that resembles an English gentlemen's club. ☎ 615-244-3121, www.thehermitagehotel.com; 231 6th Ave N, Nashville; r from $279

Margot Cafe

French and Italian peasant dishes become sublime in the hands of chef Margot McCormack at this East Nashville favorite. ☎ 615-227-4668; www.margotcafe.com; 1017 Woodland St, Nashville; mains $14-22; ☽ 5pm-10pm Tue-Sat, brunch Sun

Nashville Farmers Market

Have Southern meatloaf or Szechuan noodles at the lunchtime food court, then browse the tomato plants. ☎ 615-880-2001; www.nashvillefarmersmarket.org; 900 8th Ave N, Nashville; mains $5-10; ☽ food court 11am-3pm

Pancake Pantry

Gorge on syrup-drenched chocolate chip, blueberry and sweet-potato pancakes at this always-crowded joint near Vanderbilt. ☎ 615-383-9333; 1796 21st Ave S, Nashville; mains $5-10; ☽ 6am-4pm; ⬤

USEFUL WEBSITES

www.nashvillescene.com
www.visitmusiccity.com

LINK YOUR TRIP

www.lonelyplanet.com/trip-planner

Country Music Capital: Nashville

HISTORY & CULTURE

WHY GO For country music lovers from Peoria to Poland, a trip to Nashville is the ultimate pilgrimage. Feel yourself drawn to the neon lights, smoky honky-tonks and glitter-spangled extravaganzas like a moth to a flame. Country is not the most popular American musical genre for nothing.

TIME
2 days

BEST TIME TO GO
Jun – Sep

START
Nashville, TN

END
Nashville, TN

ALSO GOOD FOR

CITY

Start your Music City tour downtown, where the area of Lower Broadway and 2nd Ave, known as the District, is lined with honky-tonks, record stores and souvenir shops. Every bartender and diner waitress here has a story, about how Willie Nelson used to write lyrics on a napkin in the corner, or the time Elvis dropped by for a glass of milk.

Your first stop should be the ❶ **Country Music Hall of Fame & Museum**, which takes up a full city block. "Honor Thy Music" is the museum's motto, reflecting the near-Biblical importance of country music to Nashville's soul. The building, designed to look like a piano keyboard, contains written exhibits tracing country music's history from twangy hillbilly music to the slick Nashville Sound of the 1960s to today's alt-country. See thousands of artifacts, such as Elvis' gold Caddy and Maybelle Carter's Gibson L-5, and duck into private sound booths to listen to tracks from the Country Music Foundation's extensive archives. For a few extra dollars you can purchase an audio tour narrated by contemporary country stars like Vince Gill and Dolly Parton. Or you could go for the full package deal, which includes a trip to Ryman Auditorium and shuttle bus to RCA's Studio B, where Elvis recorded "Are You Lonesome Tonight."

A few blocks away is the other musical giant of downtown Nashville: ❷ **Ryman Auditorium**. It was built in 1890 by born-again riverboat captain Thomas Ryman to hold religious revivals, and was home to

BEST TRIP

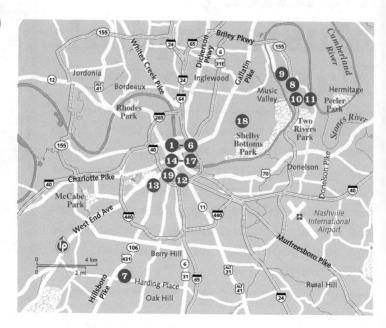

the Grand Ole Opry from 1943 to 1974. Today, the biggest names in country, rock and comedy play the Ryman, and if you can snag one of the 2000 seats, you most definitely should. While you can walk into the lobby during the day, auditorium tours are by ticket only.

Pick up a rare Dock Boggs banjo record at the ❸ **Ernest Tubb Record Shop**, the place for country and bluegrass albums since 1947. Opened by country impresario Ernest Tubb, the shop was the original home of the Midnite Jamboree, the second-longest-running radio program in America. It's now broadcast from the Texas Troubadour Theater, but you can catch it on Saturday nights on 650-AM.

Down the block is ❹ **Gruhn Guitars**, one of the top vintage instrument stores in the world. Chat with ultra-knowledgeable staff about the funky customized Gibsons and $25,000 antique fiddles. Then swing by ❺ **Hatch Show Print** for a vintage letterpress concert poster, the definitive Nashville souvenir.

Dine like a record exec at the white tablecloth ❻ **Capitol Grille** in the Hermitage Hotel, a throwback to the days of three-martini lunches and post-prandial cigars. Indulge in old-school favorites like giant Caesar salads and steak frites.

In the evening make the pilgrimage to the ❼ **Bluebird Cafe**, tucked away in a suburban strip mall. This is most decidedly *not* the place for boot stomping or yee-haws. Guests sit sedately at reserved tables, eating or sipping cocktails as they watch singer-songwriters pour out their souls on the tiny stage. Wannabe acoustic country performers absolutely have to play the Bluebird on their way up – their struggles are dramatized in the 1993 River Phoenix movie *The Thing Called Love*, filmed here. Be warned, management *will* kick you out for talking during the show. Open-mic night is legendary.

Unfortunately, visiting some of Nashville's big attractions means braving the sprawling suburban wasteland of cheap motels and chain restaurants known as Music Valley, 10 miles northeast of downtown. It ain't pretty, but, in the right spirit, it can be fun.

The ❽ **Willie Nelson Museum**, in the back of a faux-Western storefront souvenir shop, is a testament to the Redheaded Stranger's inability (or unwillingness) to pay his taxes. When the IRS seized Nelson's estate in 1990 he had no choice but to sell most of his worldly goods to the museum. The result is a bizarre collection of items, from signed guitars to ratty T-shirts. Nearby, the ❾ **Music Valley Wax Museum**, with its zombie Elvis and Minnie Pearl, rewards hardcore kitsch aficionados.

PLAYLIST ♫♪ You can't swing a chicken in Nashville without hitting an award-winning musician. Here are a few of our favorite Music City tunes from the 1930s on.

- "Crazy," Patsy Cline
- "Friends in Low Places," Garth Brooks
- "Honky Tonk Blues," Hank Williams
- "Mamas, Don't Let Your Babies Grow up to be Cowboys," Willie Nelson
- "Oh, Pretty Woman," Roy Orbison
- "Passionate Kisses," Lucinda Williams
- "Ring of Fire," Johnny Cash
- "Wabash Cannonball," Roy Acuff

The ❿ **Opry Entertainment Complex** consists of several contemporary buildings around a brick plaza. The Grand Ole Opry House is home to the legendary country music variety show on Tuesday, Friday and Saturday. The performances, which nearly always include at least one big name act, are wonderful kitschy-yet-sincere fun. Next door, the Acuff Theater, named after songwriter and founder of the Acuff-Rose music publishing firm Roy Acuff, hosts other country performances. Across the way, the Grand Ole Opry Museum has a free self-guided tour of Opry history, with hilarious life-size dioramas featuring wax figures of country stars in realistic period settings (check out the orange carpet in the model of Marty Robbins' 1970s Nashville office).

Even if you don't stay at the ⓫ **Opryland Hotel**, you've got to come gawk at the massive man-made environment, a sort of fake Delta river town under glass. Ride a flatboat through an artificial river, where musicians and comedians perform on giant lily pad stages, and snap photos of the indoor waterfalls. If you do stay, get a room with a balcony overlooking the atrium.

HISTORY & CULTURE

Head back into town for some rib-stickin' goodness at **12** **Arnold's Country Kitchen**, where meat n' threes like meatloaf with collards, fried green tomatoes and candied yams are served with both baked and griddle-cooked cornbread.

All the major record labels have offices here, many of them near the intersection of Demonbreun and Division Sts, an area known as **13** **Music Row**. Though there's not much to see on Music Row, if you're dying to lay down your own tracks this is the place – smaller studios charge between $25 and $100 an hour for personal recording sessions. Be aware that you get what you pay for.

Gear up for a long night of honky-tonk hopping. You can hear world-class bands every night of the week in the District, along with literally thousands of up-and-comers who play cheap early shows and pick out chords on the street corners, hoping against hope to be "discovered." The purple walls at **14** **Tootsie's Orchid Lounge** have borne witness to 50 years of Nashville history; it's a good place to start or end the night. **15** **Robert's Western World** is good for burgers, beer, booze and boots (seriously, you can buy cowboy boots here). Its house band, Brazilbilly, does country with a pinch of Latin heat. A mixed-age crowd whoops it up at the multilevel **16** **Wildhorse Saloon**, with its vast dance floor and free, nightly line-dancing lessons. **17** **Bourbon Street Blues & Boogie Bar**, down Printers Alley, has a rum-soaked party vibe and hip-wiggling blues.

COUNTRY'S COMING OF AGE

Country music was not born in Nashville, but it came of age here – until the 1920s it was called "old time" or "hillbilly" music. In 1925, Nashville began hosting a live radio program, *Barn Dance*, broadcast from the National Life & Accident Insurance Company building downtown. The show, which later became known as the *Grand Ole Opry*, set the foundations of the modern country music industry, drawing stars like Roy Acruff and Minnie Pearl. Music studios soon followed.

Over the river in East Nashville, the **18** **Family Wash** is a hip gastropub with live music in a former corner Laundromat. Make a pit stop here for a late-ish dinner of chorizo pizza and a pint of Hefeweizen, and dig the hyper-charged neo-country of former David Bowie guitarist Reeves Gabrels. Double back to finish out the night at the **19** **Station Inn**, just south of downtown. Inside this anonymous stone building is one of the country's top bluegrass and acoustic music venues.

Emily Matchar

HISTORY &
CULTURE

TRIP INFORMATION

GETTING THERE
From Memphis, take I-40 East for about 200 miles, exiting at 86 B onto I-24 East. Take exit 48 towards State Capital.

DO

Country Music Hall of Fame & Museum
See Elvis' gold Cadillac at this comprehensive museum of country history. ☎ 615-416-2001; www.countrymusichalloffame.com; 222 5th Ave S, Nashville; adult/child $18/10, with Studio B tour $26/18; ⊗ 9am-5pm

Ernest Tubb Record Shop
A giant neon guitar sign marks the spot for this bluegrass and country record shop. ☎ 615-255-7503; www.etrecordshop.com; 417 Broadway, Nashville; ⊗ 9am-10pm Sun-Thu, to midnight Fri & Sat

Gruhn Guitars
This renowned vintage instrument store has an expert staff and some mind-bogglingly pricey guitars and fiddles. ☎ 615-256-2033; www.gruhn.com; 400 Broadway, Nashville; ⊗ 9:30am-5:30pm Mon-Sat

Hatch Show Print
Take home a vintage concert poster, a classic Nashville souvenir, from one of America's oldest letterpress printers. ☎ 615-256-2805; www.hatchshowprint.com; 316 Broadway, Nashville; ⊗ 9:30am-5:30pm

Music Valley Wax Museum
See eerie, corpse-like replicas of your favorite country stars grinning under fluorescent lights at this kitschy attraction. ☎ 615-884-7876; 2515 McGavock Pike, Nashville; adult/child $9/6; ⊗ 9am-7pm Mon-Sat, to 6pm Sun

Opry Entertainment Complex
Yee-haw at a performance of the Grand Ole Opry, or check out the free on-site museum. ☎ 615-871-6779; www.opry.com; 2802 Opryland Dr, Nashville; Opry admission $34-51; tours $10; museum free; ⊗ box office 10am-5pm Mon-Sat; museum 10:30am-6pm Mar-Nov

Ryman Auditorium
This former gospel tabernacle is now an awe-inspiring music venue, attracting big-name acts. ☎ 615-458-8700; www.ryman.com; 116 5th Ave N, Nashville; tours adult/child $13/6; ⊗ 8am-4pm

Willie Nelson Museum
Just call it the "everything-but-Willie-Nelson's-used-toothbrush" museum, compiled of items sold to pay off Willie's IRS debts. ☎ 615-885-1515; www.willienelsongeneralstore.com; 2613 McGavock Pike, Nashville; adult/child $5/3; ⊗ 9am-5pm, to 9pm May-Sep

EAT & SLEEP

Arnold's Country Kitchen
This squat bungalow specializes in delightfully greasy Southern meat n' threes like chicken with collards, yams and fried squash. ☎ 615-256-4455; 605 8th Ave S, Nashville; mains $4-7; ⊗ 10:30am-3pm Mon-Fri; ⚐

Capitol Grille
Eat dry-aged steak with Nashville government mucky-mucks and Music Row execs in the posh Hermitage Hotel. ☎ 888-888-9414; www.thehermitagehotel.com; 261 6th Ave N, Nashville; mains $16-80; ⊗ 11am-2pm & 5:30pm-10pm

Family Wash
Try the shepherd's pie or a creatively topped pizza at this neighborhood bistro and live-music venue. ☎ 615-226-6070; www.family wash.com; 2038 Greenwood Ave, Nashville; mains $9-15; ⊗ 6pm-midnight Tue-Sat

Opryland Hotel
This enormous Dixie-themed hotel has nearly 3000 rooms and a fake indoor river complete with a paddleboat. ☎ 615-889-1000; www .gaylordhotels.com; 2800 Opryland Dr, Nashville; r from $200; ⚐

DRINK & LISTEN

Bluebird Cafe
In a suburban strip mall, the Bluebird is legendary for plucking singer-songwriters out of obscurity. ☎ 615-383-1461; www .bluebirdcafe.com; 4104 Hillsboro Rd, Nashville; admission free-$15; ⊗ early/late show 6pm/9:30pm most nights

Bourbon Street Blues & Boogie Bar
The city's premier blues venue, with a kickin' New Orleans vibe, is tucked away in tiny Printers Alley. ☎ 615-242-5837; www.bourbonstreetblues.com; 220 Printers Alley, Nashville; admission free-$10; ⊙4pm-3am

Robert's Western World
Have a burger, drink a beer, or buy a pair of boots at this divey favorite, with a house band called Brazilbilly. ☎ 615-244-9552; www.robertswesternworld.com; 416 Broadway, Nashville; admission free; ⊙11am-3am

Station Inn
South of downtown, this unassuming stone building is the best place in Nashville for serious bluegrass. ☎ 615-255-3307; www.stationinn.com; 402 12th Ave S, Nashville; admission $5-20; ⊙7pm-late

Tootsie's Orchid Lounge
The legendary Tootsie Bess once presided over this purple-painted honky-tonk, which is still a rowdy good time. ☎ 615-726-7937; www.tootsies.net; 422 Broadway, Nashville; admission free; ⊙10am-late

Wildhorse Saloon
Stomp your boots with the wild, mixed-age crowd at this multi-level club, a favorite with enthusiastic line dancers. ☎ 615-902-8200; www.wildhorsesaloon.com; 120 2nd Ave S, Nashville; admission $10-45; ⊙11am-1am Tue-Thu, from 5pm Mon, open later weekends

USEFUL WEBSITES
www.visitmusiccity.com

LINK YOUR TRIP
www.lonelyplanet.com/trip-planner

Tennessee Oddities

WHY GO Think Tennessee's all about big-hair country music and rural mountain towns straight out of a Dolly Parton ballad? After a day of indie rock and pink bouffant wigs in Nashville, and a trip out to the world's most famous whiskey distillery, you'll be singing a different tune.

TIME
2 days

DISTANCE
115 miles

BEST TIME TO GO
Mar – Jun

START
Nashville , TN

END
Lynchburg, TN

ALSO GOOD FOR

In Nashville, non-country music types will find a home on ❶ **Elliston Place**, an artsy enclave near the Vanderbilt University campus. In the middle of rapidly gentrifying Midtown/West Nashville, this hip little street is home to tattoo parlors, vintage clothing shops, coffee bars and a variety of restaurants and cafés – from haute Asian bistros to vintage student dives. At night, Elliston Place is your best bet for indie and rock music. ❷ **Exit/In** has been featuring great live rock and comic performances since 1971 – a then-unknown Jimmy Buffet was a popular early act, as was the young Steve Martin.

For new and used records, ❸ **Grimey's**, a couple of miles away on 8th Ave South, is known for its selection of CDs, vinyl and DVDs, including hard-to-find independent releases. Down the back stairs is ❹ **The Basement**, its exposed pipes hung with tapestries and old Persian rugs like an art student's cellar apartment. Up-and-coming indie acts play cheap shows most nights; bigger-name acts occasionally pack the tiny subterranean space.

For a spot of shopping, the 12th Ave South area, a couple of miles south of downtown, has an eclectic mix of boutiques, antiques shops, and home and garden stores, in a leafy, semi-residential neighborhood. Housed in a squat, 1970s bungalow with a retro, stone facade, ❺ **Katy K's Ranch Dressing** holds the mother lode of kitschy, oversized belt buckles, vintage cowboy boots and pink bouffant wigs – perfect for the rockabilly drag queen in us all. Also check out new

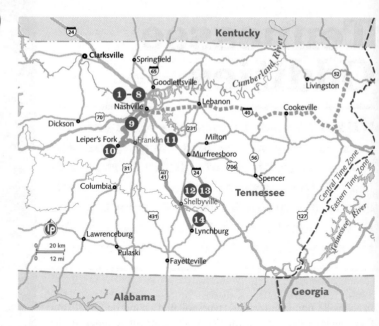

men's and women's clothes designed by Katy K, aka Parsons-educated ex-New Yorker and store owner Katy Kattelman. On a hot day (or even on a cold one) the upscale ice pops at ⑥ **Las Paletas** are an incredible treat, in flavors like chocolate-chili and hibiscus. It's tucked away in a small shopping complex not far from Katy K's.

> *"Go up to the hole in the kitchen wall and order a medium-hot leg quarter."*

For dinner, it's time to take a trip to a crumbling strip mall in the North Nashville badlands. Here, at ⑦ **Prince's Hot Chicken**, the line often snakes out the door. Go up to the hole in the kitchen wall and order a medium-hot leg quarter, extra bread and a side of baked beans. You may have to wait up to an hour, but it's worth it for the most incredible cayenne-laced fried chicken, fried up in an ancient cast-iron skillet and served with two slices of grease-soaked white bread and a couple of pickles. The medium-hot is pleasantly painful; extra-hot is like chomping down on a live wire.

Heading downtown on Broadway takes you into the heart of the country music world – an explosion of honky-tonks, rib joints and cowboy boot stores. Even if you're not a fan, it's fun to see the neon and glitz and awed tourists. Here, the ⑧ **Union Station Hotel** rises like a castle over Broadway. This Romanesque building was Nashville's train station back in the days when train travel was a glamorous affair. Timetables for trains that chugged out of the station 100 years ago are painted over the reception desk in the 65ft vaulted lobby.

In the morning, head southwest out of the city for breakfast at the **9** **Loveless Cafe**. Yeah, you can get cheaper biscuits and eggs elsewhere, but eating in the packed dining room at this big sunny roadhouse is a tradition with travelers about to set off down the scenic Natchez Trace Parkway.

Drive the hickory shaded Parkway for 15 miles or so before swinging northeast through the rural community of Leiper's Fork, where you can see live bluegrass on Friday night at **10** **Puckett's Grocery**. This restaurant and venue is no rural country store; hip types from Nashville and beyond come down to munch sweet-potato fries and watch frequently sold-out shows. Head on into the town of **11** **Franklin**, which cultivates its lost-in-time vibe with restored plantation homes and antebellum B&Bs.

From there, it's about an hour to **12** **Shelbyville**, home of the handsome, high-stepping Tennessee Walking Horse. A festival in honor of the breed has been held here every September since 1939. **13** **Clearview Horse Farm** offers trail rides through the patchwork pastureland and oak forests of Middle Tennessee.

Then on to the **14** **Jack Daniel's Distillery** in tiny Lynchburg. Here, an hour-long tour shows you how the iconic whiskey, made from local cave water, is filtered through layers of charcoal and aged in oak barrels, the same way it's been done since 1866. Tour guides – one of the favorites goes by the name of "Goose" – are slow-drawling Southerners with arsenals of country-fried anecdotes. Local laws ban liquor sales in the county, so no free samples of Old No 7. Is that not the very definition of irony?

Emily Matchar

ASK A LOCAL

"We love watching the *Doyle and Debbie Show*, Tuesday night at the **Station Inn**. It's kinda like hee-haw meets *This is Spinal Tap*. Also, having a big ol' Southern country breakfast on Saturday, and **Monell's** in Germantown, and getting ice cream at the **Pied Piper** in East Nashville. There's Banana Fanna Fo Fudding, Minty Python and its top-seller, Trailer Trash."

Sheri Lynn & Brenda Kay (the "Jugg Sisters"), NashTrash (www.nashtrash.com) tour guides, Nashville

DETOUR

Betamax cassettes, vintage crystal ashtrays, stuffed armadillos. One man's trash is another's treasure at the annual **World's Longest Yard Sale** (www.127sale.com), stretching 630 miles and five states, from Gadsden, Alabama to Defiance, Ohio. The four-day sale spans the 127 Corridor, with vendors hawking their wares from blankets and picnic tables for a slow-moving herd of festive-spirited buyers. Headquarters is in Jamestown, Tennessee, about two hours east of Nashville.

TRIP INFORMATION

GETTING THERE

From Memphis, take I-40 East for about 200 miles, exiting at 86b onto I-24 E towards Chattanooga. Take exit 48 towards State Capital and merge onto Interstate Dr.

DO

Basement, The

Check out local indie shows in a subterranean space beneath Grimey's records. ☎ 615-254-8006; www.thebasementnashville.com; 1604 8th Ave S, Nashville; ⏰ times & prices vary

Clearview Horse Farm

Take a trail ride or a private lesson at this farm in the middle of Tennessee's horse country. ☎ 931-684-8822; www.clearview horsefarme.com; 2291 Hwy 231 S, Shelby-ville; trail rides from $35

Exit/In

This loveably beat-up venue has been an alternative to downtown's big-hair country since 1971, with rock, punk, metal and more. ☎ 615-321-3340; www.exitin.com; 2208 Elliston Pl, Nashville; tickets $5-15; ⏰ most shows start 8pm

Grimey's

Buy the latest Kings of Leon on vinyl at this well-worn independent record shop. ☎ 615-254-4801; www.grimeys.com; 1604 8th Ave S, Nashville; ⏰ 11am-8pm Mon-Sat, 1pm-6pm Sun

Jack Daniel's Distillery

Tour the bucolic campus of America's oldest registered distillery. ☎ 931-759-6180; www.jackdaniels.com; 182 Lynchburg Hwy, Lynch-burg; admission free; ⏰ 9am-4:30pm

Katy K's Ranch Dressing

This boutique specializes in vintage glitter with a country accent. ☎ 615-297-4242; www.katyk.com; 2407 12th Ave S, Nashville; ⏰ 11am-6pm Mon-Fri, from noon Sat, 1pm-5pm Sun

Puckett's Grocery

This old country market and restaurant has live music most Fridays and Saturdays; some shows by reservation only. ☎ 615-794-1308; www.puckettsgrocery.com; 4142 Old Hillsboro Rd, Leiper's Fork; shows free-$15; ⏰ 6am-6pm Sun, to 7pm or 8pm Mon-Thu, later Fri & Sat

EAT & SLEEP

Las Paletas

The Mexican-style hibiscus or rice pudding popsicles from this minimalist shop are must-have treats. ☎ 615-386-2101; 2907 12th Ave S, Nashville; popsicles $2; ⏰ noon-7pm Tue-Sat

Loveless Cafe

This well-loved rural roadhouse serves biscuits and fried chicken, and sells cutesy Southern souvenirs. ☎ 615-646-9700; www.lovelesscafe.com; 8400 Hwy 100, Nashville; dishes $8-17; ⏰ 7am-9pm

Prince's Hot Chicken

Mind-blowingly spicy fried chicken is well worth braving the seedy location and long wait. ☎ 615-226-9442; 123 Ewing Dr, Nash-ville; mains $4-8; ⏰ noon-10pm Tue-Thu, to 4am Fri & Sat

Union Station Hotel

This castle-like former train station has crisp, contemporary guest rooms. ☎ 615-726-1001; www.unionstationhotelnashville.com; 1001 Broadway; r from $200

USEFUL WEBSITES

www.franklin-gov.com
www.visitmusiccity.com

LINK YOUR TRIP

www.lonelyplanet.com/trip-planner

Outdoor Chattanooga

WHY GO Surrounded by wide rivers and soaring sandstone cliffs, Chattanooga has become a destination for outdoor adventurers. Philip Grymes, director of Outdoor Chattanooga, lets us in on his favorite hiking, biking, paddling and climbing spots, and tells us where to relax with a beer at the end of an adrenaline-pumping day.

TIME
2 days

BEST TIME TO GO
Mar – May

START
Chattanooga, TN

END
Chattanooga, TN

ALSO GOOD FOR

OFFBEAT

"We live in a wonderfully remodeled town," says Philip Grymes, a wilderness guide who has made his career supporting Chattanooga's green renaissance. Called "the dirtiest city in America" in the 1960s, Chattanooga has cleaned up its act. The decaying industrial downtown has been completely transformed, with blocks of renovated warehouse lofts and grassy public parks. "The waterfront is always active," Grymes says. "You'll have large cruiser boats moored against the bank and above them, on the greens, will be people on bikes, people pushing baby strollers, picnicking on the lawns and throwing Frisbees."

The waterfront means the banks of Tennessee River, which snakes through the city on its way to the Mississippi. To best enjoy the riverfront, Grymes suggests starting in ❶ Coolidge Park, across from Chattanooga's Riverwalk. There's an interactive fountain for kids to play, a carousel and a 50ft-climbing wall attached to one of the limestone columns supporting the Walnut Street Bridge – a popular pedestrian span connecting downtown to the North Shore neighborhood.

Fuel up on the North Shore at ❷ Aretha Frankensteins, an all-day breakfast joint in a lopsided, turquoise cottage. Try the Elephants Gerald, a Belgian waffle topped with ice cream and pecans. Or just have a beer on the porch and shoot the breeze with the hipsters from the neighborhood.

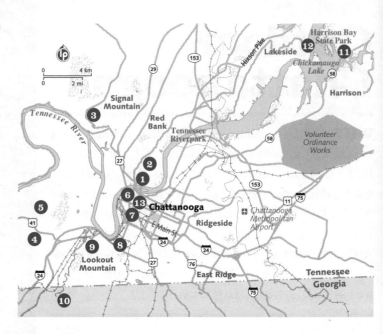

For a secluded hike, try the Rainbow Lake trail on **3** **Signal Mountain**, about 15 minutes to the northwest. "Start at the parking lot trailhead and walk through mountain laurel and rhododendron, past large boulders, and across a beautiful mountain creek," says Grymes. This area has a number of other primo trails, including a section of the Cumberland Trail, which when completed should cover 11 counties and 300 miles.

OUTDOOR CHATTANOOGA

Formerly filthy, Chattanooga's commitment to the outdoors and the environment runs deep. The city has even created a special agency, **Outdoor Chattanooga** (www.outdoor chattanooga.com), to promote an active lifestyle. Sign up for one of its many events, like Tennessee River kayaking trips and Civil War battlefield bike tours. Its helpful website has a full rundown of local recreation opportunities, with maps and directions to area hiking, fishing, rafting and climbing spots.

Southwest of town, **4** **Raccoon Mountain Caverns** appeals to both day trippers who don't want to get their feet muddy and more adventurous souls. Grymes suggests the "wild tour," where you strap on a spelunker helmet and go off-trail in the undeveloped portions of the cave, wiggling through narrow tunnels and marveling at a 75ft subterranean waterfall. You can even bunk down underground on special overnight tours. Raccoon Mountain also has fantastic mountain-biking trails. Ride around the Tennessee Valley Authority's **5** **Pumped Storage Plant**, a vast reservoir high atop the mountain. The singletrack trails, built by local bike groups, range from intermediate to extreme. Non-cyclists can hike the same trails and take in the stunning views. "Watch the Tennessee River 1000ft below you as it carves through the Cumberland Plateau," Grymes says.

After a sweaty day, Grymes recommends hoisting a cold one at the ⑥ **Big River Grille & Brewing Works**, near the waterfront. Here, a "young-oriented, active crowd" chows down on pizza, ribs and hearty salads and listens to live bluegrass and alt-country. To sleep, try the fun (but not corny) train-themed ⑦ **Chattanooga Choo-Choo Holiday Inn**, once the town's main railway terminal. The 24-acre complex includes 48 Victorian railcars-turned-guest rooms, a half dozen restaurants and a Gilded Age bar with a player piano.

Rock climbers adore Chattanooga's sandstone cliffs. The Tennessee, or T, Wall, northwest of the city, is the area's most famous climbing zone, but it's only for experienced traditional climbers. Less-advanced climbers should call the ⑧ **Tennessee Bouldering Authority** to set up a guided trip. "They'll take you to a beginner-oriented rockface like Sunset Rock," says Grymes, referring to a popular sandstone cliff in the Lookout Mountain area on the border with Georgia. ⑨ **Lookout Mountain** itself, 6 miles from downtown, has several classic attractions. A ticket will get you a ride to the top on the Incline Railway and admission to the Ruby Falls underground waterfall and the Rock City garden at the summit. And you can't leave Chattanooga without a tandem hang-gliding flight at the ⑩ **Lookout Mountain Flight Park**, just over the state line in Georgia, where you're pulled off the ground by an ultra-light aircraft and let loose to soar around above a beautiful valley.

THE CHATTANOOGA CHOO-CHOO

Post-Civil War, Chattanooga was a major manufacturing and railroad center, which made it a hip, bustling place to be. Glenn Miller immortalized the city's train culture in his 1941 hit "Chattanooga Choo-Choo" in the movie *Sun Valley Serenade*. While Chattanooga is no longer a railway hub, the **Tennessee Valley Railroad Museum** (www.tvrail.com) offers several old-fashioned train trips, including the 55-minute Missionary Ridge Local and the six-hour Chickamauga Turn.

For camping, head northeast of the city to ⑪ **Harrison Bay State Park**, where you can explore the thickly wooded shoreline of Chickamauga Lake, a reservoir created from the Tennessee River. "Fish for everything from your smallmouth and largemouth bass to crappie and catfish," Grymes suggests. On the opposite side of the lake in Hixson, TN, ⑫ **Chester Frost Park** has a sandy swim area.

To the northeast, the confluence of the Tennessee and Hiwassee Rivers is one of the best hidden gems in Chattanooga. "During the winter this is a stopover ground for more than 10,000 sandhill cranes and the site of dozens of bald eagles returning to their nesting grounds," Grymes says. Outdoor Chattanooga's ⑬ **OutVenture** program offers a sunset kayak tour of the area.
Emily Matchar

TRIP INFORMATION

GETTING THERE
From Nashville, take I-24 East for about 130 miles, taking exit 178 to merge onto Hwy 27 North towards Chattanooga.

DO

Chester Frost Park
This well-tended park has one of the few designated swimming areas on the Tennessee River. ☎ 423-842-0177; 2318 N Gold Point Cir, Hixson, TN

Lookout Mountain
See the world's longest underground waterfall and several dramatic cliff-top gardens and lookout points at this popular recreation area. ☎ 423-821-4224; www.lookoutmtn attractions.com; 827 East Brow Rd, Chattanooga; adult/child $38/19; ☽ varies by season

Lookout Mountain Flight Park
Fly tandem over the Lookout Valley, one of the country's most popular hang-gliding areas. ☎ 800-688-5637; www.hanglide .com; 7201 Scenic Hwy, Rising Fawn, GA; intro tandem flight $199

OutVenture
Go paddling on an Outdoor Chattanooga-sponsored river kayaking trip. ☎ 423-842-6629; www.outdoorchattanooga.com; 1250 Market St, Chattanooga; kayak trip from $25

Raccoon Mountain Caverns
Trips through the 5.5 miles of underground passageways range from 45 minutes to overnight. ☎ 423-821-9403; www.raccoon mountain.com; 319 West Hills Dr, Chattanooga; adult/child $13/6; ☽ call for reservations; ☦

Tennessee Bouldering Authority
Instructors from this indoor climbing gym lead guided trips to nearby sandstone cliffs. ☎ 423-822-6800; www.tbagym.com; 3804 Saint Elmo Ave # 102, Chattanooga; trips $150

EAT

Aretha Frankensteins
Hipsters and young local families dine on pancakes and beer on the porch of this funky North Shore cottage. ☎ 423-265-7685; 518 Tremont St, Chattanooga; mains $5-9; ☽ 7am-midnight; ☦

Big River Grille & Brewing Works
This rollicking brewpub attracts a 20- and 30-something crowd for burgers, brews and live music. ☎ 423-267-2739; www.bigriver grille.com; 222 Broad St, Chattanooga; mains $10-20; ☽ 11am-midnight Sun-Thu, to 2am Fri & Sat

SLEEP

Chattanooga Choo-Choo Holiday Inn
Book one of the refurbished train cars at this bustling hotel complex, in the town's old railway terminal. ☎ 423-266-5000, 800-872-2529; www.choochoo.com; 1400 Market St; r from $119, railcars $169; ☦

Harrison Bay State Park
Camp at one of the 27 campsites in this lakeside wilderness. ☎ 423-344-7966; 8411 Harrison Bay Rd, Harrison, TN; campsite $25; ☦ ☯

USEFUL WEBSITES
www.chattanoogafun.com
www.outdoorchattanooga.com

LINK YOUR TRIP
www.lonelyplanet.com/trip-planner

Mammoth Cave

WHY GO Gawk at the monstrous stone chambers, alien-looking rock formations and bottomless pits of the world's most extensive cave system. Toss in a trip to the Bowling Green Corvette factory and a night at a wigwam-themed motel, and you've got yourself an old-fashioned American road trip.

So you're driving through the Green River valley of central Kentucky, admiring the leafy countryside, the quiet rolling hills. You turn onto Park City Rd, not another car in sight. Then onto Mammoth Cave Parkway, passing under the shady branches of sugar maples and sycamores, the hum of your engine the only sound.

Then...bam! You're in the parking lot of the ❶ **Mammoth Cave National Park**. A thousand cars bake in the hot sun as visitors from all over the world kill time before their scheduled cave tour. A family of Spanish tourists snaps pictures of each other in various poses in front of the park sign, a Vietnamese mother doles out peanut M&Ms to her three bored children. As many as 7000 visitors come to the park every day, more than 2 million visitors a year. It's like the UN, in the middle of nowhere.

The only way to visit the cave is through one of the daily ranger-guided tours. Buy tickets at the visitors center, choosing from nearly 20 tours of the cave's 360 miles of surveyed passageway. Tours range from 30 minutes to 6½ hours; reserve in advance so you don't have to wait. The nearly 20 options include the ❷ **Violet City Lantern Tour**, recreating the experience of visiting the cave in the 1800s, the ❸ **Wild Cave Tour**, belly crawling through tight passageways and scrambling over jagged rocks, and the ❹ **Grand Avenue Tour** through the caves' biggest interior cathedrals and elaborate crystalline gypsum formations.

TIME
2 days

DISTANCE
50 miles

BEST TIME TO GO
May – Sep

START
Mammoth Cave NP, KY

END
Bowling Green, KY

ALSO GOOD FOR

HISTORY & CULTURE

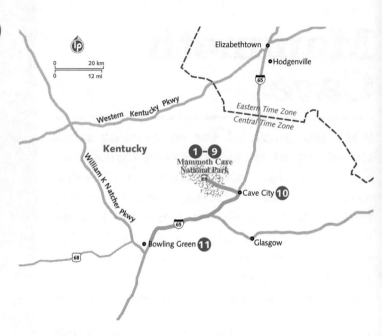

The fascinating **5** **Historic Tour** takes you through man's oft-troubled relationship with the cave.

The oldest parts of Mammoth began forming 10 million years ago. Native Americans discovered it around 2000 BC, entering to gather minerals and leaving behind slippers, gourd bowls and pottery. Tourists have been visiting the caves since the early 1800s, with guided tours offered since 1816, making it one of the oldest tourist attractions in America.

THE CAVE WARS

By the 1920s, Mammoth Cave had become such a popular attraction that everyone wanted a piece of the action and the so-called "Cave Wars" broke out. Local farmers with smaller caves on their properties began advertising their own tours, even diverting travelers headed to Mammoth by claiming it was flooded or quarantined. Other landowners blasted open new entrances to Mammoth and set up shop.

As you walk through the narrow passageways and vast chambers, a ranger in a wide-brimmed hat and tan uniform will regale you with stories of the cave's strange history: Over here are the wooden pipelines. Here are the remains of the saltpeter works, where slaves mined calcium nitrate for gunpowder, to be used against the British in the War of 1812. Here's a room known as the Church, where in the 1830s a young minister preached hellfire and brimstone to his congregation from atop a natural ledge called Pulpit Rock, his voice echoing in the lantern-lit gloom. Here's the old TB sanitarium where cave owner Dr John Croghan brought 16 tuberculosis patients in the winter of 1941. Dead bats and the corpses of some Native Americans remained for years in the cave without decaying, so the air must have some vital properties, Croghan figured. Tour groups would pass the patients lying in stone huts in their dressing gowns, growing paler by the day. Soon the patients began to die, their bodies laid out on a stone called Corpse Rock. Several succumbed before Croghan admitted failure. And over here are the blind cave fish, adapted to their dark lives. By the time you emerge, blinking, into the sunlight, you'll feel a bit like a blind cave fish yourself.

"Tour groups would pass the patients lying in stone huts in their dressing gowns."

If it's still early, you might want to shake off the subterranean shivers with a hike, bike or horseback ride along some of the park's 70 miles of trails. Bunk down in the dowdy brick **6** **Mammoth Cave Hotel** or snag one of the hotel's freestanding rustic cottages. Or rough it at one of several developed and primitive **7** **Mammoth Cave Camping** areas. The park is home to several species of endangered and threatened plants and animals, including the Eyeless Cave Shrimp and several kinds of lizards.

Dine at the park's white-tablecloth **8** **Travertine Restaurant**. The food may not be special, but there's something deliciously retro about having a sit-down meal in a national park, like in the era when people arrived here by stagecoach and stayed for days. There's also a very mid-century-looking **9** **Crystal Lake Coffee Shop**, with cafeteria-style chairs and a simple snack bar menu.

Or you could head to nearby Cave City, where the **10** **Wigwam Village Inn #2** is a cluster of concrete teepees surrounding a gift shop peddling Native American–themed kitsch. The #2 is one of three remaining Wigwam motels out of the seven built across the country in the mid-20th century (visiting all three – the others are in Arizona and California – would be a road trip adventure itself).

ASK A LOCAL

"There are caves everywhere on private land. Many of those places are still being explored. **Cub Run Cave** has a lot of formations and a really nice trail. **Diamond Caverns** has flowstone and big stalagmites. **Frenchman's Knob Pit** is one of the deepest open-air shafts in the state. They used to mine saltpeter and grow mushrooms in **Lone Star Saltpeter Cave**. **Hidden River Cave** has a cave museum; they'll take you on off-trail tours."

Pat Kambesis, geologist, Cave City

Wrap up your trip in Bowling Green, about 30 minutes away. This postcard-pretty little town is home to Western Kentucky University and the **11** **National Corvette Museum**. See more than 50 examples of the classic sports car, or watch them being made at the factory across the way.

Emily Matchar

OFFBEAT

TRIP INFORMATION

GETTING THERE
From Louisville, take I-65 south for 85 miles, exiting on exit 53 towards Cave City, and follow the signs towards the cave.

DO
Grand Avenue Tour
Hike through the caves' most dramatic caverns and gypsum-lined passageways in this 4½-hour tour. ☎ 270-758-2328; www.nps.gov/maca/planyourvisit/tour-grand avenue.htm; 4 miles; adult/child $24/17; ⊗ 2/1 morning tours summer/fall

Historic Tour
See the old saltpeter works, the tuberculosis hospital and the carved names of long-dead soldiers in this two-hour tour. ☎ 270-758-2328; www.nps.gov/maca/planyourvisit/tour-historic.htm; 2 miles; adult/child $12/8; ⊗ 9am-4pm summer, from 10am fall

Mammoth Cave National Park
In addition to the famous cave tours, this park has hiking, biking, camping and canoeing. ☎ 270-758-2328; www.nps.gov/maca; Mammoth Cave Parkway; admission free

National Corvette Museum
View vintage Corvettes and, if you register a day in advance, tour the factory where new ones are made. ☎ 270-781-7973; 270-745-8019 (to book tour); www.corvettemuseum.com; 350 Corvette Dr, Bowling Green; adult/child $8/4.50, plant tour $5; ⊗ 8am-5pm

Violet City Lantern Tour
Walk for three hours by eerie lantern light, just like a visitor from the 1800s. ☎ 270-758-2328; www.nps.gov/maca/planyourvisit/tour-violetcity.htm; 3 miles; adult/child $15/11; ⊗ 9am tours

Wild Cave Tour
Don a lantern helmet as you squeeze through narrow passageways and free-climb cave walls in this six-hour tour; ages 16 and up only. ☎ 270-758-2328; www.nps.gov/maca/plan yourvisit/tour-wildcave.htm; 5.5 miles; admission $48; ⊗ 10am daily, weekend only in fall

EAT & SLEEP
Crystal Lake Coffee Shop
This lunch-only cantina features soups, sandwiches and 1960s-style vinyl seating. ☎ 270-758-2225; Mammoth Cave National Park; mains $3-6; ⊗ 10:30am-4:30pm

Mammoth Cave Camping
The park has three developed campsites and more than 12 rustic backwoods spots (backcountry camping by permit). 270-758-2328; www.nps.gov/maca; Mammoth Cave National Park; developed campsite per person $12-30

Mammoth Cave Hotel
This park hotel has dim, spacious rooms; staying in the teensy on-site historic cottages is more fun. ☎ 270-758-2225; www.mammothcavehotel.com; Mammoth Cave National Park; cottage from $66, r from $72

Travertine Restaurant
Mains at this standard hotel restaurant range from burgers to grilled mountain trout. ☎ 270-758-2225; Mammoth Cave National Park; mains $5-16; ⊗ 2:30pm-8pm

Wigwam Village Inn #2
Sleep in a concrete teepee at this 1937 kitsch-fest. ☎ 270-773-3381; wigwamvillage.com; 601 N Dixie Hwy, Cave City; wigwams $60

USEFUL WEBSITES
www.cavecity.com
www.nps.gov/maca

LINK YOUR TRIP
www.lonelyplanet.com/trip-planner

TRIP
63 Kentucky Bluegrass & Horse Country p387
65 My Old Kentucky Home p397

48 Hours in Louisville

WHY GO Whether you call it Looeyville, Louahvul or Luhvul, the largest city in Kentucky is an under-appreciated destination, with plenty of quirky, true-blue American attractions. The lovely riverfront downtown and Victorian neighborhoods are among the nicest around. And come May, the place goes wild for the Derby.

Once a busy shipping port due to its prime location on the banks of the Ohio River, Louisville has faded into a pleasant middle age. While the Kentucky Derby brings screaming mobs to town in May, Louisville is generally an even-tempered, safe city – it's often ranked among the top 10 safest in America. It has a tranquil, slightly stuck-in-time feel, like you might turn around to see a Levi's-clad teen offering you a chili dog and a ride in his Ford Thunderbird.

Start your day in the eclectic Highlands neighborhood with brunch at ❶ Lynn's Paradise Cafe, a psychedelically-painted diner with a horse statue guarding the door and a ceiling-high tree in the dining room. Overstuffed omelets and biscuits with sorghum butter will keep you full all day. Sit at the counter and chat with the waitress to find out if there are any interesting events in town that night – Lynn's keeps good track of local happenings, from concerts to documentary premieres.

From Lynn's, head northwest into downtown Louisville, admiring the vintage brick-factory architecture along the way. The downtown area is one of the oldest established districts in Louisville, colonized by soldiers during the Revolutionary War. The Ohio River marks the Mason-Dixon line, that once-crucial invisible divider between North and South. Before the Civil War, Southern-side Louisville had one of the busiest slave markets in the country. The phrase "sold down the

TIME
2 days

BEST TIME TO GO
Apr & May,
Sep & Oct

START
Louisville, KY

END
Louisville, KY

ALSO GOOD FOR

HISTORY & CULTURE

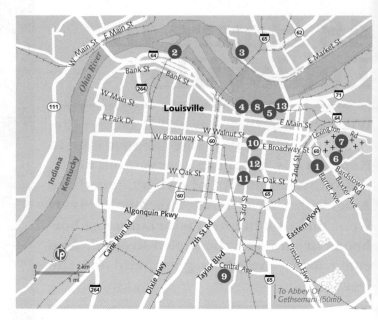

river" probably originated here as a lament of Kentucky slaves whose family members were taken down the Ohio to be sold in Louisville. These days locals jog, bike and push strollers along the ❷ **Louisville RiverWalk**, part of the city's extensive, paved trail system.

The city is located on the Falls of the Ohio, a portion of riverbed with an exposed fossilized reef formed more than 350 million years ago, when the area was the ocean floor. Today, you can visit the ❸ **Falls of the Ohio State Park**, across the river from Louisville in Clarksville, Indiana. The park offers fishing, bird-watching and fossil viewing, with a museum featuring a 14ft mammoth skeleton and a diorama of Devonian-period sea life.

The main attraction in downtown Louisville has got to be the ❹ **Louisville Slugger Museum**. After all, what says "American" more than baseball? And what says "baseball" more than the five-story-high baseball bat marking the entrance to this cool museum/factory? Hillerich & Bradsby Co has been making the iconic Slugger here since 1884. The bat rose to fame in the early 1900s when the company paid Pittsburgh Pirates hitter Honus Wagner to swing one, the earliest example of a celebrity athlete endorsement. Since then, legends Babe Ruth, Ty Cobb and Lou Gehrig have all been Slugger men, as are some 60% of all Major League Baseball players today. The modern museum offers a plant tour, a hall of baseball memorabilia including Babe Ruth's slugger, a batting cage and a free mini slugger. You can buy a customized bat in the lobby, with the message of your choice embossed on the wood. Note that bat production halts on Sunday, and on Saturday in winter.

While downtown, stick with the sports theme and head on over to the enormous **⑤ Muhammad Ali Center**. Born Cassius Clay in the segregated Louisville of the 1940s, Ali was encouraged to begin boxing at age 12 by a local police officer. He went on to become one of the greatest sports legends of the 20th century, winning three World Heavyweight Championships and an Olympic gold medal. Ali was nearly as famous for his words as his punches – his outspoken refusal to back down to anyone, including the US government (he lost his boxing license for several years when he refused to be drafted for the Vietnam War) earned him the nickname the "Louisville Lip." The museum includes an interactive boxing ring and video projections of Ali's most famous fights, as well as exhibits on segregation and the civil rights movement. Feel what it was like to be black in Jim Crow America when you step into a model lunch counter and recorded voices begin to shout at you, telling you to get out, that "your kind" is not welcome. It's truly disturbing.

For dinner, head back to the Highlands neighborhood, known for its wealth of restaurants and night spots. Pickings are especially good along the northern portion of Bardstown Rd. Try **⑥ Lilly's Bistro**, an acclaimed upscale eatery featuring "Kentucky tapas" – think catfish spring rolls, fried frogs legs in red-pepper sauce – and luscious, locally sourced meat and seafood mains, brought to you by native celebrity chef Kathy Cary.

If you're in the mood for some nightlife, wander around Bardstown Rd and Baxter Ave for a place that suits your taste – you can find anything from yuppie-friendly wine bars to sports dives popular with University of Louisville undergrads (go Cardinals!). If you're feeling morbid, you could stroll past gothic **⑦ Cave Hill Cemetery** on Baxter Ave, final resting place of Colonel Harland Sanders of "finger lickin' good" KFC fame (of course you could actually tour the cemetery during the day, if you want, but is that really as much fun as peering through the gate in the dark?).

> **ASK A LOCAL**
>
> "We've got a huge music scene. **The Rudyard Kipling** is a really, really cool little bar, with music and art shows and food. There's a bar called **Third Street Dive**, very punk rock. **Skull Alley** seems to be a younger crowd; local artists sell their stuff there. The **Monkey Wrench** is a fun bar, with lots of local bands. **Cahoots** is a rock bar, and **Headliners** is a good venue for bigger touring bands.
>
> *Jessie Sullivan, Louisville*

Bed down on Italian linens at the ultra-slick **⑧ 21c Museum Hotel**. This mod downtown space is part hotel, part cutting edge art gallery run by the International Contemporary Art Foundation. Expect serious luxury, from flat screen TV to room-service bison burgers from the acclaimed hotel restaurant, Proof.

You wouldn't go to Paris without visiting the Eiffel Tower, and you wouldn't go to Louisville without checking out the white spires of **9 Churchill Downs**. Three miles south of downtown, this most famous of all horseracing tracks is home to the "greatest two minutes in sports," the Kentucky Derby. Unless you've reserved seats for the May event years in advance (or you're the Queen of England; Elizabeth II was trackside in 2007) you're probably out of luck, but for $40 you can drink a mint julep with your face smushed into someone's sweaty back in the mobbed Paddock area. It's worth it though, just to see the outrageous hats traditionally worn by derby-goers – everything from umbrella-sized floral confections to scale models of Churchill Downs itself. The two-week Kentucky Derby Festival, which culminates in the race itself, includes a hot air balloon race and a massive fireworks display. But even if you're not in town around Derby time you can still get a $3 seat at the Downs from April to November to watch warm-up races or simulcasts from other tracks. Or you can check out the Kentucky Derby Museum by Gate 1, with displays on race history, an exhibit of winners of the annual hat contest and a behind-the-scenes track tour.

> *"The Schnitzelburg World Dainty Championship is held front of Hauck's Handy Store each July."*

Drive through the blue-collar Germantown and Schnitzelburg neighborhoods, where descendants of German immigrants have been drinking lager, playing dainty (a local version of street stickball) and going to potlucks at the German-American club for generations. Want to be sure to catch a game of dainty? The Schnitzelburg World Dainty Championship is held front of Hauck's Handy Store each July.

DETOUR Sixty-five Trappist monks live lives of silence and prayer at the **Abbey of Gethsemani**, an austerely beautiful monastery, 50 miles south of Louisville. Built in the mid-1800s, the monastery was the longtime home of Thomas Merton, famous for his writings on non-violence and his interest in Eastern spirituality. Both Catholic and non-Catholic visitors come for popular silent retreats, wandering the abbey's vast wooded property; day visitors may attend Mass. The monks sell their fruitcake, cheese and fudge at the on-site gift shop.

For lunch, you've got to try Louisville's culinary claim to fame, the rather unappetizingly named Hot Brown. An open-faced turkey-and-bacon sandwich slathered in Mornay sauce and broiled, the Hot Brown was supposedly invented to feed hungry flappers after a Roaring Twenties dinner dance at downtown Louisville's Brown Hotel.

The hotel's **10 J Graham's Cafe** features a classic version. Poking around the Brown's majestic lobby is worth a few minutes as well. Massive chandeliers hang from the vaulted ceiling and theatrically large potted ferns spill over the grand piano, recalling the hotel's glory days of the 1920s and '30s, when opera singer Lily Pons allowed her pet lion to roam free in her suite, and early film star Al Jolson got in a fight in the downstairs restaurant.

Just south of downtown, Old Louisville is America's largest Victorian neighborhood. Stroll down 3rd St, once known as Millionaire's Row, where well-heeled fin de siècle Louisville citizens built their turreted brick mansions. Duck down side streets and back alleys for peeks at hidden backyard gardens and ornate architectural details like rose windows, fleur-de-lis stained glass and wrought iron widow's walks. Don't miss St James Court, where stately homes face an open green space with a brass fountain and old-fashioned gaslights. Adjacent Central Park was designed by Frederick Law Olmstead, the famed landscape architect responsible for the park of the same name in New York City. Several Old Louisville historic homes are open for tours, including the castle-like **⑪ Conrad-Caldwell House**, complete with gargoyles, and the pink and white beaux arts **⑫ Ferguson Mansion**, with its original Tiffany lamps and ceiling murals depicting scenes from old German folktales.

THE POPE LICK MONSTER

Half-man, half-goat, this creature is said to haunt the train trestle on Pope Lick Rd in East Louisville. Either the ghost of a circus freak seeking revenge, or an undead Satan-worshipping farmer, the monster supposedly hypnotizes victims into walking out onto the 100ft-high trestle, where they're killed by oncoming trains. The legend was even the subject of a low-budget 1980s movie, *Legend of the Pope Lick Monster.*

Be sure to check out the calendar for the **⑬ Actor's Theatre of Louisville**, considered one of the best regional theater companies in America. Founded in 1964, the company produces everything from musicals to avant-garde one-acts and is home to the renowned Humana Festival of New American Plays. An evening at the theater, housed in the grand old Bank of Louisville building downtown, is a refined treat.

Emily Matchar

TRIP
62

TRIP INFORMATION

GETTING THERE
From Nashville, take I-65 North for about 170 miles and get off at exit 137 for I-64, getting off at exit 4.

DO

Actor's Theatre of Louisville
See a play at one of America's best regional theaters, in an old bank building. ☎ 502-584-1265; www.actorstheatre.org; 316 W Main St, Louisville; tickets $25

Churchill Downs
The Kentucky Derby is held every May at this most famous of all racetracks, with an on-site museum. ☎ 502-636-4400; www.churchill downs.com; 700 Central Ave, Louisville; track admission $3, museum adult/child $10/5; ⊙ race times vary, museum 8am-5pm Mon-Sat, from 11am Sun

Conrad-Caldwell House
This Romanesque mansion was once known as "Conrad's Castle." ☎ 502-636-5023; www .conradcaldwell.org; 1402 St James Ct, Louisville; admission $5; ⊙ noon-4pm Wed-Sun

Falls of the Ohio State Park
A shallow area of the river reveals ancient marine fossils at this park, just over the water in Indiana. ☎ 812-280-9970; www.fallsof theohio.org; the end of W Riverside Dr, Clarksville, IN; ⊙ adult/child $4/1; ⊙ 9am-5pm Mon-Sat, from 1pm Sun; ♿

Ferguson Mansion
Tour one of the grandest homes in Louisville's Victorian district. ☎ 502-635-5083; filsonhistorical.org; 1310 S 3rd St, Louisville; admission free; ⊙ 9am-5pm Mon-Fri

Louisville Slugger Museum
Learn about the production of this iconic baseball bat, adored by the likes of Babe Ruth. ☎ 877-775-8443; www.sluggermuseum.org; 800 W Main St, Louisville; adult/child $9/4; ⊙ 9am-5pm Mon-Sat, from noon Sun; ♿

Muhammad Ali Center
See videos and interactive exhibits on the life of Louisville's own "Greatest." ☎ 502-584-9254; www.alicenter.org; 144 N 6th St, Louisville; adult/child $9/4; ⊙ 9:30am-5pm Mon-Sat, from noon Sun

EAT & SLEEP

21c Museum Hotel
This luxe boutique hotel houses a contemporary art museum. ☎ 502-217-6300; www.21chotel.com; 700 W Main St, Louisville; r from $160

J Graham's Cafe
In the Brown Hotel, this is the birthplace of the famed Hot Brown sandwich. ☎ 502-583-1234; www.brownhotel.com; 335 W Broadway, Louisville; mains $7-16; ⊙ 7am-3pm

Lilly's Bistro
Local food gets haute treatment at this sumptuous Southern bistro. ☎ 502-451-0447; www.lillyslapeche.com; 1147 Bardstown Rd, Louisville; mains $19-36; ⊙ 11am-3pm & 5:30pm-10pm Tue-Sat

Lynn's Paradise Cafe
Linger over brunch at this art-filled diner. ☎ 502-583-3447; www.lynnsparadisecafe .com; 984 Barret Ave, Louisville; mains $7-15; ⊙ 7am-10pm Mon-Fri, from 8am weekends

USEFUL WEBSITES
www.gotolouisville.com

LINK YOUR TRIP
www.lonelyplanet.com/trip-planner

Kentucky Bluegrass & Horse Country

WHY GO A trip through the sunlight-dappled hills and meadows of Bluegrass Country is like a massage for your tired brain. Drive the scenic byways from Louisville to Lexington and beyond, stopping to tour storybook-like country estates, ride horses through the poplar forests and sip the region's famous bourbon.

TIME
3 days

DISTANCE
140 miles

BEST TIME TO GO
Apr – Sep

START
Louisville, KY

END
Harrodsbug, KY

ALSO GOOD FOR

HISTORY & CULTURE

Kentucky's Bluegrass Region encompasses the north-central part of the state, including the cities of Lexington, Frankfort and Louisville, and is home to half the state's population. Though Lexington is the capital of Horse Country, cheerful, solid ❶ Louisville has the racing world's most iconic building: the white spires of ❷ Churchill Downs. The Run for the Roses, as the Kentucky Derby is known, happens here on the first Saturday in May. Though most seats are reserved years in advance, if you're around on Derby Day you can pay $40 to get into the Paddock area, though don't expect to see much. But from April through November you can get ultra-cheap seats for warm-up races and simulcasts of racing events worldwide.

Wander over to the riverfront downtown, with its well-preserved 19th-century brick buildings. Have a mint julep while listening to live piano music in the ❸ Lobby Bar of the gilded Brown Hotel, where starlets and ambassadors got up to no good during the Roaring Twenties. Clear your head with a stroll around the ❹ Old Louisville neighborhood south of downtown, with America's largest collection of Victorian homes.

Head out of Louisville and into the Arcadian countryside, where – sorry to disappoint – but the grass is not actually blue. Poa pratensis, or Kentucky Bluegrass, gets its name from the bluish-purple buds it sprouts in early summer which, from a distance, can give fields of the grass a slightly sapphire cast.

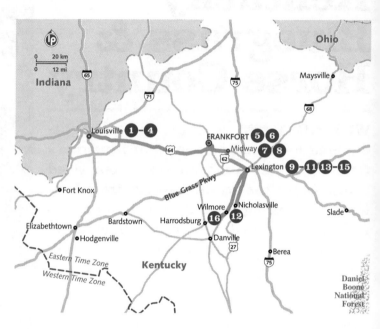

About an hour east of Louisville is Kentucky's tiny capital, **⑤ Frankfort**. This well-tended bluffside city has a gracious, all-American downtown – good for a leg-stretching stroll. A scenic overlook on Hwy 60 offers a sweeping view over the capital buildings, a popular photo op. Stay the night at the **⑥ Meeting House**, a 168-year-old Federal-style mansion in the historic district. Have a tall glass of tea on the verandah and sleep in one of four bedrooms, each decorated with quirky, hand-picked antiques.

The next day, have a decadent lunch near the village of **⑦ Midway**, at the **⑧ Holly Hill Inn**. This winsome 1845 Greek Revival estate, nestled beneath the oaks, houses one of the best restaurants in Kentucky. The married chef-owners serve a simple but elegant multi-course feast of handmade pastas, locally-raised meats and farmstead cheeses. Diminutive Midway is the state's first railroad town and home to Kentucky's only all-female college, Midway College.

"This well-tended bluffside city has a gracious, all-American downtown."

Drive the scenic oak-lined Old Frankfort Pike into stately **⑨ Lexington**, once known as the "Athens of the West" for its architecture and culture. The area surrounding Lexington, known as the Inner Bluegrass (or Horse Country), has been a center of horse breeding for three centuries. The region's ancient limestone deposits are natural fertilizers, feeding the lush meadows that in turn nourish grazing thoroughbreds.

Outside the city is the 1200-acre ⑩ **Kentucky Horse Park**, an equine theme park and sports center. The park is home to about 50 different horse breeds, from the Akhal-Teke to the Welch Cob. Catch the daily Parade of Breeds or, in springtime, watch mares and new foals nuzzle in the paddock. The park's Museum of the Horse has life-sized displays on horses through history, from the dog-sized prehistoric eohippus to modern polo ponies. Here you learn just how deep the human–horse relationship runs – Cro-Magnon man painted horses on cave walls as far back as 17,000 years ago.

To tour a working stable and training facility, visit the ⑪ **Thoroughbred Center**, where visitors get to see a day in the life of Derby hopefuls, from morning workouts to cool-down currying. You'll see exactly why blue-blooded Kentucky horses get reputations as divas. In the afternoon get even more up-close-and-personal with the horses with a guided ride at ⑫ **Sunburst Horsemanship Center**. This picturesque Lexington farm offers lessons for all levels, from basic safety to advanced jumping.

In the evening, put your money on an old-school harness race, where jockeys are pulled behind the horses in two-wheeled carts called sulkies, at the ⑬ **Red Mile**. Fans have been cheering from the grandstands at this red dirt track since 1875. Though live races are in the fall only, simulcasts are offered year-round.

ASK A LOCAL "The American Saddlebred horse was developed primarily in Kentucky and was often used to ride around the plantations. It was showy and high-stepping and pretty, and could be hitched to the wagon and go to church and show off. It was developed from a riding horse into a show horse – we have quite a strong showing contingent around here, They're beautiful horses, with long flowing manes and tails – very aristocratic."

Kathy Hopkins, Lexington

For dinner, try quirky ⑭ **a la Lucie** in Lexington's grand historical district. The funky bistro decor could have been scrounged from a Parisian flea market, but the menu is all over the map – lobster corn dogs, Mediterranean stuffed eggplant, bourbon pork. Spend the night in restored 19th-century style at the ⑮ **Gratz Park Inn** around the corner. Its leather and dark wood-paneled library makes you just itch to smoke a pipe.

If you have time in the morning, drive 30 miles through scenic pasturelands dotted with horse barns along Hwy 68 to ⑯ **Shaker Village of Pleasant Hill**. In the early 1800s these softly rolling hills were home to a communal society of 500 peace-loving men and women. Though the Shakers worshiped God through uninhibited ecstatic dancing, they practiced strict celibacy (probably why there aren't any left). See their remarkable craftsmanship in dozens of restored buildings and learn about their history at the Shaker Life Exhibit.

Emily Matchar

TRIP INFORMATION

GETTING THERE

From Nashville, take I-65 North for about 170 miles and get off at exit 137 for I-64, getting off at exit 4 for Louisville.

DO

Churchill Downs

The world's most famous horseracing track is home to the Kentucky Derby and various other races. ☎ 502-636-4400; www.church illdowns.com; 700 Central Ave, Louisville; admission $3; ☿ race times vary

Kentucky Horse Park

This horse-theme park has 50 breeds and two equine history museums. ☎ 859-233-4303; www.kyhorsepark.com; 4089 Iron Works Parkway, Lexington; adult/child $15/8; ☿ 9am-5pm; ♿

Red Mile

This 1875 red-dirt track has live harness racing and simulcasts. ☎ 859-255-0752; www .theredmile.com; 1200 Red Mile Rd, Lexington; ☿ simulcasts afternoon & evening

Shaker Village of Pleasant Hill

America's largest restored Shaker village, outside the town of Harrodsburg, has an inn, restaurant and historical displays. ☎ 800-734-5611; www.shakervillageky.org; 3501 Lexington Rd, Harrodsburg; tours adult/child $14/7; ☿ 10am-5pm

Sunburst Horsemanship Center

This school and training facility has lessons for riders of all levels. ☎ 859-224-8480; www.sunbursthorsemanshipschool.com; 1129 Durham Lane, Lexington; intro lesson $50; ♿

Thoroughbred Center

Watch champion horses go through their paces at this working farm. ☎ 859-293-1853; www.thethoroughbredcenter.com; 3380 Paris Pike, Lexington; adult/child $10/5; ☿ tours 9am Mon-Sat

EAT & DRINK

a la Lucie

This bohemian bistro has vintage furniture and an eclectic international menu. ☎ 859-252-5277; www.alalucie.net; 159 N Limestone St, Lexington; mains $18-30; ☿ 11:30am-2pm Mon-Fri & 4:30pm to 10pm Mon-Sat

Holly Hill Inn

This stately old country manse is just the place for a special dinner. ☎ 859-846-4732; www.hollyhillinn.com; 426 N Winter St, Midway; mains $30-45; ☿ 5:30pm-9pm Wed-Sat, brunch 11:30am-2pm Sun

Lobby Bar

Sip bourbon in the opulent, marble-floored lobby of the Brown Hotel, an Old Louisville institution. ☎ 502-583-1234; www.brown hotel.com; 335 West Broadway, Louisville; ☿ 4pm-2am

SLEEP

Gratz Park Inn

Draw the brocade curtains and fall asleep on a 19th-century poster bed in Lexington's historic district. ☎ 859-231-1777; www.gratz parkinn.com; 120 W Second, Lexington; r from $170

Meeting House

The quirky antiques at this Federal-style bed-and-breakfast speak of the owners' fascination with local history. ☎ 502-226-3226; www.themeetinghousebandb.com; 519 Ann St, Frankfort; r from $115

USEFUL WEBSITES

www.bluegrasskentucky.com
www.visitlex.com

LINK YOUR TRIP

www.lonelyplanet.com/trip-planner

TRIP

The Bourbon Trail

WHY GO "There is a bourbon that's perfect for everyone," says Dixie Hibbs, Kentucky bourbon historian and the former mayor of Bardstown, the "Bourbon Capital of the World." Visit Dixie's favorite distilleries and taverns in the rolling hills of Bluegrass Country, and you're sure to find the one that's right for you.

A golden inch of bourbon, silky and mellow with notes of wood and vanilla, is Southern living in a glass. Legend has it that bourbon was first distilled by a Lexington-area Baptist preacher in 1789. Between 80% to 90% of the world's supply is still produced in the state. "If it's made and aged in Kentucky, it's called Kentucky bourbon," explains honey-voiced Dixie Hibbs, bourbon expert extraordinaire and author of several books on Kentucky culture. In fact, no other state is even allowed to put its name on a bottle before the word "bourbon." While all bourbons are whiskey, all whiskeys are not bourbon, Hibbs points out. True bourbon must be made with at least 51% corn, and aged for a minimum of two years in a charred, new, white oak barrel.

Hibbs suggests you start a tour of central Kentucky's Bourbon Trail in her native ❶ Bardstown. The first major Catholic settlement west of the Alleghenies, Bardstown is located in central Kentucky's luscious, green Bluegrass Country. "Walk up and down the streets and just get a feel for a 1780s town," Hibbs suggests. With its weathered red-brick Georgian churches and fairytale stone cottages, Bardstown does seem to belong to a different era; an era of train travel and general stores, of mud-splattered frontiersmen, and of Civil War widows knitting by the fireplace.

For an overview of bourbon history, head to the ❷ Oscar Getz Museum of Whiskey History, housed in a former Civil War hospital-turned-orphanage. See a mock distillery assembly line, collections of "medicinal

TIME
3 days

DISTANCE
165 miles

BEST TIME TO GO
May – Sep

START
Bardstown, KY

END
Bardstown, KY

ALSO GOOD FOR

ROUTE

BEST TRIP

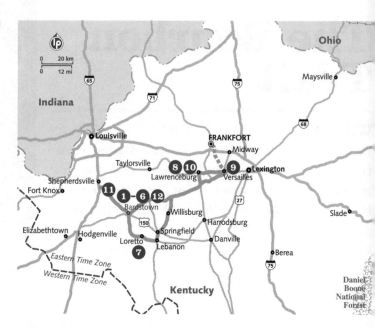

purposes only" bourbon bottles, and an ax once belonging to infamous prohibitionist Carrie Nation, who used it to vandalize taverns. Don't miss the genuine moonshine stills – Kentucky moonshiners would mix their paint-peeling hooch with tobacco juice and pass it off as bourbon, Hibbs explains.

Half a mile away, ❸ **Keene's Depot** is a general store and tackle shop where locals have been dropping by to shoot the breeze for 60 years. "It was a place where you went to get your fishing supplies, your country hams," Hibbs reminisces. Now housed in a large contemporary building, Keene's is the go-to shop for bourbon barbecue sauce, chocolate bourbon balls and bread made from leftover grain mash from bourbon production.

Grab dinner at the ❹ **Old Talbott Tavern**, welcoming travelers since the late 1700s. The gray stone building was the oldest Western stagecoach stop in America – Abraham Lincoln, Daniel Boone and Jesse James all supposedly rested their heads here. After a meal of country ham and chess pie in the dimly lit restaurant, relax at the bar with a bourbon on the rocks with water – the way the locals take it, says Hibbs. And don't feel shy talking to strangers. "Go into these bars and you'll run into people who work in the distilleries and they'll tell you all kinds of stories," she promises.

"If you have a drink and worry about driving, you don't have to," says Hibbs. "Just go next door and check into the jail!" The jail she's talking about is the

5 **Jailer's Inn**, a bed-and-breakfast housed in the Old Nelson County Jail. Here, you can enjoy the pleasures of life as a free man or woman – canopy beds, plush armchairs, antique claw-footed tubs – in the confines of the 1819 building's 30in-thick walls. Or, for fun, book the black-and-white Jail Cell, with bunk beds and original cinder-block walls. The back building housed prisoners up until 1987. Have your morning coffee in the courtyard where the condemned once swung from the gallows.

When you wake, it's time to hit the Bourbon Trail. There are seven major distilleries within a 50-mile radius of Bardstown; Hibbs suggests using your time wisely and sticking to a few of her favorites. In Bardstown proper, **6** **Heaven Hill** caters to visitors with its Bourbon Heritage Center, with displays on bourbon history, an educational film and a tasting bar inside a huge barrel. Here, seventh generation master distiller Craig Beam holds the keys to 16% of the world's bourbon supply.

When driving up to a distillery, take a deep noseful of the air. Hibbs likes to tell an old Kentucky joke about an out-of-stater catching a whiff of distillery scent and asking, wide-eyed,

THE KENTUCKY BOURBON FESTIVAL

This annual Bardstown shindig draws whiskey aficionados from all over the world. The week-long festival (www.kybourbonfestival.com), held each September, includes taste tests from local distilleries, bourbon barrel relay races, liquor-infused cooking demos, and bourbon and cigar dinners. Kids will dig the historic train rides and nighttime ghost tours of old Bardstown. And everyone can get into a competitive round of Kentucky's state game, cornhole (a sort of beanbag toss).

what the smell was. "Smells like money to me," the distiller replies. Hibbs herself thinks cooking bourbon smells like roast beef. You be the judge.

To the south, **7** **Maker's Mark** has been operating at the same site, near the town of Loretto, since 1805. "You stay where your water is," explains Hibbs. The distillery sits on a 10-acre limestone spring-fed lake, providing the pure water used in the distilling process. Touring Maker's Mark is like visiting a small, historic theme park – see the old gristmill, the 1840s master distiller's house, and the old-fashioned wooden firehouse with an antique fire truck. Watch oatmeal-esque sour mash ferment in huge cypress vats, see whiskey being double-distilled in copper pots and peek at bourbon barrels aging in old wooden warehouses. At the gift shop, you can even stamp your own bottle with the iconic red-wax seal.

From Maker's Mark, head northeast towards the town of Lawrenceburg. It's about an hour's drive, and what a pleasant drive it is. "In the spring you see the dogwoods and the horses frolicking; in the fall you get all the wonderful colors," Hibbs says. Here, the **8** **Four Roses** sits on the banks of the Salt River. Check out the unique architecture – red-roofed Spanish Mission-style buildings like these are rarely seen in this neck of the woods. For years, Four Roses was only sold overseas and some labels, like the Platinum, are still only available in Japan. But the company made a triumphant US comeback in 2002; you can now actually have a Four Roses Manhattan in Manhattan for the first time since the 1960s. Take a walking tour of the distillery and have some free sips afterwards in the tasting room. Note that the distillery shuts down in summer, but the gift shop and visitors center remain open. You can also call to arrange a free private tour of the aging warehouse, about an hour away in Cox's Creek.

DIXIE HIBBS'S WHISKEY TEA

Whiskey tea is a staple of church picnics and family reunions in the Bluegrass State. Just go by one of the distilleries and ask to buy a freshly dumped oak aging barrel. Take it home and fill it with 10 to 15 gallons of hot tea, then allow it to sit in the sun. At least a quart of whiskey will leach out of the wood, giving the tea flavor and kick.

In nearby Versailles (say it "Vur-Sails" or people will look at you funny), spend the night at an antebellum mansion at ⑨ Storybook Inn. Set amid the emerald pastureland of Horse County, the inn has three charmingly fussy knickknack-filled suites and one rather manlier hunter's cottage.

In the morning, it's back to Lawrenceburg to visit the ⑩ Wild Turkey distillery, which sits on Wild Turkey Hill overlooking the Kentucky River. More industrial and less self-consciously old-fashioned than some of the distilleries, Wild Turkey offers a frills-free tour of the facilities. If you're lucky, you'll get to meet master distiller Jimmy Russell, who's worked here since 1954. Hibbs notes that Wild Turkey is made slightly differently than most bourbons, aged in a heavily charred barrel for extra-deep amber color, with very little water added at the end of the process.

Drive back west an hour or so to catch a tour at ⑪ Jim Beam, the world's largest and best-known bourbon distiller. The tour features a video on Beam family history and a sampling of small batch bourbons. Jim Beam ages all its bourbon for at least four years, twice the legal minimum – longer aging produces a deeper, smoother character. Hibbs says you can't even call it bourbon until it's aged; until then it's called "green whiskey." Kentucky has the "perfect climate" for aging bourbon, Hibbs explains. Hot summers cause the whiskey to expand into the wood of the barrel, where it sucks up toasty, caramelized flavors, to be released when the liquid contracts during the cold winters. The barrels sit, stacked several stories high, in wood and metal "rackhouses" that dot the central Kentucky landscape like massive barns. Unsurprisingly, these facilities are highly flammable, and several distilleries, including Jim Beam and Heaven Hill, have had apocalyptic fires in the past few years.

> *"You can't even call it bourbon until it's aged; until then it's called 'green whiskey.'"*

Most widely available bourbons are aged no longer than eight years, but some ultra-premium labels are aged 14, 16, even 21 years. "Each year it gets a little darker," says Hibbs, who's partial to eight- to nine-year-old bourbon herself.

Head back into Bardstown, where Hibbs suggests a private bourbon tasting and dinner at the ⑫ **Chapeze House** as a sumptuous end to your bourbon tour. Michael Masters (known only as "the Colonel") will lead you through a tasting from his collection of more than 100 premium and vintage bourbons. Afterwards, wife Margaret Sue, president of the Kentucky Bourbon Cooking School, will serve a homemade feast in the candlelit dining room of their lavish Federal-style mansion. The Masters are so well-known for their expansive Southern hospitality (the Colonel's drawl is frequently heard on the Food Network and Fine Living) they've earned the title "the Host and Hostess of Kentucky." The Masters also rent out two dollhouse-like cottages – one pink, one blue – in Bardstown's historic district.

Emily Matchar

DETOUR **Frankfort**, the postcard-pretty state capital, sits on the banks of the Kentucky River half an hour north of Versailles. Here, in a little white house with a red striped awning, Ruth Booe invented the love-it-or-hate-it bourbon ball in 1936. For $2 you can tour the **Rebecca Ruth** factory and taste a sample of the inimitable candy. The sweets shop sells all manner of booze-infused treats, like cognac balls, mint julep candies and Kentucky Irish coffees.

TRIP INFORMATION

GETTING THERE

From Louisville, take I-65 South for 24 miles and get off at exit 112 for Bardstown. Continue on Hwy 245 for 16 miles.

DO

Four Roses

This Spanish Mission–style distillery produces great bourbon only recently available in the US. ☎ 502-839-3436; www.fourroses.us; 1224 Bonds Mills Rd, Lawrenceburg; admission free; 🕙 9am-3pm Mon-Sat, closed summer

Heaven Hill

This family-run distillery features a mini bourbon museum at the Bourbon Heritage Center. ☎ 502-348-3921; www.heaven-hill.com; 1311 Gilkey Run Rd, Bardstown; admission free; 🕙 10am-5pm Tue-Sat, noon-4pm Sun

Jim Beam

Learn a few bourbon-making secrets from the Beam clan at America's largest bourbon distillery. ☎ 502-543-9877; www.jimbean.com; 149 Happy Hollow Rd, Clermont; admission free; 🕙 9am-4:30pm Mon-Sat, 1pm-4pm Sun

Keene's Depot

This former country store is one-stop shopping for bourbon-infused foodstuffs. ☎ 502-348-3594; 8 Old Bloomfield Pike, Bardstown; 🕙 8am-7pm Mon-Sat, to 1pm Sun

Maker's Mark

Now a national historic landmark, this distillery has been going strong since the early 1800s. ☎ 502-865-2099; www.makersmark.com; 3350 Burks Spring Rd, near Loretto; admission free; 🕙 10:30am-3:30pm Mon-Sat, from 1:30pm Sun

Oscar Getz Museum of Whiskey History

Exhibits of vintage distillery vats and old whiskey ads tell the bourbon story. ☎ 502-348-2999; www.whiskeymuseum.com; 114 N 5th St; donations encouraged; 🕙 10am-4pm Mon-Sat, from noon Sun

Wild Turkey

This no-frills distillery offers simple tours of its facility overlooking the Kentucky River. ☎ 502-839-4544; www.wildturkeybourbon.com; US Hwy 62 East, Lawrenceburg; admission free; 🕙 9am-2:30pm Mon-Sat

EAT

Chapeze House

The "Host and Hostess of Kentucky" will arrange a private bourbon tasting and dinner in their immaculately restored Bardstown mansion. ☎ 502-349-0127; www.chapezehouse.com; 107 E Stephen Foster Ave, Bardstown; per guest $250, 4 guests maximum; 🕙 by arrangement

Old Talbott Tavern

Daniel Boone and Abe Lincoln passed through this old limestone tavern, now a restaurant, inn and bar. ☎ 502-348-3494; www.talbotts.com; 107 W Stephen Foster Ave, Bardstown; mains $8-20; 🕙 11am-8pm Sun-Thu, to 10pm Fri & Sat, bar to 1am Thu-Sun

SLEEP

Jailer's Inn

Sleep in a former cell in the Old Nelson County Jail, now outfitted with floral wallpaper and antique furniture. ☎ 502-308-5551; www.jailersinn.com; 111 W Stephen Foster Ave, Bardstown; r $90-145

Storybook Inn

This white antebellum mansion features a huge garden and lavish Southern breakfasts. ☎ 859-879-9993; www.storybook-inn.com; 277 Rose Hill Ave, Versailles; r $199-269

USEFUL WEBSITES

www.bardstowntourism.com
www.kentuckybourbontrail.com

www.lonelyplanet.com/trip-planner

LINK YOUR TRIP

My Old Kentucky Home

WHY GO Bourbon. Racehorses. Baseball bats. Bluegrass. Fried chicken. What do these things have in common? There's a museum in Kentucky dedicated to each one. Travel through the emerald hills and limestone hollows and find yourself lost in the state's fascinatingly eccentric past.

Every road trip needs a soundtrack, and what's more appropriate than a rollicking bluegrass fiddle tune when driving through the Bluegrass State? So start your trip in Owensboro, on a bend in the Ohio River across the water from Indiana. This town of 55,000 or so is home to the worthy ❶ **International Bluegrass Music Museum**. Bluegrass was born in Appalachia (though not necessarily in Kentucky, as some may claim) in the 1940s, mingling the mournful ballads of homesick Scotish-Irish immigrants with thigh-slapping ragtime tempos and African rhythms. The modest museum has several historical exhibits, including a Hall of Honor profiling the great pickers n' grinners. There's a special tribute to bluegrass pioneer and Kentucky native Bill Monroe, whose band, the Blue Grass Boys, gave the genre its name.

Swing east towards rural Hodgenville, birthplace of America's much-mythologized 16th president, Abraham Lincoln. Lincoln was born in a one-room log cabin here in 1809, on a farm named Sinking Springs. Honest Abe probably had his first sips of water from the cave spring that gives the property its name; you can lean over the railing and ponder his sad fate. Here, the ❷ **Abraham Lincoln Birthplace National Historic Site** features a replica of the old cabin, housed inside a faux Greek temple.

Half an hour further north is quaint ❸ **Bardstown**, "Bourbon Capital of the World." Stay at the ❹ **Old Talbott Tavern** in the 18th-century brick-and-stone downtown. Each of the five rooms is named after a former guest – including Lincoln, Daniel Boone and Washington

TIME
3 – 4 days

DISTANCE
450 miles

BEST TIME TO GO
Apr – Sep

START
Owensboro, KY

END
Corbin, KY

ALSO GOOD FOR

OFFBEAT

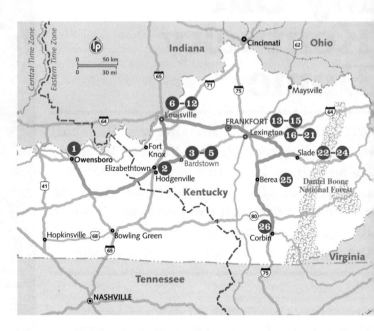

Irving. The bar downstairs has a large selection of local bourbons and is a good place to meet local distillery workers. In the morning, visit ⑤ Federal Hill, the Georgian mansion that inspired Stephen Foster's song *My Old Kentucky Home*. Though Bardstown's favorite son died young and destitute, his ballad lives on as Kentucky's state song, played before every Kentucky Derby.

An hour north is ⑥ Louisville, Kentucky's largest city. A former river port, Louisville is an unpretentious town of working-class German neighborhoods, lively college bars, and blocks and blocks of splendid Victorian rowhouses.

A block from the banks of the Ohio River in the heart of downtown is the ⑦ Louisville Slugger Museum. The five-story-high baseball bat leaning against the building makes it hard to miss. Hillerich & Bradsby Co has been making the iconic bat here since 1884. The museum has a plant tour, a hall of baseball memorabilia including Babe Ruth's slugger, a batting cage and a free mini slugger. You can buy a customized bat in the lobby.

Also downtown is the eccentric ⑧ Frazier International History Museum. See gory medieval battle tableaux and live historical re-enactments throughout the day – watch a 15th-century knight don his many layers of armor or listen to Abraham Lincoln and Stephen Douglas debate the morality of slavery. The Frazier's 3rd floor contains a branch of Britain's Royal Armories, with an astonishing collection of European weaponry and armor.

Heading south on South 3rd St, you'll see the elegant Greek Revival–style **❾ Speed Art Museum**. Kentucky's oldest and largest art museum contains more than 12,000 works of art, from Roman burial urns to 17th-century Flemish oil portraits to Kentucky silver julep cups.

Pretend you're a 19th-century captain of industry with a late afternoon stroll down Millionaire's Row. South of downtown, this stretch of 3rd St runs through the heart of **❿ Old Louisville**, with the largest collection of Victorian homes in the country. Sleep in the heart of the neighborhood at the **⓫ Rocking Horse Manor B&B**. Light pours through the stained glass into the parlor of this 1888 Romanesque mansion, where you can sip port on an antique couch before retiring to your canopy bed. Before heading out of town, snap a picture of the iconic white spires of **⓬ Churchill Downs**, home to the Kentucky Derby each May.

Head east for about an hour and you'll hit **⓭ Frankfort**, one of the smallest state capitals in America. Tucked into the steep hills along the banks of the Kentucky River, old-fashioned Frankfort's worth a stop for lunch and a visit to the **⓮ Center for Kentucky History**, with its self-guided tour through the state's history from prehistoric times through the exploration of the Cumberland Gap to the present. Take a picture in front of the nearby Greek Revival **⓯ Old State Capitol**, which housed the legislature from 1827 through 1910.

THE CIVIL WAR IN KENTUCKY

"I hope to have God on my side, but I must have Kentucky," said Abraham Lincoln, testifying to the strategic importance of this border state during the Civil War. Literally on the border between North and South – the Ohio River marks the Mason-Dixon line – Kentucky was deeply divided between slave-holding plantation owners and secession-squeamish Union loyalists. All in all, 64,000 Kentuckians fought for the Union and 30,000 for the Confederacy. Union president Abraham Lincoln and Confederacy president Jefferson Davis were both Kentucky-born.

Roll through the heavenly hills of Kentucky's horse country, and into **⓰ Lexington**, once called the "Athens of the West" for its wealth and culture. Contemporary Lexington is still a cultured city, with stately Victorian architecture, many museums and a walkable downtown. Settle into a worn booth at **⓱ Billy's Hickory Pit Bar-B-Q** and order a massive platter of pulled pork, beef or smoked mutton. Try the burgoo, a Kentucky meat and vegetable stew, with a side of corn bread.

In the quiet countryside off Old Frankfort Pike, is the quirky **⓲ Headley-Whitney Museum**, the private collection of the late George Headley, a successful jewelry designer during Hollywood's Golden Age. Wander roomfuls of carved bibelots, handmade dollhouses and ostrich-egg candlesticks. The wacky garage-turned-"shell grotto" is a testament to Headley's eccentric energies – he spent a year gluing seashells to every surface, including the chandeliers.

Back in town, take an afternoon to tour a few of Lexington's historic homes. Splendid 19th-century **⑲ Ashland** was the estate of Henry Clay, the golden-tongued Kentucky senator known as "the Great Compromiser" for his diplomatic skills. **⑳ Waveland**, an imposing brick plantation house, is now run by the National Park Service as a museum of antebellum life. Guided tours walk you through both masters' and slaves' quarters of the Greek Revival mansion, built by Daniel Boone's grand-nephew on land said to be originally surveyed by Boone himself. Visit the 1806 **㉑ Mary Todd Lincoln House**, where the first lady was born fourth of 16 children to a prominent Lexington family. Raised in privilege, feisty Mary Todd took solace from her later life's tragedies in the growing Spiritualist movement, attending séances and consulting fraudulent mediums. The house museum contains furniture, housewares and dolls from her childhood, as well as items from her marriage to Lincoln.

> **ASK A LOCAL**
>
> "The **Battle of Perryville**, in October, is a very good Civil War re-enactment. The camps are open – you can literally walk through them and ask questions. **Munfordville** has its re-enactment around mid-September. You'll have cannons, you'll have horses. There might be a medical tent, with fake blood and fake arms being cut off. There are also very interesting driving tours of fortifications around **Bowling Green**, the Confederate capital of Kentucky."
>
> *Michael Trapasso, Civil War re-enactor, Bowling Green*

Spend the night in the deep wilderness of the 707,000-acre Daniel Boone National Forest. The **㉒ Red River Gorge** area, near the hamlet of Slade, is a world-class rock climbing destination. At bohemian **㉓ Miguel's Pizza**, climbers relive the day's ascents over veggie slices and local Ale-8-One sodas (it's a dry county) before crashing in their tents in the backyard. A more scenic place to sleep is the **㉔ Koomer Ridge Campground** inside the park, with a bathhouse and access to trails leading to numerous gravity-defying sandstone arches.

Heading back south on I-75 you'll hit the tiny town of Berea and the **㉕ Kentucky Artisan Center**, visible from the highway. This airy, contemporary building is part travelers rest stop, part crafts fair, where vendors sell local pottery, bourbon barbecue sauces and folk art sculptures. The café serves state favorites like Louisville Hot Brown sandwiches (open-faced turkey-and-bacon sandwich slathered in Mornay sauce and broiled) and bourbon bread pudding. Craft-making demos are held on Friday and Saturday.

Further south is Corbin, home to the biggest Kentucky icon of them all: Colonel Harland Sanders. The Colonel ran a gas station here, frying chicken for travelers to nearby Cumberland Falls. While his chicken became massively popular, he didn't begin to sell the Kentucky Fried Chicken franchises until he was 65 You can visit the **㉖ Colonel Sanders Cafe & Museum**, with original 1940s kitchen equipment and a creepy life-size statue of the Colonel himself.

Emily Matcher

TRIP INFORMATION

GETTING THERE

From Nashville, take I-65 North for just over 50 miles and take exit 20 onto William H Natcher Parkway North for 70 miles to Owensboro.

DO

Abraham Lincoln Birthplace National Historic Site

See a replica of Lincoln's birthplace cabin, and his childhood farm. ☎ 270-358-3137; www.nps.gov/abli; 2995 Lincoln Farm Rd, Hodgenville; admission free; ☾ 8am-4:45pm, to 6:45pm summer

Ashland

This Italianate brick mansion was the home of statesman Henry Clay. ☎ 859-266-8581; www.henryclay.org; 120 Sycamore Rd, Lexington; adult/child $7/3; ☾ 10am-4pm Tue-Sat, from 1pm Sun

Center for Kentucky History

View stunning black-and-white photographs and other artifacts from the state's history. ☎ 502-564-1792; www.history.ky.gov; 100 W Broadway, Frankfort; adult/child $4/2; ☾ 10am-5pm Tue-Sat

Federal Hill

The brick plantation house is set in the My Old Kentucky Home State Park, with campgrounds and cabin rentals. ☎ 502-348-3502; parks.ky.gov/findparks/recparks/mo; 501 E Stephen Foster Ave, Bardstown; ☾ 9am-5pm

Frazier International History Museum

The three-story museum has wandering historical re-enactors and a huge collection of weaponry. ☎ 502-753-5663; www.frazier museum.org; 829 W Main St, Louisville; adult/child $12/9; ☾ 9am-5pm Mon-Sat, from noon Sunday; ♿

Headley-Whitney Museum

The late George Headley created this collection of marvelous miniatures and bejeweled oddities in his family's estate. ☎ 859-255-6653; www.headley-whitney.org; 4435 Old Frankfort Pike, Lexington; adult/child $7/5; ☾ 10am-5pm Tue-Fri, from noon weekends

International Bluegrass Music Museum

Learn where this uniquely American genre of music came from at this small museum. ☎ 270-926-7891; www.bluegrass-museum .org; 207 E 2nd St, Owensboro; admission $5; ☾ 10am-5pm Tue-Sat, 1-4pm Sun

Kentucky Artisan Center

Find local handicrafts and foods in this contemporary building, just off the highway. ☎ 859-985-5448; www.kentuckyartisan center.ky.gov; off Hwy 75 at exit 77, Berea; ☾ 8am-8pm

Louisville Slugger Museum

See where this iconic baseball bat is produced and take one home for yourself. ☎ 877-775-8443; www.sluggermuseum.org; 800 W Main St, Louisville; adult/child $9/4; ☾ 9am-5pm Mon-Sat, from noon Sun; ♿

Mary Todd Lincoln House

Lincoln's wife spent her comfortable childhood in this two-story home, now filled with artifacts from her life. ☎ 859-233-9999; www.mtlhouse.org; 578 W Main St, Lexington; adult/child $7/4; ☾ 10am-4pm Mon-Sat, closed Dec & Jan

Speed Art Museum

This stately museum contains works from classical Greece to contemporary Kentucky. ☎ 502-634-2700; www.speedmuseum.org; 2035 S 3rd St, Louisville; admission free, suggested donation $4; ☾ 10:30am-4pm Tue-Sat, noon-5pm Sun

Waveland

Find out what pre–Civil War life was like at this plantation-turned-historical park. ☎ 859-272-3611; parks.ky.gov/findparks /histparks/wl; 225 Waveland Museum Lane, Lexington; adult/child $7/4; ☾ 10am-5pm Mon-Sat, from 1pm Sun

EAT

Billy's Hickory Pit Bar-B-Q

It's all meat, all the time, at this casual joint – order burgoo (a Kentucky meat and vegetable stew) and a side of corn bread. ☎ 859-269-9593; 101 Cochran Rd, Lexington; mains $6-15; ☾ 11am-10pm Mon-Sat, 11:30am-9pm Sun; ♿

Colonel Sanders Cafe & Museum

View the Colonel's original 1940s kitchen, then eat some finger lickin' chicken at the attached KFC. ☎ 606-528-2163; 688 US Highway 25 W, Corbin; mains $2-6; ⊗ 10am-10pm; ⚅

Miguel's Pizza

Tired climbers fill their bellies and swap stories at this yellow-painted pizzeria. ☎ 606-663-1975; 1890 Natural Bridge Rd, Slade; mains $10-24; ⊗ 7am-10pm Mon-Thu, to 11pm Fri & Sat

SLEEP

Koomer Ridge Campground

In the wooded Red River Gorge area, this 54-spot rustic campground has grills, picnic tables, drinking water and showers. ☎ 606-668-9214; www.fs.fed.us/r8/boone/recreation/campcumb.shtml; off Mountain Parkway near Slade; campsite s/d $18/22; ⚅ ⚘

Old Talbott Tavern

This 1700s inn and tavern has old-fashioned guest rooms and a great bourbon selection. ☎ 502-348-3494; www.talbotts.com; 107 W Stephen Foster Ave, Bardstown; r from $69

Rocking Horse Manor B&B

Wake up and have breakfast in the garden of a restored 19th-century mansion on Old Louisville's Millionaire's Row. ☎ 502-583-6408; www.rockinghorse-bb.com; 1022 S 3rd St; r incl breakfast from $105

USEFUL WEBSITES

bluegrasskentucky.com
kentuckytourism.com

LINK YOUR TRIP

www.lonelyplanet.com/trip-planner

Day Trips in Kentucky & Tennessee

Drive into the countryside around Louisville, Nashville or Memphis to find Civil War battlefields, spooky old plantation houses and quirky small towns loaded with antiques shops and historic bed-and-breakfasts, as well as get-away-from-it-all wilderness areas.

OTTER CREEK PARK

About 35 miles southwest of downtown Louisville in the town of Brandenburg, Otter Creek Park is 2600 rambling acres of riverside forest and wildflower meadows. While some parts of the park feel deeply secluded even in high summer, others have a busy Boy Scout–camp vibe. For solitude, hike on trails through the silent, hardwood groves or wade on the banks of the Ohio River or numerous small, rocky creeks. If you're feeling more social, see if you can get in on a game at the disc golf course, or bring a lunch of pulled pork and pecan pie to eat at one of the many sheltered picnic areas. You can camp here too, in the backcountry or at drive-up tent sites, or rent a furnished cabin. **From Louisville, take I-264 East to Louisville and get off at exit 5b for Cane Run Rd. Take Hwy 31 West towards Louisville/Fort Knox, making a right after 13 miles at Hwy-1638. Turn right at Otter Creek Park Rd.**

SHILOH NATIONAL MILITARY PARK

It's hard to imagine that these peaceful fields and forest once soaked up the blood of 3400 soldiers. The Battle of Shiloh, fought just north of the Mississippi border, was the second major engagement of the Civil War and was, at the time, the bloodiest battle ever fought on American soil. Ulysses S Grant, leading the victorious (though not by much) Union army, noted that the corpses lay so thick you could almost walk across the battlefield without touching the ground. Today the Shiloh National Military Park commemorates that battle and the fallen soldiers. The only way to see the vast park is by a 9.5-mile self-guided driving tour. Head to the visitors center first to get a map and watch the documentary *Shiloh: Portrait of a Battle*. Grim sights along the route include the Shiloh National Cemetery, the death site of Confederate General AS Johnson, and Bloody Pond, where soldiers came to clean their wounds, dying the waters deep red. **From Memphis, take I-240 South and merge onto Hwy 385 East. Follow Hwy 72 towards Collierville, entering Mississippi. Stay on this road for about 65 miles before merging onto Hwy 45 North. Follow Hwy 57 to Hwy 22, which will take you into the park.**

See also **TRIP 11**

LAND BETWEEN THE LAKES

On the border of Tennessee and Kentucky, the Land Between the Lakes National Recreation Area is the peninsula formed when the Cumberland and Tennessee Rivers were damned to create Kentucky Lake and Lake Barkley. The 170,000-acre emerald wilderness is a refuge for hikers, campers and outdoor sports enthusiasts. Bikers adore riding the old logging roads through the forest or bouncing along miles of singletrack, while the 300 miles of shoreline are big with fishermen casting for bass, catfish and bluegill –16 boat ramps throughout the park make access easy. But the coolest part of the park may be the 700-acre Elk and Bison Prairie. Here, scientists and non-profit agencies are trying to resettle the herds that were hunted out of the area more than 100 years ago. For a $5 fee you can drive your car through the prairie to see them up close and personal (through the windshield, that is – stay in or near the car, as bison are known to charge). **From Nashville, take I-24 West into Kentucky to exit 53. Take Hwy 68/80 West past Cadiz and across the Lake Barkley Bridge.**

FRANKLIN

With its quaint 19th-century downtown, little Franklin looks like the movie set for a Civil War romance. Antiques lovers could spend days poring over vintage lithographs, delicately painted gravy boats and estate jewelry in the town's numerous antiques shops. There are a number of historic homes open for tours. The Carter House, built in 1830, was used as the command headquarters for the bloody Battle of Franklin in 1864. Today you can tour the house and battlefield, where you can see traces of more than 1000 bullet holes. Nearby Carnton Plantation, a white-columned brick manse, became the field hospital for scores of wounded Confederate soldiers. Take a guided tour of the house and see the rows of graves in the Civil War cemetery. **From Nashville, take I-65 South towards Huntsville and take exit 65 to Hwy 96 for Franklin/Murfreesboro. Continue on Murfreesboro Rd into downtown.**

See also **TRIP 11**

Behind the Scenes

THIS BOOK

This guidebook was commissioned in Lonely Planet's Oakland office, and produced by the following:

Product Development Manager & Commissioning Editor Heather Dickson
Coordinating Editor Dianne Schallmeiner
Coordinating Cartographer Andrew Smith
Coordinating Layout Designer David Kemp
Managing Editor Geoff Howard
Managing Cartographer Alison Lyall
Managing Layout Designer Celia Wood
Assisting Editors Simone Egger, Charlotte Harrison, Anne Mulvaney, Diana Saad
Assisting Cartographers Pablo Gastar, Margie Jung, Sophie Reed
Series Designer James Hardy
Cover Designers Gerilyn Attebery, Jennifer Mullins
Project Managers Chris Girdler, Craig Kilburn
Thanks to Imogen Bannister, Yvonne Bischofberger, David Burnett, David Carroll, Jay Cooke, Catherine Craddock, Laura Crawford, Owen Eszeki, Jennye Garibaldi, Suki Gear, Mark Germanchis, Michelle Glynn, Brice Gosnell, Martin Heng, Liz Heynes, Lauren Hunt, Laura Jane, John Mazzocchi, Darren O'Connell, Paul Piaia, Kirsten Rawlings, Averil Robertson, Julie Sheridan, Glenn van der Knijff, Jeanette Wall

THANKS

Alex Leviton A special thanks to travel companions Matt Reagan and Len 'Il Muffino' Amaral. Thanks to friends and helpers along the way: Wit Tuttell, Jennifer Francioni, Theresa Watts, Marc Rapport, Rah Bickley and John O'Brien, Molly Matlock, Todd Mason, Diana Bello and my neighbors at the Bullington Warehouse, Alison Satake and Mike Polito, and Dave Barnes. Thanks to the Lonely Planet team: Heather Dickson, Dianne Schallmeiner, Andrew Smith and Charlotte Harrison.

Emily Matchar Thanks to Dixie Hibbs and Philip Grymes for their excellent advice, and to all the local experts who added their voices along the way. Thanks to Alex Leviton, Heather Dickson and Jay Cooke at Lonely Planet, and to Jamin Asay for being my human thesaurus and co-barbecue taster.

Kevin Raub Thanks to Georgia, whom I miss dearly. My wife, Adriana Schmidt. At Lonely Planet, Jay Cooke, Heather Dickson and Alex Leviton. Along the way: Kelly Norris, Beth Parker, Hannah Smith, Edith Parten, Patrick Saylor, Emily Saliers, Scott Peacock, John T Edge, Stefanie Paupeck, Jason and Jennifer Hatfield, Dave Corbett, Jeff Richard, Erica Bacchus, Carey Ferrara, Harriet Sharer, Mary Wallace, Steve Klein, Brian Jones, Brian Casey, Paul Butchert, Susann Hamlin and Amber Moore.

Adam Skolnick Thanks to Jordan Johnson at CJRW, Vicki at Little Rock Tourism, Grace Wilson at New Orleans Convention & Visitors' Bureau, Mike Mills of the Buffalo Outdoor Center, Caroline, Kelly and the guys at Shack Up Inn, Red, Semmes, Steve Martin at Tourism Mississippi, Lani at Monmouth in Natchez, Keith, Melissa and crew at Under the Hill. Thanks also to Alex Leviton, Heather Dickson, Kevin Raub, Emily Matchar and the Lonely Planet production team.

ACKNOWLEDGMENTS

Many thanks to the following for the use of their content:

Internal photographs p16 (top) Steve Bly/Alamy; p13 (top) Charles O Cecil/Alamy; p13 (bottom) Danita Delimont/Alamy; p17 Thomas R Fletcher/Alamy; p15 (bottom) M Timothy O'Keefe/Alamy; p21 (bottom) Bob Pardue - SC/Alamy; p15 (middle) RagApple Lassie Wines; p12 Martin Shields/Alamy; p19 (top) H Mark Weidman Photography/Alamy. All other photographs by Lonely Planet Images, and by Jerry Alexander p8 (bottom), p14 (bottom); Richard Cummins p6 (top), p7 (top & bottom), p8 (top), p16 (bottom), p23, p24 (top); John Elk III p5; Lee Foster p7 (middle), p9, p10 (bottom), p16 (middle), p18 (top), p20, p21 (top), p22 (top), p24 (bottom); Richard I'Anson p15 (top), p19 (middle), p22 (bottom); Lou Jones p6 (bottom); Ray Laskowitz p11 (top & bottom); John Neubauer p19 (bottom); Carol Polich p10 (top).

All images are the copyright of the photographers unless otherwise indicated. Many of the images in this guide are available for licensing from Lonely Planet Images: www.lonelyplanetimages.com.

SEND US YOUR FEEDBACK

Got feedback? We'd love to hear your corrections, suggestions, compliments or complaints, so feel free to use our feedback form: **lonelyplanet.com/contact**.

Note: We may edit, reproduce and incorporate your feedback comments in Lonely Planet products such as guidebooks, websites and digital products. If you send it in, then that counts as permission for us to use it. If you don't want your name acknowledged, please let us know.

To read our privacy policy, visit **lonelyplanet.com/privacy**.

Index

See also separate GreenDex p422

000 map pages
000 photograph pages

000 map pages
000 photograph pages

000 map pages
000 photograph pages

n

000 map pages
000 photograph pages

000 map pages
000 photograph pages

GreenDex

Tourism can giveth, and tourism can taketh away. The South is fiercely proud of its historic treasures, and more often than not, sustainability means historical and cultural preservation. In this book, we skip the national motels and chain restaurants for places that best help local communities preserve the culture, history and environment of the regions we cover. From 175-year-old restaurants to inns run by the same family for generations, almost all of our listings preserve a piece of history in the South. You'll find several locations with an additional commitment to sustainability marked in the text, and listed below.

We might not have it 100% right yet, so that's why we're including you — our readers — in the process of helping us figure it out. Visit us at www.lonelyplanet.com/responsibletravel and tell us what you think makes a location "green."

LONELY PLANET OFFICES

USA
150 Linden St, Oakland, CA 94607
☎ 510 250 6400, toll free 800 275 8555
fax 510 893 8572
info@lonelyplanet.com

Australia
Head Office
Locked Bag 1, Footscray, Victoria 3011
☎ 03 8379 8000, fax 03 8379 8111
talk2us@lonelyplanet.com.au

UK
2nd fl, 186 City Rd,
London EC1V 2NT
☎ 020 7106 2100, fax 020 7106 2101
go@lonelyplanet.co.uk

Published by Lonely Planet Publications Pty Ltd
ABN 36 005 607 983